DON'T
BELIEVE IT!

HOW LIES BECOME NEWS

Published by:
The Disinformation Company Ltd.
163 Third Avenue, Suite 108
New York, NY 10003
Tel.: +1.212.691.1605
www.disinfo.com

Library of Congress Control Number: 2004114768

ISBN 1-932857-06-0

Printed in USA

Design: Hedi El Kholti

10 9 8 7 6 5 4 3 2 1

Editor: Jason Louv

Distributed in the USA and Canada by:
Consortium Book Sales and Distribution
1045 Westgate Drive, Suite 90
St Paul, MN 55114
Toll Free: +1.800.283.3572
Local: +1.651.221.9035
Fax: +1.651.221.0124
www.cbsd.com

Distributed in the United Kingdom and Eire by:
Turnaround Publisher Services Ltd.
Unit 3, Olympia Trading Estate
Coburg Road
London, N22 6TZ
Tel.: +44.(0)20.8829.3000
Fax: +44.(0)20.8881.5088
www.turnaround-uk.com

Attention colleges and universities, unions and other organizations: Quantity discounts are available on bulk purchases of this book for educational training purposes, fund-raising, or gift giving. Special books, booklets, or book excerpts can also be created to fit your specific needs. For information contact Marketing Department of The Disinformation Company Ltd.

DON'T
BELIEVE IT!

HOW LIES BECOME NEWS

ALEXANDRA KITTY

disinformation®

Table of Contents

Section **One**

Introduction to Evaluating the News

| Introduction

Can you get what you want? Can you get what you need? It's hard to get either without information: facts and evidence are the tools you use to choose the best option for you. Do you invest your life savings in a blue chip company with record-breaking profits based on what your financial planner tells you, or do you turn to a psychic for advice? Which form of cancer therapy do you choose: the one that showed promise in carefully controlled clinical trials, or the one that was touted by a D-list celebrity in an infomercial? Why did you decide to enroll in a particular college? How do you decide which presidential candidate you will vote for? How do you choose your doctor or lawyer?

Each decision is based on finding the right information and then weighing your options. No matter how you get your information, it has to come from somewhere—hopefully, that information source is accurate, relevant, useful, timely and truthful.

News is accessible any time, any place, from the corner store to your hotel room to your living room. Journalists cover a wide variety of topics— politics, business, health, education, technology, entertainment, crime. They report on local, national and international issues that are relevant to their audiences. Whether the topic is a product recall or a recall election, most expect the press to give the right information for us to make informed decisions.

Yet an increasing number of us don't quite trust journalists, despite the fact that most of us rely on at least one form of media for our news. Journalists have been accused of bias, distortion and outright deception. So how did the journalistic profession go from the heights of Woodward and Bernstein to the lows of Stephen Glass, Jack Kelley and Jayson Blair? Why don't we trust journalists, regardless of their qualifications or solid track record? What have those who work in the news media done to arouse such a level of suspicion in the public?

Maybe it was the media's lack of safeguards that helped blemish its image. You don't have to reach far into the memory pool to find an example:

in the August 2002 edition of *Details* magazine, an article carrying the byline of *Spy* magazine founder and former *New York Magazine* editor Kurt Andersen was a breezy, if somewhat pointless piece on male gossips. In his surprisingly lackluster story, the writer began with the kind of colorful anecdotal opening that magazine editors love to see:

> In Washington not so long ago, the postmodern airhead Goldie Hawn called for Americans to recognize how hurtful—how manly!—gossip can be. Speaking on behalf of a poignant anti-dish campaign called *Words Can Heal*, which disgracefully exploited the culture's 9-11 neo-Amishness, Hawn told of her wrenching experiences at the hands of male rumormongers. "I have sat around dinner tables where they have done nothing but talk about people the whole dinner," she bleated. "You can actually talk about real stuff... Or you can be just a gerbil running in a cage with that little roundy roundy toy and going nowhere."

It wasn't the only thing going nowhere. The story was quickly forgotten—that is, until Andersen made a call to *Details*, asking how an article he hadn't written could have his byline on it.

It turned out that Andersen didn't write the piece or have any connection to it at all. Someone had apparently written an article with Andersen's name attached, without his permission. This debacle led to some disheartening conclusions:

• Fact-checkers didn't get in contact with Andersen;

• The editor-in-chief ran with the story without speaking directly to Andersen or procuring a signed contract;

• No one at the magazine could account for how someone—inside or outside the publication—could bamboozle the magazine without a sweat.

Then again, the article was a useless and fluffy canard printed in an otherwise disposable men's fashion magazine. Hoaxes may sneak into glossies, but not into the finger-staining pages of newspapers whose staff diligently tell their readers about the issues of the day. Small community and large metro newspapers will weed out the lies and the frauds. Right?

Not quite. Mike Barnicle was a newspaper columnist for the *Boston Globe*, known for his engaging columns and slice-of-life takes on the city; that is, until questions arose about one of his 1998 columns. Barnicle was first suspended from the *Globe* for lifting jokes from a book penned by comedian George Carlin. After an investigation into Barnicle's previous stories, there were more questions swirling around his October 8, 1995 column about a nine-year-old boy who was battling cancer:

Their son struck up a friendship with another boy on the floor, a ten-year-old who—like him—loved baseball. And on those dreamy summer nights when the Olde Towne Team was home, the two of them would sit by a window on an upper floor in a hospital ward and listen to games on the radio as they looked at the lights of the ballpark off in the distance, washing across the July sky like some brilliant Milky Way all their own.

These two sick children became thick as thieves, joined by their passion for the Red Sox along with the anchor of their cancer. Naturally, their parents became friends, too.

Sadly, the nine-year-old died from his illness and his parents struggled both emotionally and financially, until a mysterious letter arrived at their home—which read, in part:

"We will never forget the kindness you showed our son at Children's… We heard about your difficulty from a nurse and want you to accept what we have sent. Your son gave a lot to our son. We think about him every day and we still hear his beautiful voice singing his favorite song, 'The Star Spangled Banner,' when we watch the Red Sox. You gave to us. Now it is time for our family to give in return. May God bless you."

They had enclosed $10,000… Not that it matters, but the people from Connecticut are white while the parents who lost their nine-year-old boy are black. And in their common voyage, there might be an American verdict we can admire.

But the verdict Barnicle received from his editors was guilty—of writing a bogus story. The information couldn't be substantiated. Barnicle was fired, though he maintained that the hospital's nurse had told him the tale. If that's the case, Barnicle pinned his entire column on a single secondhand source and then embellished that shaky information with bogus, but colorful details to spruce up an otherwise empty and saccharine story.

To make matters worse, the *Globe* wasn't the first organization to discover that the story had corroborating problems with it: *Reader's Digest* wanted to reprint the column, but editors dropped the idea after they couldn't verify the yarn (however, no one at the *Digest* bothered to clue in the *Globe* on their findings).

So newspaper reporters make mistakes just like those working for magazines, but we can expect that news editors are skeptical and vigilant enough to be able to weed out truth from fiction. Right?

Not always. In a letter to the editor published in the *Charleston Daily Mail* on September 10, 2003, Sgt. Shawn M. Grueser, a U.S. soldier stationed in Iraq, told readers in his own words about the current situation in the tumultuous country:

I have been serving in Iraq for over five months as a soldier with Company A, 2nd Battalion of the 503rd Airborne Infantry Regiment, otherwise known as "The Rock."

We entered the country at midnight on March 26.

One thousand of my fellow soldiers and I parachuted from ten jumbo jets (C-17s) onto a cold, muddy field in Northern Iraq. The parachute operation was the Army's only combat jump in the war and opened up the northern front.

Things have changed tremendously for our battalion since those first cold, wet weeks spent in the mountain city of Bashur.

The letter described that many Iraqis purportedly welcomed American troops:

After nearly five months here, the people still come running from their homes into the 110-degree heat, waving to us as our troops drive by on daily patrols of the city. Children smile and run up to shake hands, and in their broken English, shout: "Thank you, mister."

At least it was assumed those were Grueser's own words. As encouraging as the letter sounded, the same words were repeated in other letters from other soldiers. Not only did the letter appear in the *Daily Mail*, but identical ones were published in at least a dozen other papers, such as the *Everett Herald*, *Tulare Advance-Register*, the *Snohomish County Tribune* and the *Boston Globe* —all under different names. A case of mass plagiarism? No, but in an effort to win the public relations war, apparently a commander in the 2nd Battalion of the 503rd Infantry Regiment took it upon himself to draft the letter and canvass the troops for signatures, resulting in soldiers putting their names on letters they didn't write. It wasn't until the Olympian noticed two identical letters with different names that the ploy came to light.

So even the letters to the editor section can be suspect—but with the vigilant eye of the camera lens, at least we can trust television news won't get the facts wrong. Right?

Wrong. A camera's eye can be as easily fooled as its human counterpart. KLAS, a television station in Las Vegas, stunned its viewers with a multi-part series about a company that allowed men to shoot paint balls at naked women. The "game," called "Hunting for Bambi," caught international attention and outraged women's groups.

But while the story made great copy for countless other media outlets, no reporter had actually investigated the company's claims. It took a small website dedicated to urban legends to debunk the story with a little common sense and observation. Even then, many in the media were reluctant to declare the scheme a hoax.

Perhaps TV reporters can be duped as easily as their print colleagues, but at least events broadcast on television news outlets, such as "town hall meetings" and the like aren't staged—right?

CNN's November 2003 "Rock the Vote" was supposed to be a debate between eight candidates vying to win the Democratic presidential nomination, with university students asking the candidates tough questions. So it came as a surprise when Alexandra Trustman, a first-year Brown University student, asked the eight presidential hopefuls: "I'm a freshman at Brown University. And going to college this year, I was confused with an important decision. My mom advised me one way, my dad the other. And so my question for you all is... Macs or PCs?" Needless to say, many people questioned aloud whether Brown had suddenly lowered certain entrance requirements for their students. Other media outlets, such as the *Eagle Tribune*, made reference to the question in their coverage.

After feeling the heat for her asinine question, Trustman confessed in a column in the *Brown Daily Herald,* the college newspaper, that she wanted to ask the candidates a technology question, but was instructed by a CNN producer to ask the scripted question instead, to "encourage a light-hearted moment" during the debate. CNN later confirmed her account of events. Planting questions in an attempt to set the tone during a debate is manipulative: if this is supposed to be an unscripted event, then how can viewers believe what they see in the future?

If print and broadcast can't be trusted to spot hoaxes and scams, then there's always the pure and unfiltered information flowing from the Internet—with countless websites, the truth has to be easy to find. Right?

Just ask those who sympathized with "Kaycee Nicole," a teenager who kept a website chronicling her battle with cancer. People sent messages and began to feel a connection with the girl whose photo and brave words touched so many. Sadly, readers discovered that young Kaycee had succumbed to her illness in May 2001.

Events then took an even more unsettling turn after the young girl's mother refused to divulge the details of her daughter's funeral; some supporters began to look for more information, and discovered that the sob story was a hoax.

With established reporters bulldozing away at their own credibility and many Internet denizens following suit, at least we can expect that college and university journalism programs (affectionately or lazily referred to as "j-schools" by those in the business) are taking drastic steps to ensure that the new generation of chroniclers are skeptical news-gatherers who can thoroughly research and question the information they receive.

Childlike innocence can still be readily found in those who aspire to make a career in this hard-bitten profession. Student reporter Kim Na wrote a front-page story that ran in the October 3, 2002 edition of Washington State University's student newspaper, the *Daily Evergreen*:

> The month of October is officially observed as Filipino-American History Month. On Oct. 18, 1587, the first Filipinos landed on the shores of Morro Bay, California on a Spanish galleon called the Nuestra Senora de Buena Esperanza, which translates to "The Big Ass Spanish Boat."

If accounts are to be believed, she wasn't trying her hand at ethnically offensive humor, but she wasn't trying to double-check her information, either. Na found her info on a website and assumed that if it was on the web, it had to be true, even if it sounded bizarre. The punch line was that the information on the site was a joke.

Not only did the paper have to apologize for the blunder (which outraged a number of the student body at Washington State), but it turned out that the student reporter plagiarized her information from the following passage on Pinoylife.com:

> Filipinos landed on the shores of Morro Bay, CA serving as crewmen/navigators/slaves on a Spanish galleon named the *Nuestra Senora de Buena Esperanza*, which loosely translates to "The Big Ass Spanish Boat."

Didn't *Evergreen* editors question Na's unique translation? Even the most linguistically ignorant of us can see that "senora" means "lady" and "buena" means "good," but somehow those words didn't appear anywhere in the translation (for those who are clueless, the phrase means "Our Lady of Good Hope"). Was it even remotely likely that the phrase "big ass" was in common usage in 1587? Was it that hard to get a Spanish-English dictionary (online or in print) to double-check five little words? One editor did question the veracity of the passage, but since Na found the information on a "legitimate-looking" website, the rest of the staff assumed it had to be true and the translation remained untouched.

The *Evergreen* printed a somewhat misleading retraction on October 4, 2002:

> Parts of the story, including the translation above, were plagiarized from an inaccurate website.

In fact, the website wasn't inaccurate—it was a farce. The student reporter didn't just steal someone else's words, she also took a single questionable source as fact.

If these cases were the only blunders in the news media, it could be argued that a few errors in judgment on the part of a scattering of individuals shouldn't taint the news media's credibility. However, within the last few years, countless media outlets have been repeatedly scammed and tricked by everyone from brilliantly cunning con artists to frightened little kids. Some highlights of media professionals being duped include:

• A *New York Post* reporter believing that two lawyers with similar names were the same person;

• Several large media outlets reporting that blondes were in evolutionary peril;

• A well-respected paper publishing embarrassing and intimate information in an obituary that turned out to be false;

• Hundreds of media outlets telling their readers that a music group was wanted by the FBI;

• A child of average intelligence being touted as a genius;

• Several local outlets and one wire service reporting that human parts were found in a can of food;

• Several newspapers reporting that a tombstone was equipped with an ATM machine;

• Many reporters believing an ordinary family was being terrorized by an extraordinary stalker;

• A decadent cult receiving prominent media coverage after it claimed it cloned a human baby;

• A teenager's sob story that enemy soldiers were killing babies becoming a rallying cry for war;

• A pyramid scheme huckster being portrayed as a competent businessman;

• A security guard who helped victims during a bombing later being portrayed as possibly the bomber himself;

• A woman dependent on painkillers being transformed into a desperate and dying crime victim, prompting hundreds of people to donate money to her.

And the list goes on. From being lied to about kidnappings to being lied to about a multinational conglomerate's illegal dealings, news producers have been hoaxed at a troubling rate. This steady stream of erroneous and false reports can lead many people to ask whether reporters know what is happening around them. The sad answer is that some reporters don't even know much about the companies for whom they work.

Some news consumers may at least hope that journalists are still honest, if sometimes naïve. That illusion has also been smashed within the last twenty years, with a disturbing stream of reporters being caught in the act of lying, cheating and stealing. For instance:

• The *New York Times* was rocked to its core when one of their own troubled reporters plagiarized and fabricated over three dozen stories.

• The *New Republic* magazine kept a journalist on staff who fabricated the whole or parts of twenty-seven of his forty-one articles.

• A Kentucky newspaper ran front-page columns from a reporter who lied about having a terminal illness so she could make friends.

• An Emmy award-winning television reporter faked a multi-part story after a lead she was given fell through.

• A wire service reporter fabricated interviews in his articles.

• A Pulitzer-nominated reporter at a national daily was caught fabricating parts of his stories.

Some disenchanted news consumers find comfort in getting their information from the Internet. After all, if several websites report the same information, then it must mean the information is true. But here, too, in this electronic Wild West, inaccurate information and hoaxes, such as the following, can run unchecked:

• Several websites displayed a yearbook photo of a teenaged girl who was identified as the woman who accused Los Angeles Lakers star Kobe Bryant of sexual assault. All of these sites had, in fact, found a picture of the wrong woman.

• A website proclaiming to originate from a group called "Anarchists for a Better State" was a bogus site set up by a writer in an attempt to fool his fellow journalists.

• A website touting the launch of a new slacker men's magazine was a hoax set up to fool unsuspecting reporters.

If newspapers, magazines, radio and television broadcasts and websites are all prone to hoaxes, frauds and inaccuracies, then journalists, producers and editors should be taking steps to correct these problems—and even if they are slipping back into their lax ways, technology can protect consumers from errors and lies. Besides, with the sheer number of media outlets, the number of reporters covering a single event will keep reports accurate. Convergence and the Internet should ensure more accurate reporting. Right?

Not exactly. Historically, though there may have never been as many news outlets before, the problem is that today's outlets rely on surprisingly few news gathering services for their information—after all, gathering data and harmonizing those strands can be an expensive proposition. If you look up a single news item using a basic Google News search, you will notice something unsettling: that even though hundreds of media outlets are covering the same story, most of those same outlets rely on the same wire service and not on in-house reporters (the most common wire services are the *Associated Press* and Reuters, along with the *New York Times* wire service). The implications are obvious: a single misleading, exaggerated, biased, inaccurate or fraudulent news story can spread to hundreds of media outlets without opposition within seconds.

Then again, what can be considered misleading, exaggerated, biased, inaccurate or fraudulent? Many people accuse the media of "smearing" them, but it doesn't mean that the accusations are true. While there are those who gripe about reporters, many of these people are resentful because reporters don't share their delusions of grandeur. For some actors and politicians, only positive fluff pieces that would describe their subject in the most nauseatingly superlative terms would be their idea of fair and balanced. Just because a cult leader's mom thinks he is the most wonderful darling in the world, it doesn't mean the rest of us think that his disturbing temper tantrums and negligent behavior are adorable. Reporters get rapped for writing the truth as much as they are rapped for falling for lies. Even criticism is no barometer for determining a report's truthfulness.

We need information, but determining how accurate our information is can be tricky. Falling for lies, misinformation, hoaxes and scams can lead to humiliation, bankruptcy or even death. Perhaps that may be true for older generations who are overwhelmed by the glut of facts and factoids and grew up in more trusting times, but computer-savvy generations who grew up in the Information Age are supposedly skeptical and educated enough to know how to evaluate information.

Then again, a large portion of the new generation honestly believes that Germany fought along with the Allies during the Second World War, that the pill prevents HIV infection, that stock market losses are insured and that pharmaceutical companies can only advertise "completely safe" drugs—the young can be as easily bamboozled as the old.

No matter how old you are, being uninformed doesn't only make you a desirable pigeon for scam artists—it can kill you, too. Not knowing what is going on around you is a dangerous and pathetic way of living life. Are the pills you are swallowing killing you? Is the company you work for a front for a swindler? Is the person you are donating money to a con artist? Is the tax shelter you are investing in a fraud? Maybe media reports seem reassuring, as are websites, but how can you be certain that all those information gatherers know what they're doing? What if they believed what they were told without question the same way you did?

The Information Age is a minefield: unless you have credible and up-to-date facts, your ignorance is likely to blow up in your face. Who do you trust and how do you know you can trust them?

Some people think that the best way to protect themselves is to believe nothing they hear in the media—but if a news anchor reports that a tornado is headed to town, is that the time to accuse the media of scare-mongering, while refusing to budge from the recliner? To think that all reporters are biased liars is equally naïve as believing that reporters never lie or make mistakes. The problem isn't that the media is always biased and inaccurate, but that it mixes truth in with the fiction.

If you can't evaluate the information you hear, you can set yourself up for heartache or even disaster. Believing or distrusting the wrong sources can get you into all sorts of trouble, such as:

• Investing your life savings in a sham;

• Avoiding or boycotting innocent businesses, organizations or places;

• Changing your vote in an election;

• Ingesting dangerous products or ceasing to take helpful products;

• Supporting criminals or condemning innocent people;

• Supporting questionable or extreme actions, groups or organizations;

• Donating your money to fraudulent causes.

If the information we receive isn't all lies, then how can we know what is real and what is fake? How can you tell if there are any lies or misrepresentations in an article or broadcast? Are there ways to separate good information from the bad? Is it possible to expose hoaxes from a single news report without outside knowledge?

Yes.

Just knowing what questions to ask and how to break down information can help you separate lies from the truth. By looking at pictures and listening to words, you can evaluate news reports to determine whether the information you just read or watched is real or a hoax. What information was left out and why? Studying expressions, body language, events, words, pictures and even camera angles can give you the information you need to determine whether the news report is accurate, incomplete, exaggerated or flat out false.

This book will show you how to critically and quickly evaluate the information you see, hear or read in order to make informed decisions. Some con artists are brilliant deceivers, but by knowing what to watch out for, you'll have the knowledge you need to smoke them out, even if journalists who heard the story before you couldn't. Some of the biggest hoaxes in history could have been exposed within seconds if people asked the right questions.

How can it be possible to expose a hoax without seeing the event first hand? Think of a bad news story as a cluster of symptoms. If a doctor can diagnose an illness based on physical signs, then a news consumer can diagnose a bad news story by looking for the telltale signs or symptoms.

A suspect story is very much like a persistent cough. The cough by itself may hint at an underlying problem, but by itself you don't know what the illness could be—maybe you have a cold, flu, bronchitis, acid reflux or even lung cancer. But if you also identify the other symptoms, you can better pinpoint what the problem is.

The same logic can apply to evaluating news reports. By knowing what signs to look for and where to look for them, you'll be able to evaluate the news and reduce your chances of being fooled by a con artist or an unscrupulous journalist. While we may be dependent on others for our information, at least we'll have the tools to sift through their findings and get what we want and what we need to make better decisions in our lives.

Sometimes you don't even need that much—sometimes a single, but subtle clue will tell you that something is seriously wrong with the story. This book will show you what red flags to look out for and what those warning signs mean.

This book should help you spot lies, inaccurate information and hoaxes and learn how to easily spot and confirm suspect information or stories to avoid being misled and manipulated. Not only will you learn how to evaluate information, but also how to become an information connoisseur to learn how to absorb healthy information and not swallow harmful misinformation.

Once you train yourself to think differently and not believe everything you read, see or hear, evaluating the news may become easier and lies become more obvious—but before you can evaluate the news, it's a good idea to know how reporters gather it in the first place.

Chapter Two

| Definitions

Every profession has its own jargon: retailers talk about end-caps, POP and price leaders; psychologists talk about dissonance, CERs and Mignon delusions and police talk about recidivism, LKAs and summary offenses. Not surprisingly, journalists talk about embargoes, ECUs and news holes. The lexicon for any industry can tell you how that industry sees the world around it.

News consumers also need their own set of definitions to see the news in a new way. How are media outlets vulnerable to lies? What do they take for granted? What processes are considered important to journalists, producers and editors? What's the industry's mindset and values? What's important to reporters? How do reporters interpret their surroundings? What assumptions do reporters make? Where and how can an unscrupulous person manipulate the news media?

Hoax Definitions

Lies make their way into print and onto the airwaves, and it helps to be able to distinguish between a rumor, hoax, scam, urban legend and culture jam, since their nuances can give you valuable clues as to whether a news story is factually sound, or if someone is manipulating the press for their own ends.

Rumor

A rumor is a disseminated piece of information (or more likely dirt or gossip) that has not been confirmed or verified with either documentation or corroboration. Many times, the source of the rumor is unknown, making substantiation difficult. In the news world, the rumor is often referred to as an "unconfirmed report," as in the phrase "An unconfirmed report from rescue workers at the scene said three people were apparently killed in the blast," or "unconfirmed reports suggested [disposed Iraqi leader Saddam Hussein] had been moved to another country."

A rumor is not necessarily wrong or misleading; many times the unconfirmed detail turns out to be true. However, a false rumor can cause embarrassment and harm to not only the target of the rumor, but to the disseminator as well. The person spreading a rumor may be doing it for personal gain, but others disseminate rumors simply because they believe the rumor to be true.

Hoax

A hoax is a deceptive story told in the hopes that the story will lead to some personal, political or financial gain by the storyteller. Unlike rumors that have some chance of being true, hoaxes are meant to be deceptive. Hoaxes can be as sophisticated or as simple as the teller; the story may be logical or fantastic; it can be well planned or spontaneous and it can involve a single person or a group of people.

Unlike rumors, which may seem factual in nature, hoaxes rely on emotional manipulation to evoke a response in the listener that would benefit the storyteller. While hoaxes are false, they may be based on a partial truth, though that truth will be indirect and irrelevant to the hoax itself. For example, during wartime, many people (or governments) will claim that an extremely gruesome atrocity has been committed by the enemy side. While the hoax may be based on a partial truth (that violent, bad things are happening in the location in question and are being committed by the enemy), the over-the-top claim itself will be false. Another example would be parents who claim that their child was kidnapped: while the child may be missing, the truth is that the parents murdered their child and, to avoid arrest, have concocted a story to cover their tracks.

Urban Legend/Urban Myth

An urban legend is an oft-told "friend of a friend" story about allegedly real life events. An urban legend isn't necessarily false in its origins: in fact, some urban legends are based on real events, but the story changes names, dates, locations and even key details. Legends are meant to frighten or warn people about unknown lurking danger, warm the hearts of listeners with feel-good tales of good deeds or are used as morality tales where everyone gets their just desserts.

A myth is used interchangeably with legend; however, the word myth has supernatural underpinnings, while the word legend does not. Legends are usually told as fact by friends or relatives, by word of mouth or forwarded e-mail, but many times, legends find their way into news reports.

Vector

In nature, a biological vector—such as insects—can spread disease. In folklore, a vector is someone or something (usually a website or publication) which passes on or disseminates an urban legend. The term was coined by

Jan Harold Brunvand, a folklore expert. But by extension, a vector could be more than someone who spreads a rumor or a hoax: it could be anyone or anything that pollutes the information stream.

A news outlet can be a vector of bad information, as can governments, websites, private citizens and scam artists. Some vectors are inadvertent spreaders of misinformation, while others deliberately spread lies—however, the end results are usually the same.

Mark/Pigeon

This is a con artist's victim, or the person "marked" for a scam. In the carnival days, the sucker's back was literally marked with chalk, to let other cons know that the person could be taken in by means of a swindle and had money for the taking. These days, the term refers to anyone who is targeted for a scam.

We can take it one step further: a mark can also include those who are marked for media hoaxes, meaning the intended victim isn't simply a single mark. Journalists (usually more than one) can also be pigeons, as can editors, producers and, ultimately, the public. Mass marks may include specific targets such as law enforcement (to throw police off of a con artist's trail) or followers of a certain religion (to encourage them to donate money to the hoaxer's cause).

Misdirection

A misdirection is a choreographed and pre planned trick, distraction or ruse to draw the audience's attention away from the sleight of hand that would expose the trickster's real methods. Magicians use misdirection so that their audiences don't see the obvious and ordinary way they perform their tricks. Criminals use misdirection to draw attention away from their faces or their make of car. Scam artists use it as a way to get their marks from noticing a story's gaping plot holes and inconsistencies. The misdirection can be physical, emotional or psychological in nature, but its purpose is always to prevent the mark from using logic and common sense to unravel a scheme or trick.

Begging/Pity Scam

This type of scam's sole purpose is to extract money from a mark by playing the pity card. The scam artist will feign hardship and then rely on the mark's compassion to give money (in the form of a donation) to the beggar. Traditional begging scams have adults or children faking homelessness or physical hardships (anything from a physical handicap to a terminal illness), but modern begging scams are more sophisticated: the con may use a media outlet to claim hardship for himself, a relative or a group of people, hoping to increase his take with less effort. Regardless of the method, the scam artist must play the role of a vulnerable, kind and honest person who is inferior to the mark: the pigeon must feel good about making a "donation" to someone who is deserving of the mark's generosity and pity. While the mark doesn't expect tangible returns for his investment, the payoff to the pigeon is the feeling of helping the less fortunate in their time of need.

Investment/Greed Scam

The opposite of a begging scam is an investment scam; i.e., chicanery that is based on the mark's desire to get rich quick. While a begging scam hinges on a mark's sympathy, this scam is dependent on the mark's self-indulgence, greed and ego. For example, in the mid-1990s, one popular pyramid scheme making the rounds across North America was a home-based "seminar" called "Women Helping Women," where women would be allowed to "invest" several thousand dollars while recruiting a certain number of other women to invest and recruit. Women who met the requirements were given "Queen Bee" or "Birthday Girl" status and a supposedly generous return on their investment. It wasn't just the allure of fat dividends, but the title that hooked thousands of women into the scam.

Some investment scams appear to be based on legitimate businesses and practices, such as investing in stocks or in a known company, while other scams are openly based on shady practices. In either case, these scams work by the con artist stroking the pigeon's ego and praising their business savvy while assuring the mark that with minimum effort and risk, a fat return awaits.

Culture Jamming

Literally, jamming refers to the interference of television or radio reception. The related term, "culture jamming," is the use of the media to make a statement against the shortcomings of the media. Culture jamming includes hacking, graffiti, pie-throwing, streaking, defacing billboards, forgery, the interruption of public forums, social protests, ad parodies and other forms of public subversion. Media piracy of this sort is usually initiated by performance artists, activists and publications like *Adbusters*.

Though jamming is essentially scamming, it can also be a method of making a social statement against advertising, capitalism and the perceived defects (real and imagined) of the mass media. The use of parody is a defining aspect of jamming. However, one jamming method is staging elaborate hoaxes to fool the news media: some pranks pulled on reporters stem from jammers making a statement against the gullibility and sensationalism of the press.

Media-Related Definitions

Unlike those of many other trades, many journalism-specific words either tend to sound like slang or actually come from other professions. Since journalism did not originate from an academic tradition, the terms are more informal, but still reveal what's important to the profession—mostly advertising, information, clinical detachment, style and audience reaction. In other words, journalism is a study of contradictory values duking it out for supremacy and a larger audience.

Objectivity

One of the key tenets of the profession, the concept of journalistic objectivity (as opposed to scientific objectivity) has changed over the years. Objectivity meant emotional detachment and getting "both sides of the story"; however, the idea that it is possible for anyone to be completely detached or that seeing the world without feeling is a healthy or accurate way of reporting is questionable. The assumption that there are only two sides in a story also seems overly simplistic.

While many reporters still adhere to that definition, others prefer to think of objectivity as a reporter being "fair and balanced." Again, this definition is slippery: fair to whom? How do we determine "fair" reporting? What is balanced? If a balanced report means giving equal time to both sides, how can we ensure balance if one side has more resources and is more media-savvy than the other side?

It should be noted that journalists and those who teach journalism haven't conducted much research to determine whether their definition of objectivity is a better way of disseminating information (i.e., if it is a more accurate or efficient way for an audience to understand information). It's an ideal—rather than a well-defined—term.

The concept of journalistic objectivity began to take shape during the "Penny Press" era of the 1830s and came into its own in the nineteenth century. Objectivity was not a concept born out of morals, ethics or academics, but born out of economic necessity: politically neutral newspapers were more likely to find a wider audience than partisan ones. Before the age of objectivity, editors and reporters were openly biased, mostly in the hope of snagging a lucrative patronage position from the political party the newspaper supported. These days, while there is debate over whether objectivity exists or is the best way to cover the news, the *ideal* of objectivity still thrives in the newsroom.

Newsworthiness/Gate-Keeping

Another vague term crucial to the media profession, newsworthiness generally refers to what editors, producers and journalists consider worthy of their collective attention and, ultimately, what will grab the collective attention of the news audience. So what makes news? Is sensationalism equivalent to newsworthiness?

Not really. News is what deviates from the ordinary, whether it's better than normal or worse. Horrendous tragedies or extraordinary achievements make news. Crime, politics, disease, war and celebrity stories can be considered newsworthy ones—these are people and events that most ordinary people don't experience on a regular basis. On the whole, bad news will get more coverage than good news—however, new trends are also considered newsworthy events.

For an item to be newsworthy, it also has to be informative or amusing, as well as timely and relevant to the target audience. Events happening close by will be more newsworthy than those that happen far away; new legislation that has a direct impact on the target audience will be more newsworthy than laws that do not affect the news consumer. What happened yesterday is less important than what's happening now. In other words, newsworthiness is a relative concept.

Because producers and editors have to make choices as to what will make news, some potential news items have to be excluded. The game of inclusion and exclusion is known as gate-keeping (although the term is more commonly used by media critics and communication and sociology professors than by reporters in their newsrooms). Certain people, issues and events get more coverage than others, but access comes with an expiration date: once a story is deemed "resolved" or "passé" by the press, the gate can abruptly close to those who once were considered newsworthy. A sitting president can find more media access than one that has left office. It's the elite nature of the gatekeepers that has them being accused of bias and discrimination. Sometimes the charge is warranted—but other times, it's just the nature of the media beast.

Fact

This is a piece of information that can be independently verified and tested (i.e., it can be proven right or wrong). Did the crime or unemployment rates rise or fall? How much money did a company make or lose last quarter? What chemicals were found in a river? Who's running for mayor? What new laws have been passed or repealed? Was a defendant convicted or acquitted of a crime? Did more people file for bankruptcy this month than last month? How many people were killed in an explosion?

The mandate of most news outlets is to present new facts to the public as they become available, but what facts are presented and how they're presented is up to the individual outlet. How facts are uncovered depends on the thoroughness, doggedness and tenacity of the individual reporter. Some will interview eyewitnesses, experts and other key players while unearthing classified documents; others are content with what's handed to them on a press release or police blotter. There are no uniform standards in journalism as to how many facts any given news item must contain.

Opinion/Spin

Opinion is a personal feeling or belief that is dependent on a person's own worldview. Nevertheless, many people confuse opinion with fact. Facts are dry; opinion is subjective. Opinion can be backed by facts or be an interpretation of what a certain set of facts mean, but not necessarily so. In journalism, reporters are supposed to convey facts alone, while columnists convey opinion supported by facts. "A spectacular fire broke out in the industrial district," "A large rally occurred in front of city hall," "The gunman's motive appears to be distress over his firing," "Soft laws have contributed to the rise in crime in the area," "The city's economy is suffering because of the governor's do-nothing approach." These statements all express opinion.

In the simplest terms, spin is also the interpretation of what a fact or cluster of facts mean. In many ways, spin is opinion—but there is a key difference: spin is a public interpretation of facts that tries to portray a person, company or event in the most positive light and/or rivals in the most negative light. Spin tries to enhance or salvage one's own reputation and denigrate or ruin an enemy's reputation based on recently published information. Spin is usually a reaction to current and relevant news items.

Suppose the unemployment rate in a city suddenly increased from 2% to 8%. The increase is a fact, but the mayor's office may try to put a spin on what the sudden rise means. They may wish to deflect criticism by either suggesting that the city's rate is lower than other cities or that someone else is to blame for the rise. Large businesses may blame the city's "restrictive" bylaws for the increase. Regardless, each side will try to make itself seem blameless.

Unlike opinion, spin is predictable: there are only so many ways to make yourself look good. For example, if a person or company is rocked with negative publicity, there is only so much he can say to save his reputation:

- It's not as bad as it looks;
- It's a lot worse for the other guys than for us;
- It could have been worse if it wasn't for our hard work and competence;
- It's not our fault;
- It's the fault of our various rivals or enemies;
- If it wasn't for our rivals meddling with their wrong-headed policies, this never would have happened;
- We told you this would happen if our policies weren't implemented the exact way we wanted them;
- It will get better quickly;
- Though we didn't get our way, we learned valuable lessons and gained connections and experiences that will help us improve in the future.

Lead

The lead is the first sentence of a news story. Most leads are short—and traditionally, the first sentence is supposed to contain the latest, most important and most newsworthy information in a powerful way, to "hook" the audience into wanting to know more. The practice of placing the most important information first and then adding increasingly less important information is known as the "inverted pyramid" style, and the reasoning behind it is simple: if a copy editor had to chop an article because of space constraints, then the last paragraphs can be removed without the editor even reading the bottom half of the story.

The inverted pyramid isn't strictly adhered to these days; some leads may open with an interesting quote, a colorful description or an unusual anecdote, but the concept that the first sentence must serve as a hook remains.

Source

A source is the person the reporter relies on for information. A good source is open, intelligent, helpful and knows the workings and power structure of his surroundings. Some sources have agendas, while others are merely publicity hounds. A reporter is dependent on the source for accurate information; but it doesn't hurt for a journalist to independently verify the source's information or claim. Some reporters go by the "three source rule": if three people confirm a piece of information, then the information is likely true and therefore can be published.

Angle

This is the way a reporter decides to present a story: what slant or perspective will the reporter use to disseminate information? Does a story focus on a victim, villain, hero, witness or society? An angle can also determine which facts ultimately make it into the story, and which ones are excluded.

Correction

Corrections are a newspaper's mea culpa and usually appear in the front section of the newspaper or in the letters of the editor section in a magazine. Interestingly, there is no universal corrections protocol: some publications, such as the *New York Times*, add online corrections to the bottom of the offending story; however, many online databases do not include corrections. Some other publications will correct the mistake within the article before it's added to the database, or in some cases of gross inaccuracy or fabrication, the publication will remove the articles from their archives entirely.

The correction may be minor in nature, such as a name being misspelled (this may happen because a soft-spoken interviewee comes across a reporter who is hard of hearing); other times the mistake is a doozy, such as the wrong person being identified in an article as the neighborhood child molester.

News Peg

A news peg is an element or hook that will draw the audience into wanting to read or watch a story. The peg has to be timely, relevant, important, newsworthy or colorful. If an event or fact doesn't have a wide or definitive impact on an audience, it can't be used as a peg, and hence the news item won't be published or broadcast. Many issues and events may be important, but only a few can serve as a news peg at any given moment. For example, AIDS is no less deadly than before, but since it's not seen as a timely topic, it won't make the same headlines as it did twenty years ago.

News Hole

A news hole is the amount of space a newspaper, magazine, radio program or TV news cast has to fit news items after the advertising has been laid out. In other words, ads come first and the news has to fit within those constraints. When a newspaper boasts in its advertising that it now carries more news or has a bigger news hole, what they're really saying is that they have fewer advertisers buying space or at least those advertisers aren't spending as much money as before.

Breaking News

Breaking news is news that is being reported on as it happens, such as coverage of a hostage crisis.

Hard News

This is considered serious news: anything that can greatly impact an average citizen's life and well-being. Tax increases, the spread of potentially fatal and contagious diseases, election campaigns, natural disasters and environmental hazards are some of the items that are considered to be hard news. Has a child gone missing? Is war breaking out? Has the electricity gone out? Has a killer been convicted?

Soft News

If the news item is interesting, but its impact won't have serious consequences for an average citizen, then it is considered soft news. These are the stories found in the lifestyle, arts, celebrity, life, fashion, gardening and sports sections of the newspaper or newscast.

Color

Simply put, color is the liberal use of adjectives to describe small but inessential details of a scene, and the use of human-interest anecdotes to liven up a story.

Scoop/Exclusive

A scoop is an important and significant story, fact or interview a journalist has uncovered first (or more likely it is a piece of information or interview given to the reporter by a source). A scoop is something that hasn't been spoon-fed to a group of reporters via a press release or press conference, but may have been spoon-fed to a reporter by an angry, frightened or calculating individual who may have something to gain by publicizing information. Other times, the reporter has uncovered something because he has heard rumors and through his investigation had found the rumors to be true. A reporter may have come across new information while reporting on a related matter and may have discovered the scoop through serendipity.

In its purest form, an exclusive means that a piece of information, interview, footage or document has been discovered by a single media outlet. These days, the term "exclusive" has been watered-down to mean "rare"—an "exclusive" interview may simply mean that a person has agreed to talk to only one major network, but has given interviews to several magazines. With interviewees making promises and then breaking agreements with journalists, there is very little a reporter or news outlet can do to ensure an exclusive stays an exclusive.

With media convergence becoming a reality, an exclusive may now mean that a person has agreed to release information (such as giving an interview) to a single media conglomerate (for example, a person may agree to an interview that will be covered by "CNN Headline News" as well as *Time* and *People* magazines). The interviewee may also agree to a multi-platform deal with a media conglomerate (a convoluted way of saying the person will get rewarded or paid if he agrees to an exclusive deal, such as seeing his life story turned into a movie of the week by the same network who will interview him on one of their TV newsmagazines).

Scrum/Pool

The term "scrum" refers to a group of reporters from various media outlets dispatched to cover the same event. Images of scrums are fairly common sights for TV news audiences: a crush of reporters surround a newsmaker with their microphones, tapes and cameras thrust in front of the interviewee. Scrum behavior has been compared to everything from a pack of wolves to a group of descending vultures.

A media pool is a select group of reporters who have access (usually by invitation) to a certain event, who then "feed" the information and footage they gathered to other reporters outside the pool; in other words, other media outlets are dependent on the pool reporter for their information.

Beat

This is a reporter's area of expertise. Reporters covering a particular institution or area have developed their own sources and report on the happenings of that specialty. Beats include crime, courts, municipal government, state politics, federal politics, education, business, environment, health, sports, defense, entertainment and foreign affairs.

Column

A column is an article not based on straight reportage, but is instead the writer's opinion on current events. Newspapers use an increasing number of columnists as "name" writers to attract readers. Becoming a columnist is considered a feather for any reporter's cap, not only for the prestige, but also because the reporter's mug appears in print. Columnists may do their own legwork, but others more or less write in response to the news of the day and rely on previously published reports for their research.

Columnists are considered to have superior writing skills and have better developed views than reporters. Columnists usually come in two varieties: the hard news and the soft news columnists. Hard news columnists cover city affairs, politics, crime and business, and tend to be hard-nosed and opinionated. Many columnists aren't even journalists by trade but may be former politicians or political advisers (think Dick Morris and Tony Blankley) to lawyers (think Ann Coulter). A columnist is more than just a writer: he needs to have personality or have been an "insider" to a certain institution's workings. If covering politics or government, the columnist will either be left or right-winged (moderates need not apply).

Soft news columnists cover topics like advice, health, humor, home improvement, sports, law, finance, movie reviews, arts, entertainment and "slice of life" stories. Like their hard news counterparts, many soft news columnists were never journalists, but were professionals in other fields. These columnists are promoted by their various personalities, from domestic frump to pop culture geek. These scribes will be more casual and may have nicknames like "The Movie Guy."

Correspondent

Generally speaking, this is a reporter covering a region outside the media outlet's mandated geographic area. If the reporter is a foreign correspondent, sometimes he can speak the language in the area; but some reporters rely on interpreters. Some correspondents are dispatched to an area for the outlet, but many times, the reporter is a freelancer who already lives in the region.

Editor

An editor is the newspaper or magazine's manager: he or she oversees the day-to-day journalistic operations. The editor assigns and edits stories, determines the editorial direction and content of the publication and oversees the hiring, firing, promotion and demotion of journalists. There are different levels of editors who oversee different aspects of the publication (editor-in-chief, managing editor, senior editor and section editor, for example); however, a copy editor has the most thankless and unglamorous job in journalism: he or she edits stories for factual and grammatical errors.

Pundit

Television pundits are the columnists of the television world: their reason for being is to share their opinions on the current events of the day. Most pundits are former politicians, advisors, military generals and lawyers of note who made their name elsewhere, though some newspaper and magazine columnists may also become TV pundits. These personalities are expected to be talkative and opinionated, and although they are supposed to have areas of expertise, most will form opinions on topics on which they have no experience (or clue). Pundits also tend to shout and be loud and obnoxious. Some do their jobs with dignity, while others shrill their way to lucrative book deals.

Interview Subject

The person a reporter interviews for a story. The interview subject can be used for color, information or analysis. The interviewee may be an expert, hero, victim or witness to an event. Reporters may gain knowledge through an interview or they may gain bragging rights if the interviewee is normally press-shy.

Though the interview itself can be conducted in person, by phone or less commonly (and less recommended) through other means, such as an e-mail interview. The reporter asks the interviewee a series of questions in the hopes of getting valuable or at least interesting answers from the individual.

Though the interview structure is as unique as the journalist conducting it, there are certain rules that reporters follow. "On the record" means the reporter can publish or broadcast everything discussed during the interview, as well as the name of the source. "Off the record" means that the journalist can use the information for his own background research, but can't publish either the information or the name of the person who gave him the information. In other words, everything is off limits. In the middle of these two extremes is an agreement that the information is not for attribution, meaning the reporter can use the information without naming the specific person who gave it (this is more commonly known as using an anonymous source). Finally, on background means the reporter can use the information, but only use a general title for attribution (such as "a senior official" or "a military official").

Eyewitness

An eyewitness is a type of interviewee who has seen an event first-hand and is asked to describe what he or she has seen.

Leak

This occurs when a reporter receives information that other individuals or organizations do not want to be made public (or at least publicized at that moment) but someone within the group gives the information to the reporter anyway. The person leaking information will most likely demand that his or her name not be used in the article, hence demanding to be labeled as an anonymous source. Some leak information to reporters for altruistic reasons, while others do it for self-serving ones. Some facts given to journalists are pseudo-leaks—that is, the source that provided information to a reporter then pretends to object to the information being publicized.

Byline

The reporter's name, appearing under the headline or under the article that he or she wrote. The byline wasn't created for the benefit of readers or to reward journalists for good reporting, but began during the Civil War as a way for Union Army generals to keep track of which reporter had writtn each story. A byline strike occurs when journalists withhold their names from articles (usually stemming from a contract dispute with management or to protest a despised new policy). Short articles and many advertorial stories don't carry bylines.

Traditionally, no more than two reporters were given credit for the same story; however, these days it is standard practice for newspapers and magazines to credit all reporters who were involved with the story. This does not mean all reporters credited wrote the story, but that some reporters (and interns) contributed to research and interviews that were used in the story. For those who did not contribute to writing the story, their names may appear after the article with the tagline "contributed to the story" or "additional reporting by."

Embedding

Embedding means that an institution will allow select reporters to conditionally cover an extended event by having reporters assigned to certain units of that institution. Though the term was popularized during the 2003 Iraq war when reporters were allowed to join and travel with certain military units and cover events as they unfolded, it has also become a term used during election campaigns.

Convergence

Media convergence is defined as the fusing and pooling of various media outlets through technology. With media conglomerates seeking expansion, convergence allows for flexible media partnerships. This allows outlets to pool resources, stories, technology, brand names (such as titles) and editors and journalists to streamline operations. This type of pooling is also referred to as synergy. The downside is that convergence means fewer outlets and jobs, and constricts the number of ideas and voices heard.

Wire Service

This is a news gathering organization that sells stories to newspapers, magazines, Internet, radio and television stations. Most media outlets subscribe to wire services for all or much of their news. Some wire service agencies include *Associated Press (AP)*, *United Press International (U.P.I.*—now owned by the Unification Church), Reuters (British-based), *Bloomberg, Canadian Press (CP)*, Getty Images and *Agence France-Presse (AFP)*.

Contrived News Definitions

News is supposed to be informative, important and substantial, but there are people and organizations that are paid to strategically disseminate material that is favorable to their client's best interests—they call it "public relations." Because the material originating from these organizations is preprocessed and edited to be media-friendly, this type of information can be seen as contrived news. This view of public relations may be cynical, but these guys aren't paid to slag off their employer or client. These people also have their own groupspeak, which it doesn't hurt to know:

Public Relations (PR)

Individuals or companies may need to improve or maintain relations with the press and need more media-savvy individuals to help them deal with the news media; hence these individuals will need experts who specialize in public relations. Companies may have their own PR department or hire a PR firm, but both are paid by a company to either disseminate positive information about a person or company or to stem negative publicity. Many former journalists go on to work in public relations and hence have contacts and know the media industry intimately.

PR firms may organize contrived events, set up press conferences, compose and disseminate press releases and coach clients in media relations. Some PR firms deal exclusively with small companies, while others specialize in crisis communications. Larger firms handle accounts from multinational conglomerates, celebrities and even countries.

While those working public relations will say their job is to inform the public about a company or individual, PR firms are paid to present one-sided information and spin negative information in order to present their clients in the most favorable light.

Press Release

This is a statement that originates from a company or organization that is sent to journalists in order to generate publicity for the company. They mimic news articles with datelines, the inverted-pyramid style of writing and even quotes, though the information is one-sided and ignores any negative aspects of the announcement, making the release a form of advertising. Press releases are sent in the hope that the news outlet will not only pursue the story, but that journalists will pursue it with the same slant presented in the news release.

Video News Release (VNR)

The VNR is a prepackaged digital tape sent to journalists via satellite feed from public relations firms or departments. Like the press release, VNRs are sent with the sole purpose of getting media coverage for a person, product, organization or event. News outlets don't pay for VNRs—these packages are created by former journalists, who now work for public relations companies, and are paid for by the client company. VNRs may include "interviews" (obviously since the VNR originated from the interviewee, the questions will show the person in the best light), demos of new products, press conferences or product demonstrations. VNRs may run from a minute and a half to two minutes, making it easy for hundreds of newscasts to use them.

Some news outlets rely on VNRs to various degrees and use them without verbally attributing where the footage came from, though they will more likely label the footage on the screen. Free VNRs are cheaper to use than paying for a cameraman and journalist to drive to various locations to shoot footage and interview people. For radio stations, some companies may also provide an audio news release (ANR).

Government agencies have VNRs available on their websites, as do universities and many larger corporations. Some companies specialize in the making of VNRs: while some VNRs are common for business, technology and medical related stories, they are used for hard news stories as well. Another common use of VNRs is celebrity interviews; entertainers promoting a new film or CD may have a VNR sent to the news media in lieu of sitting down for a face-to-face interview with journalists, meaning the interviewee has near-full control of both the content produced and the questions they answer. Not surprisingly, these videos are a regular part of local and national stories: footage seen on newscasts isn't filmed by the station's cameraman or videographer, but is supplied by the company profiled in the story.

Press Conference

This is a canned event with at least one speaker, moderator and several journalists, whereby the speaker makes an announcement, then has reporters ask questions, while the speaker presumably answers them (though some conferences do not have a question and answer period, making the trip a wasted one). Conferences may be used to announce political candidacies, retirements, mergers, acquisitions or product launches. Press conferences are also used by police departments for investigation updates, and by governments and companies during a crisis. This is a staged news event with prepared statements where only certain journalists may be invited. The journalists who do attend may not be acknowledged or properly answered.

Advertorial

Also known in some circles as the "fuzzy bunny," this is an advertisement that looks like an actual magazine or newspaper article. This will be in the form of an article, many times with a byline that mimics a news report in every way, except that it will be extremely positive about a product, service, destination or location. Advertorial articles may be delegated to freelance writers and young, novice journalists, though other reporters may write advertorial copy as well. Advertorial topics are diverse, ranging from the benefits of prearranging your funeral to tips on how to get the most out of your wedding photographer. Many special sections and inserts, such as bridal, automotive or travel, are in fact paid advertising. While smaller community papers and local magazines rely heavily on advertorials, larger publications also feature these ads as well.

Television and radio stations also carry fuzzy bunnies; many "travel shows" and "health shows" are nothing more than advertorials. When a program starts off with a disclaimer, it's a sure sign that the program is nothing more than paid advertising, even if it's hosted by one of the station's anchors or hosts.

Stunt

A stunt is a feat or trick performed for the express purpose of getting media attention. It's any tactic used to bring attention to a person, product or cause. Stunts can include (but are not limited to) picketing, using props, storming government meetings or media events, chanting or even using trickery. Stunts themselves aren't truly news or newsworthy since they won't change anyone's lives, but stunts hinge on journalists' thirst for the interesting and unusual. Some people use stunts to generate publicity for a cause or to draw attention to social problems and some use them to promote products or companies, while others use them to bring attention to themselves. An example of a media stunt would be a politician hanging a "sold" sign on a government building.

Junket

A junket is a free trip given to reporters by a company or organization to promote an event or product. Though many media outlets ban their reporters and editors from accepting junkets, they are still used. Some other events may be borderline junkets, such as the practice of having reporters on campaign buses during elections. Junkets are more commonly used for celebrity reporting, such as promoting a new movie, CD or film festival. Though companies will pay for a reporter's travel expenses, most executives expect that the reporter will write a positive piece about their vehicle.

Graft/Freebie

A freebie is a gift given to reporters from political or corporate interests, ranging from a free dinner to an expensive keepsake. The gift is given in the hopes that the reporter will take a liking to the gift giver and thus downplay the negative or focus on the positive—but technically the gift comes without any strings attached. Graft, on the other hand, is given to all reporters during special events, such as political conventions. Graft can range from t-shirts to mugs to customized cell phones with logos to pens. The theory is that reporters won't be swayed by toys, but graft is a standard way to try to soften up a journalist. Whether the journalist falls for this ploy or not depends on the moral fortitude of the individual reporter. Some news organizations prohibit reporters and editors from accepting freebies and graft.

Chapter Three

| How News is Created

In the news world, time and space have to be continually filled with new, attention-grabbing information, and filling this never-ending void can be easy or complicated, depending on the story, the reporter's deftness and the resources available to the news outlet. Some stories can be produced within minutes, while others can take months. The trick for reporters is to truthfully present reality while being just engaging and entertaining enough to sustain an audience's attention. It's a bizarre and awkward balance that reporters and editors have to strike every day.

Creating news stories isn't a simple process: the reporter, producer or editor has to first decide on which story to pursue. Then the reporter has to research the story, observe the surroundings relevant to the issue and interview people who can provide information, opinion, context or analysis. He then has to decide how he's going to cover the story and what angle he will use. Creating the final package is the last step in the process.

Still, some parts of the reporter's job are easier than others. For instance, presenting the news is easier than gathering raw information. Writing or producing stories is fairly straightforward: news outlets have their own set formats and styles that reporters follow. Print reporters have stylebooks and their writing style has to "fit" the publication's editorial mandate and voice. Radio and television news scripts are short and to the point; the journalist actually says very little, and illustrates his story with interviews as well as footage or sound.

That's not to say telling a story is always simple; some news items are harder to present than others. How much violence should be shown? How much intimate or embarrassing information should be disclosed? Despite these questions, most news stories aren't too complicated to package to an audience.

What is more complicated is getting access to relevant information. The more potentially life altering and important the information, the harder it is for journalists to find it. Finding information about an accessible and popular actor's latest film is a breeze; finding key documents and sources about a foreign government's secret weapons program is going to be difficult.

From language barriers to intimidation to censorship to threats of law suits, gathering important news can be frustrating, even dangerous at times. When it comes to soft, happy news, there is no shortage of people throwing information in reporters' faces. It's the hard news that's the most difficult to gather.

The Basic News Gathering Process

The way a national network news show gathers news won't be the same as the way a rural weekly newspaper does it, but both will have some things in common. Most news organizations have regular editorial meetings to debate and decide what stories will get covered, who will cover them and how, as well as where those stories will be placed. Newspapers will also have regular meetings or at least keep in close contact with the circulation department to decide what stories are likely to attract the most readers and how those stories will be promoted.

A print editor or radio or TV producer may assign particular stories to certain journalists, depending on the reporter's specialty, contacts or abilities, or the reporter may find or come up with stories on his own. While most news outlets have full-time reporters on staff, some stories are produced by freelancers. Newspaper editors usually assign stories to freelance writers, while freelancers pitch ideas to magazine editors.

Once a reporter sets upon a story, she needs to gather as much information as she can—but there will be a time limit, from a few minutes to several months. How she gets her information depends on her ability and ambition, but there are common places where reporters look. She may read press releases or media advisories to determine whether a story or angle is worth pursuing. Some news events happen at regular intervals, such as city hall meetings or an Attorney General's weekly news conference.

Reporters also read newswires or watch satellite feeds of images of international news to get information. Some television reporters will rely on VNRs for visuals or for information for their stories, and some will attend press conferences. Most news outlets read, listen to and watch other media outlets to get ideas and to compare their coverage to that of their rivals.

Information may also come to the reporter through rumors, contacts with regular sources, leaks, phone calls or e-mails from readers or viewers who may have first-hand experience with a news story. Reporters also get leads and information from police scanners, government reports, research studies, coroner or fire marshal reports as well. Court trials, government meetings, conferences, protests, combat zones and campaigns will also attract reporters looking for dirt.

Other information can come from the self-reporting of people or organizations. What book, CD or film is a best seller? Who was promoted

CEO? How many jobs were lost this month? Who was arrested? Who won the World Series? Who was voted president?

There will be experts, officials, players or eyewitnesses to interview; however, not all of them will want to see their names publicized. Some of those individuals will be those directly involved in the story (some of these individuals may also be known as newsmakers); others may be witnesses, heroes or victims of events. Some will be experts. Many will agree to speak to the reporter only on condition of anonymity. The reporter may also choose to interview people not directly involved in a story to get their opinion on the topic (known as "streeters").

The print reporter's story will be read by at least one editor before it's published. The editor will change the wording and ask the reporter questions to make sure the information is accurate and in context, and then come up with the story's headline. If the reporter works for a magazine, she will submit materials and the contact information of sources to the fact-checker, who ideally will follow up on the information to ensure that none is fabricated or incorrect. Radio reporters and TV reporters' stories will be vetted by producers before being broadcast. The radio host or TV anchor will introduce the story from a prepared script.

Each news story starts with a lead: this is the first sentence in a news report, a hook to lead the audience into wanting to know more. Usually, the most important and newest information comes first. Print reporters may add color to their stories; that is, they may embellish their stories with vivid details and descriptions of people, places or events. Color may come in the form of a telling anecdote about a newsmaker's legendary temper or a detailed description of a crime scene. The theory is that dry, straightforward news turns readers off. Color is an essential part of the news that helps readers visualize and understand a story better. Radio reporters use certain sounds for the same reason that TV reporters use powerful visuals.

This is a simple and condensed explanation of news gathering, and the above description doesn't capture the entire story, such as the media's use of consultants and focus groups to boost circulation or ratings. Each media outlet has its own standards and idiosyncrasies.

The Process of Gate-Keeping

Just as you can't let everyone into your house, editors and producers can't let everyone onto their property, either. Some people, issues and events can expect the red carpet treatment, while others will be shut out of the back pages, let alone the headlines. Those who are snubbed by the press will complain bitterly about the silent treatment, claiming everything from media bias to a vast diabolical conspiracy. Bias may very well be a reason why some groups and people are shut out, but other times, these people simply aren't newsworthy—or, if they are newsworthy, there are more important stories, issues and newsmakers who've beat them out for limited time and space. Additionally, some invisibles simply don't know how to properly present themselves as media-friendly commodities.

Some people know how the gatekeeper thinks and what the keeper is looking for when granting access. They can package their message into amusing sound bites and look good on camera. Call it elitism, the caste system or even the pecking order, but people who know how to work the press can nab more headlines than they deserve. Other people can work the news audiences, too. Slap one person's face on a magazine cover, and the publication sees a significant increase in single copy sales. Princess Diana was a trusty circulation booster in her time, regardless of the fact that her private life had virtually no impact on the audience. Slap another person's visage on the same cover, and the sales will plummet. This rule applies to everyone from A-list actors to politicians to accused murderers.

Danger, impact, innovation and social change will open the gate. Will the story affect lives? Can audiences relate to the main players? Does the story surprise or shock viewers or readers? Is the story outlandish? Are the events taking place nearby? Can it evoke strong emotional reactions in a jaded audience? If the answer is no, then the gate closes shut. There are too many stories and issues competing for limited space and resources.

Immediacy and impact are important elements a story needs to grab media interest, but the story also has to appeal to a wide audience, since most media forms depend on advertising and subscriptions for their very survival. The bottom line is that the bottom line greatly controls what will make news.

Put bluntly, give the public what it wants: the public wants to know about danger, from natural disasters to rampant crime. They want to know what laws and government policies will affect them. The public also has an interest in education, business, health and entertainment. Audience tastes do change, though—the 1970s had a focus on labor news; by the 1990s, the shift was towards business news.

People and corporations who understand what makes the media tick have an easier time getting past the gatekeeper, who is always looking for new ideas and stories, despite having only limited space to fill. They can hire consultants and public relations firms to help get their point across in a more media-friendly way. Those who either don't have the money or the savvy to hire outside help may find themselves left standing in front of a locked gate.

But don't think that the media-savvy can persuade journalists and editors to give them air time every time. Some editors and producers will run with whatever stories their rivals are pursuing. The news peg is the journalist's version of peer pressure: if other outlets think someone or something is newsworthy, then they will follow the crowd. It used to be fashionable to report on world hunger and domestic homelessness, yet these stories have all but disappeared from the mainstream press. Why? Have these problems been eradicated? No, but they did become passé media topics. This isn't to say that news outlets can't be trendsetters or go against the grain but, to a degree, editors and reporters do look to their peers and rivals for direction.

Once a person, issue or event makes it past the gate, it's up to news producers to decide how to present the story. Marshall McLuhan said that "the medium is the message," and he was right. Papers cover the same news differently from radio and television, simply because of the built-in strengths and constraints each media form has.

How Stories Are Packaged

Radio is about sound and convenience. Radio stories aren't heavy on information; most people listen to radio news in their cars or while concentrating on other tasks at home. They will be short and easy to digest. Stories will make use of both natural sound and interviews. Radio excels at reporting breaking news, but it can't deliver in-depth coverage, since audiences may lose interest or become distracted. News delivery is quick, punchy and to the point. Newscasts usually start with serious hard news such as crime, and end with a kicker—a strange, funny or amusing story to lighten the audience's spirits.

Television, on the other hand, relies on images and personalities. Though TV is a medium of moving pictures, it is still highly dependent on sound for its impact: a viewer can still follow the news even if he isn't watching. News stories need powerful images combined with bare bones reporting.

Even though large-screen televisions have become commonplace in American households, the types of images seen on newscasts, surprisingly, haven't greatly changed. Most news anchors sit behind the news desk with only their head and shoulders visible. Anchors will be perky, though the male anchor will probably be much older than his female co-anchor. Even though newscasts use violent images to tell stories, the footage is still highly sanitized and edited: you won't see the rotting corpse of a murder victim on the six o'clock news. Television can also cover both breaking news and traumatic events effectively.

Background music is a staple of prime time news magazines, and not just for stories profiling musicians. While "60 Minutes" doesn't rely on background music, newsmagazines like "20/20" seem to use mood music for almost every story. Happy news gets whimsical music; scary news is accompanied by dramatic scores; sad news is mixed with soft piano music.

Newspapers rely on words and reader investment. Sounds and sights have to be described. Still pictures can be a powerful way to capture a news event, but it is still the written word that rules. Stories can be long or short, but they will be more in-depth than stories covered by radio or TV outlets. On the other hand, newspapers have a harder time covering breaking news, since other media can report these stories more quickly.

Newspapers tend to be bulky and finger-staining, and are considered disposable: once the reader is finished reading, the paper is either left behind for others to read or is thrown out. On the plus side, newspapers can cover a wider range of topics and can excel at investigative stories. With the explosion of Internet sites using wire stories, newspapers publishing those same reports make the paper seem one step behind, since papers will publish the same stories a day or two later.

Magazines rely on format and style to tell their stories. News magazines have a fairly predictable format: the first few sections of the magazine deal with shorter stories, newsmaker quotes, graphs and quick observations. Later sections contain longer articles, with accompanying photos, graphs and illustrations. While many newspaper stories don't rely on visuals, most longer magazine articles will have at least one illustration. Pictures in magazines must be high quality, clear, large and preferably in color.

Finally, Internet news sites are more closely related to television (viewers stare at a screen, whether it be a computer screen or a cell phone screen), but unlike TV, websites still heavily rely on text to disseminate information. In that way, they share close ties to newspapers and magazines. Moving images and sounds can also be featured—meaning the Internet borrows from radio and TV. Breaking news can be posted and disseminated to an international audience quickly.

Yet websites have quirks that eluded their precursors. Audiences can choose what stories they read, and in what order. Users can post messages reacting to stories and they can also gain access to a large number of stories on a particular topic very quickly. While some sites have web logs from their journalists, most sites still rely on other media outlets—such as newspaper and wire services—for their content.

What should become clear is that reporters use many tools *that do not directly relate in any way to the facts of the story*. For example, what informational value does using morose-sounding violins as background music have? Why do we have to know the color of someone's dress? These parlor tricks are used to spice up stories, but they also have a more questionable purpose: they are ways to bolster a factually weak story with window dressing. These tricks can also be used to manipulate the audience's emotions, which leads to the question: how do news outlets expect angry, frightened or depressed audiences to make rational decisions and judgments?

Still, most news packaging is not done in a deliberate attempt to fool the public. Most news producers do honestly believe the information they are reporting is fair, balanced, truthful and accurate (and many times, it is). But information can be manipulated—music directs the audience to feel a certain way, even an extreme close up of a newsmaker can make a normally honest person look shifty and dishonest.

You should keep the above points in mind when watching the news. Be aware of the background music, story placement and camera angles. However, problems with news reporters don't just stem from their normal, everyday way of doing business—it's also the journalists' constraints that make them vulnerable to lies.

Chapter Four

Media Realities

The news media isn't a public service—it's a business. Its survival depends on both consumers buying and using its services and its ability to generate profit. That profit comes from two main sources: advertising and paid circulation. Yet even the rates outlets can charge advertisers depend on the size and demographic make-up of the audience.

Producing news can be an expensive proposition, considering the price of newsprint, technology, travel and labor. The cost of producing investigative stories can be prohibitive to many smaller news outlets, especially during economic recessions. Customer satisfaction also drives the media machine: when readers and viewers complain or tune out, their anger or apathy can at times impact what news is delivered and how it is packaged. Worse, if a punitive advertiser pulls its dollars out of the "offending" outlet or if someone decides to slap the outlet with a lawsuit, a newspaper, magazine or station can be financially crippled.

This means each news outlet has to make due with the resources it has: larger outlets have the resources to invest in manpower and technology, while others get by with a shoestring budget and a resourceful and dedicated staff who can deliver hard-hitting investigative pieces and exposés. Most news outlets also rely on freelancers and unpaid interns to produce content.

If attracting an audience and securing advertising dollars and subscribers wasn't enough, news outlets are faced with other constraints and barriers that can limit what they can produce in terms of quality, investigation and diversity of voices. While journalists are supposed to be detached, objective observers who chronicle the world around them, their surroundings and ground rules do influence what issues they can report and how they will cover events and issues.

What Factors Can Restrain Journalists

Media Concentration: Most major cities have at least one daily newspaper, a few TV stations, several radio stations and an assortment of news and alternative websites. That alone seems to show a town's democratic health and media diversity—this is, of course, if you ignore the fact that large conglomerates probably own more than one of these properties and their parent companies probably don't live in the same city. Significantly fewer newspapers are owned by independent companies. Gannett, Clear Channel, News Corporation, Tribune, McClatchy, E.W. Scripps, Hearst, New York Times Company, General Electric, Viacom and Walt Disney Company are some of the better-known media titans, though companies such as Community Newspaper Holdings, Liberty Media Corporation and Freedom Communications are also notable media players.

With the Federal Communications Commission (FCC) considering loosening media cross-ownership rules, a single company can own different media platforms in the same market. So whoever owns your city's local television and radio stations could also own your town's newspaper, too. It could even be conceivable that with weaker limits on media ownership, the US landscape could one day see the same high level of media concentration as in Canada, a country where most news outlets are owned by less than a handful of players. So much for diversity of voices and opinions.

When one media company owns a slew of properties, they tend to "streamline," "integrate" or "centralize" operations, meaning that individual outlets will have fewer local reporters keeping watch on unfolding events and have to rely more on shared resources. Even now, newspapers and broadcasters disseminate identical news stories; i.e., the same stories which are produced by the same wire services are used by rival media outlets. Having fewer media players means that fewer stories are produced. For example, why bother having one hundred newspapers writing their own editorials when they can all print the same editorial produced by head office?

And what happens if one conglomerate eventually collapses on its own weight? True, its assets will be divvied up and absorbed by other conglomerates—but that means there would be even fewer voices, stories and ideas presented. If other companies are also financially strapped and couldn't afford to take on any more properties, then those unsold outlets would be forced to shut down. With Hollinger International's recent troubles with its majority shareholder Conrad Black seemingly using company assets to fund his own lavish lifestyle, how credible would they seem if they didn't see what was going on right under their noses?

Even if a media conglomerate is in excellent financial health, reporters still have to be careful not to burn their bridges. Can a reporter dare criticize his employers, then expect to find work as a journalist elsewhere, especially if the parent company owns most of the radio, television or newspapers in that region?

A final byproduct of media concentration is the homogenization of a company's product. Just as every Wal-Mart and Holiday Inn looks alike, news outlets owned by the same parent company will have a similar "feel," but to achieve that consistency means taking out quirks and ending up with a blander product. What this all means to reporters and editors is that news outlets are allowed fewer voices, fewer types of voices, less creativity and less autonomy to produce the news. Outlets also have to rely on shared news copy and direction from the head office. Controls and checks fall into fewer hands.

Convergence: One byproduct of media consolidation is the popular buzz-word "convergence." Though the melding of different media is still in its infancy, one way convergence is changing journalism is that future reporters will have to be well-versed with multiple media platforms, such as television, print, radio and the Internet. While having multi-talented journalists is always beneficial, good reporters without TV or radio-friendly personalities or faces may be left out in the cold.

Another consideration is that with technology allowing media outlets to disseminate information quickly, stories will have to be completed faster than before, giving the multi-tasking reporter less time for minor considerations, such as depth, reflection, investigation, accuracy and thoroughness. Finally, whether reporters will suffer from burnout more quickly (since journalists will be asked to take on the jobs of several people) still remains to be seen.

Circulation/Ratings: A media outlet's survival depends on how many and even what type of people use its product. Any declines in circulation or ratings means that media outlets will have to lower the rates they charge to advertisers. Thus, story placement and inclusion do depend to a certain degree on what is likely to attract the largest audience.

Worse, if younger audiences aren't using the product, advertisers may not wish to give their patronage to that outlet. Advertisers tend not to like audiences who were born in the 1950s or previously. It's blatant age discrimination, but advertisers have a right to spend their money any way they choose, even if a sizable percentage of their customers happen to have gray hair.

With that in mind, what story will make it on the front page: the one that is complex, but important, or the one that will attract the most viewers? Sadly, you'll get to find out which disposable Hollywood couple slept together before you'll find out whether the food you are eating may be killing you.

Advertising: It's hard to run a media outlet without sufficient funds. For news outlets, the problems of maintaining steady funding and the threat of advertisers pulling their funding if certain news stories offend them always looms.

The other side to advertising in the news media is "advertorials." These "articles" look like news items, but in fact are just puff pieces paid for by companies that tout their products and services. For years, general interest magazines have increasingly blurred the line between advertising and editorial content, but newspapers also have their own fuzzy bunnies in the soft news parts of the paper, such as the home improvement, travel and automobile sections.

Competition: Media outlets, especially network television news programs, fight hard to gain audiences and one way to secure higher ratings or circulation is to be the first to publish or broadcast breaking news. In the news world, competition is fierce, meaning a reporter doesn't have time to double check information, fearing that his colleague and rivals might also find the same information and out-scoop him.

Then there is the question of the "get"; being the first reporter to nab an exclusive interview with a newsmaker. How far reporters or hosts will go to secure an elusive newsmaker has been debated and put under scrutiny. In the quest to be the first to interview the latest "get," many reporters and personalities have crossed ethical and moral boundaries. Pandering kiss up letters, telling white lies, assuring positive press coverage and even promising TV movie deals have all been used in the ongoing bloody war to interview the hip newsmaker of the week.

Story Structure: Whether it be a radio story or a newspaper feature, writing styles and story types need to "fit" with the outlet's mandate and vision. Still, there are certain rules journalists have to follow when writing or producing a story; for example, any quotes a television or radio reporter uses will be short—one or two sentences at the most, lest the audience become bored with the speaker. These are referred to as "sound bites"; long, thoughtful quotes may shed light on a topic, but will have to be cut to make the final product.

Furthermore, important stories that don't fit with an outlet's editorial vision will be nixed, as are stories not conforming to the protocol. That may mean that certain facts and angles will be excluded from the final story. Reporters who wish to flourish at any outlet understand the rules, even if they don't agree with them. While many reporters fight hard to bend the rules, others follow docilely.

Time/Space Constraints: There are many important stories that get little or no exposure—not because of malice on the part of the editor or producer, but because there are only so many stories that can fit in a single newscast or publication. Even when a story does make the cut, some important details have to be sacrificed for brevity's sake. Journalists and editors have to decide which elements can be included and which can be left out.

Complicated stories don't translate well to television or radio. Dry topics such as constitutional law make for boring news with poor graphics (how interesting is it to show documents lying on a wooden table)? While television news producers have been accused of favoring sensational stories, such as murders, violence and celebrities, the truth is that these stories lend themselves to dynamic, gripping images. A hunky, uncooperative and somewhat depraved drug dealer being carted off by hunky and somewhat peeved police officers makes for better visuals than a roomful of aging aldermen debating the merits of banning smoking.

Uncooperative or Difficult Sources: The maddening irony in journalism is that the people who have the most intimate knowledge about the most dangerous, immoral and corrupt practices and scams (whether it be a murder, environmental violations or corruption) are also the ones who have the most to lose if their identity becomes public. That's why many of these people keep quiet: they either don't want to endanger themselves or they still somehow benefit from these unethical practices, even if they don't agree with them. Reporters trying to uncover corruption hit brick walls with sources, either refusing to speak or making demands that the reporter cannot grant.

In addition, people change stories or exaggerate. Reporters have to deal with arrogant, temperamental and even mentally unstable sources. Some other interviewees can back out at the eleventh hour, making the reporter's job that much more frustrating.

Lack of Knowledge/Training: You don't need a license to practice journalism. Technically, you don't actually need a high school degree to practice it, either. Not to indulge in elite snobbery, but considering that journalists are supposed to uncover facts, it would help if they had some training. Today, many journalists do have journalism degrees, but sometimes that may not be enough for their area of expertise; for example, while many media outlets have medical and health reporters who actually have a medical or science degree, others do not. You don't need an MBA to cover business and finance. Journalism programs across the country are currently seeing a decrease in funding, meaning fewer classes and professors are available to students.

What journalism schools, or "j-schools," excel in is teaching students how to write stories and perform well in front of a mike or camera. Some, but not all schools thoroughly teach students the art and science of researching. Most j-schools do not teach future journalists how to think critically or how to avoid getting bamboozled by a fraudulent source. Statistics, scientific methods, forensics, anthropology, psychology, criminology and reasoning—all critical mental tools a journalist needs to negotiate with his subjects, are not taught to students. Unless the student has a degree in one of these areas or takes these electives on his own initiative, he will have gaps in his knowledge. The exception may be Columbia University's Graduate School of Journalism, which has attempted to address this issue by revamping its journalism program with a more academic and philosophical focus, much to the chagrin of many old-school reporters.

For the most part, while j-schools do a splendid job of refining their students and teaching them "the craft," they do nothing to teach them the rough and tumble ways of con artists—whether the con in question runs a three-card monty racket on the street or is the CEO of a multinational conglomerate.

Focus Groups/Consultants: Consultants and focus groups are used by outlets to help maintain and increase their number of readers and viewers. It's ironic for an industry whose very job it is to know what's going on to have to hire others to tell them what's going on. Outlets rely on companies that tell them how to increase their numbers; however, consultants don't bother themselves with how to improve the content of the news product, their mandate is to help boost numbers, whether the boosting improves the news gathering process or not.

To wit, one research group suggested that for newspapers to attract more under-thirty readers, they should focus more on celebrity news, make sections and stories easier to find (calling the process "navigability"), and make the paper more "user friendly" (the astute bunch offered papers this sage advice: "Magazines are highly successful among younger adults because they are bright, colorful and full of pictures!") While that may get a few additional young readers in the short term, the problem is that the consultants didn't actually stop to think whether it is a news outlet's mandate to report on trivialities. Aren't there important topics that interest the young also?

The consultants assumed that the young like celebrity news because of the glamour factor, but didn't seem to consider that perhaps young people like celebrity because celebrities tend to be people who are in or near the same age group as the young audience member. That means that papers could just as well be attracting younger readers if their hard news focused on issues relevant and important to youth. After all, there is a difference between the headline "Are your children safe at school?" versus "Are you safe at school?" The fact that the research group didn't consider an obvious alternate explanation shows that media outlets don't always look for critical thinking skills from their paid advisors.

Reporters and editors work mostly within these rules and boundaries. Many can do this while producing quality and accurate work, while others have faltered and made embarrassing mistakes. If these constraints weren't enough to impede the journalistic product, the industry's inherent vulnerabilities have also caused journalists to make some serious mistakes.

| **Breakdowns**

News is supposed to be an accurate and truthful account of events; how editors and reporters ensure that the stories they present meet those criteria is another question. Some editors and producers are strict and vigilant, some are lax and a few others are corrupt. There are reporters who are meticulous, others who are lackadaisical and some who are crooked and have an agenda. How rigorously editors and journalists apply their trade varies from outlet to outlet, but even the most respected and revered newspapers and TV news magazines have fallen for hoaxes and scams. With advancements in information technology, one would think finding accurate information would be an easier task, yet news producers still fall for simple and illogical hoaxes. The truth is repeatedly ignored; lies are repeatedly believed.

Journalists should look inward to find the reason why they not only fall for lies, but also why a disturbing number of reporters deliberately spread them. The organizational and rewards systems in most newsrooms are constructed in such a way that speed is more important than accuracy, and finding a fresh deviate to display is rewarded over using critical thinking. This is a profession that has tolerated, promoted and even fawned over reporters who deliberately lied about facts and plundered other reporters' stories, passing them off as their own. With each new scandal, journalism loses that much more credibility, but news producers still insist that their rotting and crumbling structure remain untouched.

When too much leeway is given to reporters, the results can be damaging to the industry's reputation. Jack Kelley was a well-respected foreign correspondent for *USA Today* for twenty-one years. He was the first *USAT* journalist to be a Pulitzer finalist and was the paper's de facto poster boy. Though there were internal rumblings about the star journalist's work, to the tune that he had few restrictions when it came to using unnamed sources, Kelley's reputation for intrepid reporting was well known in industry circles.

Then, in May 2003, an anonymous letter from a journalist accused the reporter of fabricating and embellishing stories he filed in Israel, Cuba and the Balkans. Kelley was known to produce stories with succinct, meaningful quotes, a remarkable feat considering that Kelley almost always needed translators whenever he was working abroad—many times in chaotic, war-torn hot spots. While some of Kelley's stories were confirmed to be true after an internal investigation, one article led to his ouster.

The front-page article in question, appearing on July 14, 1999, was about Serbian atrocities committed during the Kosovo War. What was particularly explosive was that Kelley had heard a damning and tangible admission by one Serb soldier of the horrors committed against his declared enemy:

> U.N. war crimes investigators have found Yugoslav army documents containing what they say is the strongest and most direct evidence linking the government of Yugoslav President Slobodan Milosevic to "ethnic cleansing" in Kosovo, *USA Today* has learned.

Kelley described the three-ringed "black vinyl notebook" whose scribbled Cyrillic contents were "examined by *USA Today*" as containing "dozens" of names of Serbian soldiers who were actively partaking in atrocities as well as detailed records of war crimes committed by the Serbian soldiers. It seemed as if Kelley spoke to one of the investigators directly:

> "This is proof that Belgrade directed the operation," the investigator who found the items said. She refused to allow her name to be used for fear of reprisals. "It is the strongest single piece of evidence (against Milosevic) to date."

The story had not been scrutinized until the May 2003 investigation began. Though the July 14 article was not listed on the secret detractor's letters, an independent complaint about the article surfaced nearly four years after the original story was published. Kelley maintained that the story was true. He gave his editors the name of the unnamed activist whom he used for the article—Natasa Kandic, a well-known Serbian lawyer and outspoken critic of the Yugoslav military and government. He also said another UN investigator had shown him the book in front of Kandic.

One *USAT* editor contacted Kandic, but she said that she had not seen the diary in question. Editors pressed Kelley, who gave them the name of Danielja Jacamovich, one of two translators who Kelley said also saw the diary in question, but no one at the paper could locate the woman. Editors looked at telephone and expense records, but even then couldn't verify Kelley's claims.

Kelley then claimed there was a second translator present during his interview with Kandic; the original translator said she had not seen the diary, nor was there a second translator. Feeling the heat, Kelley said that he had located Jacamovich and that she would call them. A woman claiming to be the elusive translator did call *USAT*, but her odd behavior did not quiet suspicion.

USAT editors hired a private security firm that discovered that "Jacamovich" was in fact a Russian translator who had posed as Jacamovich at Kelley's request. Confronted with his deceptions, Kelley confessed that the Russian translator had posed as Danielja. Faced with termination, Kelley opted to resign on January 6, 2004. *USAT* editors had shown how powerful investigative reporting can be; unfortunately, it took place only after a reporter's credibility was called into question. The safeguards to catch nebulous sourcing should have been in place across the board for all reporters.

For journalists who are careful, it's still a tricky process of getting accurate, balanced and attention-grabbing information disseminated quickly without goofing up or facing the business end of a lawsuit. For journalists, the job-related stresses are numerous, from war zones to death threats to jail time for refusing to name confidential sources. Abusive sources and unpleasant editors can beleaguer even the most stoic of journalists.

Others can get in on the act, too. Viewers get offended over war images on television (they should try imagining how offensive it would be if they had to live through it). Reporters deal with self-righteous special interest groups, overzealous PR firms and thin-skinned suits, all of which are convinced that they are keepers of the Truth. Yet those distractions don't give reporters the excuse to gloss over ugly truths in fear of receiving complaints. Journalism shouldn't be a process where the reporter is merely a stenographer for spin doctors and publicists. Many reporters don't question what they hear, and many editors don't question what they read. The question is, why don't news producers think critically when it really counts?

What Makes the News World Vulnerable to Hoaxes and Scams

Time and Budget Constraints: An irony of the information age is that news can now be disseminated more quickly than at any other time in history, yet gathering raw information is still a long and laborious process. Investigative journalism costs money and may take months to complete. New information does not come prepackaged on an easily accessible electronic database. Investigative journalism requires researching, getting many people to open up, getting access to secret documents. It takes legwork, cajoling, persuading and digging—and none of this can be done on the fly or on the cheap.

The reality is that news holes have to be filled quickly, and that newsrooms simply don't always have the necessary funds needed to turn over every rock. Important stories are either ignored or they are not done as thoroughly as they should be. A con artist who knows a reporter is pressed for time or is desperate to find an exciting story can use these weaknesses to his advantage.

The second budget advantage a hoaxer has is that reporters, producers and editors, on the whole, are not paid very well by their employers. Entry-level reporters may make only the minimum wage, and freelance writers may be paid a couple of hundred dollars for a large article. Some interns and outside writers may work for free in the desperate hope of securing a paying position with the media outlet later on. Reporters, producers, editors and anchors that are paid in the millions make up only a small percentage of the entire journalistic community.

What this means is that many reporters are asked to produce accurate articles on a paltry budget. A freelance writer, for example, may want to conduct more thorough research, but is it worth his while to spend his entire fee on digging deeper into a story or is it better for him to cut corners and present a less probing piece? However, while a hoaxer can take advantage of a writer's financial status to disseminate a lie, wealthy journalists working for financially healthy outlets have also been conned.

Upset Advertisers and Interest Groups: Advertisers don't get mad; they pull their money out of a news outlet. Irate audiences don't get mad, they boycott the outlet instead. Virginia Gerst, an arts and entertainment editor for twenty-seven local papers owned by Pioneer Press in Chicago, resigned when she said management allowed the publisher's marketing manager to write a glowing review for a restaurant. Apparently the restaurant owner, who was also a former advertiser, took exception with a negative review published earlier—and the Pioneer Press decided to write a fluffy review to mend fences.

When a news outlet has been burned by bad publicity or the loss of hundreds of thousands of dollars or hundreds of readers or viewers, those scars may inhibit editors and reporters from taking on risky stories. People will complain about unflattering portrayals of their heroes and leaders. Reporters and editors may simply ignore red flags and nagging doubts, so as to not upset advertisers and audiences.

Color: Most editors and reporters wouldn't classify "color" as a breakdown, but as a valuable writing tool used to describe people, places, feelings and events. How did a murder suspect react when the reporter asked an unnerving question? How did firefighters react when they saw the tiny bodies of preschoolers found in a burned out preschool?

Let's say a newspaper reporter interviews a woman whose husband was mysteriously gunned down and asks the woman how she feels about the crime. If she said, "I feel devastated," and the journalist reported only her verbal response, the reader has no choice but to take the quote at face value.

Yet what if she was smirking or grimacing when she said it? What if she was crying and her voice broke as she trembled with pain? What if her reaction was emotionless? What if she was laughing? What if she was red in the face and barked her answer while slapping the reporter? Each scenario points to a very different mindset. She may be a grieving widow or a prime murder suspect, depending on her behavior. It's the nonverbal cues that can give more information to the reader.

Clinical descriptions of events won't get the point across in a print story, and that's the upside to color. But if misused, it can also be a way for lazy, naïve or unscrupulous reporters to lie, or to hide the fact that they have done little research for their story. The more color a reporter uses, the less information the article contains and the more likely that the reporter hasn't done a thorough job.

Evaluating color is so important that it will be one of the best tools you can use when you're evaluating the truthfulness of a news report. Some of the most telling signs of dishonesty can be found in a reporter's use of color.

Reporters are in the information business—it's their job to give enough useful information for a news consumer to understand the situation clearly. When reporters clutter articles with flowery details, they have a need to spruce up the piece with interesting details and descriptions because that's pretty much all the information they have.

When reading color, think of the color red—as in red flag. Dishonest and indolent reporters just love to use color—it's their way of trying to make their dubious and ridiculous articles sound more legitimate. But you can use color to turn the tables and smoke out suspect stories.

Unconfirmed Reports: Rumors that can't be pinned down are referred to as unconfirmed reports, and they are usually used for sketchy, breaking news stories happening in foreign countries, usually during disasters, unrest and war. The phrase simply means that no one has been able to verify the information, but reporters want to seem knowledgeable and they can't resist running with it. Whenever you hear "unconfirmed report," treat it as you would treat gossip told by a nosy acquaintance: you don't know enough about the person to trust him, but it's impossible to dismiss it outright.

Unnamed Sources: All sources have names, it's just that journalists know who these people are—and you don't. Unless a reporter made up the source, a journalist would never suggest that the interviewee should keep his name out of the story unless the person had explosive information, but seems reluctant to divulge it. It's usually the interviewee who insists on being a secret source, and the reporter who relents. There are various reasons why secret sources want to remain nameless; sometimes there is fear of reprisals—while other times, the person doesn't want to lose his job.

Some people keep their identities hidden because they have an agenda: they want to cause trouble and do not want to pay the consequences. Some interviewees are in a power struggle and the interview is a strategic leak to firm their grip; and sometimes the source is a liar and wants to scam without getting caught. With an anonymous source, it's hard to tell what their game is, and many reporters don't try hard enough to persuade these interviewees to speak on the record.

Questionable Experts: An expert can be a reporter's brainy best friend: a good one has knowledge the reporter doesn't and can help the reporter, and the audience, understand a complex and tangled issue. Yet the reporter has to find the right expert for the story, and has to rely on other means to find their sage. Websites such as Sources.com, Profnet and Megasources are some of the common sites reporters use to find their experts. When a reporter double checks the expert's credential and asks the right questions, the expert can make a dry and dense story become accessible.

If reporters don't do their homework in finding the right expert, not only can they report biased and inaccurate information, but they can cause other damage as well. One of the more popular experts was Christopher Byrne, who was considered an expert on children's toys. He had a typical nickname for his times—"The Toy Guy"—and he appeared on countless media outlets as well as publishing his annual list for the year's best toys.

Who could question an expert who calls himself the "Toy Guy"? Most reporters didn't, but they should have. It turned out the Toy Guy wasn't an objective, impartial observer of toys. Toy companies, such as Hasbro and Mattel paid Byrne to promote their products. His recommendations almost exclusively included toys manufactured by his generous benefactors. *New York Daily News* busted the Toy Guy's cloak of impartiality, but other reporters who interviewed Byrne said they had no idea the Toy Guy was paid by toy companies to recommend their wares.

When a media story relies on experts, look for clues as to whether the expert is qualified, impartial, truthful and knowledgeable. Not all experts are equal and it's not a good idea to take all experts at their word.

Media Concentration: Media companies seem to be getting bigger every year. The problem with big media is these behemoths are more likely to rely on the same source for information across their news holdings. They also tend to try to maintain the same editorial voice. What this means for you is, one, a single lie can spread quickly to many outlets, two, what seems to be many outlets covering an event is deceiving and, three, the same biases and assumptions will permeate through multiple media outlets. If you rely on the "strength in numbers" approach to verifying information, you might wind up believing hoaxes and scams.

Over-Reliance on Wire-Services or Niche Web Sites: Many reporters and talk show hosts in radio and television rely on certain websites for their information, such as the Obscure Store, the Smoking Gun, Buzz Flash and the Drudge Report. *New York Post*'s "Page Six" is also a popular site for reporters. While those websites have their place, when a reporter almost exclusively uses those sites as part of their regular research, this is lazy cribbing.

Wire services can also be problematic since most media outlets from radio, Internet, TV and newspapers use them heavily and regularly for their information without always verifying whether the information is accurate. A single hoax propagated by a wire service can disseminate quickly to hundreds of outlets, giving the appearance that hundreds of newsrooms reported on the same story, when in fact none of them did. When reading a news story, check to see whether the article was written by a newspaper's reporter, or was culled from a wire service.

Pop Culture References and Slang Over Utility: In their desperation to attract a young readership, news outlets do their best to be "with it"—which, in this case, has been defined as using street slang, writing shorter pieces and peppering stories with loads of pop culture references, all in the hope of attracting younger news consumers. Watching news outlets trying to be hip, though, is like watching Betty Davis in *Whatever Happened to Baby Jane?*

Space and time in the news world are precious commodities: for every pop culture reference used in a newspaper or magazine article, that much less real information is going to make the final cut. Filler doesn't give you information; it can actually distract you from spotting suspect information. When judging a heavily laced news story, don't take those soon-to-be-dated tidbits as fact—just ignore them.

Authority Figures: Authorities aren't infallible. Some reporters rely heavily on them, particularly on the nameless ones, anyway. Take these examples:

• "... [said] a Turkish oil official at the Ceyhan terminal... speaking on condition of anonymity..."

• "'From what I've seen, this is not conclusive evidence,' said the expert, who also spoke on condition of anonymity. He said that the tubes were not suitable for manufacturing into high-speed enrichment centrifuges because their diameters were too small and the aluminum they were made from was too hard."

• "Quoting unnamed officials, the Times said cities include Baghdad and Basra, as well as Athens, Istanbul and Manila."

Who is the expert? What are his or her qualifications? Why does this expert insist on not being named? When reporters treat an authority's word as gospel, it doesn't mean that the reporter tried to verify that information. Read each authority's quote with caution.

Spin: Facts differ from opinion, or spin. Reporters may not question a source's spin on a particular fact. Just because an opinion isn't challenged or labeled as such by the reporter, don't assume that a pearl of wisdom is true.

Press Releases, Public Relations and Publicists: Spinmeisters aren't paid to give the objective truth. Everything about their client is just positive, positive, positive. Every cloud has a silver lining, every glass is half full and every scumbag exhales carbon dioxide to help plant life sustain itself.

These are the people who speak vaguely about their "deepest condolences" and about "win-win" situations. They limit a reporter's access to important sources and make demands, from vetting a reporter's story beforehand to sitting with their client during the interview to even demanding that crucial questions not be asked. Some demand that the reporter sign a waiver barring the journalist from writing any negative or unflattering information about their clients (a common demand from certain A-list celebrities).

PR firms are hired by "regular folks" too—from crime victims to murder suspects and even to parents of multiple births. Just because someone isn't a "corporate" or "celebrity" type, doesn't mean you're seeing these people as they are; they've been trained to handle the media, behave in front of cameras in a certain way and give controlled interviews.

Image consultants can do wonders to help even the most repulsive person seem warm and cuddly. With the right power suit and hand gestures, anyone can learn to look honest and likable without having to be honest or likable.

Press releases are also problematic if the reporter doesn't independently double-check the information or look at the problems associated with the announcement. When judging the news, think whether the person has had media training or a makeover or whether the news you're hearing came through a reporter or through someone parroting a news release.

Worse, many journalists use words and images in their stories that are not their own. In March 2004, the General Accounting Office raised questions over the Bush administration's use of VNRs for television newscasts. The VNRs in question were produced by the Department of Health and Human Services and addressed a new law targeting Medicare. One woman who was hired to pose as a "journalist" in the VNR for the segments was a former reporter who left the profession to run her own public relations company. The releases gave a one-sided view of the new law, but not only did forty TV stations use these VNRs, the news releases were dubbed "news package" or "reporter package." As one government-prepared script read in part:

> In December, President Bush signed into law the first-ever prescription drug benefit for people with Medicare. Since then, there have been a lot of questions about how the law will help older Americans and people with disabilities. Reporter Karen Ryan helps sort through the details.

WBRZ, a television station in Baton Rouge used the package on its January 23, 2004 noontime newscast with the ersatz journalist:

> When President Bush signed the Medicare Prescription Drug Improvement and Modernization Act into law... millions of people who are covered by Medicare began asking how it will help them... Medicare will offer some immediate help through a discount card... Officials urge people to call 1-800-MEDICARE for more information about the new law.
> In Washington, I'm Karen Ryan reporting.

When news stories are written and produced by the newsmakers themselves, they cease to become news, but instead become advertising. In a somewhat shrill attempt to save face and justify her actions, Ryan defended her tattered honor in a March 29, 2004 *Television Week* commentary:

> But dumb me, little did I think about how this is an election year and Medicare is a politically charged topic. The story took on a life of its own totally based on rumor, innuendo and, "Well, if the Times ran it, guess it must be true." Shame on me for practicing my profession and engaging in a standard, acceptable practice, namely, narrating a VNR.
> I did nothing wrong. Nothing...

VNRs are pseudo-news stories narrated by pseudo-journalists. If those involved with these productions don't see the problem with passing advertising off as news, then it's up to the news consumer to separate the ads from the news for himself.

"Rent-a-Quotes": Some people get quoted in the media more often than others. One of those people is Robert R. Thompson, a professor at Syracuse University who is likely to be interviewed whenever a reporter needs an expert about a popular culture phenomenon. He is a knowledgeable expert and he can deliver pithy quotes. There are other pop culture professors, but Thompson is the one most journalists know about. On the one hand, Thompson is a good source; on the other hand, experts with different takes on the same issue tend not to get interviewed. When reporters have settled on an expert, other voices don't get equal time. Alternate explanations or new information doesn't get through.

Sometimes the dispenser of the *bon mot* has an expertise in a given area, but other times the rent-a-quote simply knows how to play the press to get attention. Greg Packer, a highway maintenance worker from Huntington, New York, was outed by Ann Coulter when she reported that Packer was an unofficial rent-a-quote—for streeters.

Though most reporters never realized it, Packer had given numerous "man-on-the-street" interviews. In a state with millions of people, it was nothing short of bizarre that one man would catch the eye of so many reporters looking for a good, benign filler quote. Among Packer's cameo performances:

• He wore a green wig and colored his mustache green while watching the St. Patrick's Day parade. ("I'm representing Ireland and New York today. It's a day for happiness and to be together.")

• He attended Lamertville, New Jersey's "Zora Andrich Day," in celebration of the "winner" of the Fox-TV program *Joe Millionaire*. ("The show mostly had to do with money. But being the down-to-earth person she is, Zora put this small town on the map.")

• He was the first in line for a White House tour during President George W. Bush's inauguration. ("I'm disappointed, but obviously he can't greet everybody.")

• He was also first in line for several New York City signings for Senator Hillary Clinton's book *Living History*. ("I'm a big fan of Hillary's and Bill's," he said, and, to another reporter, "I want to know if she is going to run for President.")

• He waited in line to see the Pope at the Giants stadium. ("The Pope is appealing to everybody of all religions and backgrounds. I believe it'll be inspirational and something I'll never forget.")

• He was at Times Square for the NYC New Year's celebrations.

• He wore a "2000 Subway Series" shirt, while casting multiple votes at Shea Stadium at a 2001 All-Star game.

• He visited Ground Zero in New York City.

• He was in line for the premiere of the film *Star Wars: Episode I*.

He was quoted in at least ten *Associated Press* stories, two *USA Today* articles, as well as *Newsday*, the *London Independent* and the *New York Times*.

Packer simply insinuated himself into situations that would serve as easy fodder for reporters: he strategically slipped himself in crowds and did things to draw attention to himself.

After Packer's terminal quoting became public knowledge, he found himself being quoted by the press again: this time with a barrage of stories about his hobby. He was suddenly known as a professional man-on-the-street; the guy who excelled at giving those short, bland comments reporters needed.

Though reporters found his exploits amusing, Packer's unchecked infiltration is unsettling: if a laborer knows how to manipulate the media (by a series of simple, yet calculated tricks), then what are public relations firms or even hoaxers doing to ensure their sound bites are being covertly disseminated? Are they also planting people at key events?

So why choose Packer? As *Newsday*'s Sheryl McCarthy mused, "I think the reason Packer is quoted so often is that journalists hate man-on-the-street interviews. It's demeaning to have to scan a crowd of total strangers, searching for someone who looks like he or she might have something quotable to say, and won't tell you to get lost."

What's demeaning about talking to another human being, who also happens to be your listener, viewer and reader? If reporters have this little respect for people who do not hold a position of power or are a celebrity, then how much respect do they have for their audience? If reporters asked the right people the right questions, then maybe they would get more thoughtful and interesting answers from those peasant plebs they are forced to interact with once in a while.

No Uniform Agreement on What Journalistic Qualifications are Needed for the Job of Reporter, Editor or Fact-Checker: Many journalists do not have a high school diploma, while many might hold PhDs. Fact-checkers may be unpaid interns. Some media outlets require that applicants have a college or university degree in journalism, but others do not. Not all reporters are created equal.

Not Double-Checking Information: In the drive to be first to break a news story, some reporters run with what they have without double-checking the information. Technically, they're not supposed to—but then again, your parents probably told you that you weren't supposed to smoke cigarettes, either. In both cases, common sense was abandoned to look cool—and in both cases, abandoning common sense won't seem like it was such a good idea when bad judgment causes grief later on. Just because a story made it to print or onto the air, doesn't mean anyone actually bothered to make sure that piece of information was true.

Not Including Enough Information in Stories: With media outlets focusing on shorter stories in a bid to attract younger audiences, important information has to be sacrificed. Not only is the news consumer not getting enough information, but the lack of details make a hoaxer's scheme much easier to execute. The focus on shorter news items also means reporters need to conduct even less research than before, making reporters more vulnerable to chicanery.

Colorful Personalities Over Informed Sources: A smart, boring source is going to get pushed aside in favor of a bubbly, perky attention-seeker. A con artist who is a likable character will find it that much easier to grab media attention.

Rivalry and Bragging Rights: In the race to be the first and the best, reporters will push ethical boundaries to trump and upstage their colleagues. What this means is that con artists can use a reporter's desperation and ambition against him. When a reporter or outlet crow about an exclusive "get," it's a good idea to pay close attention to the story and the interview to see whether the reporter may have been manipulated or bamboozled by a cunning scammer.

Assembled News: These days, newsgathering can be a group effort. A stringer interviews unnamed Washington, DC officials; an intern interviews survivors on the West Coast. Two reporters in the East Coast office write the story, relying on wire copy and the information gathered by the intern and the stringer.

Everything seems all right, but what if the intern made up the quotes or asked the wrong questions? What if the stringer made up quotes, got his information wrong, didn't follow up key comments or interviewed a fake official? What if the reporters writing the story embellished parts or relied on unconfirmed reports? Could anyone in the chain spot shady information? Probably not.

There is no shortage of problems with the media machine. Blind faith, adherence to old rules and the need to be first can lead reporters and editors astray. But exactly how do these weaknesses harm journalism? The next section shows just how these and other problems make journalists vulnerable to lies.

Section **Two**

Rumors and Misinformation

Chapter **Six**

Rumors and Common Knowledge

The Internet has been a cruel blow for proud factualists: obscure trivia and up-to-the-second slang used to be their domain, but now everyone can verse themselves in foreign swear words and obscure movie trivia within seconds. Any schmuck with Internet access can become fairly well-versed in almost any topic in a short period of time. A ninety-year-old woman from Stockholm can now learn to speak fluent hip hop, while leaving those who reveled in their insider status pouting that anyone can play in their clubhouse. In one real way, the Internet has become the great cultural and intellectual equalizer.

Yet the Internet can't equalize determination, perseverance and critical thinking skills. What separated the factualists from the rest wasn't the mere knowledge of Blue Beetle's alter ego, but the length they would go to find even the smallest piece of information. These are the people who would scour secondhand and remainder book stores, spend hours in the library or listen to knowledgeable people to glean new information for their own mental encyclopedia. The slang aficionado would hang out with and eavesdrop on the in crowd, while the trivia buff would hunt down every obscure book and magazine he could find. Neither type was shy about doing the legwork or digging to get the payoff. With practice, they even learned how to differentiate a good piece of information from a bad one.

The information connoisseur wants good information. He compares information and then decides what data he will ingest and which he will ignore. It wasn't just his vast knowledge that impressed (or irked) others; it was the quality of the information he stored in his head that did it.

On the other hand, people who accept any information will swallow the good information with the bad; these are people who believe in the benefits of diet and exercise, but they also believe that aliens came down and made crop circles. Worse, they will pass on bogus information to friends, family and coworkers who believe them.

It's not just factoids and common knowledge that get passed on from person to person—it's the juicy stuff, too. Gossip and rumors are also hot commodities to be savored and passed on to the less hip and clueless. How many everyday sentences begin with the phrase "Did you hear that...?" It's a bitter disappointment when the answer is, "That's old news." Gossips pride themselves on knowing dirt first.

Journalists also love to break stories first—it's a professional rush when a reporter can nab that exclusive interview or scoop. A titillating, salacious or important tidbit can make a reporter's career. Other times, the shocking news happens to fall into a news producer's lap.

Such was the case of C.J., an African-American woman who became Dallas' one-woman nightmare. The deadly and mysterious C.J. had her origin in September 1991, when she wrote a letter to *Ebony*, recounting how she became infected with AIDS and what she would do to avenge her suffering: she would have unprotected sex with as many black men as she could. So far, she had slept with forty-eight men. C.J.'s vendetta caught the attention of reporters and citizens alike as recounted in the September 24, 1991 Knight Ridder wire story appearing in the *Seattle Times*:

> She calls herself C.J. Nobody is sure who she is. But everybody fears they know her.
>
> Before she dies, she says, she wants to kill as many men in this town as she can.
>
> C.J. is infected with the AIDS virus, which she says she contracted from a white bisexual man. Since then, this angry woman, whose dreams of getting married and having children collided with her illness, has launched a deadly mission to infect the men of Dallas.

Her *Ebony* letter wouldn't be C.J.'s last public statement. "C.J." called a radio call-in host on KKDA-AM in Dallas confirming her HIV status and restating her intention to infect men with AIDS. C.J. called other radio and television programs with the same brazen threat.

Dallas police investigated the letter and the calls and managed to locate C.J.—at least two of her, anyway. *Ebony*'s C.J. was a fifteen-year old girl who wasn't HIV positive. She had concocted the hoax as a misguided way of warning readers about the dangers of the disease. The radio call-in C.J. was a copycat: she was a twenty-nine-year-old Dallas woman who had called the station as a joke. In both cases, neither woman was HIV positive.

The C.J. hoax sounded similar to many legends based on a victim being seduced by a stranger who then departs, but not without leaving a note informing the hapless lover that he or she has been infected with a deadly disease. But AIDS myths do not always involve the exchanging of bodily fluids; sometimes the victim gets infected by doing normal, everyday things, such as pumping gas or using a pay phone. When these rumors make the rounds, businesses may suffer greatly as a result. The August 17, 1998 edition of the *Toronto Star* tried to dispel such a rumor:

Unsuspecting patrons enjoying an evening out on the town, the story goes, have suddenly been jabbed with a needle and handed a note that reads "Welcome to the World of HIV."

Metro police say they've never received a single report of such an incident from clubs or club-goers, and staff at the clubs often named in connection with the needle scare—The Docks, The Guvernment, Atlantis and The Joker—have never fielded any complaints, either.

Rumors, unconfirmed reports and common knowledge are plentiful on the Internet, but they still make their way into mainstream news reports, too. Most people are familiar with the Neiman-Marcus cookie hoax: parent and child go to Neiman-Marcus' restaurant, eat cookies, ask for recipe, agree to buy recipe for "two fifty," get shocked when the credit card bill comes for $250 instead of $2.50 and get revenge by posting said cookie recipe on the Internet. Though known for years by many to be a hoax, it didn't stop one weather anchor on "CBC Newsworld" from falling for the hoax on an October 27,1995 broadcast, vowing to share the recipe with viewers.

Another legend that fooled some reporters was a spin on the classic mix-up legend: two opposites who happen to share the same name get confused with hilarious results. As the December 18, 2003 edition of the *San Diego Union-Tribune* recounted:

> At least Purdue won't have to worry about keeping new basketball signee Jason Smith eligible. Whether he can run the offense or not is another story.
>
> On the first day of the early signing period for high school basketball players, Purdue used their one available scholarship to sign Yorktown High's 5-foot-6, 128 pound Jason Smith, an honor student who has never played competitive basketball in his entire life.
>
> Purdue had intended to sign Yorktown's OTHER Jason Smith, a 6'6" 215 lb. point guard who averaged twenty-six points and eleven assists per game last season. This Jason was named to *Blue Chip Magazine*'s top fifty players in the nation.
>
> [...]The Boilermakers have a serious problem on their hands. They cannot force Jason Parker Smith to give up the scholarship without facing a great deal of bad publicity for cutting a player who has not violated team rules, and the young man does not plan on giving it up voluntarily.

Problem was, the story was a joke. The *Hoosier Gazette*, the website where the *Union-Tribune* sports editor found and culled the article verbatim (and then incorrectly claimed the story came from "Union-Tribune News Services"), carried the tagline "Indiana's first source for inaccurate news" at the header of its pages in big blue letters. Perhaps the phrase and its placement was too subtle for the *Union-Tribune*. No one who ran the story bothered to call the university for confirmation.

Rumors and urban legends taint the knowledge pool, but so does common knowledge—those pearls of wisdom almost everyone spouts freely, yet no one can remember the origins or the evidence. Common knowledge tells us that humans use only 10% of their brains, or that reading in the dark will ruin our eyesight. Neither factoid is true, but sometimes those ersatz facts make it into news stories, anyway: the common mistaken belief that suicide rates increase during the Christmas holidays was mentioned in an article in the December 14, 1998 edition of the *Bergen Record*.

When someone uses "common knowledge" without checking his facts, embarrassment ensues. When singer Barbra Streisand gave a speech during a Democratic fundraiser in October 2002, she quoted what she thought was a line from William Shakespeare's *Julius Caesar* that began, "Beware the leader who bangs the drums of war in order to whip the citizenry into a patriotic fervor, for patriotism is indeed a double-edged sword."

The quote had been making its rounds on various websites, but it was not from Shakespeare or even Caesar himself. Her mistake was quickly noted, from the *Washington Post* to the *Drudge Report*. Strangely enough, the quote had been used by readers writing letters to newspaper editors, though many editors did not correct or edit the letters before publication (such as the *Morning Call* and the *Roanoke Times* and *World News*).

Traditional media outlets aren't the only places that disseminate fraudulent information. While forwarded e-mail and bulletin board messages are notorious for spreading lies, scams and hoaxes, even the most legitimate and credible-looking website can fool thousands of people with ease. In August 2000, Newton, Kansas resident Kaycee Nicole Swenson, a beautiful, talented, articulate and athletic seventeen-year-old battling leukemia, kept a website called "Living Color," which told readers about her struggle to survive. Kaycee's picture and thoughts touched thousands of people, who often wrote to her, encouraging the young girl to fight, or who sent cards and gifts.

Kaycee's eloquence made quite an impression, and she was even mentioned in an August 10, 2000 article in the *New York Times* about college students and computers (unrelated to her illness):

> Kaycee Swenson, a high school senior in Wichita, Kan., who took several courses at her local college last year, said she talked to people online every day, most of whom were not at her campus. But she said she also hung out with friends in the physical world, listening to music and playing basketball. "You have to balance it," she said.

This fall, she will enroll full time at the University of Cal' Diego, and she plans to take a new computer with her, ev already has one equipped with a Pentium II processor. "It's "but not fast enough."

[...]When she talks to her mother about what she took to ᴄᴏ decades ago, she cannot believe what students had to put up with. "She thought it was great...that she was able to take a calculator to college or a cassette player to tape lectures." And when her mother said she had to stand in line to register for classes and to wait for professors to open their offices, she said she could hardly imagine it. "I laugh at those things... but I'm sure it wasn't fun, you know?"

By May 2001, one person who followed the girl's website wanted to come and visit her. The girl agreed to see him after she returned from a Florida trip, but the meeting was not to be: Kaycee had succumbed to her illness, as her mother announced on her late daughter's web diary. Unlike her candid daughter, Kaycee's grief-stricken mother would not divulge private details, such as her address or the details of her child's funeral (she claimed her daughter was cremated two days after she died).

That's when the really sad news hit: Kaycee wasn't dead or alive. Skeptical readers could not find any death notices in Kansas for Kaycee. After doing a little more digging, they discovered the truth about Kaycee: she didn't exist, but was the invention of a forty-year-old woman named Debbie Swenson living in Peabody, Kansas. Kaycee's pictures were of Swenson's unsuspecting neighbor. Swenson would also pose as "Kaycee" on the telephone, as she did when she gave an interview to the *Times* as Kaycee.

There were signs that Kaycee wasn't real: her points of reference were more consistent with an older individual than a teenager and there were inconsistencies with Kaycee's medical history. Still, it was the poignant way Swenson described "Kaycee's" battle that made it easy to ignore the blaring signs of a hoax.

Another popular form of rumor is the overnight starlet: an unknown performer (usually a female) suddenly becomes a white hot celebrity by mere serendipity. One of the most successful examples of the overnight starlet is the "discovery" of actress Lana Turner in a malt shop. The story was bogus, but it made great copy.

Flamboyant health and beauty millionaire Stewart Fason told the media that he was looking for a young promising female violinist he had met by chance. He was so impressed that he wanted her to play at Carnegie Hall. The story had a happy ending as recounted in the October 15, 1981 edition of the *Boston Globe*:

It is a tale of star-crossed music lovers—he a millionaire, she a nineteen-year-old street-corner violinist whose mastery riveted him. He heard her once, then lost her. Now, with the help of a $1000 reward, he's found her—and booked her to play on one of the world's great stages, Carnegie Hall. "I can't believe what has happened, it's like a fairy tale," said Stewart Fason, forty-eight, of Palm Beach, Fla.

The story proved to be a hoax only days later. Fason later admitted he already knew the violinist, Kerry McDermott, and had already auditioned her. Fason simply made up the story in order to help boost tickets sales, since he couldn't get media attention for his latest enterprise (Fason has a history of playing around with the truth: he was convicted of tax evasion, claimed his wife was cured from cancer thanks to the miracle pills he peddled and had used aliases).

While many rumors, urban legends and faux pearls of wisdom are ignored or debunked by journalists, others are wholeheartedly embraced without question. Tidbits, gossip, factoids and buzz can and do make their way into news stories and columns as truth and escape detection for days or even years. As a news consumer, look carefully at the story or fact to determine who the original source of information was. Sometimes the original source isn't obvious in the news story, but other times it can be misleading, as the next case study shows.

When Bored Narcissists Have Free Time and Internet Access

Gossiping about babes and studs is a good way of getting attention for yourself, and knowing where to find the beautiful people can score you points with your leering friends. Journalists also like to report on beefcakes and cheesecakes: models, athletes and actors all make news simply because a pretty face and a firm tush sell papers and grab eyeballs.

Not all the hotties embark on a sports or entertainment career, but the good news is that even they can get some media attention, too. Bonus points can be given if the babe in question can garner some attention in an unusual way. The *San Francisco Bay Guardian*, an alternative publication, found just such a looker. A May 31, 2001 article entitled "'Gorgeous Guy' is San Francisco's new cyberlebrity" introduced the world to Dan Baca, a man who was generating buzz on the Internet because of his attributes:

When lusty mid-May rolled around, this digital ecosystem also spawned what's become known as the "Gorgeous Guy" phenomenon. It began innocuously enough, when a woman posted to the Missed Connection board that she wanted to meet this "gorgeous guy" she saw every day at the bus stop, carrying a gray bag. Another poster chimed in, saying he'd seen the hunk and offering encouragement: "Why are you ladies so afraid to go up to him and say Hi?"

The article described how Baca slowly transformed from being a techno-geek to a smoldering Adonis:

[...]Blissfully unaware of the Craigslist Missed Connections maelstrom, a twenty-five-year-old network engineer lounged at his usual bus stop, carrying his gray bag of technical books. Two women were staring at him. There was something odd about the conversation they were having. "She knew things about me," he told us after we contacted him over e-mail.

...[The] next day it was a group of five people at his bus stop. The next day, ten. "One guy was holding a camera." As he approached them, they all stopped talking suddenly. He confronted the admirers, who eventually spilled the beans about Craigslist. He'd never used the site, though now he's pretty impressed. People would look at him, check their watches, and stare. Yep, 5:30. Must be Gorgeous Guy.

Other media outlets got in on the story. Baca soon became a popular topic of media conversation. Suddenly, Baca's dates included interviews and even an appearance on CNN on June 3, 2001:

JAMES HATTORI, CNN CORRESPONDENT: Dan Baca, a twenty-nine-year-old computer network engineer, considers himself an outgoing guy.

But these days you wouldn't blame him for being a little shy or paranoid.

DAN BACA: Well, I had mixed feelings. It was more of like anger, a little bit of outrage.

HATTORI: Why?

BACA: Because I felt like I was being targeted.

USA Today's Janet Kornblum also got in on the Gorgeous Guy act on June 19, 2001 when she wrote about the cyber stud:

Every afternoon for a year, Dan Baca, a mild-mannered network engineer, left work at a downtown bank, walked to his bus stop and waited. Then he'd get on the bus to go home, just like thousands of other commuters who trek across the Bay.

Only he was being watched.

And Friday, May 11, at 12:15 p.m. PT, someone who just wanted to meet this "gorgeous guy" posted a note to a popular local website. Baca's metamorphosis into "The Gorgeous Guy" had begun, but it was a few days before he figured out what was going on.

It seemed as if every detail of Baca's life became fodder for his legion of lascivious huntresses:

> They discussed his looks (agreeing he was gorgeous), his facial expressions and his commuting habits. They gave out his schedule and his physical description. Some said he was gay, others insisted he was straight and married. He had children. He was single. They fought over who would date him first.
>
> And that was just the first day.

Then the ugly truth came out.

After the reporter who broke the original story became suspicious of Baca's inconsistent statements, he did what he should have done before he broke the story: he went back to Craigslist and began inspecting the posts more carefully. The e-mail addresses of posters who mentioned Baca were fakes. Baca finally admitted that he was the one who posted over fifty fawning messages about himself on Craigslist. Furthermore, the same reporter later admitted that Baca had "consistently lied" to him in the ten hours he interviewed him. If so, then why run with the story in the first place? Was the reporter suspicious before he wrote it?

How did Baca manage to fool the press? No one had initially bothered to verify the e-mail addresses of the alleged admirers. Had they, the hoax would have been uncovered almost immediately. Vanity, not lust was the primary motive of the message writer, but this subtle difference never dawned on journalists covering the story.

Auctioning Malarky

Cute little anecdotes are a reporter's best friend. Those "did you know...?" factoids give color and spunk to dry stories, such as business or technology news. But even these stories-within-a-story have to follow a strict set of rules: they have to be playful and light, they have to be quirky and they have to be revealing of an interview subject's true nature.

The online auctioning company eBay was a new economy reporter's dream story: the company was innovative, well-known, successful, media-friendly and most importantly, eBay's public relations department had a really good, colorful anecdote for journalists to use. The *San Jose Business Journal* used the whimsical anecdote in the journal's November 13, 1998 edition:

> If it weren't for Pierre Omidyar's fiancee and her penchant for collecting Pez candy dispensers, eBay Inc. might not exist.

Over dinner one night, Mr. Omidyar listened to his significant other bemoan the difficulties she faced in connecting with other Pez collectors. And so he turned his attention to solving her problem.

Thus was born eBay, the first online auction service.

The *Silicon Valley Daily* also led with the colorful factoid:

How eBay was founded is already part of Silicon Valley lore. Pierre Omidyar was a young programmer whose fiancee was a collector of Pez candy dispensers. She wished there was a way she could trade Pez items with other collectors and also communicate with them over the Internet.

Based on his fiancee's wishes, Omidyar went out and launched eBay on Labor Day, 1995, naming the site after the Bay Area. EBay would eventually lead an entire industry of online auctions.

The Pez story, which began to circulate in 1997, was repeated without question in publications from *USA Today* to the *New York Post* and even to the *Wall Street Journal*. Some publications, as the two above examples, opened their stories with the quirky lead. Others, such as *USA Today*, made reference to the story without attribution, making it sound as if the Pez connection was a fact. The story quickly became a part of technology folklore: a goofy childhood rite of passage mixed in with true love and vision, equaled big hefty profits.

As sweet and touching as the story sounded, there was just one problem: it was made up. Adam Cohen, a reporter who wrote a book on eBay, decided to look into the Pez connection and discovered the source of the factoid was eBay's PR department. The lie was concocted by Mary Lou Song, eBay's PR manager. Song made up the story to get media attention and positive press for the company. Reporters fell for it hook, line and sinker.

The story was too sugary and cutesy to be real. The real origins for eBay were more mundane, but since reporters wouldn't have a colorful story if the truth was told, Song came up with a media-ready version that would give journalists the color they needed to write a positive piece. Unfortunately, Song's sophomoric ploy worked beautifully. Most reporters used the story without ever double-checking to see whether the improbable tale was true.

They've Fingered the Wrong Company

Stories that play up on our secret neurotic fears will make news, such as crazed stalkers and accidental poisoning with household products. Whispers alone won't be enough to bait reporters, but if someone has concrete evidence of our worst fears coming true, he can expect media coverage for his nightmare.

One of those strange back-of-the-mind fears is inadvertent cannibalism. What would happen if someone fed you man-meat and you didn't even know it? That was the question posed to readers in the January 5, 1987 edition of the *San Diego Tribune*:

> A man discovered an object identified by a pathologist as part of a human finger in his plate of a canned Mexican stew after his family had already consumed some of the food for dinner, police said.
>
> The discovery of the two-inch body part with a fingernail prompted a supermarket to pull cans of Juanita brand menudo—a Mexican stew made with tripe—from its shelves, Lt. Mike Skogh said yesterday.
>
> Freddie Ureno, thirty, who lives with his brother and their wives in the Los Angeles suburb of Azusa, told police he found the finger in his portion of the menudo Friday night while the family was having dinner.

The family took the contents of the can to the Glendora Community Hospital, where someone confirmed that the object was indeed a finger. News spread quickly: *U.P.I.* also picked up on the story, as did local radio and television stations. The store where the offending can was sold recalled the product from the shelves. Juanita's Foods lost roughly one million dollars from the negative publicity.

But then federal food inspectors examined the "finger" and found it to be from the connective stomach tissue of a cow. Since menudo is made from bovine stomach tissue, there was nothing in the can of stew that shouldn't have been there. There was no human finger, only tripe.

How did the story gain credibility even though there was nothing amiss with the can of menudo? Reporters took the word of the family instead of waiting for inspectors to examine the tissue. If journalists had waited, they would have discovered the tissue wasn't human and that there was no story to tell. Furthermore, the pathologist who allegedly told the family that the tissue was a human finger did not actually deem the object to be a finger, but advised the family to take it to police.

The *U.P.I.* and *Valley Tribune* reporters got much of their information from a single police official who claimed to have seen the finger in question, but he could not officially inspect or confirm the nature of the tissue. The family misinterpreted the facts; the original pathologist wasn't interviewed, and the only official interviewed wasn't qualified to make judgments about the tissue's origins. Put together, while journalists were seemingly thorough in their reportage, they did not interview the people who in fact would have the information the reporters would need.

Nothing Suspicious About a 104-Year-Old Swearing Parrot

Factoids are readily available at the tail end of newscasts and as filler in newspapers. These stories serve as "want-to-know" fodder and don't tell the news consumer anything important—they just serve as mild and fleeting amusements. One category of disposable amusement is the cute animal with an extraordinary history. Charlie was one of those animals who made the media cut.

Charlie was Winston Churchill's parrot, who apparently was still around, according to the January 19, 2004 edition of the *London Daily Mirror*:

> She was at Winston Churchill's side during Britain's darkest hour. And now Charlie the parrot is 104 years old... and still cursing the Nazis.
>
> Her favorite sayings were "F*** Hitler" and "F*** the Nazis." And even today, thirty-nine years after the great man's death, she can still be coaxed into repeating them with that unmistakable Churchillian inflection.
>
> Many an admiral or peer of the realm was shocked by the tirade from the bird's cage during crisis meetings with the PM.

Charlie's current owner was Sylvia Martin, manager of a nursery where Charlie had been living for twelve years. Charlie was owned by one Peter Oram, whose father-in-law originally sold Churchill the bird. The *Mirror*'s exclusive also gave a quick history lesson to readers:

> Churchill bought Charlie—giving him a boy's name despite the fact she was female—in 1937...
>
> He immediately began to teach her to swear—particularly in company —and she is keeping up the tradition today.

World Net Daily explained to readers how Charlie ended up at Martin's nursery on January 20:

> Charlie was purchased by a pet shop owner, Peter Oram, when Churchill died in 1965. But the London-area man was forced to remove the bird from the shop after she kept swearing at children.

Other media outlets, such as *U.P.I.*, FOXNews.com, *Chicago Sun-Times*, the *Washington Times* and the *New York Post* soon picked up on the story, most using the *Mirror* as their source. What was there to question? It was known that Churchill had a menagerie of animals, from albino kangaroos to even a leopard. Reuters also made mention of Charlie on January 20:

British war leader Winston Churchill's foul-mouthed... parrot refused to surrender to news hounds Monday after a British newspaper tracked the bird down and discovered it was still alive.

"They've been trying to get him to talk all day, but he's not saying much," said Sylvia Martin, who manages Heathfield Nurseries where parrot Charlie has lived for the last [twelve] years.

Charlie, who kept Churchill company during World War II, was famous for occasionally squawking four-letter obscenities about Hitler. But Martin told Reuters the bird has mellowed.

This little piece of trivia would have probably been forgotten except that Churchill's daughter denied that her father ever had a colorful parrot named Charlie (though he did have a gray African parrot named Polly). Others who knew Churchill also said that colorful Charlie wasn't Churchill's. No records could be found to support the theory that Charlie belonged to Churchill. In this case, reporters hadn't bothered to confirm whether Churchill ever had a parrot named Charlie and, if he did, if this parrot was the same one.

It was only after people who were familiar with Churchill's personal life came forward to debunk the story that reporters corrected themselves. Did *Mirror* reporters look for confirmation (historical or biographical references, photographs, etc.)? No, but why bother with the details when a story about a former titan's 104-year-old parrot falls into your lap?

A Joke So Subtle That No One Gets It

Quirky businesses are always newsworthy: innovation, personality and the ability to find a new niche makes for exciting news since these entrepreneurs tend to be characters in their own right. These are the people of vision who can fill a consumer's oddest needs.

One such quirky business that *Esquire* magazine profiled was a company known as Freewheelz, an Internet company that would allow clients to drive free cars in exchange for listening to specialized streamed ads—and drive around in cars with bumper to bumper ads. The business was described this way in the April 2000 issue:

There's something profoundly unfair about picking a posh suburb as the test market for free automobiles. As if one of the nation's most affluent towns, already strewn with Lexuses and Land Rovers, didn't have enough going for it, residents are now driving free cars. For that, they can thank Skip Lehman, a Chicago native who applied his Stanford M.B.A. to creating the new economy's boldest giveaway. For the past three months, the village of Barrington du Lac, Illinois, has served as the beta market for FreeWheelz, a new e-business Lehman hopes will soon ply America's roads with thousands of new, Internetpumped, self-financing, free cars. Talk to any of the "FreeWheelerz" who paid zilch for one of Lehmans's cars and they tell you their hero will transform the auto industry more than Henry Ford did. The revolution will get rolling in full on April 1, when FreeWheelz launches on the Web for real.

The April 1 reference was no coincidence: the colorful story was a spoof satirizing oddball Internet businesses. Though there was an impressive Freewheelz website, it was created by the article's author, who let visitors know the concept was a gag. Yet it didn't stop advertisers from contacting the hoaxers, asking to enroll in the program. Other fledgling entrepreneurs contacted the site, letting them know that they had also planned a similar business. To top it all off, there were businesses who already offered vehicle financing in exchange for the driver to have his car bubble wrapped in ads.

The satire was too subtle for some, despite the strange turns in the story: Freewheelz' lengthy online questionnaire demanded that potential "customers" answer medical questions ("Does hair loss concern you?") to educational ones ("When you applied to college, what was your safety school?"). Even the alleged precursor to Freewheelz wasn't enough to clue some people in on the joke:

Inspired by the local board of health's closing of a favorite Palo Alto taco joint, Lehman and Raj Ramanujan, now on the board of FreeWheelz, proposed I-Coli.com. The service invited restaurants to post their health reviews and other ratings... He and Lehman peddled their plan to number-two Microsoft billionaire Paul Allen—who, according to Lehman, "must have just had some bad oysters or something"—and he put up launch money. I-Coli.com was a local hit.

After *Esquire* let readers in on the gag, the article's author sold his domain name to a similar real-life business for $25,000, splitting the proceeds with Hearst, owners of the magazine. The bizarre questions and the silly businesses mentioned in the article were red flags, but the prospect of making money, no matter how ridiculous, was too big of a lure for those wanting to do business with Freewheelz. One simple rule for the news consumer is to always be aware of stories with an April 1 dateline.

How to Spot Rumors and Fake Common Knowledge

What these above cases share is that they all were reported as fact. Charlie the parrot's fake pedigree was as easily believed as the existence of Kaycee Nicole Swenson, C.J. and the two Jason Smiths, or even that suicides increase during the winter holidays. There are facts and statistics bandied about in the news, yet there is not a shred of evidence that these numbers and details are based in fact. Whether it's a too-good (or bad)-to-be-true yarn or an obscure "whatever happened to...?" pop culture tidbit, news consumers have to carefully listen to the information before they determine whether the information is real or fake.

While not every false fact can be rooted out, there are some signs to watch out for when listening to or reading rumors and common knowledge:

1. The story or factoid is repeated, but the original source is nebulous.

If a fact is repeated enough times, people tend to believe it's true, regardless of whether it's based on myth or misconceptions. Unless we know who or what the original source of the information was, we can't make judgments as to the truthfulness of the story. Think about some of the conventional wisdom you hold: where did that information come from? What proof is there that the factoid is true?

For example, some people believe that a captain of a ship can perform weddings—but what is the proof? While the captain-as-minister myth is popular in movies, the truth is that captains can't perform legally binding weddings. We hear the myth, but who do you know who was married by a captain? What law gives captains the right to marry couples? It's common knowledge, but it's wrong.

In psychology, there is a phenomenon called the sleeper effect: even if people hear information from an unreliable source, they will eventually forget who the original source was, but will remember the factoid. Because people have forgotten the source, they also forget that the source wasn't credible, leading to them deeming the fact to be true. That means lies told to us by liars eventually become our truths.

When reading or listening to a story, pay attention to how much common knowledge is used by the journalist. What assumptions do they make and what sources do they rely on for the facts? Are they credible sources, or the word of someone who may also be relying on rumors? In the eBay case, most reporters who quoted the Pez connection did so without ever attributing where they got the information. Had they looked into the origin of the factoid as Cohen did, they too would have discovered that the story originated from a PR professional, a source who was both media-savvy and had an agenda.

2. The story is the result of a miscommunication or a prank.

When a reporter relies on a single source for a story, there is a good chance that the source will misremember details, or worse, make details up. In the case of "Gorgeous Guy," the reporter who broke the story relied on anonymous bulletin board postings on an unfiltered website. In the Juanita's Foods example, reporters relied on the family's account of events as well as the word of one police officer. The family made an erroneous deductive leap (assuming that the pathologist said the tissue was human since he advised them to show it to police), while the police official misinterpreted what he saw.

Pay attention to the number of sources a reporter uses and how accurate those sources are likely to be. Has the reporter actually interviewed all the sources or has he allowed someone else to speak for that source? Is it possible that the source could misinterpret what was said or seen? Could he be exaggerating or lying?

3. An unknown entity becomes popular overnight not by chance, but by professional or amateur marketing.

True overnight sensations are rare. When someone you've never heard of suddenly becomes a white-hot commodity, it's a good idea to question how he managed such a stunning feat. For example, in the Gorgeous Guy case, why was it that one man was the focus of so many e-mail messages from strangers? What was so different about this man that over fifty people would notice him in the morning by a bus stop? How gorgeous would he have to be for passersby to see him, remember him and feel compelled to write about him in a public forum? In the Stewart Fason hoax, an unknown violinist suddenly became a mysterious and alluring celebrity. As we'll see in Chapter 14, an untested entity getting sudden media coverage may be a red flag that the overnight sensation is the figment of a reporter's overactive imagination.

4. There is an element of dark or twisted humor in the story.

Twisted humor is a common trait in urban legends; while that fact alone is not enough to dismiss a story's truthfulness, it is enough to look for other red flags that may indicate that a story is just a myth. While life has its humorous moments, they aren't usually perfectly contrived. In the two Jason Smiths saga, the story played on people's beliefs that colleges are a haven for irreversible mix-ups. What are the chances that two young men with identical last names would be polar opposites of each other? The story sounds like a punch line for a reason: because it is.

5. A convoluted and complicated tale is too neatly tied together.

Television mysteries are unfailingly predictable: no matter how dire the situation or twisty the mystery, the heroes will always finger the right culprit about fifteen minutes before the next program is about to start. The same cannot be said of real life. If a complex story gets tied up too neatly, there is an excellent possibility that the story is a fraud. In the Kaycee Nicole case, no one had ever seen her, but just before anyone could have a face-to-face meeting with Kaycee, she immediately died from her illness. One explanation could be a cruel twist of fate; the other was that Kaycee was a hoax and the perpetrator did not want this fact to be revealed. The latter explanation turned out to be the right one.

6. The report has an overly just ending where justice is swift, sure and severe.

These types of stories are fun and not only play upon our sense of fear, but our sense of justice as well. But swift, sure and severe justice or vigilantism rarely happens. Morality tales where the ends are too neatly tied together may indicate that a story is false. Just because a story conforms to our beliefs, that doesn't make the story true. In the C.J. saga, a woman who was infected by a callous man sought revenge by turning the tables on other casual men. While the deliberate spread of diseases is nothing new, few people do it as revenge.

7. The sourcing of the information is nebulous.

A news consumer needs a way to be assured that an actual person directly related to an event was interviewed, or that documents relevant to an event were obtained. It's the only way for reporters to be able to draw conclusions about a story's truthfulness. To be able to know whether a piece of information is true, you have to know where the information came from.

When reading or listening to a story or news item, pay careful attention to who is the original source of information. Does the reporter or storyteller explicitly identify who it was they interviewed? Did the reporter trust an anonymous source? If so, there is a good chance the report is wrong; after all, why does the source wish to remain anonymous? What is the advantage to being hidden? In the case of the "Gorgeous Guy," there were many anonymous posters who marveled at Baca's beauty, but reporters didn't know the specific identities of the posters—they just assumed these messages were from a lot of different people and did not consider the possibility they all came from a single source who had a vested interest in spreading the news that an available man could be found at a certain place everyday (i.e., wanting to gain attention from passersby who may be looking for a date).

8. The time, day, location and principles are vague and impossible to track down.

Information can be better verified when an exact location is given; the more specific the location, the easier it is to double check to see whether a certain person exists or an event has taken place. Finding a particular Bob Smith is harder when someone tells you "He lives somewhere in North America," than when they tell you he lives at 123 Military Road in Niagara Falls, New York. If a story's main players can't be tracked down, it's a red flag that they do not exist, as in the case of Kaycee Nicole and C.J.

9. If a location is given, it is usually wrong.

Urban legends and other fake stories don't give precise locations, if any. These stories aren't meant to be verified; if they were, they'd fall apart. Sometimes the storyteller won't mention an address, but other times they may mention a state or city as the location, without going into greater detail. Some bolder con artists will give addresses, but they turn out to be wrong. If a location is mentioned in a story that interests you, it's not a bad idea to see whether the location exists.

In the Kaycee Nicole case, Debbie Swenson claimed Kaycee lived in Newton, Kansas, yet no records existed for the girl. Interestingly, Swenson herself did not live in Newton, but Peabody—a subtle way of distancing herself from the location of her hoax. In the C.J. example, "C.J." claimed to live in Dallas, but her exact location wasn't actually known. In the needles at nightclubs example, various clubs were mentioned as possible targets to lend the hoax credibility, yet none of the aforementioned establishments had encountered a needle-pricking incident.

10. Even if it is not found on an urban legend website or book, the story has the markings of a "friend of a friend" tale.

News stories need references as proof that the event took place as described; without concrete evidence, there is a chance the story is an exaggeration or a flat out lie. Anecdotes are cute, but they are not to be confused with concrete evidence. When there is no one who can directly verify a story's truthfulness, but there are people who "heard" about the story, that is a sign that the story is a hoax.

In the Kaycee Nicole case, there are thousands of people who saw Swenson's web log and photos of a seventeen-year-old girl, but no one had actually seen Kaycee in the flesh. Since "Kaycee" had an online presence for two years, it stands to reason that someone would have actually seen her at some point. In the Gorgeous Guy case, there were fifty e-mails that made mention of an average-looking man standing on the street corner, a truly fantastical claim that sounds like a romantic comedy plot for a film rather than a plausible turn of events. The story of the two Jasons also has the feel of an urban legend.

11. Sourcing and details seem certain (mentioning of Neiman-Marcus or even a city or region), but other details are missing (e.g., police reports, security video, autopsy reports).

Vagueness is a liar's best friend: if you can't prove his story to be false, then logically, you should come to the conclusion that his story is therefore true. That piece of faulty logic comes up short: if you don't have enough information to be able to determine a story's credibility, it does not mean the story is real. Regardless of whether a story is from a mainstream media outlet or a forwarded e-mail message, look for specifics: any piece of information that can nail the truthfulness of a story. Details are potent clues that can tell you whether the story you read or heard is accurate or a fraud. Are there information gaps? Does the story have chronological or logical holes? Can you pinpoint an event's location, date or time? Sometimes you think you've been given concrete details, when in fact you've only been given sketchy ones.

For example, suppose you lived in Buffalo, New York and one of your friends tells you that he will be "out of the country" this weekend. Without questioning your friend, you may assume he is going to Europe or Asia, since he says he's going out of the country. If you ask "Where are you going?" he may sheepishly tell you, "Niagara Falls, Canada," which is literally right across the bridge. Of course, he didn't tell you from the onset exactly where he was traveling—he wanted to brag and make you envy his ersatz jet set life.

On the other hand, he might have said "Brazil," and his vagueness was just his way of communicating. Vagueness isn't an automatic sign of deception, but without asking a couple of questions, you don't know whether the information is accurate or not. What you are looking for when listening to these stories are omissions—what information has been left out and why? What isn't mentioned in a news story is often more important than what has been said.

In the Neiman-Marcus hoax, the fact that specific details aren't given point to the storyteller's deceptiveness. In the Kaycee Nicole saga, no one had actually seen the girl, nor had any revealing information been given. In the C.J. case, the lack of details known about the vengeful woman also pointed to the story's weaknesses. In the Churchill parrot case, the fact that no one could find references or photos of Churchill with Charlie strongly hinted that the story was a fake.

Chapter Seven

| The Competitor's Myth

The concept of objectivity is important in many information-gathering industries; however, the definition of objectivity varies from profession to profession. In science, objectivity means making sure the researcher's biases and beliefs don't taint the results of the study. Scientists and researchers build fail-safes, such as placebos and double blinds, into their studies to make sure their hopes don't taint the final product.

But objectivity in journalism is not the same concept. Journalistic objectivity means getting both sides of the story, being fair and balanced and keeping a reporter's personal feelings out of a story. Though many reporters hold to this view of objectivity, there is no empirical evidence to support that this is the best or most reliable way of disseminating the truth to a wide audience. It's assumed that objectivity will prevent a reporter's or media outlet's ideological biases from creeping into a news story.

Objectivity in journalism hasn't prevented biases from creeping into the news product—but, more importantly, it hasn't exactly prevented lies from tainting stories, either. Many hoaxes thrive in journalistic objectivity simply because this form of objectivity requires simple roles, and journalists reporting information in a passive manner. One type of hoax that manipulates objectivity is the competitor's myth.

A competitor is not necessarily a business rival, but can be someone who has competing interests with the target of the rumor or hoax. The competitor's plan involves taking something of value that is not rightfully his by means of lying about a person or company. In other words, malign your victim and then rob him, too. If done correctly, the true villain will be seen as the victim who deserves the spoils while the victim is seen as the villain who deserves to be robbed.

This sort of scheme takes advantage of the reporter's concept of objectivity: the con artist assigns himself the role of the victim, making the true victim seem like the villain by default. The fact that the con artist will strike first by posing as a victim will set the tone of the story. The true victim will have no idea that he was targeted for a scheme, making him poorly prepared to defend himself. This lack of planning makes the victim seem even more guilty and the con artist seem more credible.

Since reporters are asked to look at only two sides of an issue and give both sides equal time, the side with the carefully thought out plan will make his story sound more convincing while the victim will be too busy defending himself—thus making himself look even more guilty. In these cases, the con artist has the advantage. The only hope a targeted person or company has is that a trusted institution will investigate and uncover the hoax.

When reporters actively engage in investigative journalism, a competitor's manipulative tactics can be stopped before they ever begin. In 1989, one activist group called for a boycott on Nestlé products because the company had continued to distribute free infant formula to developing nations, making newborns vulnerable to malnutrition and death since mothers would use the formula over breast-feeding, depriving infants of vital nutrients while exposing them to untreated water used to mix the formula. The practice went against guidelines set by the World Health Organization and the activist group called for a boycott of the company's products until Nestlé abandoned the practice.

Did Nestlé consider changing their unhealthy practices? Don't be silly: they hired the advertising company Ogilvy and Mather to help rehabilitate their image. The firm's report, dubbed "Proactive Neutralization: Nestlé Recommendations Regarding the Infant Formula Boycott," in essence, advocated that the company "monitor" grassroots organizations and "inoculate" the public against any negative accusations by cultivating a "do-good" image in order to make the charges seem groundless. The confidential report was leaked to the media, and Nestlé quickly abandoned the project. The moral of the story is: don't correct your mistakes, just make your critics look like fools.

But belittling rivals and competitors can also involve spreading false information. When the mudslinging rumors are released into the public, the targeted company can see its fortunes quickly flounder. In 1987, Corona Extra, an imported Mexican beer that was quickly becoming a popular brew with the in crowd, suddenly saw its sales decline when rumors that the beer was made with human urine began to spread across the country. The rumor was unfounded and not disseminated by the press; however, many people who spread the rumor falsely claimed that news programs such as "60 Minutes" reported the story in an attempt to lend credibility to the rumors. Importers of Corona fought back, accusing competing beer importers of starting the rumors to damage Corona's sales. While all companies denied wrongdoing, Corona's importer sued a rival importer and settled the matter out of court: while the rival importer denied any wrongdoing, as part of the settlement they issued a statement saying that Corona was contaminant-free. In this case, the mainstream press did not fall for the bait, and helped debunk the myth.

When it comes to grabbing easy money, many people will happily resort to spreading lies to get what they want. Slander, libel and innuendo can be powerful tools in a rival or subversive's attempt to steal from a target. It's difficult for companies to cope when the rumor spreads by word of mouth or through e-mail warnings, but when those lies are passed as truth on newscasts, the damage can be more severe and come even faster.

A Soft Drink Company's Own Version of the Crackerjack Box

Supposedly unpleasant surprises make for easy news stories, particularly if an upset person purchased an All-American product only to find the product tainted with a dangerous or revolting object. Audience reaction to these stories can be fairly predictable—fear, anger and disgust—but one reaction many reporters don't consider is cold calculation.

Pepsi drinkers were in for a rude shock when they found out that somebody found more than just fizzy liquid in his soda can in the June 11, 1993 edition of the *Seattle Times*:

> A... Pierce County couple say they found a used hypodermic needle in a can of Pepsi they bought at a Tacoma store, in a case that has been turned over to the federal Food and Drug Administration.
>
> Earl and Mary Triplett found the needle Wednesday in a can of Pepsi they consumed Tuesday night, according to their attorney, Frank Ladenburg of Tacoma.
>
> Ladenburg said both Earl Triplett, eighty-two, and Mary Triplett, seventy-nine, consumed part of the can of Pepsi before Earl discovered the needle when he shook the empty can the following morning.
>
> Ladenburg said he checked with a registered nurse who told him it appeared to be the type of syringe and plunger used by diabetics. The tip of the needle was bent as if it had been used, he added.

News of the tainted pop can spread quickly across the country, including TV outlets such as CNN. The story affected millions of consumers: what if the needle was tainted with the HIV virus? What if children pricked themselves on the needles? But by the next day, worse news came to Pepsi drinkers in a June 12 *Associated Press* article:

> A syringe has been found in a second can of Diet Pepsi, this time by a Federal Way resident.
>
> Alpac Corp., the regional Pepsi bottler, learned of the second syringe Friday night when it was called by a consumer who asked not to be identified, Carl Behnke, president of the South Seattle firm, said yesterday.

Alpac and the federal Food and Drug Administration are conducting an investigation into the apparent product tampering, a felony under federal law.

"It has to be some sort of sabotage because there is no way that type of a foreign object could enter our product in the normal course of events," Behnke said.

How did the syringes find their way into the cans? Who would be sick enough to harm innocent people and children? The questions couldn't be answered, but people were warned how to prevent themselves from being the next victim in a June 14 *USA Today* news brief:

Diet Pepsi drinkers in the Northwest are being told not to sip from the can. The warnings came after Seattle area residents found hypodermic needles and syringes in two cans of Diet Pepsi last week. The Food and Drug Administration warned consumers Sunday in Washington, Oregon, Alaska, Hawaii and Guam they should inspect cans of Diet Pepsi for signs of tampering and pour the contents into a glass before drinking.

The news went from bad to worse for PepsiCo when scores of other consumers—over fifty reports across the country—began finding booby prizes, such as rocks, cocaine vials and even a bullet in their cans, though it was strange that only a single report of a contaminated can was reported on June 9. Considering the popularity of Pepsi, how was it that multiple reports of product tampering suddenly exploded only *after* the first report received media attention?

The question wasn't important—the fact remained that others had also been victimized by an anonymous urban terrorist. Outlets outside Washington state were eager to localize the Pepsi scare by reporting that their own citizens were also victims of product tampering without verifying whether the claims were true or not. The *Milwaukee Sentinel* reported that one of their own had been victimized, too: Kitty Wuerl, a part-time telemarketer for the paper, gave an interview when she found a syringe in her can of Pepsi. Her first person account was published June 17:

I still can't believe it. I saw on television how syringes were showing up in Pepsi cans in New York, but I didn't expect to find one in my can. I was eating in the *Journal/Sentinel* TV lounge at 6:45 p.m. Wednesday when I opened a can of Pepsi I purchased from a vending machine at 3:30 p.m. outside Kmart, 6900 W. Greenfield Ave., West Allis. As I was pouring the soda from the can into a glass filled with ice, I noticed something float to the top of the can.

Other media outlets continued to report on other cases, as they did in a June 15 news brief in *USA Today*:

> More cases of syringes and needles in soft drink cans were reported Monday. New Orleans shipyard worker Lenny Schouest said he cut his lip on a bent needle in a can of Pepsi, one of two cases reported there.

The Pepsi scare continued until the FDA had a chance to examine those other cans and determined that cans were neither tampered with nor contaminated. By June 19, the news media reported that most of the cases of tampering were hoaxes. Once those people who made false claims were arrested and faced prison sentences, reports of tainted Pepsi cans suddenly stopped. As for Kitty Wuerl, the telemarketer for the *Milwaukee Sentinel*, she confessed that she made up her story in a bid to get attention. For her duplicity, the paper fired her.

How did a single complaint balloon into a mass panic? Reporters simply didn't question the truthfulness of the complaints. The scare had all the elements of a boffo story: good visuals, frightened average citizens and a benign product turned into an unpredictable menace. Without questioning the motives of those who made their claims, reporters simply let a minor story balloon into a national hysteria.

Reporters didn't ask the hard questions: were the cans manufactured at the same time? At the same plant? Would it be possible to tamper with the can in that manner? Did the people making the claims have proof? What would be their gain in lying? Were these individuals planning to sue Pepsi? Why was it that only a single complaint of a contaminated can was lodged on June 9? If there were other spiked cans, wouldn't it be more likely that several reports would be lodged at the same time, independent from other media reports? Without answering those questions, the news media allowed hoaxers and saboteurs to spin their stories freely, leading to a needless mass panic.

Taking the Plunge Into the Shallow End

A sizable percentage of a news outlet's stories come from wire services. Media companies subscribe to several services which provide articles, photos, footage and audio to hundreds of media outlets every day. Wire services make it possible for local outlets to report on national and international news stories and national outlets to report on events happening in smaller regions. These services are a cheaper and more efficient way of gathering news. Outlets rely on wire services for breaking news, features and any other story imaginable. Sometimes, wire services rely on other wire services for their information.

That inter-wire service trust was evident when the following press release distributed by Internet Wire on August 25, 2000 made its way to other wires:

SEC Launches Investigation Into Accounting Practices. Paul Folino Steps down as CEO.

[...]Emulex Corp... the world's largest supplier of fibre channel adapters, announced that last quarter's earnings will be revised and will fall short of previously announced Net income for the fourth quarter of fiscal will be revised to a loss $0.15 per diluted share, compared with net income of $3.0 million, or per diluted share, for the same quarter a year Earnings for Q4 were reported as $0.25 per share, due to compliance with generally accepted accounting principles, revisions were made. Net Earnings for fiscal 1998 and 1999 will also be revised. A press release with more detail will be submitted today at 5:00 pm EST.

The news made its way onto the Dow Jones, Business Wire and Bloomberg wire services in the morning, as well as CNBC. Stockholders who read the online news release panicked and began to sell their shares in the company. The news sent Emulex stock tumbling over 60%—costing the company over two billion dollars. Nasdaq halted trading of Emulex shares.

Emulex brass quickly responded to the panic—the news wasn't true and the release did not originate from the company. A few days later, the FBI found and arrested the mastermind behind the hoax: a twenty-three-year-old former Internet Wire employee named Mark Jakob who had worked for the company until August 18—leaving a mere week before the hoax.

Jakob knew the workings of Internet Wire and also had a motive for spreading the rumor—Jakob played the market and would gain financially if the Emulex shares fell sharply. As a result of one man's greediness, an unsuspecting company saw its shares plunge while Jakob made a quarter of a million dollars with his simple scheme. Fortunately, the company managed to regain most of its losses while Jakob lost all of his.

Did Internet Wire, Dow Jones or Bloomberg wire services double-check the bogus press release? While the sheer volume of releases received can make it extremely difficult for one media outlet to verify them, no one at any of the wire services had someone call the company or the SEC to verify the claims. A story of this magnitude would have warranted a precursory check on the accuracy of the press release. Didn't anyone find it curious that this unexpected turn of events happened at Emulex? The wire service simply repeated what they read without following up on the surprising details.

Money for Nothing

Big lottery pay outs seem to be a favorite story for many reporters: a regular Joe winning millions appeals to viewers since many wish they too could solve all their financial problems in such a fast and easy way. Viewers can relate not only to the winners, but lottery stories can also be presented in quite a suspenseful way: did anyone win the lottery? Who? How poor were they? Why haven't they come to claim their prize yet? How will they spend their newfound wealth?

There is also one neurotic question to ponder: what happens if someone looses his winning ticket?

That was precisely the question reporters around the country asked when Elecia Battle tearfully claimed that she lost the winning ticket worth $162 million. Her report seemed credible: a single winning ticket had yet gone unclaimed, and then she reported the missing ticket to police. As the January 5, 2004 *AP* story recounted:

> A Cleveland woman has told police she picked the winning numbers for the $162 million Mega Millions lottery jackpot but lost the ticket before the drawing, according to a police report.
>
> Elecia Battle told police she dropped her purse as she left the Quick Shop Food Mart in suburban South Euclid last week after buying the ticket. She said she realized after the drawing last Tuesday that the ticket was missing.
>
> The Ohio Lottery said last week that the winning ticket was sold at the store, about fifteen miles east of Cleveland.
>
> "I feel like crap right now," said Battle, who cried while speaking to the *Associated Press* at her home Monday night.
>
> Police say Battle also was in tears when she came to the station Friday to file the report and did not hesitate when asked to write down the winning numbers.

Battle's word was good enough for over a dozen people: they braved the cold winter and went to search for her missing ticket with flashlights in hand, hoping to cash in on her misfortune. As one treasure hunter told the *Associated Press*, "I decided to come back to see if I could find the winning ticket." The woman also said she'd keep the millions for herself. Her story made local (e.g. WEWS-TV) and national news (e.g. CNN).

Then came Act Two.

A woman named Rebecca Jemison came to lottery officials and claimed the winning jackpot—and had the ticket to prove it.

The media attention might have ended there, except Battle, true to her last name, retained a lawyer and attempted to pursue her case in court. News outlets continued to report the story and referred to Battle as the "lottery loser." Technically, she was a lottery loser since she didn't win the jackpot, but the implication was that she lost her lottery ticket. Soon after, the website the Smoking Gun obtained Battle's rap sheet. Battle admitted that the winning ticket wasn't hers and dropped her suit. She was charged with filing a false police report.

How did this non-story gain national attention? The too-bad-to-be-true elements were simply too outré for reporters to ignore: a working class stiff losing a multi-million dollar jackpot was a story of heartbreak. The fact that police seemed to believe Battle's story was enough confirmation for reporters to pursue the hoax without digging deeper. When Jemison came to claim her rightful prize, reporters still pursued the story, even when one wasn't there.

However, Jemison's ticket showed no signs of being weather-damaged (in the cold and snowy winter of 2004, a ticket staying in pristine condition would have been nearly impossible). She not only provided a second ticket she purchased from the same store, but also an older ticket she played with the same numbers. Jemison was the clear winner and Battle was trying to claim some of those millions for herself. It was an unsuccessful gambit—but she managed to gain temporary credibility thanks to the news media.

How to Spot a Competitor's Myth in the News

A person or company can have scores of secret enemies or competitors—and all of them willing to lie to get what they want from their target. Sometimes the detractors aren't even aware of each other's intentions. It may sound like a paranoid conspiracy theory, until you consider the Pepsi tainted can scare: the copycat hoaxers did not know each other nor were they known to have any previous axe to grind with Pepsi. What these fraudsters saw was a rare opportunity to spike their own cans, claim distress and then possibly sue Pepsi for negligence and emotional distress.

Without asking critical questions, the media can give legitimacy to these types of con artists. The news media has the power to take a small problem and distort it into looking like an unstoppable epidemic. The trick for news consumers is to determine whether an unsavory rumor is real or is the work of an unscrupulous rival or saboteur.

Uncovering a competitor's likely story isn't as difficult as it first appears; by considering the motives of known or hidden competing interests, you can consider alternative explanations for a company or person's apparent faux pas. What would someone have to gain by spreading harmful rumors?

But there are other signs to look for when considering these types of news stories.

1. The story is inflammatory or slanderous, but has the feel of an urban legend.

Real dangers should sound plausible and logical—hoaxes, on the other hand, are made to frighten and discourage customers from wanting to patronize a product or company. That means that the danger will sound severe, imminent and virtually unavoidable. Over-the-top stories may serve to frighten us, but they won't make much sense. When listening to a news report (or any e-mail warning) that sounds frightening, but illogical, there is a good chance that the warning is a hoax meant to ruin someone's reputation.

In the Pepsi can scare, how likely was it that so many cans could be contaminated with syringes and rocks? Since the syringes were found in cans, not bottles, how would someone bring in over two dozen items into a factory and slip the items into cans undetected at the processing level? What would be his or her motive?

Obviously, extortion did not play a factor since no one claimed responsibility. It could have been an act of urban terrorism, but then again, wouldn't it be easier to covertly slip poison or a foul-tasting liquid into the cans rather than bulky and noisy garbage? The risk of detection would be great—plus it would most likely have to be an inside job, also increasing the risk of the culprit getting caught in the act of sabotage. Besides, wouldn't the items, particularly rocks, make noises as the cans were being shipped, unpacked and purchased? If a can made a clanging noise as you picked it up to buy it, would you have bought the suspect can? While product tampering is not unheard of (such as the 1982 Tylenol terror when several bottles in the Chicago-area had been tampered with and the contents were spiked with cyanide), the act of tampering still has to conform to what is physically and logically possible.

While technically it could have been possible for someone to tamper with cans of soda at the factory level, the alternate explanation that people were deliberately spiking their own pop cans in a bid to sue Pepsi turned out to be correct.

2. The original source can't be pinned down.

When adults become the victims of a dubious business, they will usually report their troubles to some official institution, whether it be a hospital, police station or the courts. Some people report a bad business because they believe it is their duty, while others report corporate negligence for the chance to sue and win a sizeable settlement. In either case, there should be some form of official complaint.

It may be possible that a single person won't complain about being the victim of a shady business practice or that ten people won't put their displeasure on official record, but if hundreds or thousands of people refuse to lodge a complaint against a single business, then it is almost a certainty that the rumor is hoax.

Similarly, if someone is aware that a company is involved in an immoral or disgusting enterprise and they make the company's questionable practices public, there should be a way to trace the rumor to either the original source, or at least be able to determine whether the accusation is true (i.e., by inspecting or investigating the company). If there are only vague and unproved rumors, it is a sign that there is no basis to the whisperings. In the Corona case, while there were rumors that the brewery used urine to make their beers, the original source could not be traced, making the veracity of those claims suspect. Why wouldn't those people who had first-hand knowledge come forward to blow the whistle on the company? If Corona did use urine, a simple lab analysis on several cases of the beer could confirm or refute the outrageous claim.

3. The target of the story is competing with someone else and there have been prior instances of mudslinging.

When hearing any negative rumor about a person or company, first think very carefully about the person's probable competitors: what would they have to gain if the public believed the rumors? Corona Beer had managed to become one of the most popular imported beers in the U.S.—an up-and-comer gaining on someone else's turf would be motive enough for some rivals to start vulgar rumors against their competition. While the source of the original rumors wasn't ever discovered, the rumor was most likely started by someone who did not want to see the Mexican brewery make any further strides in the U.S. market.

4. Allegations could permanently ruin the target and there is little or no evidence to back up the claims.

The more damaging the rumor, the more important it is to look for corroborating evidence to substantiate the allegations. Our first instinct may be to believe the rumor, after all, common sense tells us that "when there is smoke, there is fire." Sure, there may be fire, but the fire doesn't necessarily point to a company or individual's wrongdoing, but to the company's bitter rivalry with a less ethical competitor. In other words, if there is smoke, in what direction do you see the fire?

No matter how bombastic the rumor, look for tangible evidence to support the rumor's truthfulness. If there is no solid evidence, chances are, the rumor is meant to hurt an innocent party. In the Emulex, Corona and Pepsi cases, each had faced serious accusations, but none of the rumors were backed by any evidence. In the lotto hoax, a single individual claimed to have lost a winning ticket, but she did not provide any hard evidence of her claim.

5. The source of the claim has something to gain by making the allegation.

Jealousy and greed are two powerful motivators for starting vicious rumors, and you shouldn't overlook those motives when you hear damaging allegations against a person or company. Is it likely that someone will benefit by spreading the rumor? If so, by how much? Is the payoff great enough for the vector to risk detection?

In the Pepsi can scare, complainants had a motive to come forward: they could sue Pepsi for negligence, mostly likely as part of a class action lawsuit. Since there would be strength in numbers, those who spiked their cans would hope they could blend in with those they assumed were genuine victims of product tampering. In the lotto hoax, Battle's motive was to try to gain a part of the lottery winnings—if she reported her ticket missing before the winner came forward, she may have thought she would have a better chance of gaining credibility. In the Emulex hoax, the source of the fraud had a motive for spreading his lies.

Next time you hear an unsavory rumor about a company or person, think about the invisible competitors; if there is a possibility that a story is false, who would have something to gain by besmirching that person's reputation? Rumors shouldn't be listened to passively and uncritically: a good dose of critical thinking can help you determine whether you should take the warning seriously, or simply ignore it. Are you in danger when you are drinking your cola, or is someone spiking his own can for profit? Should you go out in the freezing elements to look for someone's missing lottery ticket or should you stay indoors and laugh at those who've fallen for someone's ridiculous hoax? Do you sell your stock and risk losing thousands or millions of dollars based on a panicky rumor, or do you hold on to your stock until cooler heads prevail?

People have self-serving motives for starting harmful rumors and hoaxes, and if it means ruining someone's livelihood or bamboozling customers, then so be it. Playing into these people's hands can't lead to any good—so think about the rumor before you take any action.

Chapter **Eight**

| **The Winner**

Crime, war, poverty, abuse, discrimination, illness, death and taxes are all downer topics, and, for many people, these trusty news themes alone are enough to make the queasy and the chronically offended avoid the news altogether, lest the reporting of reality wreaks havoc with their sparkling auras. For some folks, it's difficult to admit that bad things happen to good people, or that wonderful things happen to bad people. These are the people who complain loudly and bitterly to the news media when graphic images and gut-wrenching stories fill pages and television screens.

News outlets hear these people loud and clear, and in order to keep their patronage, will make certain that there is an ample dose of happy news. "Happy news" is the pastry puff of the news world: it's light, flaky, devoid of anything nutritious—and when you condense it, there really isn't any substance there. Simply put, happy news is there to keep the moral masturbators gratified.

But it wasn't a happy news story when media outlets around the world reported that a massive earthquake struck northwest Armenia and killed 25,000 people in its wake. The images and consequences were devastating and the world's focus shifted to other events; that is, until over a month later, when word came out that some newly found survivors lived through the quake and its aftermath with barely a scratch to show for it.

International media reaction was simply glowing, as in the case of a January 13, 1989 article in *USA Today*:

> Six Armenians are living proof miracles still happen.
>
> The men were pulled from the rubble of a nine-story apartment building in Leninakan, the Soviet Union, on Wednesday—thirty-five days after the Dec. 7 earthquake...
>
> The six... survived on canned vegetables, fruit, pickles and ham stored in the basement. One had a broken arm, but there were no serious injuries, the Soviet news agency TASS reported.
>
> "Not for one minute did we lose confidence that we would be saved," survivor Aikaz Akopyan, fifty, said.

Akopyan became an overnight media amusement, giving interviews about his ordeal. His story made it to A-list media outlets like "NBC Nightly News." However, the Russian daily Izvestia found inconsistencies with Akopyan's yarn: where were his neighbors? How could he survive the bitter cold for an entire month without any shelter? Why hadn't he developed frostbite?

While Akopyan maintained that his story was true, the Russian news agency TASS, which originally broke Akopyan's story, had done its own investigating and found the story could not stand up to scrutiny. The man who could defy Mother Nature's odds turned out to be an attention-seeking fraud.

Winners in the news should almost always trigger a silent alarm in your head: winners and heroes may not be all that they appear, especially if they are the ones who blatantly push themselves as the hero or winner. A little positive press may not have ever hurt anyone, but many unscrupulous people have their own agendas and it doesn't hurt to try to figure out why these heroes and winners are seeking media attention in the first place. What's in it for these people to draw attention to their heroic or impressive deeds?

Sometimes in their zeal to lionize someone, many journalists will inadvertently embellish a person's story, even though the person in question never made the claims. In March 1988, fifteen-year-old Joey Philion suffered burns to 90% of his body when his home suddenly caught fire. Media outlets in North America claimed the young man had run back into his home to save his younger brother Danny. Though none of the Philions ever denied or confirmed this account, the story made its way into the media until one television reporter began following up on the story. It was then when reporters finally realized their error.

When you are evaluating winner stories, keep these two clichés in mind: "nobody's perfect" and "everybody loves a winner." People who come off as above reproach in news stories need to be looked at with extra skepticism: they may be the real deal, but perhaps they were adept manipulators or the reporter simply did not dig deep enough to unearth contradictory information.

Journalists tend not to ask winners the tough questions, mainly because they know there will be people who will complain if anyone questions a hero or winner. In our minds, nice people shouldn't have to defend their actions or credibility. Unfortunately, that type of thinking gives con artists a patina of protection to lie without having to prove their claims.

Winners can be charming, with equally charming stories. Heinz Braun was living in East Germany during the last days of the Cold War. With a little ingenuity and a lot of bravado, he managed to fool the border patrol, as was recounted in the August 11, 1986 edition of *Time* magazine:

> It wasn't a movie, but it probably will be. As he told it, Heinz Braun, an
> East Berlin tire salesman, last week painted his auto to resemble a Soviet

patrol car, dressed himself and three mannequins in Red Army uniforms, and coolly drove through a Berlin Wall checkpoint to West Berlin.

Braun claimed that he and a cohort had photographed soldiers during routine patrols and then created their own uniforms based on the photographs. After this spectacular escape, media outlets from around the world wanted to interview the intrepid East Berliner. The story made sense: East Germany was immersed in Soviet-style obedience. These soldiers, who were used to obeying authority and not questioning anyone wearing official regalia, would see nothing amiss with the homemade uniforms on three mannequins.

Two weeks later, Braun and his partner confessed that their story was a hoax, supposedly as a homage to those forced to live on the east side of the Berlin Wall, but others questioned aloud whether Braun and company wanted to sell the rights to their story to a movie studio. Regardless of their motivations, few reporters who initially interviewed Braun or his conspirators asked for any corroborating evidence; why would they? They escaped to the other side of the Wall, didn't they? Why would anyone lie about their bravery and resolve? The story was too good to be true, but the allure of an average Joe turned cunning escape artist was just too much for reporters to pass up.

Just as it was hard for Thailand journalists to resist the charms of taxi driver Sompong Leudtahan, who claimed to have returned $25,000 that was accidentally left in his cab by a foreign tourist in 1997. For his act of altruism, Leudtahan received money from politicians, an award from the Thai royal family, and got to appear on countless media outlets. It was a feel-good story, until the cab driver was arrested for defrauding the public. Leudtahan's good deed had taken place exclusively in his mind. While the Thai press gave him accolades, the police could find no witnesses or evidence to corroborate his version of events. Even his family said that he tried to pull a similar stunt a couple of years before, but journalists didn't follow up on those leads.

A past record of real bravery doesn't mean the hero won't try to invent a fake crisis to hold on to the glory. James Pearson was a Los Angeles police officer assigned to keep a vigilant eye on events during the 1984 Olympic Games. Pearson had a glowing record of bravery, including being shot in the chest in 1978, but nothing compared to his brave deed as recounted in the August 14, 1984 edition of the *Daily Oklahoman*:

> A sharp-eyed police officer discovered a pipe bomb aboard a bus carrying the baggage of the Turkish Olympic team Monday and disarmed it moments before it was to explode, authorities said.
>
> About 6,000 people were evacuated from three terminals after the bomb was discovered aboard the bus headed to Los Angeles International Airport.

[...Police Chief Daryl] Gates said Officer Jim Pearson "pulled the device out of where it was located, determined it was about to go off.

"He has some knowledge of that kind of device," Gates said.

The officer then carried the pipe bomb to the tarmac, put it down and pulled some wires loose "and ran," apparently successfully disarming it, the chief added.

While Pearson was hailed a hero by the press and the public alike, his superiors became suspicious and soon discovered that Pearson himself planted the bomb on the bus to gain attention and impress his superiors, with whom he had been having problems. Pearson confessed and was later charged in connection with the hoax.

Why and how do reporters fall for these types of stories, and why do some scammers choose to play the winner?

Why Scam Artists Can Pass as Winners in the Media

A hoaxer has to choose which role will suit his own ends very carefully. Playing the villain is definitely out, since the con artist is not likely going to get what he wants by evoking mass ridicule, and he is trying to hide his villainy in the first place.

The freak is a dicey role to take on: no one really wants to be the laughingstock of a city or country. But if someone paints himself in a corner by getting caught in the middle of a scheme, it's better to be thought of as a freak than a villain, and the person may try to save face by portraying himself as a sympathetic oddball.

This isn't to say that cons always avoid the freak role: some actually thrive when they portray themselves as someone who has supernatural powers, such as clairvoyance or telekinesis. Whether the pseudo-power in question is predicting the future or talking to the dead, in these cases, the con is not claiming to be just a freak, but a super-freak. The upside is that the person may get media coverage and a devoted following which will financially support the con artist. The downside is that the hoaxer is dependent on parlor tricks that are usually easy to detect and expose. For those who don't know parlor tricks or who don't have the right mindset, this role isn't a viable option.

That leaves two roles to choose from: the victim and the hero. The victim role is a safe bet and, for many con artists, this is the role of choice. A victim inspires sympathy, which, in turn, inspires protection and, in many cases, generous donations from the public; besides, most people become angry at those people who would question an alleged victim's truthfulness. For those who don't have credibility, but need to establish it quickly, playing a victim in the media may be a viable option.

The victim role isn't foolproof: if a hoaxer cannot evoke sympathy, then the scam falls apart, since only those who have likable personalities can play this type of role convincingly. For some people, no amount of doe-eyed stares or hunched postures will help them gain the public's trust. For example, suppose two people in the same city get stabbed to death by the same unknown indiscriminate killer: a comely teenaged girl who is an honor student and hospital volunteer, and a rough-looking gang member with a rap sheet and loaded gun. The fallen teen will invariably be seen as the victim in the press, while the gang member will be seen as someone whose lifestyle led him to his horrific fate.

Even if the con can maintain a lovable demeanor, an observant skeptic might unravel the scam in other ways, and if the hoax is discovered, the same compassionate public will suddenly turn angry towards the scammer. While playing a pseudo-victim is a tricky proposition, it can work only if the person can pull the right heartstrings and keep his story straight.

The final role for the scam artist is the hero. This role can also yield superb dividends if the hoaxer plays his cards right. Being the trusted altruist who can save the day or save lives can translate to prestige, credibility and a lucrative career. To save a life, company or murder investigation takes bravery, skill and spirit—all the qualities that most of us would consider to be indicative of a trustworthy person.

The advantages to playing a hero are numerous: even a modest person can transform himself into a hero (who we would describe as an "underdog"). The public generally trusts heroes, and rewards them with praise, publicity and, in many cases, financial incentives. Heroes don't need to present themselves as weak and sympathetic; in fact, heroes can be crude and obnoxious—so long as they deliver what they promise. In fact, obnoxiousness can be seen as an endearing personality quirk on someone who has just saved an infant from a pack of hungry wolves. Finally, to catch a fake hero can be harder than it is to catch a fake victim—but it's not impossible.

The 1980 Boston Marathon seemed as run of the mill as previous ones. The winner of the women's marathon seemed to be twenty-three-year-old Rosie Ruiz, and photos showed the triumphant young runner hamming it up for the camera. With a laurel crowning her head and arm muscles flexed, who could question whether or not she was the winner?

But even the photo revealed troubling inconsistencies: why wasn't she sweaty after running for hours? How could she stand up at all? Her leg muscles seemed relaxed, hardly what anyone would expect from a runner who just completed a grueling marathon.

If the photo itself wasn't enough to rouse suspicions, it was other evidence that finally led marathon officials to revoke Ruiz's standing. First, no runners or spectators saw Ruiz actually running the marathon. Second, some witnesses claimed to have seen Ruiz jump out from a vehicle near the finish line. Finally, Ruiz did not appear in any photos or video footage of the race. As winsome as her bright smile was, Ruiz's shoddy planning was quickly exposed.

Heroes vs. Winners

Closely related to the hero is the winner: this is the person who can turn a near-bankrupt company into a money-making machine, win marathons without breaking a sweat, cure incurable diseases with little effort, attend university classes when most of his peers are in preschool or break flying records with only a little experience and a lot of pluck. There is nothing a winner can't do; after all, he has the know-how, the perseverance, the pearly white smile and the magic touch.

Still, there are differences between a hero and winner: a hero needs a specific event to catapult himself into the media spotlight, while the winner may grab attention for possessing an alleged ability. The hero role is a short-term proposition, since a single heroic event can't maintain media interest for a prolonged period; the winner may receive media attention for weeks or years. A hero has to seem noble for a single instance, while the winner needs good press for the long haul. Finally, a hero needs to muster the nerve to scam for a short period of time, while a winner needs the guts to perpetrate his hoax over a long period.

For those who are good at long-term deceptions, the winner role is superior to the hero role, mostly because the financial rewards can be substantial. After all, because the winner has a "proven" track record, we can not only take the winner at his word, but we can also entrust the winner with billions of dollars and expect those billions to turn into trillions. Winners defy gravity, logic and common sense; they are the creative innovators who can somehow turn that worthless straw into pure gold.

Of course, you can't turn straw into gold, and the "winner" clearly knows this, but the winner also knows something else: that people deep down believe that straw might somehow be turned into gold if only the right person came along with the right recipe. We can send a cloned animal into space, so why can't someone turn water into gasoline? Winners play on our optimism and desire for better days, which is what makes the winner so effectively manipulative and, at times, even dangerous.

Many con artists who choose to play the winner can escape detection for years if he or she is media-savvy. Why? First, because winners make for good copy. What reporter can resist writing a profile about a person who took a hemorrhaging company and turned it into a lean business making monster profits? Second, with the right publicity and image consultant, almost any anonymous jerk can be transformed into a winner.

If the pseudo-winner is able and willing to make a small investment, he can opt to hire a public relations firm to help maintain his winsome image for him; after all, these are the companies that specialize in making almost anyone look better than they are in real life. Those who work in PR are professional window-dressers, which makes the journalists' task of weeding out a fraudulent winner that much harder: even if the hoaxer gets careless, he has seasoned professionals at his disposal to clean up his messes or even coach the scammer on how to behave publicly before the slip up happens in the first place. Of all the roles an adept con artist can play, the hero or winner can be the safest bet.

The winner role is safer for another reason. Journalists need to cover a variety of stories: if every news report was depressing, infuriating and frightening, the news media would lose a significant share of their audience, who cannot stomach a stream of stories whose moral is that life is hard and unfair. People are still looking for heroes and winners to uplift spirits and inspire others. The press needs winners to counterbalance stories of crime, death, disaster, terrorism and illness. A fake winner has the advantage: he is the welcome relief whose golden aura may rub off on the rest of us.

Though a fake winner can gain credibility if he can gain media attention, he still has to concoct and maintain a fairly believable story of his prowess. Finding the right ability in the right field isn't easy, but it's not impossible. If a person claims to be able to perform any of the following feats, there is the possibility that the person is, if not exaggerating or taking sole credit for a group effort, flat out lying:

• Can dramatically turn around the fortunes of a faltering company in a short period of time;

• Can perform physical feats that no one else can do;

• Breaks a world record or is the first person to accomplish a particular feat, though there are no independent witnesses to verify the claim;

• Claims to be the best in his profession;

• Claims to be able to cure illnesses that most experts in the field cannot cure;

• Can perform impossible tasks or portrays himself as a profession's last resort;

• Claims to be able to make a fortune with minimum effort and can make others as wealthy with minimum effort as well;

• Claims grand success in a field by completely ignoring or violating that field's "old rules."

Anytime you read or watch a story about a "winner," it is a good warning sign that the story should be evaluated carefully. Everyone loves a winner, and someone pretending to be one can bask in praise and positive press without having to prove the truthfulness of his claims. This isn't to say that everyone who is portrayed as a winner is lying, but there may be clues that the person is exaggerating or hogging all the glory for himself. Media-friendly winners know how to package themselves and can think in terms of camera angles. Winners in the news usually can avoid the journalist's critical eye, at least in the beginning (which many disgruntled former winners term the "honeymoon period").

One breed of fake winner is the capitalistic maverick: this is a person who claims the power of making billions with his business acumen, guts, vision and mastery of cunning strategy. On the face of it, the business winner is telling the truth: the company is making millions or billions of dollars. Investors and stockholders seem very happy with their returns. Rivals and financial analysts alike concede that this tycoon can turn straw into gold. Quarterly earnings reports are flush with profits and the company's stock climbs to new heights. What's there to question?

Not much, since the tycoon will receive positively glowing and unquestionably fawning media coverage in the beginning. This winner may be seen as a savior or an avatar of the business set. New economy, old economy, it doesn't matter: this is a person (usually a middle-aged man or a young turk) whose genius can overcome any barrier to make money. Yet it takes a little digging, courage and skepticism to question someone whose daily earnings surpass your yearly income. If everyone is making money, how could anything be wrong?

Ron and Loren Koval seemed like business winners: their upscale private health clinic, called the King's Health Centre, was Toronto's version of the Mayo Clinic. The Kovals' elite medical center seemed like a surefire winner, as the *Canadian Medical Association Journal* touted in its February 15, 1997 edition:

> Located in a newly renovated building in downtown Toronto, King's was the brainchild of Ron Koval, a merchant banker and a group of private investors. Koval lauds the relationship that King's has developed with the Mayo Clinic in Rochester, Minnesota. Over an eighteen-month period, King's paid a consultant's fee that allowed it to tap into the Mayo's administrative, marketing, computer and medical systems. The physical layout, right down to doctors' offices and the "pods" used by support staff, follows the Mayo Clinic model.

But the Kovals had no previous experience in running a medical center, though Loren Koval worked as a nurse for fourteen years at a psychiatric hospital. Nor did the couple have the kind of funds needed to make their vision a reality—but no matter, Ron Koval assured everyone in an April 2, 1997 article in the *Financial Post*: "Koval and [president Doug] Quirt won't disclose who the initial investors are or how much money they've put into King's until a prospectus is issued."

Why didn't Koval disclose who his investors were? True, it could have been because his investors wanted to remain anonymous or because Koval himself may have wanted to keep his strategies secret.

That may have been the end of it except that it was discovered several years later that there were no investors, just loans from both Canadian and U.S. banks—loans which were repaid with other borrowed money. The Kovals simply created bogus companies and applied for—and received— millions of dollars in loans, which helped keep King's afloat and supported their lavish lifestyle. While King's did offer many of the services advertised, it was never a moneymaker, and the Kovals kept borrowing under fake corporations in order to keep up appearances and live it up.

Not only was King's not all that it appeared to be on the financial front, but its relationship with the Mayo Clinic was grossly overstated. King's was never affiliated with Mayo: Mayo Medical Ventures served as consultants, but relations soured once the Koval's touted on King's brochures that the center was the "Mayo Clinic of the North." Reporters covering King's in its heyday had not called the Mayo Clinic to confirm whether the implied relationship actually existed.

Ironically, though King's was supposed to promote healthy living, its owners were overweight chain-smokers who regularly dined on red meat, expensive drinks and other unhealthy fare (a fact brought up by journalists only after the Kovals were arrested for fraud). Ron and Loren's behaviors struck many as unrefined, but were shrugged off as the expected quirks of visionary entrepreneurs. As one former King's physician admitted in the wake of the scandal, "I knew he was a cagey entrepreneur, as most entrepreneurs are." The doctor added that Koval seemed like a shrewd businessman who "made a lot of money. A lot of rough diamonds make a lot of money, but they're not crooks." The Kovals' shenanigans turned out to be one of the biggest business scams in Canadian history. Why they could dupe those in the medical, financial and banking communities for so long was simple: they seemed to be able to make a lot of money. With some journalists seemingly backing up the notion that the Kovals were cunning entrepreneurs, the couple could continue to swindle while maintaining their capitalistic image.

The Kovals weren't the only ones to use a seemingly legitimate business for suspect ends. Home-Stake Oil was a well-respected, fearless and innovative oil-drilling company based in Oklahoma, whose CEO was a lawyer named Robert S. Trippet. From the 1950s to 1970, Home-Stake's oil-drilling ventures were seen as profitable tax shelters for the country's upper crust: celebrities like Candice Bergen, Liza Minelli, Bob Dylan, Jack Benn and Mike Nichols invested, as did countless lawyers and executives.

The investment seemed like a surefire winner. Home-Stake's brochures showed the company's oil-drilling operations taking place right in the field. Early investors saw fat returns and endorsed the ventures to their well-heeled friends. Trippet himself seemed straightforward, capable and honest. And many investors were those who worked in the upper echelons of the banking industry. Who could even consider that Home-Stake was anything but a legitimate company?

Very few people investing their money in Home-Stake questioned where the money to pay investors actually came from: all had assumed profits came from oil drilling and recovery, even though Trippet himself admitted there were delays and complications which were delaying oil production. Perhaps there were delays; oil recovery wasn't a predictable business.

The annual reports from Home-Stake also looked extremely odd. It seemed as if every year, a new accounting company would sign the report; sometimes Trippet himself would sign, a highly disturbing development for a supposedly legitimate company. Even this irregularity didn't set off too many alarm bells.

However, Trippet's company never drilled for oil; what they did is buy land near another company's drilling site and take a picture of a fake derrick emblazoned with a Home-Stake logo, giving the appearance that it was Home-Stake workers who were the ones drilling for oil. Accounting companies did notice Trippet's deceit and resigned. Though investors were lawyers, celebrities and business executives, most had not been suspicious of Trippet's shifty tactics. Not only did investors lose their initial investments, but they owed the IRS back taxes and penalties as well. All signs pointed to a pyramid scheme that would eventually collapse on itself, but even the most savvy investors didn't suspect that anything was wrong until the pyramid collapsed.

Even today, many people invest in various businesses and schemes that seem solid and are run by winners, without looking at what is logical, nor at the warning signs that all is not what it appears to be. During the Internet boom of the 1990s, many could also get away with pretending to be shrewd new economy tycoons. What was appealing to many was the idea of getting rich quick by surpassing old school rules. Both traditional business and new economy reporters alike dumped kudos on the new breed of tycoon, though many Internet companies had shaky business plans and precarious financing. While some journalists truly believed the hype, others knew they were merely playing cheerleader and did not try to dispel the myths.

Wherever there is a record to be broken, a camera to mug in front of or money to be made, someone will try to win admirers and gain instant credibility by pretending to be a hero or winner. Fake winners can be found in almost any profession or recreation: sports, business, academia and even law enforcement, as the following case study shows.

A Dog and His Bogus Bones

Cute animals are trusty attention-getters for both print and television outlets. Animals warm hearts and rarely offend the public. Unless it is a story of animal abuse or cruelty, animals are almost always happy fodder in the news world, especially if that adorable fuzzy can also help people and save lives.

Sandra Anderson had such an animal at her disposal: her dog Eagle wasn't just her faithful companion; he was her not-so-secret weapon in her war against crime. Anderson was part of an organization called Canine Solutions International, where she worked as a director for "detection services" and had worked on over a thousand cases for police and other law enforcement officials. Anderson had an international reputation and media coverage, with her abilities profiled everywhere from the *Washington Post* to the *St. Petersberg Times*.

Eagle had the unique ability to find the smallest bone fragments, even if other dogs and detection devices had overlooked them. There were many murder defendants who were convicted with the help of Eagle's sensitive nose and Anderson's role as key witness. As one writer recounted in the September/October 2000 edition of *Archeology*, Eagle was in a class all by himself:

> Gifted with unusual olfactory abilities, [Eagle] is the star of Canine Solutions Inc., Anderson's Virginia-based company that trains dogs for all manner of tracking and cadaver search. Anderson directs the company's Michigan detection task training division. Sniffing out ancient remains is a field pioneered by Eagle—the only dog in the world certified for ancient human remains detection.

The *St. Petersberg Times* described Eagle as "a Doberman mix owned by... Anderson, known throughout the world for his ability to detect small traces of human remains, authorities said." What authorities vouched for the dog's uncanny ability is left unsaid. In the February 26, 2002 article, a typical Eagle outing was described in melancholic detail:

> In less than five minutes, a Michigan cadaver dog sniffed out bone fragments in a field west of Brooksville Monday that authorities believe could be the remains of Megan LeeAnn Pratt, a three-year-old who disappeared eleven years ago.
>
> Sheriff Richard Nugent said a cadaver dog named Eagle, who arrived by plane Monday morning with his handler, led them to bone fragments scattered across the wooded lot. The bones appeared to have been burned, which authorities said matches their story about Megan's death.

This feat was astounding, since area police had already used "ground-penetrating radar, cadaver dogs and earth moving equipment" but came up with nothing except for a few animal bones. Even prison inmates were sent to clear land in the area, but they too found nothing. Eagle's keen canine senses seemed to find what scores of others missed.

The find was obviously the break the police needed and the sample was taken for DNA analysis but, in an October 12, 2002 follow up article in the *Times*, it was sadly revealed that even though the bone fragments were of an adult human, they were not from three-year-old Megan. What other poor soul perished in the area was unknown: it seemed that the police now had two puzzles to solve.

It was a similar story in July, 2001, in Wisconsin. Eagle was dispatched to look for the remains of Beth Kutz, whose husband was convicted in her disappearance and murder. After hours of searching, Eagle's keen sense of smell helped locate a finger at what police believed to be the crime scene. Though Eagle again was praised for his fantastic abilities, tests later showed that the finger was human, but not from Kutz. Again, not only were police officers' hopes dashed, but now there was an added mystery and another unaccounted-for person to identify. How was it that only Eagle could find bone fragments at thoroughly examined crime scenes, and why had the dog found unaccounted-for human bones?

The answers to those questions didn't seem to matter: what counted was that Eagle could track down the dead, and that ability in and of itself was enough to grab the interest of the news media. In the June 13, 2002 edition of the *Washington Post*, one feature article examined the abilities of cadaver dogs, which included an interview with Anderson:

> Eleven-year-old Eagle, a celebrated Doberman-pointer mix from Michigan, recently surveyed a golf course on Mackinac Island where American and British troops fought a bloody battle nearly two centuries ago. "We don't know what is too deep, what is too subtle," said Eagle's owner, Sandra Anderson, who several years ago took him to Panama to look for victims of Manuel Noriega's terrorizing reign. "We just don't know about that olfactory."

There were other things that people didn't know about Anderson or Eagle, either: why was it that Eagle had a tendency to find bones from other bodies that could not be accounted for through other means (i.e., missing persons reports or other ongoing criminal investigations)? That question may have gone unanswered; that is, until one police investigator claimed to have seen Anderson taking a "recovered" bone fragment from her sock. Though she denied any wrongdoing, Anderson was charged with obstructing an investigation. Since her arrest, dozens of other cases in which

Anderson was involved have been reopened. In one case where a defendant was convicted of murdering his wife, blood samples were found by Eagle; DNA testing has shown the blood to be from Anderson herself.

How could a news consumer have spotted any trickery? In this case a single news story about Eagle's "discoveries" probably wouldn't have set off alarm bells. On the other hand, stories about those found body parts belonging to someone other than the known victim gave readers an unwitting clue that all was not as it appeared (a simple search on one online news database showed that this was not an uncommon occurrence for Anderson). How could Eagle find blood and bone fragments when multiple searches using equally reliable means couldn't? In some cases, the crimes were committed over twenty years before, making any new discovery unlikely. Readers or viewers who followed more than one news story about Anderson would have a better chance of detecting the problems with Anderson's claims and methods. In one case, Eagle had found a "toe" of a missing man; however, when the man's body was eventually found, all his toes were still attached to his feet.

Anderson's claims about Eagle's abilities could have been called into question if news consumers had paid attention to what Anderson claimed versus what results the dog actually produced. Anderson claimed that Eagle's ability to find cadavers and body fragments was near perfect; however, her dog didn't always find the bone fragments as Anderson claimed. In many other cases, the suspect was already convicted with other evidence. In the Kutz case, her husband was already convicted of murder. In the Megan LeeAnn Pratt case, the girl's stepfather had already confessed to the murder.

As for Anderson's "fame" as being a helper of last resort, it was Anderson herself who let various media outlets know of her assignments with law enforcement. How Eagle became the "only dog in the world" certified to detect "ancient human remains" was never properly explained. Who does the certifying? What's the process of certification? Why aren't other dogs certified? How reliable and credible is the certifier?

Anderson herself brought attention to Eagle; hence her credibility hinged on self-generated publicity, giving her a possible motive for wanting Eagle to perform seemingly impossible tasks. A cadaver dog that could perform the extraordinary would be in greater demand than one that smells and tracks as well as an average dog. Anderson's vested interest in promoting her poochie was never scrutinized by journalists: if they had, they may have found other troubling parts to her story as well.

Sure, This Gate-Crashing Elvis Messiah Can Shimmy, But Can He Run a Company?

Maverick business tycoons can almost always expect to get positive press, and lots of it, from business reporters. There is something alluring about a winner who has the knack of making money with seemingly little effort; in fact, the ability to make money just seems to stem from the person's natural inclinations. The executive can just be himself and suddenly his company's profits start to soar.

One company blessed with such a leader was Enron Corporation. Started in 1986, Enron made its mark as an energy and commodities company, and in its fifteen year history became one of the ten largest companies in the U.S. The company's profits were exceedingly healthy (with revenues of $101 billion in 2000) and its vision was considered innovative: that energy could be a traded commodity on the open market. It also seemed that Enron's Chairman and CEO Kenneth Lay had the capitalistic Midas touch: everything he touched turned to golden profit.

Lay was the darling of the business world: he was a former economics professor who had his own theories about how energy markets should be managed. Unlike many other professors, Lay had the opportunity to test his theories in the real world with stunning results. As Enron became the company to beat, Lay became the "It Boy" of both Wall Street and the business media. The air-kissing kudos for "Kenny Boy" (a nickname used by President George W. Bush) did not cease in an April 17, 2000 issue of *Fortune* magazine, which began this way:

> Imagine a country-club dinner dance, with a bunch of old fogies and their wives shuffling around halfheartedly to the not-so-stirring sounds of Guy Lombardo and his All-Tuxedo Orchestra. Suddenly young Elvis comes crashing through the skylight, complete with gold-lame suit, shiny guitar, and gyrating hips. Half the waltzers faint; most of the others get angry or pouty. And a very few decide they like what they hear, tap their feet… start grabbing new partners, and suddenly are rocking to a very different tune.
>
> In the staid world of regulated utilities and energy companies, Enron Corp. is that gate-crashing Elvis.

While there might not have been a single factual tidbit in the first couple of paragraphs, readers nevertheless got a colorful description of the Houston-based executive and company. The article went on to describe Lay as "an august and serious fellow, look[ing] like Patrick Stewart, the actor who portrayed Captain Picard in *Star Trek* (only with more hair and without the British accent)."

Fortune also let readers know how various authorities and colleagues felt about the beloved and revered company:

> Paine Webber proclaimed [Enron] had "one of the deepest and most inno vative management teams in the world." (That opinion is shared by Enron's peers, who've given it the highest score for innovation of any company on

Fortune's Most Admired Companies in America survey four years in a row. Enron ranked first this year in quality of management too.)

The *Economist* magazine was also busy heaping on the plaudits. A June 3, 2000 article fawningly entitled "The Energetic Messiah," also went to considerable lengths to describe the blazing CEO with this opening anecdote:

> Exactly a year ago, the top brass from big oil and gas companies gathered in London. They brainstormed a bit, gossiped a lot and drank too much coffee. But when Kenneth Lay rose to speak, there was pin-drop silence. As the chairman of Enron sketched his vision for how liberalization and deregulation would transform the world's energy markets, his rivals were busily scribbling notes. Some nodded dumbly. Others shouted out half-baked questions. Having expanded Enron's market capitalization nine-fold over the past decade, asked one boss, could he possibly top that? "We'll do it again this coming decade," he responded coolly. Mouths fell agape.
>
> But that wasn't the end of the story:
>
> After his speech, Mr. Lay commented to an aide, with some surprise, that "some of these guys finally seem to get it." Yes, she responded smugly, "they were even using some of our language!"

The *Economist* and *Fortune* weren't the only media outlets handing out Lay and Enron accolades. While some articles did note that Lay's faults were occasional arrogance and a reluctance to admit weaknesses, these qualities didn't seem to stand in the way of monster profits for the company. On the whole, Lay was the cool kid to be admired, as one journalist dutifully noted: "The response from investors has been astonishment, followed by praise. Enron's share price has rocketed far faster than those of other energy companies. Analysts continue to gush."

As Enron's stocks continued to rise, so did Lay's reputation. The year 2000 was a high point for the white-hot company. Anything Lay did became news. In the March 27, 2000 issue of *Barron's*, one article on Lay began this way:

> When the Houston Astros officially open their new ballpark on April 7, the first pitch will be tossed out by Kenneth L. Lay, Enron's chief executive. It's one of the perks you get after you lead the drive to build a retractable-domed stadium in downtown Houston and get your company to chip in $100 million to make sure the park is named Enron Field.

The love affair between Lay and the media sometimes took eyebrow-lifting turns, with one presumably objective publication suddenly starting to read like a Lay fanzine:

Such bold moves aren't surprising to anyone familiar with the passion that Lay has displayed for being a "first mover" in his fourteen years at Enron's helm.

Lay was a winner through and through, and he was in demand. A CNBC interview with anchor Mark Haines, broadcast on October 27, 2000, started off by Haines asking this gushy, leading question:

HAINES: I was struck by the headline on the release of a few days ago. "Enron's Earnings Jump 31% as Web Boosts the Volume." So you are an old economy company using the new economy to great effect?

LAY: We are making the shift, Mark. As a matter of fact our e-commerce business is growing very rapidly. We launched it last November, at the end of November. It is a business-to-business platform. It has now, it has been spread around the world and indeed currently we are doing between $1.5 and $2 billion of business a day on that platform and well over 3,000, 3,500 transactions every day, and that makes it by far the biggest e-commerce platform in the world.

Though Enron's profits surged, there was trouble in Utopia: one executive resigned for "personal reasons," even though the company he thrived in was supposedly thriving itself. In six short weeks, the company's fortune would take a nosedive. After one energy company pulled out of a takeover bid in late 2001, citing its reservations towards Enron's tottery finances, Enron sued the company and then filed for bankruptcy.

Finally, the extent of Enron's troubles came to light when correspondence to Lay from one Enron vice president and accountant named Sherron Watkins gave a different account of the company's true health. Her publicized correspondence claimed Enron brass inflated its profits, used dubious accounting practices and claimed that $700 million dollars could not be accounted for.

Further investigation suggested that company executives also partook in suspicious tax schemes. Arthur Andersen, Enron's accounting firm was convicted of obstructing justice by shredding vital Enron documents. Enron brass were accused of bribing tax officials and inflating profits (since many executives had stock options, this puffery served to thicken their wallets). In 2000, Lay's yearly salary jumped from $15 million to almost $170 million even though the company finances were far from rosy; however while Watkins maintained that Lay was duped by the company's other executives, other observers were not convinced. Lay resigned from the bankrupt company and was indicted for his part in the scandal, though the investigation into Enron's shady dealings has not been completed as of this writing.

From a gate-crashing Elvis to a crash and burn has-been within a year, Lay's downfall may seem puzzling. Though he was credited with creating a powerhouse from near scratch, in the end, he was accused of everything from being clueless about the moral and financial health of the company to being a shifty and greedy con artist.

Lay was dubbed a messiah by many journalists and analysts alike, though few actually scrutinized Enron's bottom line. The appeal of his free market theories fit in nicely with the mindset of those on Wall Street, though whether those theories were actually implemented at Enron was another matter completely. What Lay advocated *sounded* right, and for business journalists, his capitalistic allegiance was enough. Whenever glowing adjectives replace substance in a news story, it is a red flag that the subject of the profile was taken at his word—or that at least that his PR machine was getting their message across without difficulty.

If Horatio Alger Ever Went Into Telecommunications...

If Trippet, Lay and the Kovals were the only tycoons whose hype fooled or distracted the news media, those lapses in journalistic judgment could be easily forgiven: the Kovals, though they defrauded U.S. banks, lived in another country. Trippet's company had a solid reputation from the 1950s to the late '60s, but Trippet himself didn't seek the limelight. In the waning days of the twentieth century, Lay's abilities didn't match the hype. But Lay wasn't the only executive to hold the title of media "It Boy."

Figuratively speaking, business journalism is a profession whose workers are being bombarded by "subliminal" messages: every day, business journalists report about people whose job is to sell commodities, whether the commodity is a product, service or idea. These reporters spend their days interviewing and mingling with people who excel at the art of the sale. The journalists' sources and interviewees make their living by pushing their products, their companies and themselves in the never-ending quest to boost the bottom line. These are the people who know how to package and promote their products.

What this means is that, more than any other type of reporter, business journalists are immersed in a flood of commercials, advertising, PR campaigns, trade shows and press releases—and the purpose behind most of these messages is to promote the Next Big Thing and the "brilliant minds" behind it. A good business reporter is aware of the incessant propaganda that surrounds him, day in and day out. He knows a source that he is interviewing will try to use him to secure free advertising and publicity to promote his company or himself. When he interviews a spokesman or executive, he knows he is dealing with someone who may be one of the most persuasive professionals in his town, state or country. He knows the people he is covering are trying to sell an image as well as their product: the trick for the business reporter is to disseminate an informative news article without being influenced by the relentless hype. Added to this quagmire is that many companies advertise in the very same media outlets that report on them.

But not falling for carny tricks isn't always easy. Shameless promotion will slip into a news story. If the business reporter isn't careful, his article will promote a person or company in the same way a PR firm would promote its client.

Telecommunications giant WorldCom, of Ashburn, Virginia, got its start in 1983 when Bernie Ebbers, the company's CEO, supposedly scribbled his business plan "on the back of a cocktail napkin." Before his foray into business, Ebbers was a former high school basketball coach and purchased and managed nine Best Western motels in Mississippi.

The company quickly turned from napkin doodle to a new economy powerhouse, and for his prowess Ebbers received lavish praise from business journalists. A *USA Today* headline described him as a "cowboy-boot-wearing maverick." The same October 2, 1997 article described Ebbers this way:

> Bernard Ebbers may be the first person ever to move from the western Canadian town of Edmonton, Alberta, to Jackson, Miss., to make a fortune. He certainly is the first to realize his dream.
>
> At fifty-six, the bearded CEO of WorldCom has become, in less than a decade, one of the biggest names in telecommunications simply through the savvy of his dealmaking.

Ebbers' star was rising, particularly during the Internet boom of the 1990s. He gave a speech to the National Press Club. He named his first yacht "Aquasition." His yearly bonuses ranged from eight to ten million dollars a year. News reports described him as having a "cult-like following," and being a "savvy dealmaker" and "corporate cowboy."

He was also described by journalists as "fearless," a "superstar," a "shark" and a "country boy tycoon," who ironically did not "carry a cell phone, pager or use E-mail." What else could one expect from a classically quirky corporate titan? Ebbers was both a unique and an archetypal figure, as Jeffrey Kagan wrote in the October 6, 1997 edition of *InternetWeek*:

> Bernard Ebbers is the proverbial Horatio Alger, rags-to-riches, all-American, entrepreneurial success story. About fifteen years ago he was a high school basketball coach turned small-time motel operator.
>
> Then in the early '80s when Ma Bell was breaking up, anyone who could scrape together $50,000 to buy a switch could lease lines from AT&T and get into the phone business by offering long distance service.

Ebbers bought into one of these little firms called LDDS, short for Long Distance Discount Service. From those humble beginnings sprang one of America's most unlikely success stories.

A few days earlier, in an October 1, 1997 article from *Reuters Business Report*, the Alger comparison was again made by Kagan, who was an interviewee this time:

"It's a great Horatio Alger story, a great entrepreneurial story," said consultant Jeffrey Kagan of Kagan Telecoms Associates in Atlanta. "There were thousands of small companies like WorldCom. But Worldcom just kept on gobbling, instead of becoming a gobblee," Kagan said.

The same Reuters article described the colorful personality of its subject:

With forty deals in the past five years alone, Worldcom chief executive Bernard Ebbers has made the company's headquarters in Jackson, Mississippi, an international telecoms center and delighted Wall Street with spectacular stock performance. But Ebbers, fond of cigars and golf shirts, claims that his successes and personal wealth, approaching $600 million, are based on thin knowledge of fiber optics, the Internet backbone and telecommunications overall.

Ebbers' personality was also the focus in an article from the September 22, 1997 edition of *Time*:

Ebbers is as low frequency as any telecom executive can be. He favors faded blue jeans and golf shirts and on-the-road Willie Nelson tunes. While his 1.8% stake in WorldCom is worth more than $560 million, he likes to aw-shucks his own role in his company. "The thing that has helped me personally," he says, "is that I don't understand a lot of what goes on in this industry." So he relies on executives who come along with acquired companies.

Ebbers seemed to be a fearless, lovable tycoon that was as well known as any A-list actor. *Newsweek* magazine described Ebbers "as the man everyone knows as Bernie." Everyone? Could there possibly be a few people who didn't nod knowingly when someone asked if they knew "Bernie"? The exaggeration was a minor quibble, though, and Ebbers had big plans to oversee. Within the year, WorldCom would merge with MCI, making it one of the biggest mergers in American corporate history. While the MCI/WorldCom was still in its honeymoon phase, Ebbers already had his roving eye on acquiring Sprint, too.

But this time the Justice Department put its foot down, and the $140 billion merger was called off. Adding to Ebbers' woes was the decreasing value of WorldCom stock. Though the situation looked bleak, Ebbers was a stoic man, as recounted in a January 22, 2001 edition of *Fortune* magazine:

> You'd think someone in his position would be pretty stressed out. Yet on a recent snowy day at the sprawling Ashburn, Va., campus that houses WorldCom's Internet operations, Ebbers seemed relaxed and confident as he opined on matters that could have made him dejected, or at least defensive-like his company's performance or the swirl of regulatory and technological changes that confront the beleaguered telecommunications industry. He cracked a few jokes about his reputation for draconian cost cutting. He offered *Fortune* a candid assessment of his qualities as a manager. He talked bluntly about WorldCom's options, which include the possible sale of the company, and the challenges that he faces.

Perhaps Ebbers wasn't all that candid. Internal auditors discovered and reported that WorldCom's earnings had been grossly inflated—the company simply postponed reporting nine billion dollars in expenses by mislabeling them as expenditures. Investors lost billions, such as many retirees who either invested their life savings in the company or had their state pension funds invested in the company. Five WorldCom executives were charged, with four pleading guilty. Ebbers resigned as CEO in April 2001. Tens of thousands of MCI/WorldCom employees lost their jobs.

Like Enron, WorldCom filed for bankruptcy—the largest in U.S. history. Months later, despite reporting a debt of $33 billion, the company emerged from Chapter 11 and dropped the WorldCom from its name, leaving only MCI appearing on the company stationary. Eight months after being barred from bidding for government contracts, the ban was conditionally lifted. Ebbers was charged with defrauding investors in Oklahoma (to which he pleaded not guilty), though the charges were dropped until the trial of another WorldCom executive was resolved in New York. In March 2004, Ebbers was indicted for fraud.

Stories about business tycoons should be read carefully: what is the angle the reporter decides to use? An angle focusing on evidence of a company's health or one that focuses on the leader's personality? The angle will determine what information and facts the reporter will use; a report centering on the character traits or pet peeves of a leader means more important information will have to be left out. Describing someone as eccentric, crass, lovable and difficult means the reporter will be looking for evidence to support his assertions: he will not focus on whether the CEO is inflating the bottom line.

Not all winners gravitate toward business or finance. Academia also has prestige, and some winners may try to make their mark there. Though many winners love to bask in the limelight, some may not want to hog all the glory for themselves, as the following case study shows.

Having the Brains to Know When You've Outsmarted Yourself

Preternaturally gifted children make common news fodder: in one way, they make sunny, uplifting, awe-inspiring news—and they deviate from the norm. In another way, these children are unwitting players in a freak show: audiences are asked to see children behave like miniature grown-ups.

Profiles of the child prodigy seem similar: these children are precocious, afflicted with a nervous laugh, are pleasers and are almost always home schooled. These children do not live normal lives: many are pressured by parents to study and practice honing their talents day and night. And behind every great child prodigy, there's an overambitious parent drilling them to the top of the kinder heap.

Kids absolutely hate these soft news stories: nothing is worse for children than having mom and dad demand to know why, despite years of paying for expensive piano lessons and sports equipment, and driving their children at ungodly hours to the hockey rink, their offspring are still not as gifted as the kid profiled on "Good Morning America." The folks don't seem to ever ask what price those gifted children had to pay to get to the top. Despite having young faces, these special children are not ones that ordinary children can relate to; these types of stories are strictly for adult audiences.

These stories are supposed to be soft, happy news, and thus are invariably positive toward the child: the child will be praised for her talents and gifts in a lighthearted manner. If the gifted child is profiled in a documentary or in a hard news piece, the parents' behavior may come under scrutiny. In rare cases (such as the case of Augustin De Mello, who faced scrutiny for his pushing his eleven-year-old son to graduate from university), is the child's gift or genius called into question.

Stories on young prodigies typically range from minor feats, such as spelling bee winners (a popular venue for home schooled children) to the more high profile artistic endeavors of child performers (singers, actors). But one favorite staple among reporters is the young university student. Getting accepted at any university is difficult enough for a young adult, but if a *child* can be accepted and excel, then the youngster has to be someone extraordinary. The child has to be a winner.

Even here, the baby genius in question will almost always be a home-schooled boy who excels at one particular discipline. He may live with both his parents, but sometimes the child will live with one parent. The genius will be a child who is so unquestionably gifted that he or she will skip multiple grades in school, but the accelerated advancement will almost always be at the parents' insistence. The parents know the child is gifted and many believe teachers are holding the child back for selfish reasons.

Though smart children being enrolled in colleges isn't a common occurrence, it has been done enough times to become a somewhat clichéd story. The little genius has to trump the baby genius before him; after all, if a kid going to university has been done in the past, then what makes this smart kid special? What this means is that the current contender will have to be younger than the reigning champ.

When a baby genius gets media attention, the images evoked will be typical: the child will be photographed sitting in a lecture room, busily and studiously writing notes in class. What won't be shown is the reporter asking that the child be given a test to verify his genius. Nor will he ask if the child is happy. Is the child being abused if he or she isn't performing up to task? If the child is gifted in one subject area, does it justify the accelerated pace, even if he or she is average or sub par in other academic areas? Does the child perform better at take home assignments or in-class assignments? Could the child be receiving extra tutoring or help from another source?

But the journalist who dares to ask the above questions will find himself being accused of jealously, pettiness and being mean to a little kid. Besides, how could someone be so cynical toward someone just so darn cute?

Few were as cute as Justin Chapman, a sweet young boy who was six years old when he enrolled at the University of Rochester, making him the youngest person to enroll in an American university course. He scored 298 on an IQ test, the highest score ever recorded. Justin seemed attentive and bright, as this *Associated Press* article showed on February 16, 2000:

> A six-year-old boy who began reading at age two has enrolled in three college classes.
>
> Justin Chapman began taking a four-credit introductory history course titled "The Ancient World" at the University of Rochester this semester. He has already earned a B for a paper on Babylonian creations myths and the Greek epic poem "The Iliad."
>
> Justin says he finds the class challenging. "I only got a B on my last paper," he said, "but I am learning a lot, and I have a few things to work on."

Justin's extraordinary accomplishments attracted attention from local media outlets as the November 4, 1999 edition of the *Rochester Democrat and Chronicle* profiled the young man:

[...]On Mondays and Wednesdays, Justin is at the University of Rochester, learning introductory college physics along with about thirty traditional students in Dr. Paul Tipton's class.

If he were actually enrolled in the course for credit, he might qualify for the "Guinness Book of World Records" as the youngest college student ever.

As it is, Justin's mother says the home-schooled Penfield boy is doing tenth-grade work and he could be ready to take the SAT by next summer.

The endearing boy lived with his mother, Elizabeth, who kept a watchful eye over her only child, as the same *Democrat and Chronicle* article noted:

Outside the classroom, Justin and his mother, twenty-seven-year-old Elizabeth Chapman, are creating a stir. The Penfield Central School District is skeptical of how gifted the boy is. Chapman, who has set startlingly high academic goals for her son, has not allowed the district to test him.

She doesn't believe public school would challenge Justin.

"The problem is the standards are way too low in the schools," Chapman said.

[...]When Justin attends class, his mom sits near the back row of Hoyt Hall, a large lecture room. Justin usually sits up front and says little, according to students in the class.

The *Democrat and Chronicle* did notice some discrepancies in the Chapman juggernaut: while Chapman insisted her son attended Montessori school at a year of age, the school's records showed he attended classes a year later. Nor would Chapman divulge how she managed to enroll her son in kindergarten before age three when school policy was to admit students only after receiving a copy of the child's birth certificate.

But with such a remarkable child, Chapman must have been given the green light by *some* school official. Besides, thinking about the alternatives could have ruined the colorful anecdote used by one journalist in the November 17, 2000 edition of the *Albany Times Union*:

Laughing and crawling under a table as he's being chased by a producer from the British Broadcasting Co., Justin Chapman looks like any typical seven-year-old kid from upstate New York.

As the BBC guy grabs Chapman to fasten a portable microphone on the child's collar, the boy playfully swipes and tugs at the adult's beard.

"He's seven, what do you expect?" laughs Mary-Ellen Seitelman, a member of Advocates for Gifted and Talented Education, a group pushing for more opportunities for precocious learners.

A few minutes later, Chapman is dead serious as he stands beside an overhead projector, which on top of a table is a bit taller than he is.

Using bell curves, charts and quoting Eleanor Roosevelt as well as Ralph Waldo Emerson, Chapman makes a case against age discrimination.

Justin was duly rewarded for his mental agility: he was featured in a Bell bicycle helmet ad, he was front-page news in the *New York Post* and he was part of a BBC documentary on child geniuses. He had his own syndicated column after one editor read a story about Justin in the *Post*. He met New York governor George Pataki and wrote an article in the *Christian Science Monitor*.

With so many tangible accomplishments beneath his belt, who could question Justin's genius? He scored 800 on the math portion of his SAT; he scored well on the Wechsler Preschool and Primary Scale of Intelligence-Revised. He enrolled in online high school courses at five. Psychologists who specialized in dealing with gifted children praised him lavishly. All this pointed to the young man's brilliance.

Or did it? In fact, there was no independent testing done to confirm the boy's genius. When Johns Hopkins University offered to test Justin, his mother declined. When audiences asked Justin questions after his speeches, Justin couldn't answer them. Many of the advanced courses he took were offered online, meaning that someone else could have conceivably done his assignments for him—but who could quibble about these details when the boy was accepted and thriving at a university? Most reporters who covered Justin didn't question the veracity of his mother's various claims.

Sadly, Justin's life soon took a disturbing turn. The boy exploded in a theater while watching a *Harry Potter* movie and had to be removed. Eventually, Justin was hospitalized and both his mother and hospital psychologists reported that the boy threatened suicide. It seemed that Justin was perilously close to crossing the line between genius and insanity.

Then, in a stunning twist, Elizabeth Chapman admitted to the *Rocky Denver News* that she had taken Justin's tests and completed his assignments for him after the paper began to investigate claims about her son's intelligence. Later independent tests revealed that the boy was gifted with average intelligence, and the *Denver News* could not confirm tests that had been conducted before the boy's breakdown. Even many of Justin's supporters admitted that they had only corresponded with the boy through e-mail and had not seen the child face to face. The juggernaut known as Justin the boy genius was a sad hoax. Chapman was charged with neglect, but she was later convicted of second-degree forgery (stemming from faking her son's test scores), and sentenced to four days in jail and a small fine. Justin was initially removed from his mother's custody and placed in a foster home, but reunited with her over a year later.

Though Chapman maintained her belief in her son's brilliance, much of what she did indicated otherwise. Why didn't she want to confirm her son's abilities by agreeing for him to take independently administered tests? Why did she decline offers of independent testing? The answer was obvious, but no one voiced concerns over Chapman's trickery. While some reporters pointed to some inconsistencies with Chapman's claims, none had asked for her to submit her son to an independent test—or ask to see the boy's work, such as an in-class essay or test.

The Chapman hoax is a throwback to another supposedly extraordinary mind, this time in Germany, in 1907: Clever Hans, a horse whose owner maintained could perform addition by stamping his hoof. The horse could stamp his foot the required number of times when his owner "asked" him the questions, but when his owner was removed from the scene, Hans couldn't get the right answer. The trick was subtle: the horse was looking at his owner's face, following the old man's cues. When Hans' owner wasn't present, there were no cues to follow and Hans turned out to be a cute, but average horse. Chapman attending the same classes as her son should have tipped off reporters and university officials alike that something was amiss.

How to Spot the Fake Hero

Happy news is more advertising than news: there isn't much usefulness in the information given (unless a large group of consumers win a class action settlement and the article details how those wronged can reclaim their money), but these reports serve as rewards for good behavior or as relief from more somber news. Because happy news serves as a diversion from bad news, it is usually placed at the tail end of a newscast or out of the front section of the newspaper.

When the happy news is about someone who has done something extraordinary, journalists tend not to look for information that would be unflattering to the "hero." One reason for the kid gloves is that it seems rude and paranoid to question someone's accomplishments if the person produced "proof" of his deeds, whether that proof is real or fabricated. The other reason is that reporters and editors know there will be backlash from some readers or viewers who think the reporter is being rude by questioning the intelligence of a young boy or business maverick. What this means is that if someone wants to present himself as a hero or winner, there is a good chance the reporter won't attempt to dispute the claim (though as we'll see in chapter thirteen, not all reporters operate this way).

Good news needs a different kind of evaluating: since good news mimics advertising, it should be evaluated as if it were advertising. Just as not every product or service can live up to its hype, not everyone who is lavishly praised in a happy news story is going to be as good as the reporter claims.

Deceptive or misleading advertising tries to make grand claims without having to commit to anything: for example, an ad may claim a product is "Virtually 100%"—but the word virtual means almost, but not quite. In other words, the advertisers have flat out admitted that the product is not 100% effective! What we're left with is hype, but no promises and no information about the product.

Happy news stories about winners can play out in much the same way—what you are looking for are signs that the winner is not being straightforward with his claims, or that reporters haven't tried to independently confirm those claims. Here are some of the other signs to look for when reading about a hero or winner:

1. There is no independent evidence to prove that the hero or winner has accomplished what he claims to have accomplished.

A winner will almost always provide "proof" of his feats, but on closer inspection, the evidence isn't good. In the Justin Chapman case, even though it seemed as if he had taken high school courses at five years of age, in fact, he had never set foot in an actual high school. If all his assignments were done through e-mail, then how much of the work did Justin do himself? How much help did his mother give him? If young Justin's genius was genuine, then one would expect that his mother would insist on having her son independently tested to have his results on the record. In Eagle's case, although the dog "found" bone fragments and blood smears, many times the samples did not match the victim. With multiple false hits, how could Anderson claim that her dog was a reliable cadaver dog?

2. The person claims he can do something that no one else can.

Some people have rare talents, but one-of-a-kind talents are harder to prove. For some, there is an allure to being so special that no one else in the world shares their unique gift. Enabling these delusions should not be the role of either reporters or the audience. When someone says, "I am the only one in the world who can do this!" the best response should be, "Interesting theory. Prove it."

In the Eagle case, his owner claimed that her dog could detect fragments that other detection dogs or devices would miss. It may be true that Eagle has a more sensitive sense of smell than many other dogs; however, how realistic is it to assume that no other dog could detect small fragments? Eagle was also supposed to be the only dog in the world to be certified in ancient human remains detection, but who certified Eagle and why no other dog had shared this certification wasn't ever made clear.

3. Alternate explanations can explain the winner's uncanny abilities.

In Justin Chapman's case, his mother was attending the same class as her son and was taking notes during the lecture. Justin also took online courses. If the child was as gifted as his mother claimed, why not have him enrolled in a private school? One explanation was that she believed that traditional public and private schools weren't challenging for the boy. The alternate explanation—that the mother was taking notes and doing her son's assignments—turned out to be the correct explanation. What would have been interesting is if the reporter had asked to see Justin's lecture notes: what do the jottings of an alleged boy genius look like?

In Eagle's case, the dog found bone fragments that others missed, but the DNA from those fragments didn't match those of the victims. One explanation was that someone else may have been murdered in the area. The other reason, that Anderson planted evidence for her dog to "find," seems to be the better explanation. Both Enron and WorldCom were young companies that made record profits by defying old school rules. Perhaps it was because these CEOs were simply the best at their jobs, but the alternate reason, that the executives cooked the books until they got numbers they liked, ended up explaining the results. Maybe Rosie Ruiz was in such great physical shape that she could run marathons without breaking sweat; but she just inserted herself at the tail end of the run.

4. The hero or winner's claims cannot be confirmed or falsified.

When someone makes a claim, there has to be an independent way to confirm or refute those abilities: if someone can't disprove the claims using unbiased, reliable methods of testing, then there's a good chance that there is trickery involved. For example, if someone claims to be able to see the future, then there has to be a way for others to test those claims; otherwise, the person is just trying to scam gullible people. One easy method is to have the person write his "visions" or predictions for specific events and seal those guesses. The sealed envelope should be given to someone who is not in cahoots with the psychic and other measures should be put in place to ensure that there is no cheating. Then, at a later date, those predictions should be compared to what actually happened.

If the predictions are wrong, the person claiming to be a psychic is wrong about his abilities—and if the self-proclaimed psychic refutes those claims with convoluted explanations (claiming bad vibes, or that testing can't work since it interferes with psychic visions), then the person is now trying to explain away failure. If a claim can't be proven right or wrong, the safest route is to assume the claim is wrong. The burden of proof rests with the winner.

In the Chapman case, Justin's intelligence wasn't tested by outside, independent testers, making his scores suspect. Add his online schooling and his mother's attendance to the mix, and suddenly the boy's genius comes into question. In the earthquake survivor hoax, though Akopyan claimed to have survived in freezing temperatures without shelter, he had none of the signs that such a survivor should have had (exhaustion, frost bite, dehydration, scratches). In the Ruiz case, though she claimed that she had run the marathon, Ruiz did not appear in any of the video footage of the race.

5. The article focuses on the personality rather than confirming the winner's feats or accomplishments.

News stories obviously need facts to support the reporter's assertions, but many journalists focus on softer, less important elements of a story. One favorite focus is a winner's personality. While there is nothing wrong with informing audiences about the temperament of a person, too much focus on personality suggests that the reporter is not looking for information that is harder to find. A personality is easy to stumble upon: just hang around a person long enough and you'll soon discover if the person is nice or snobby, kind or rude, easy-going or prone to tantrums. Finding out whether the CEO is setting up shell companies to embezzle or launder money takes much more work.

When there is too much personality, and not enough information in a news report, think about what information the reporter has missed. Why is the reporter flattering the winner: has the winner charmed the reporter? Did he use his powers of persuasion and salesmanship to ensure good press?

In the Justin Chapman hoax, reporters focused on Justin's personality rather than on his mother's telling behavior. In the Enron fiasco, reporters were taken by Lay's maverick behavior. In the WorldCom debacle, journalists also were so amused by Ebbers' "corporate cowboy" persona that they failed to ask the obvious questions.

6. Deference is mistaken for good reporting.

A good reporter tends to be a rude one. He is going to ask the impudent questions and will have no trouble confronting even the sweetest of winners to ensure that he's not being taken in. If the winner is genuine, he won't crumble under pressure.

But rude reporters tend to get chastised by the soccer mom set, and for other journalists, it's not in their nature to ask critical questions. It's not easy for some television anchors to ask tough questions while maintaining that warm, dazzling smile. Cheerleading is the path of less resistance, but it also tends to let scam artists present themselves as winners and heroes without problems. In the Enron and WorldCom cases, reporters described both men in glowing terms and ignored signs that both companies were in serious trouble. In the Eagle and Chapman sagas, reporters could have asked to set up demonstrations to prove both Eagle's and Justin's abilities: if Andersen or Chapman declined, the reporter could have been clued in that both women had something to hide.

Just because someone gets good press, it doesn't mean the person deserves it: all it might mean is that the person has a talent for getting himself positive coverage by charming or bamboozling reporters. With CEOs who can make billions only on paper, the bottom line is never the bottom line. The phony appearance gives investors and employees alike a false sense of confidence, and encourages others to decline job offers from other companies or turn down stocks from other companies to align themselves with the winner. Without journalists using forensic accounting techniques and asking critical questions, they abet those who scam millions of people and cost the economy billions of dollars. Had unscrupulous executives been exposed sooner, countless individuals would not face personal bankruptcy or ruin later on.

For every copy inch or broadcast minute devoted to praising a winner, that's one inch or minute less that is used to investigate whether the winner could be a scammer.

Chapter **Nine**

Fear, Stereotypes and Myths

Xenophobia is the fear of foreigners, and it's easy to blame outsiders for our woes: the less we know about a group, the more mysterious, unpredictable and dangerous they seem. We don't know their weaknesses, their fears or even their humanity and kindness. The new kids could be nice but, then again, they might just want to destroy us. Because we don't have enough information to make a decision, it just seems safer to hate and fear outsiders.

On one hand, that anxiety can sometimes be healthy for our very survival: fearing an untested or unknown group can prevent us from getting too close to the danger. If the strange group means to harm us, keeping our distance may save our lives. This hardwired apprehension is what has kept our ancestors alive and thriving long enough to reproduce.

On the other hand, our evolutionarily-wired fear doesn't always help us: crime statistics indicate that our in-group members are still more likely to cause us harm than outsiders. Whites prey on whites, Asians prey on Asians and blacks prey on blacks. Interracial crimes and hate crimes do make up a percentage of violent offenses but, as a rule, criminals tend to target whoever is closer, more predictable and more trusting.

In a real way, the idea of a hate crime seems silly: a stab wound delivered by someone of the same ethnic group as us hurts the same as one given by someone from another creed. Regardless of the illogic of their fears, people still tend to look toward their tribe for safety, while casting a weary eye on strangers who look and behave differently.

But con artists are all too aware of our instincts, and take advantage of our prejudices to orchestrate hoaxes for their personal gain. Hoaxers who play upon the race, gender or ethnic card will claim that they were abused by a person or group of people who were outsiders.

This type of hoax hinges on one or more people spreading rumors based on ethnic, racial, ageist or economic stereotypes, hoping that the target group's latent prejudices will give the con artist a layer of credibility. Some hoaxers will claim the act of racism or sexism was videotaped or even broadcast. Rumors that designers Tommy Hilfiger and Liz Claiborne made bigoted remarks on "Oprah" endured, even though neither one had ever appeared on her program.

This type of false story may seem dramatic and convincing, but the evidence to support the claims is either scarce or inconsistent, and there is no sourcing to support the allegations.

In the early 1990s, residents, institutions and media outlets received dire warnings of national gang initiation rites. Some of the warnings claimed that young gang members would kill innocent motorists who flashed their headlights, while others would hide underneath cars and prey on unsuspecting women in mall parking lots. None of these alarms panned out, nor were there any documented cases of these heinous acts, but people still checked under their cars, just in case.

For this type of scam to work, the con artist casts himself as the victim and appeals specifically to his "in group," while shaming not only the designated outsider villain, but any outsider who dares to question the "victim's" story. In-groups tend to be defensive and protective of one their own; hence, if someone makes allegations that the scammer is lying, members of the in-group won't believe the outsider and will stand by the hoaxer, even if the hoax seems obvious. In fact, many con artists who later admit to concocting a hoax can still count on the support of the true believers, who continue to believe that the scammer was "forced" into recanting his story. For many scam artists, manipulating in-group loyalty has its advantages.

For this type of hoax to make news, it takes a little more finesse and believability: the hoax can be effective if the scammer attaches his claims to real instances of racially-motivated crimes; after all, if five cases of attacks are proven to be true, then why would anyone assume the sixth was a fraud? One journalist seemed to make that assumption in an April 29, 2002 *Associated Press* story printed in the *Seattle Times*:

> Black and Hispanic men enlisted in the Coast Guard here have been the targets of numerous racial taunts and vandalism, according to a Coast Guard report.
>
> Nine incidents since last fall were outlined in a report by the Port Angeles Coast Guard station's commanding officer, the *Peninsula Daily News* reported yesterday.
>
> In one case, a black petty officer's car was vandalized twice with scratches and racial slurs while parked in a retailer's parking lot. The petty officer requested and received reassignment to another command.

Make that eight incidences: over a year later, the coast guardsman who claimed to have found a racial slur written on his car admitted that he himself had written the note. A more thorough reporter would have asked to see the notes or ask someone to read the notes to him: if the notes didn't sound authentic, it would have given the reporter a clue that at least one of the charges was false.

For many journalists, questioning the veracity of someone claiming to be the victim of a bigoted attack is difficult, since skeptical reporters may be accused of being bigoted themselves. To avoid accusations of bias or insensitivity, journalists may cover the story without questioning the alleged victim of the attack. The in-group looks only for evidence that confirms their views of outsiders and the emotional poignancy of the story itself—logical inconsistencies are ignored completely. Ironically, while the in-group rallies around the fake victim and laments the coldness of outsiders, the group's own biases and prejudices blind them from seeing the obvious. It's the group's own stereotypes that give the hoax longevity and credibility.

If journalists don't question the in-group's assumptions, the hoax can be believed for months or even years. A savvy news consumer doesn't have to fall for hoaxes based on stereotypes: by ignoring emotional manipulation and race, ethnicity or gender, a news consumer can determine when the alleged act is real or a scheme.

Only the Strong Survive

Crime and tragedy befall many people, yet not all their stories make the news. So what separates newsworthy grief from the nameless variety? The newsworthy misfortune should be violent, cruel, unexpected and have a photogenic and winsome victim.

A crime meeting those requirements befell a young, attractive, upwardly mobile Boston couple expecting their first child. A husband and his pregnant lawyer wife seemed to be doing everything right, yet something went horribly wrong on their way home from the hospital. To the middle class posse, it was an unspeakable crime: nice, well-heeled couples weren't supposed to get attacked after attending a birthing class.

The chilling details were recounted in the October 24, 1989 edition of the *Boston Globe*:

> A Reading man and his pregnant wife were shot in Roxbury last night by a gunman who forced his way into their car after the couple left Brigham and Women's Hospital.
>
> The woman, thirty-three-year-old Carol Stuart, was in critical condition at that hospital last night with a gunshot wound to her head. She delivered a baby boy, who was placed in intensive care. Police said she was between five and seven months pregnant.
>
> Her twenty-nine-year-old husband, Charles, was in stable condition at Boston City Hospital with a gunshot wound to the abdomen, a hospital spokesman said.

The heinous crime shocked Boston: if an expecting, affluent couple wasn't safe near a hospital, then who was? Charles' frantic 911 call to police was replayed on news broadcasts, and images of a mortally wounded Carol, heavy with child in her car, were also available for public consumption. The Stuarts' horrible plight mesmerized millions.

With Carol Stuart fighting for her life and her husband in rough condition, questions swirled: why were the Stuarts targeted? Police were convinced that "the gunman who robbed the couple apparently thought the driver was a police officer, perhaps because he saw a cellular phone in the car, said Boston Deputy Supt. Joseph Dunford," (to put things into context for those too young to remember or at least pretending to be too young to remember, in 1989 cell phones were a rare and expensive toy that only the relatively well-to-do could afford). Was it because the criminal wanted to rob a mon-eyed couple who drove a "late model Toyota"?

Tragedy was only beginning for the Stuart clan—Carol died from her head injuries; her infant son was fighting for his life in intensive care. While Charles Stuart was recovering from his abdominal injuries, the hunt was on for Carol's killer. Stuart wasn't in the best condition, but he was alert enough to provide police with the details of the assailant—a young African-American man in a jogging suit. The media spotlight became intense, the Stuart case found its way into the *San Diego Tribune*, the *Boston Globe*, the *San Francisco Chronicle*, the *Austin American-Statesman* and the *Richmond Times-Dispatch*. Journalists wondered what kind of person would harm such a couple, especially a heavily pregnant woman. As the *Richmond Times-Dispatch* noted in a December 6 story, headlined "The Triumph of Evil":

> Although crime-reporting has become mostly a body-count from the drug war's combat zones, some crimes still carry a shock value that claims national headlines. That was the instance not long ago when a pregnant woman and her husband were abducted and shot in Boston after leaving a childbirth class.

Within days of the killing, the police arrested a black man in the process of breaking into a house; with the burglar's arrest, police began to see whether he was the Stuart shooter. The *Boston Globe* reported on the city's tensions in an October 30, 1989 article:

> At services at the Morning Star Baptist Church in Mattapan, [Mayor Ray] Flynn told the congregation of about 250 black people that the city should feel the same sense of outrage whether the victim of violence is black or white.
>
> Flynn also cautioned against strained racial relations. "No one group or community should be singled out because of the actions of a few," he said.

During a later interview, Flynn said many black people have expressed resentment that the murder of a white suburban woman gains far more attention than the murder of a black city resident.

"It's an overreaction on both sides, so I'm out telling people that it's a time to come together, not divide," he said.

In mid-November, the *Boston Herald* reported that another African-American man had been arrested on a traffic violation and he, too, was considered a suspect in the shooting. When police showed Stuart the picture of William Bennett, Stuart had a "strong physical reaction," according to the *Boston Globe*, which quoted "sources close to the investigation." However, Stuart could not make a positive identification. He left the hospital six weeks after his ordeal; sadly, his infant son Christopher died seventeen days after the shooting.

Amid all this gut-wrenching misery, the turning point in the investigation came when Stuart visited the police station, as recounted in the December 29 edition of the *Globe*:

> Charles Stuart yesterday singled out William Bennett from a police lineup, saying that Bennett looked "most like" the man who shot Stuart and his wife, according to sources close to the investigation. One source said Stuart made additional comments during the lineup that convinced investigators that Stuart's reaction to Bennett, the chief suspect in the shootings, was a "positive identification. It was absolutely crystal clear. That's the guy."

Despite the emotionally textured and touching stories journalists gave their audiences, there was one unsettling problem: why would a robber shoot a pregnant woman in the head, but shoot her husband in the abdomen? The question may sound absurd, but it's important. Suppose a strong man (not to be sexist, but the accused shooter was a man), is faced with having to battle another strong man and a pregnant woman and the villain has only one bullet. Who does he shoot?

If the shooter stops the woman, he would have to tangle with the man, who is tall, young, healthy and probably could hold his own in a fight. He may know how to fight, he will likely slow down the shooter and he may wound or even defeat him.

If the shooter stops the man, he is left to contend with the pregnant woman. She may be strong and a good fighter, too, but she has a built-in vulnerability which the attacker can use to his advantage. She's pregnant and she's not going to be as dexterous or as fluid in her fighting. She may be afraid of harm coming to her unborn child, too. With the woman, there is a physical and possibly psychological advantage. This isn't to say the woman couldn't defeat an attacker, but if the criminal is to take his chances, he is best off making sure that his male opponent is incapacitated.

This same thinking must have gone through the killer's mind during the Stuart shooting: if he were to hedge his bets, should he take down the young man or the pregnant woman? Most criminals would try to maim the greater threat, which would have been Charles Stuart. Carol's pregnancy would have put her in a vulnerable position, and therefore she would be the lesser threat. If the shooter saw Stuart's cell phone, as the police suspected, it would then make it a virtual certainty that Charles would be inflicted with more severe injuries.

But in the Stuart case, this didn't happen. Why not?

Most reporters hadn't considered this question. But police did discover, among other details, that Stuart had taken out a hefty insurance policy on his wife. Suddenly, Stuart had a motive for wanting his wife dead.

The case unraveled quickly, and Stuart killed himself by plunging into the Mystic River, after his brother implicated him in his wife's killing, on January 4, 1990. The aftermath of the Stuart hoax inflamed race relations in Boston: the black community openly demanded to know why Stuart's story was so easily believed. Stuart had the motive and the means to commit the crime, and parts of his story simply didn't make sense. Yet his story was easily believed by both police and the news media, who were quick to label him a victim. The black men of Boston were treated as a pool of suspected killers.

When the emotional and racial elements were ignored, Stuart's lies became apparent, but some in the news media still couldn't shake their latent prejudices. Even when Stuart's role in his wife's death became amply clear, the January 5, 1990 edition of the *Bloomington Pantagraph* ran the following headline: "Victim of Boston double shooting kills himself."

With Mothers Like These...

Stories focusing on the fear of the unknown not only warn audiences about real dangers lurking around the corner, but they also serve as macabre mysteries. Tales of abductions and kidnappings fit into this category of news story: What happened to the person? Are they being hurt, frightened, tortured or killed? We may even try to speculate on the missing person's fate, depending on the person's age, gender, race and wealth. A group of affluent young teens missing after a wild party on a boat may have had a boating accident—but when two small children get snatched away from their own mother, the game of speculation takes a sickening turn. We want the children to be found safe and in the care of kindly strangers but, deep down, we know the worst has probably happened.

It was this kind of dread that a young single mother named Susan Smith faced when she told police a black carjacker snatched her two young sons—Michael, three and Alex, fourteen months—as she helplessly watched, on October 26, 1994. Smith had been driving on a deserted road in the evening, when a carjacker forced Smith to stop the car and then ordered her to get out. Before Smith had the chance to rescue her sons, the driver took off with them. Helpless, she screamed, "I love you all!" before going to find aid.

The guilt of leaving her sons behind ate at Smith, as she was quoted as saying in an October 27, 1994 *Associated Press* story:

> While police keep up the hunt for her small sons, Susan V. Smith is tortured by doubt that she was right to allow a carjacker to drive away with the boys. "I just feel hopeless. I can't do enough. My children wanted me. They needed me. And now I can't help them," she said. "I just feel like such a failure."

Though an October 29, 1994 article from the *Greenville News* and the *Associated Press* reported that Smith failed a lie detector test, her credibility wasn't seriously questioned by many reporters. After over a week, many black men in Unionville and the surrounding areas were still being questioned by police. The details of Smith's ordeal were recounted without skepticism in the November 1, 1994 edition of the *Atlanta Journal and Constitution*:

> Susan Smith said she was on her way to visit Sinclair last Tuesday night when a gunman commandeered her car at a traffic light. She said the abductor forced her to drive several miles to a desolate stretch of road, made her get out and sped away with the toddlers strapped in the back in their car seats.

The next day, the same newspaper described Smith's televised plea to her children's kidnapper:

> With a promising lead dashed as quickly as it was raised today, the mother of two young brothers missing for eight days pleaded tearfully for their return. "I would like to say that whoever has my children, that they please, please bring them home to us where they belong," said Susan Smith, flanked by her husband, David, and other relatives at a news conference crowded with reporters and Union residents.

NBC and CNN, as well as many other networks and stations, followed the painful search for the missing boys, as did NPR, which profiled the Smith case on November 2, 1994:

LINDA WERTHEIMER: One of the things that people have talked about in this case is that the parents of the two boys are estranged. And questions have risen about the possibility that one or the other of the parents might have arranged for this—for this to happen in order to get custody of the children, the sort of thing that happens, more often I think, than we generally know. The sheriff seems to think that this is not the case. Are you all still proceeding on the assumption that the story happened the way Mrs. Smith said it did?

ANNA BROWN: That's all we have to go on, and he has been questioned about that. He said that the separation seems to be amicable, that he's noted no tension between them, not tension enough to cause one of them to try and make some sort of an abduction here. And they've been together. The night this happened, when they were filmed, they were holding hands. Today [at] the news conference, they were together.

WERTHEIMER: Their appearance is of two people who are—who obviously are very upset by what has happened.

BROWN: Distraught and united, wanting to have their children back.

While many people wondered what happened to the young boys, rumors that Susan Smith may have had a role in her children's disappearance changed the course of the story. Police eventually got Smith to confess that there was no carjacker: she drowned her two sons by locking them in the mini-van and rolling the car into the river. She had been looking for a new lover, but the one she was seeing casually rejected her, claiming he did not want to date a woman with children.

Susan Smith pleaded guilty to killing her two sons, but how and why journalists were fooled was a question that needed answering. Why would Smith not put up a bigger struggle? Where were her defensive wounds? Why didn't she try to hold on to the car, in a frenzied bid to save her sons from certain death?

There were also questions surrounding her claim that a black man was responsible for her children's disappearance. Here too, there were holes in Smith's story. Her description of the abductor was vague and generic. Unionville's black community was outraged, and Smith's brother apologized for the hoax and its consequences.

Getting Messed Up in More Ways Than One

Despite the insistence that they do not get emotionally involved in their stories, reporters will rally behind an underdog. Whether the person is behind bars for a crime he maintains he did not commit, or was forced to move out of his farm because the government foreclosed his home, reporters will generally side with the party whom they have deemed to have been mistreated.

With an underdog story, reporters will ignore their rules about emotional detachment to deliver a compelling, heart-wrenching story. For these stories to work, the underdog has to seem helpless, but sympathetic. The victim can't seem to be too aggressive, unlikable or dishonest.

Adelaide Abankwah was a young woman from Ghana who spoke little English, broke immigration laws and had no friends or family to turn to for support. In other words, she was like scores of other illegal immigrants negotiating their way around the United States.

Her plight might have been ignored, except that the women's magazine *Marie Claire* took up the young woman's cause in a May 1998 profile. Suddenly, Abankwah became the press's latest *cause celébre*. The *Washington Times* also took up Abankwah's plight on Christmas Day, 1998:

> December is a time of celebration for people of many faiths. It is a time when countless Americans join their families to honor their religious traditions and mark the holidays with good cheer.
>
> But not Adelaide Abankwah, a young Christian woman from Ghana. She will continue to languish in Wackenhut, a detention center in Queens. Her crime? Seeking asylum on U.S. shores to escape female circumcision in her home country.
>
> Adelaide's mother was queen of her tribe. When she died unexpectedly, it was assumed Adelaide would take over, but she was not considered "holy," as she had a boyfriend. As punishment for her misconduct, she was threatened with female genital mutilation, so she fled. Upon arriving [in the U.S.] she was shackled, strip-searched and sent to Wackenhut, a maximum-security facility (more secure than Rikers Island), where she has remained. At Wackenhut, there is no privacy, inmates share sleeping and bathroom facilities, which are basically in the same room (so the sounds and smells permeate), and are allowed one hour a day in a confined, outdoor courtyard for fresh air.

The article also noted that "on one level, Adelaide is 'lucky.' Yet, she has been detained longer than most (longer than many felons, in fact), and it is predicted that she will stay in detention for many more months, if not years, to come."

Sad it was, agreed other reporters who wrote for both left- and right-wing publications. Journalists began to weigh in on the matter in earnest, as the *New York Times* did in their April 25, 1999 edition:

> For more than two years, Adelaide Abankwah's waking hours have felt like living nightmares. Slumber, she said, is her only refuge.
>
> "I dream that I am stepping out of a dark, dirty room into a light, beautiful room, where everyone is eating a lot of food," she said, closing her

brown eyes as if trying to keep the vision from getting away. "When I sleep, that is when I feel free."

[...]Sobbing and speaking in broken English, she told United States officials that she had fled her homeland because the elders of her village were going to cut her genitals. She had lost her virginity to a man who was not an approved mate for her, which violated her tribe's customs.

Outlets from *New York News Day* to the *Washington Post* followed the woman's plight, the latter of which profiled Abankwah in a July 21 article:

"My grandmother told me I have to watch myself because if I don't, they will not forgive me. They will cut me," [Abankwah] recalled. "So I have to leave, so I am safe."

Happy times were ahead for Abankwah, as the *New York Times* noted in their August 20 follow up:

Ms. Abankwah, twenty-nine, flanked by Gloria Steinem and other supporters, spoke haltingly at a news conference at Marie Claire magazine on West Broadway. Since her plight was detailed in the magazine's May 1998 issue, it has attracted the attention of scores of women's rights organizations, politicians and celebrities.

Last Friday, Ms. Abankwah received final word that her ordeal had ended. The Board of Immigration Appeals granted her petition for political asylum on the grounds that she feared being subjected to genital cutting if she returned to Ghana. She is one of only a few women to be granted asylum in the United States for that reason.

"There are really no words that can express the way I'm feeling," she said yesterday. "I am so happy to be free. I don't have to worry about being deported or dying in jail. Today, I am surrounded by my friends and supporters, who have all helped me attain my freedom."

The *Times* also noted that one reporter asked Abankwah to describe the genital mutilation process she would have endured if she were deported. Before the teary Abankwah could respond, her lawyer interjected and stated Abankwah would not answer the question.

NPR also covered Abankwah's victory with detailed color in an August 19 broadcast:

MARGOT ADLER: Adelaide Abankwah, her hair pulled back, wearing a conservative suit and exhibiting a fragile, stately grace, stood surrounded by supporters, including Nancy Weisman, the photo editor for *Marie Claire* magazine who had championed her cause, and Gloria Steinem, who had brought her case to feminist organizations and to members of Congress. When she rose to speak, her words were simple.

By December 20, 2000, things wouldn't be so simple for either Abankwah or the press, but this time both INS and the *Washington Post* conducted their own separate investigations and reached the same startling conclusion: Abankwah's story was a hoax, starting with her name.

Abankwah was in fact Regina Norman Danson, a thirty-one-year-old former hotel worker. The real Abankwah was a woman in her 20s whose passport had been stolen four years earlier, but who had not reported it stolen, fearing deportation. Danson was arrested and convicted of perjury, among several other charges.

So how did the media get fooled? First, there were the usual oversights: reporters did not try to verify Danson's identity, nor did they try to locate her alleged tribe to see whether it existed or if she was who she claimed she was. Was genital mutilation part of this tribe's punishments? Were there other refugees from the area making the same claims? Had they threatened Danson? Almost no one in the press tried to confirm or refute Danson's over-the-top claims, giving the false impression that journalists did their homework and Abankwah was credible.

Second, there were stereotypes of African nations that tainted reporters' accounts of the story: since Abankwah claimed she would face a misogynistic punishment, and since it is well-known that some places in Africa are known to mete out such punishment, then it stood to reason that what Abankwah said had to be true. She must have fled her homeland and risked so much to live in America: land of the free, home of the genitally intact. Had reporters been a little more skeptical, they could have verified whether Ghana still practiced this loathed ritual.

With both factual and cultural ignorance blinding many journalists, Abankwah managed to bamboozle the public and bypass her dues. In fact, Danson's court battles were not successful until the press took up her cause; unfortunately, they had not done enough background research before they decided to support a con artist.

Who Can You Trust?

Some media hoaxes reveal a disturbing white in-group shorthand: when a white person commits a heinous crime against a loved one and wants to deflect suspicion, the best way is to blame a threatening black man for the deed. But what happens when white men are the outsiders?

On November 28, 1987, the residents of Wappingers Falls, New York would learn that one of their children had been the victim of a horrifying crime. The sickening violation was recounted in the February 11, 1988 edition of *USA Today*:

> Tawana Brawley, sixteen, was a popular honor student in the quiet village of Wappingers Falls, N.Y. A high school cheerleader, she also ran track.
>
> Now she's a recluse who's been unwittingly thrown into the national spotlight, drawing the support of black leaders like entertainer Bill Cosby.
>
> The reason: She was found Nov. 28 curled in a fetal position inside a plastic bag, racial slurs scrawled across her torso. Her body was smeared with feces and her hair was cut off.
>
> Brawley says she was kidnapped and sexually assaulted by six white men, including one wearing a badge. The case has shocked this upstate village of 5,000, leading to charges of racism and cover-ups.

Brawley's vicious rape drew national attention and interest: the NAACP took up her cause, as did Rev. Al Sharpton, Alton Maddox Jr. and C. Vernon Mason. Outlets from across the country reported on the young girl's story without much skepticism.

Yet there were problems with Brawley's background and version of events: why would an offender who had everything to lose by being exposed as a rapist, let the young girl live, especially if he spent a significant amount of time with her? Couldn't she identify him? Wouldn't it be safer to kill her rather than risk losing his career and freedom? Why would someone "with a badge" be so careless with a living eyewitness, considering he would be familiar with police procedure?

Journalists covering the story discovered that those who knew the girl said she had run away from home before, only to face a beating by her strict mother. She was seen "partying" in an unsavory part of town the night she was supposedly attacked. Suddenly, Brawley had a reason to make up the story of being kidnapped and assaulted: the girl did not want to face her mother's wrath again. A grand jury determined that Brawley's story was a hoax.

Yet her supporters still believed the girl, and were convinced that there was a cover-up to protect her assailants. The former prosecutor in the Brawley case successfully sued Sharpton for defamation—Sharpton had accused the prosecutor of being one of Brawley's attackers. What lent Brawley's accusation credibility was that she claimed to have been attacked by someone "with a badge": if her allegations were shown to be false, then it would be easy for Brawley and her defenders to claim there was a police cover up. That fail-safe device in her story made it easy for her supporters to continue to believe her long after evidence pointed to her fabricating her ordeal.

Who Would've Guessed That Terrorists Eat at Shoney's?

After the terrorist attacks on September 11, 2001, reporters and the public were suddenly put on high alert that the United States wasn't invulnerable to grand scale threats. Journalists were even more uneasy about terrorism than the public: several media outlets were sent anthrax-laced letters, which resulted in eight media employees contracting the disease.

Needless to say, many journalists became sensitive to stories about possible terrorist attacks, particularly as the first anniversary of the attacks approached. When September 11, 2002 came and went uneventfully, everyone breathed a sigh of relief.

That relief would be short lived. Two days later, another potential terrorist threat landed on American soil, as was recounted in a September 13, 2002 *Associated Press* story:

> Officials shut down the main east-west highway across the Everglades, and [three] people in two vehicles were detained after a possible terrorist threat, police said.
>
> Bomb-sniffing dogs alerted authorities to material in both vehicles, said E.J. Picolo of the Florida Department of Law Enforcement. Explosive charges were used to blast open what appeared to be a backpack taken from one of the vehicles.
>
> [...]The Georgia Bureau of Investigation...issued an advisory for two cars Thursday after a waitress in Calhoun, Georgia...told police she overheard three men of Middle Eastern descent discussing terrorist plans Wednesday night.
>
> The Georgia woman said the men were talking about amounts of explosives and warned that Americans would "cry on 9/13," said Miami Police Lt. Bill Schwartz...

CNN also covered the threat on their September 13 "Breaking News" broadcast:

> KYRA PHILLIPS: We want to get the latest on the events on Interstate 75 in southern Florida. Two cars have been detained since early hours of this morning. It started with a tip in Georgia from a woman who told authorities she heard three men discussing a possible terrorist plot. Many hours later, one of the cars sped through a Florida toll-booth and was stopped by police. The other car halted as well.
>
> CNN's Mark Potter is in Collier County, Florida, to bring us the very latest—Mark.

MARK POTTER: Hi. We are standing on the highway right now. Some of the officers are in front of us, the scene is beyond these officers here. They have been here for hours searching these cars, and that search continues.

Let me bring you up to speed on where we stand now. The first of the two cars was searched and cleared by the authorities on the scene.

Three young men of Middle Eastern decent were held in police custody for seventeen hours until the truth emerged: they were medical students interning in Florida and, no, they weren't terrorists. The woman who claimed to overhear the men plotting was not a waitress but a customer, a nurse named Eunice Stone. Though Stone maintained that she heard the three men make "alarming comments," no one else in the restaurant could confirm her account. The three men denied making any such comments and accused Stone of spicing up her comments, a charge she denied.

In any event, the men carried no explosives and had no history of terrorist sympathies. The assumption that three young Arabic men would automatically be terrorists makes this episode all the more troubling.

How to Spot Hoaxes Based on Stereotypes

Whenever you see or read a story that invokes an over-the-top "in group" versus "out group" dynamic, do not automatically assume that this is a story about good versus evil. Try to determine whether the story has logical inconsistencies. If there are problems, consider what one person has to gain by maligning an outside group.

This isn't to suggest that attacks based on race or gender never happen. The trouble is that hoaxers sneak in their stories with the real ones and use fear and stereotypes as devious and lazy rallying points: they have no difficulty preying on the fears of people who trust. When their hoaxes are exposed, not only will the scammer's supporters lose credibility, but other groups will refuse to believe legitimate cases of attacks or abuse, or worse, real cases of abuse will be overshadowed by a fake report.

So how can you determine if this type of news story is truthful? First, ignore the emotional distractions—these are the least important elements in a nonfiction story. There's no point in feeling compassion toward someone who is trying to con you. What you are looking for is facts and more than one of the following signs that can confirm or refute a person's claims:

1. The story is based on racial, ethnic or gender clichés.

Though it sounds obvious, it nevertheless is a good indicator that someone's tale of abuse by an outsider is a hoax. Here, brutal and menacing black men are out to get white women; groups of psychopathic white men in positions of power are out to get everyone else. When pressed to describe what his alleged black attacker said, the hoaxer will almost always claim her young assailant used bad-assed street slang—but the slang will sound outdated and awkward.

If a hoaxer has little contact with someone of a different race or ethnicity, he won't be able to give a realistic description of either the "offender's" behavior or even a physical description: he is going to have to guess how this particular phantom stranger will talk, think and behave. The hoaxer will most likely base his lies on what he has seen on television or on the myths he has heard from members of his group. In either case, the descriptions won't sound authentic.

Hate crimes and racially motivated abuse do exist, but the vast majority of crimes are intraracial. Whites attack whites, blacks attack blacks and Asians attack Asians. In the Charles Stuart and Susan Smith cases, both had claimed their assailants were menacing black men. What is interesting about Smith's description of her phantom carjacker is that he had no distinctive characteristics. In the Abankwah hoax, she relied on Americans' ignorance of her country's practices to galvanize support for her refugee status. In the fake terrorist scare, reporters believed that there was a possible threat simply because the three young men were of Arabic descent.

2. Though there are reports of "mass" attacks, there are no specific accounts, despite efforts to track down specific instances.

Many people may be too afraid or ashamed to step forward after being victimized, but chances are, someone will swallow his fear and his pride and publicly acknowledge that he was a crime victim or at least a witness to one. If not a single person comes forward after rumors of mass attacks become widespread, even despite public pleas to do so; the rumors are a hoax. In the case of rumors surrounding various gang initiation rites, no one has come forward to report the crimes, nor was there any hard evidence that they ever happened (such as surveillance cameras or eyewitnesses).

3. The sourcing of the story is difficult to pin down.

If there is an attack where it is reported that victims survived, we'd expect at least one of those victims to come forward or for police to confirm that they have spoken to at least one of the victims. Reporters may find documented proof through public records, but the origin of the story is known. If the rumor's origin can't be pinned down, it's most likely because the crime or attack doesn't exist. Believers will claim the silence is a direct result of a complex cover-up, but if the event allegedly happened in an open area or to hundreds of victims, this is a harder excuse to swallow.

There are other hard to believe scenarios: if several people are missing, it's highly unlikely that all these people's loved ones will keep silent about the abductions. Even if police aren't cooperative in certain cases, the wronged party can use other avenues to gain public attention. In the gang initiation rite cases, the origins of the rumors couldn't be pinned down, making their truthfulness questionable.

4. Though most crime statistics show that perpetrators prey on victims who are the same race as they are, the story implies the opposite.

Crime statistics show that you have much more to fear from people belonging to your race or ethnic group than from an outside group. According to the Federal Bureau of Investigations, in 2000 almost 94% of black murder victims were killed by a black offender and 86% of white murder victims were killed by a white offender. Getting attacked by someone outside your own race is rare.

In the Brawley, Stuart and Smith hoaxes, each had claimed that they were attacked by someone from a different race. While it was possible that their offenders were another creed, they created offenders of a different race to gain sympathy and lend credibility to their stories, even though, ironically, their chosen scenarios were less likely to happen.

5. No witnesses are found and there is no forensic evidence to corroborate the victim's story. Furthermore, the crimes could not have logically taken place as described. Even if there are witnesses, their accounts are too similar, even though they may claim to have been at different places.

Bigots may have the power to destroy lives, but they don't have the power to destroy the rules of reality. They can't be in two places at once, nor can they destroy every shred of evidence of a crime in a short period. In the Charles Stuart case, the pregnant wife (who would be far less of a threat than a male), not the husband, received the fatal injuries. In the phony terrorist hoax, the "threat" was based on the word of a single witness—a witness who was the only person to hear the threats in a public place. In the Brawley hoax, Brawley was left alive, even though she would be able to identify her attackers.

6. There are chronology problems.

Any crime story requires a plausible timeline: certain things have to happen in a certain order. If a victim's story seems as if it were out of order, there is a high probability that the story is a fake. Time elapses are also important—walking up ten flights of stairs takes more time than opening an unlocked door. Try to keep the timelines straight in your head: if they sound confusing, that means the victim is most likely lying or exaggerating. In the Brawley hoax, witnesses had placed her at another location at the same time she was supposedly attacked.

7. Incidents were first said to be "seen on 'Oprah'" or any other talk show.

Television is all about ratings. If a popular celebrity had made a racial slur in front of a studio audience with cameras rolling, chances are that the tape will be made public. With websites showing bootleg copies of unreleased movies and the like, embarrassing footage of a bigoted entertainer would not be difficult to procure. In the Liz Claiborne and Tommy Hilfiger cases, the accusers' credibility hinged on nonexistent television appearances.

8. There are allegations of a vast conspiracy to keep the information quiet when no evidence is found to support these claims.

A favorite ruse among the diehard believers is the claim that a "cover up" is preventing the truth from coming out. For the believers, cover-ups explain a lack of forensic evidence (destroyed), victims (silenced or bribed), eyewitnesses (silenced, bribed or killed) or documents (destroyed). Cover-ups happen and happen frequently, but cover-ups are like a mop—they can clean up small spills, but they cannot clean up a flooded room. Sooner or later, somebody breaks, brags or gets careless. Many murderers get caught because they confess or boast to another person who, in turn, tells the police.

In both the gang initiation and Brawley hoaxes, the lack of evidence and action were attributed to a vast cover up, even though there were other troubling problems with the stories.

When reading or watching a news story that plays up to racial tension, ignore the emotions and the ethnic labels and pay attention to the facts: what information is missing? Where is the smoking gun? If the story doesn't make sense, it probably means the story is a lie.

Chapter Ten

War Propaganda

War is a reliable audience grabber, even if the war is not a direct threat to the reader or viewer. Violence, danger and macabre tales of evil can captivate audiences and invoke strong emotional responses. In one way, bloody battles on the small screen are the equivalent to a rollicking action flick—except that soldiers can't rely on stunt doubles to do their dirty work.

Unlike other violent news stories, war stories have their own set of rules. Wartime is a different reality than peacetime: chaos and the drive for mere survival taints the way people see the world around them. Lawlessness isn't just present on the battlefield, but also in the way people communicate with each other. If it takes lying to defeat the enemy, then so be it.

Brutality and cruelty are expected byproducts of war and it was certainly a brutal and cruel end that one poor solider met during World War I, as recounted in the May 10, 1915 edition of the *Times of London*:

> [The soldier] had been pinned to a wall by bayonets thrust through his hands and feet; another bayonet had then been driven through his throat, and finally, he was riddled with bullets.
>
> The wounded [soldiers] said that the Dublin Fusiliers had seen this done with their own eyes, and that they had heard the officers of the Dublin Fusiliers talking about it.

Though there were allegedly witnesses to the event, the lack of corroborating evidence eventually proved that the story was an effective piece of propaganda meant to rally public support for the war.

Gaining support for the home team and discrediting the opponent is the main reason why propaganda is used. How else can a country frighten all its citizens into compliance on short notice? Why else would a foreign country agree to spend time, money and human life for strangers, unless there was a compelling reason? How else can a nation goad millions of people to wish death on an enemy?

Propaganda has to be effective on the first try, but how do armies or governments disseminate their lies? By using the media to spread the message of hate and despair. A powerful news report can lend credibility to propaganda, especially if the reporter can interview a sympathetic false witness.

Many media critics assume that reporters are willing and deliberate spreaders of false information. While some journalists do intentionally lie in their stories (and not just during war time), many are simply too lazy to go out and verify a war rumor, too ill-prepared to negotiate through a foreign and lawless country, or too naïve to question a sobbing witness. What this means is that the reporter's intentions are irrelevant: what the news consumer has to do is listen to the report and look for signs that the report is a fake. But to know what signs to look for, it is important to understand both war and propaganda first.

Basic Truths About War

Whenever reporters are brought to task for misreporting information during wartime, they will usually quote U.S. Senator Hiram Johnson who said, during the First World War, that "The first casualty when war comes is truth" or maybe it was "The first casualty of war is truth" (though whether Johnson actually said either isn't known for certain). In any case, it's a convenient mea culpa, that loosely translates to "There's propaganda everywhere; so don't expect me to endanger myself even more to find out what's really going on."

That means war coverage is likely to be tainted and biased, depending on which side the journalist is assigned to cover, especially if the reporter is witness to real atrocities committed by one side. False accusations slip in with stories of genuine suffering and horror. Tensions flare; emotions are manipulated and scores of normally rational people are whipped into a frenzy. Institutions that reporters heavily rely upon to get their information are either scuttled or taxed to their limits trying to restore order. Foreign reporters are parachuted into this mess, thinking they will not be dragged into the hatred.

Atrocities happen in war, but it's important to keep one point in mind: not all of the worst offenses are committed by regular citizens or regular soldiers. For example, are convicted criminals and the criminally insane separated from the rest of the population, or are they free to wander the streets without supervision? Yet this is hardly considered by the enemy side nor by many journalists who may lump the psychopaths with the rest of the criminal's race or ethnic group. In war, fear and hatred will lead many people to exaggerate what they've seen or heard to justify their side's hostilities, even when exaggeration isn't exactly needed—as if ten slaughtered innocents isn't as despicable as a hundred.

All these factors make covering any war objectively nearly impossible. Many "eyewitnesses" will honestly believe the false information they are feeding reporters actually happened and lie only to boost the credibility of the story. It's only natural: in mortal danger, people will do anything and stoop to any level just to survive, because that is what all of us have been primed to do on an instinctual level. That is why the number of casualties reported may be inflated or suppressed, either to compel foreign intervention or to confuse the enemy, respectively.

Covering wars isn't easy, particularly if the reporter finds himself in a foreign country confronting a foreign language and different cultures. Warring sides have a frenzied hate for one another and will not question some of the more ridiculous tales of terror they've heard from their military, government, family or friends. What people hear are legitimate warnings; they may have no idea that those stories are meant to incite hatred, fear and loyalty. What people assumed to be legitimate forewarnings may in fact be war propaganda. While it is understandable that warring sides are oblivious to this manipulation, foreign reporters have no excuse for also swallowing these over-the-top lies, but they do anyway.

Why War Propaganda Works

War propaganda is not a well-understood form of communication (even when it is being effectively used), but there seem to be recurring themes: the enemy is made to be faceless and melodramatically inhuman, and the warring side is made to seem evil *en masse*. The enemy side is accused of starving, freezing, torturing, raping and killing their opponents with ease and glee. The enemy side may be accused of reproducing and multiplying at the expense of the opposing side. Women and babies will be seen as likely targets of the enemy side—meaning that the enemy isn't only gaining physical ground, but reproductive ground as well.

With this never-ending stream of scary stories preying on our most basic fears, it is difficult for reporters to get the truth; after all, each side will claim total innocence and their enemy as the only ones doing the killing—unfortunately, war takes at least two hostile forces. Conflicts in Asia, Africa and Europe have shown us that it is important to look at all sides and look at as much of the forensic evidence as possible without being swayed by emotional pleas.

This is no minor point: some people who recount the horror stories of war may be frightened children or weeping adults. There is real trauma and fear written on their faces. The people who make these allegations may be well meaning, but under the circumstances, they are not unbiased or without an agenda. They may believe that inciting intervention by any means necessary will save their lives, their families, their properties or their country. They want to win a war—not necessarily for the glory, but for mere survival (real or perceived). Under the circumstances, many of these vectors aren't regular hoaxers; they don't necessarily have a malicious intent. Yet if thousands of people unnecessarily suffer as a result of the hoaxer's lies, the hoaxer's intentions don't matter.

Many propaganda stories, for the most part, make little or no sense: they defy what is physically or logically possible, but those stories will be believed anyway. The stories may revolve around threats to life, health and freedom, and rely on emotional manipulation to make them sound real. These stories may be told by sympathetic-looking people and be based on partial truths— but that doesn't mean they are true.

To add to the difficulties, reporters may fully believe what they are told by citizens, as well as government or military officials. While the 2003 Gulf War saw U.S. reporters "embedded" within U.S. military units, the practice did nothing to sharpen reporters' critical thinking skills. False information was still reported, as it had been in wars past.

Since news consumers cannot always verify the information they get independently, they have to evaluate the information received through logic and lateral thinking. So if the first casualty of war is truth, then the news consumer's first line of defense is skepticism—but that isn't easy, as the following case study shows.

Babies, Weeping Teenaged Girls and Faceless Soldiers

Advertisers have figured out long ago that certain fresh-faced teenaged girls make excellent product sponsors. They are young, innocent, pretty, soft, not yet corrupted by life's harsh nature and, unlike their male counterparts, seem too dignified to be amused by flatulence. These girls seem honest and their ingenue quality gives them enough credibility to sell anything from music to toothpaste. The undisputed marketing prowess of teen girls is so remarkable that it's no wonder that this lucrative demographic has been tapped to be the face of political causes, such as making the case to go to war.

When the 1990 invasion of Kuwait by Iraq first made the news, most people who heard about the annexation reacted with one part ignorance and one part apathy. Kuwait was a small country, known mostly for its royal family's decadence and its oil-rich resources. While Kuwaitis pleaded for international intervention, many citizens in outside countries simply shrugged their shoulders.

Yet all hope for Kuwaitis was not lost: news of various Iraqi atrocities began to seep into Western newscasts; for example, the September 5, 1990 edition of the *London Daily Telegraph* told readers that one exiled Kuwaiti minister had made claims that Iraqi soldiers had ripped Kuwaiti newborns out of their incubators. The accusation was made again two days later when a Reuters story recounted the traumas Kuwaitis faced at the hands of Iraqi soldiers (including that the fleeing Kuwaitis would have their ears cut off by the soldiers). One of the anonymous sources the Reuters article relied on was an American woman who had returned from Kuwait. The woman, who would identify herself only as "Cindy from San Francisco," gave her account of events:

> [...]Iraqi troops took premature babies out of incubators in Kuwait. "Iraqis are beating people, bombing and shooting. They are taking all hospital equipment, babies out of incubators. Life-support systems are turned off... They are even removing traffic lights," Cindy said.

While there may have been some stirring into wanting some sort of military intervention, the accusations were still too nebulous: how could anyone relate to anonymous eyewitnesses named "Cindy"? No sympathetic face from Kuwait had attempted to make an appeal for international intervention. After all, the ghost named Cindy may have heard the story from others and not have seen the atrocity itself. Unless there was someone who had actually seen the horror, the stories may have been apocryphal.

That anonymity would change on October 10, when a young girl named Nayirah (she was too afraid to give her last name, it was claimed) testified before the U.S. Congress' Human Rights Caucus that the rumors of Iraqi barbarity were true. The *Los Angeles Times* recounted the girl's story in an article dated October 11, 1990:

> Nayirah also described a friend whom she encountered after he was tortured by the Iraqis. "He is twenty-two, but he looked as though he could be an old man," she said. "The Iraqis dunked his head into a swimming pool until he almost drowned. They pulled out his fingernails and applied electric shock to his body."

Maclean's magazine concurred with the *Times* account of events, but added that shock was applied to "sensitive" parts of the young man's body and that Nayirah felt that her friend "was lucky to survive." But the torture of Nayirah's rapidly aging friend wasn't the only atrocity she witnessed. The tour de force of this young girl's account was her first-hand account of how Iraqi soldiers snuffed out the life of helpless Kuwaiti newborns as the October 11 edition of the *Atlanta Journal and Constitution* recounted:

> A witness identified only as Nayirah said she was working as a hospital volunteer when Iraqi soldiers with guns entered a room where fifteen babies were in incubators.

"They took the babies out of the incubators, took the incubators and left the babies on the cold floor to die," Nayirah said. "It was horrifying."

Maclean's magazine went into more detail in its October 22, 1990 issue:

[...]Nayirah... said that she was vacationing in Kuwait with her mother when the Iraqis invaded. Her voice breaking with emotion, Nayirah described a horrific incident at the Al-Adan hospital in Kuwait city, where she was working as a volunteer. Said the teenager: "I saw the Iraqi soldiers come into the hospital with guns..."

It was heavy stuff for a teenaged girl to witness, and the American news media and public responded to the story with anger. President George Bush, the United Nations and Amnesty International all cited the story as proof of Iraqi brutality (by some accounts, over 300 premature babies were killed in Kuwait by this method). By 1991, the U.S. and its Allies went into Kuwait and successfully drove back Iraqi troops from the annexed country.

Despite the victory, there were questions surrounding the mysterious Nayirah: why would a fifteen-year-old who was vacationing in Kuwait work or volunteer at a hospital? What forensic proof was there to support her claims? Who else saw the Iraqi soldiers remove the infants from their incubators? Why would soldiers take the incubators, as opposed to more important hospital equipment? Why wouldn't she give her last name, yet be willing to show her face to the world?

The most important question still remained unanswered: who was Nayirah? A refugee? A Kuwaiti citizen? An American citizen? Where did she live if not in Kuwait, since she claimed that she was vacationing there? How did she manage to leave the hospital unscathed?

Nayirah's smooth, tearstained face was seen around the world, including on CNN, NBC, CBS and ABC. But what most news consumers didn't know was that Nayirah wasn't filmed by a television news crew or ever interviewed by reporters. If reporters weren't filming her during her testimony, then how did they get hold of the footage?

Nayirah's testimony was disseminated through a video news release (VNR) provided by Hill and Knowlton, a prominent public relations firm specializing in handling radioactive clients and crisis communications. While the origin of the VNR should have roused journalists' suspicions, the girl's powerful emotional testimony in front of "Congress" made her seem credible, even though she technically didn't give congressional testimony in front of the caucus.

Since reporters aired her story uncritically, many people assumed that Nayirah's background and story had been double checked by the press.

There was one small problem: journalists didn't look into her background—that is, until *Harper's* magazine publisher John R. MacArthur took a look into her story. Hearing rumors that Nayirah was Nayirah al-Sabah, member of the Kuwaiti royal family and daughter of Saud al-Sabah, Kuwaiti ambassador to the U.S., MacArthur confirmed the worst: the girl's family had a vested interest in her testimony. Other reporters and activists also discovered that the stories of dead babies couldn't be confirmed, and it soon became obvious that the story was a hoax.

Those who wonder why a teenaged girl would lie to someone in authority should think why many girls lie to parents and teachers about their boyfriends, the decency of their friends, their experiences with drug use, their reasons for not finishing their homework, their arriving late at work and the status of their virginity: because many girls have something to gain by hiding the truth. In Nayirah's case, inciting Americans to support Kuwait would go a long way to restoring her family's former power base.

War propaganda is used as an extreme form of stereotype and myth, with one key difference: this form of propaganda is meant to incite the troops to hate enemies enough to want to kill them. Though war does bring atrocities, some of the more inflammatory tales are just too bad to be true.

All the Fine Young Cannibals

No matter how sophisticated or pampered a person may be, the threat of starvation by an enemy can be a powerful motivator for people to react strongly against the foe. The threat can become a rallying cry and a legitimate reason to ask for outside intervention. No food means certain death—so how far will people go to survive?

The civil war in the former Yugoslavia made headlines in the early 1990s: the patchwork European country disintegrated into bloody chaos, but the reports of macabre atrocities committed seemed to multiply daily. Though this was the war that helped coin the term "ethnic cleansing," there was one particularly gruesome outrage that shocked even the most jaded journalist: people in the region had taken to cannibalism.

One account of Balkan cannibalism as a method of Serbian torture upon Muslims was reported in the October 18, 1992 edition of *New York Newsday*:

> [One Bosnian Muslim detainee] told *Newsday* he had twice witnessed forced cannibalism at Keraterm camp. On one occasion, he said, guards cut off a prisoner's ear and forced another man to eat it. The second time, a guard cut a piece of flesh off a wounded prisoner and told him to eat it. He refused. "Why not? It's cooked," Hamuric quoted the guard as saying. Hamuric could not say whether the man ate his own flesh. "All I know is that they took him away and we never saw him again."

Though Serbs were also accused of cannibalizing Muslims, the January 13, 1993 edition of the *Washington Post* also told of the Muslim populace resorting to the sickening act out of desperation:

> "There is the threat of cannibalism soon," ... said [one Bosnian Muslim man]. "There are suspicions that it has already happened." Nothing Heljic said could be independently confirmed, since Zepa—situated in mountainous terrain about 40 miles east of Sarajevo—has been cut off by Serb nationalist forces since Bosnia's factional war began nine months ago.

This variation of the rumor was repeated in the February 17, 1993 edition of the *Press of Atlantic City*:

> Bosnia's U.N. ambassador, Muhamed Sacirbey, told reporters in New York that some besieged Muslims have turned to cannibalism to survive. "I received a call from the military commander in Tuzla who told me that people in these besieged enclaves in eastern Bosnia were now eating the dead in order to survive," he said. He did not elaborate and the claim could not be confirmed.

By May 1996, Serbian officials claimed that Muslim soldiers had cannibalized four missing Serb woodcutters since the bodies of the men couldn't be found. With claims and counterclaims of enemies feasting on victims, victims forced to feast on other victims or enemies forcing victims to eat themselves, the bloody Balkan region would have been Hannibal Lecter's idea of paradise.

As in the Gulf War incubator hoax, there was no forensic evidence to sustain that anyone was indulging in or forced to participate in the eating of man-meat. The charges on all sides eventually fizzled out. The stories were used to shock, incite fear and hate of the enemy, and rally foreign support for military intervention, but it was hardly the first time that false claims of cannibalism were made in a battlefield, as the next case study shows.

When There is Nowhere to Hide

Infants and young girls are powerful symbols of a country or race's evolutionary survival. Infants represent a country's success in reproducing the next generation, while young, fertile girls represent the potential to make sure that the next generation can exist. As crude as it may sound, any threat to either is a threat to a country or race's very survival. It can be argued that an enemy who attacks babies and teenaged girls is committing a form of genocide.

World War One was marked by stories of man's inhumanity to his fellow man, but one particularly horrifying atrocity occurred in the Belgian city of Liege in August 1914. As the story went, German soldiers overtook the city, murdered thousands of civilians, publicly raped young Belgian girls, used bayonets to kill infants and then ate a dead infant in front of the horrified Belgian crowd. Not surprisingly, the incident helped to rally U.S. support for military intervention.

Some began to doubt the incredible tale of depravity, but Belgian officials were adamant that the claims were true, according to a September 25, 1914 edition of the *Washington Post*:

> As a proof of the contention that German soldiers have been guilty of barbarity, the Belgian government will shortly send to America two beautiful young Belgian girls, now patients in the Paris General Hospital recovering from mutilations inflicted by German soldiers.

There were some problems with the accusations: why didn't the crowd try to help the girls? How convenient is it to sadistically torture people in front of a large crowd in a war zone? After eight years, the over-the-top story still couldn't be corroborated and it was eventually agreed that most of the story was a hoax.

Propaganda has to work fast and decisively: the audience has to react quickly and in favor of the propagandist. Any chance to think or to reflect on the meaning of the information reduces the propagandist's effectiveness. The Liege saga had the desired effect on foreign audiences: people outside Belgium were outraged and wanted to stop the Germans before they had the chance to overrun their nation.

However, if propaganda was all about threats, it would scare the public into uncontrolled fear. A good propagandist has to outline the dangers, but then offer a solution to the public; otherwise, a terrified race or nation may want to surrender. The solution has to be in the form of a competent and powerful army that will drive the enemy away and withstand almost any threat, as the following case study shows.

The Truth About Helmet Hair

A war story without a brave soldier is like a superhero comic book without a superhero: within all that violence, lawlessness and chaos, there has to be some shining knight who can withstand war's tortures without whining or complaining. How can you maintain the support of the folks back home unless the folks in the trenches are calm and intact? A mass panic or revolt caused by the sight of broken and depressed soldiers cannot do governments any good. A war hero has to withstand extraordinary pains without a scratch. Supernatural agility or endurance boosts morale at home and increases support for military spending and action.

One British soldier stationed in Iraq seemed indestructible, or at least he was wearing an indestructible helmet. In any case, his close call with death captured world attention, as reported in the March 27, 2003 edition of the *Daily Record*:

> Smiling Royal Marine Commando Eric Walderman yesterday showed how he cheated death after being blasted in the head four times.
>
> Eric's life was saved by his kevlar helmet which deflected the bullets and clearly displayed the force of the impacts...
>
> He was caught in the sights of Iraqis during a savage firefight in Umm Qsar.
>
> The twenty-five-year old was helping to drive out the last elements of Iraqi fighters from the key port. The bullets ripped through the outer camouflage covering of the standard-issue helmet but were stopped by the kevlar.

Newspapers weren't the only media outlets fascinated by Walderman's intact head. CNN's "Inside Politics" made a mention of the lucky solider in a March 27 newscast:

> WOODRUFF: There is a British Royal Marine in Iraq who is one lucky man. Eric Walderman was shot in a helmet four times during a firefight in Umm Qasr, but his helmet has a bullet proof Kevlar shell inside which stopped the bullets. And the reports are that he is doing just fine. We can think of all sorts of analogies here, but suffice it to say he's doing well and we're pleased.

CNN apparently couldn't get enough of the story—it was repeated in the following days. A March 28 story broadcast on "CNN Newsnight" also made reference to the helmet incident:

> BRUCE MORTON: And sometimes war is just amazing luck. Royal Marine commando Eric Walderman's Kevlar helmet—Kevlar replaced the old steel pot in the 1970s—took four rounds during a firefight, and he wasn't hurt.
>
> Let's hope they let him keep his dented hat. He will be telling that story for the next fifty years.

Walderman's preternatural good fortune also earned a mention on March 27 on the FOX News Network:

> BRIT HUME: And now the most engrossing two minutes in television, the latest from the "Wartime Grapevine." Kevlar, the hard, plastic fiber seems to have saved the lives of at least four coalition soldiers.

[...]Sky News reports that Royal Marine Commander Eric Walderman was shot four times in the head by Iraqi fighters inside Iraq's port of Umm Qasr. But his helmet's Kevlar shell stopped all four bulls while doing some damage to its camouflaged cover.

The helmet incident wasn't just covered from the soldier's point of view: the March 27 edition of the *Birmingham Post* also included an interview with Walderman's significant other, who had heard about the episode from the press:

Yesterday [Walderman's] relieved partner Lindsey Robinson, aged twenty-five, at home with their son Danny, aged two, said: 'He's the luckiest man out there. I'm just so glad he's still alive.' The twenty-five-year-old had the incredible escape as the Marines drove out the last elements of Iraqi fighters in the key port town.

The four bullets ripped through the outer camouflage of the standard-issue helmet but were stopped by the ultra-tough protective Kevlar shell.

Just an inch lower and the father-of-one could have joined the list of British casualties.

The military angle of the story may have started to sound old, but a celebrated incident like that couldn't just be dropped by some journalists. The *Sun* revealed Walderman's lottery number picks. The staunch helmet also made an unexpected appearance in an April 7, 2003 article in the *San Francisco Chronicle*'s business section:

Although there is no such thing as an invincible bulletproof vest, the protective gear—helmets lined with Kevlar and body vests that use Kevlar and one-inch-thick ceramic plates—has reduced the number of injuries to coalition forces.

In one well-publicized example, British Royal Marine Commando Eric Walderman took four shots to the head during a firefight at the port of Umm Qasr, but was not hurt because the bullets did not penetrate his Kevlar helmet.

The helmet episode also made its way to the *Tulsa World*, the *Times of London*, BBC and the *St. Paul Pioneer Press*. The March 27 *Daily Mirror* described the helmet as "ultra-tough" and quoted Walderman's mother as saying "I'm shocked. I just want him home..."

There was one strange thread that all the above stories had in common: Walderman wasn't interviewed. The "Luckiest Soldier in Iraq," "Stay Lucky" and the "Miracle Marine" wasn't the source of the story, nor were any of his fellow soldiers. That meant that the ubiquitous photo of the smiling solider wearing the cratered helmet wasn't taken by any media outlet's photographer.

So how did journalists find out about the incident in the first place? The British Ministry of Defence had posted Walderman's smiling picture on its website, touting the miracle properties of its Kevlar helmets. Reporters took their cue from a government website without double-checking to see whether the story was true.

The *Daily Mirror*, a British tabloid, decided to write a follow up story on Walderman, and it was only then that the paper discovered the truth: the story was a hoax. According to the new account from the soldiers in question, the helmet was shot at by British soldiers—while the helmet was on the ground.

How did the hoax manage to gain credibility when none of the principles of the story were interviewed? Some reporters simply cribbed their information from a government website without double-checking or questioning the information—then other journalists simply got their information from the cribbers. What's also interesting is that reporters who did make mention of the story never told their audiences where they found their original information, or give credit to who shot the picture of Walderman (meaning the story was essentially plagiarized). Government sources aren't infallible, especially when they are focused on winning a war. While government officials had maintained they were also duped by the story, it was reporters who helped spread the hoax around the world without an ounce of skepticism—or attribution.

How to Spot War Propaganda in News Reports

Many problems confront journalists who are reporting in a war-torn area, especially if a reporter finds himself in a foreign country: different cultures, languages and customs can add to the tensions. If two or more of the warring sides have a frenzied hate for one another, the journalist can only hope that the stories he is told are true. He has to hope that he isn't being used as a propaganda tool and a vector. Unfortunately, most times, that's exactly what he will be used for. Under these circumstances, it is difficult for reporters to get to the truth, since each side will claim total innocence and that their enemy is the only one committing the atrocities.

Because the news consumer doesn't have the tools to confirm or refute the information independently, he has to evaluate the information received through logic and common sense. But how does he do that? By looking for any of the following red flags that the war zone story is being used as a way of gaining sympathy:

1. The villain is demonized while the victim is deified and made to seem preternaturally altruistic, even with contrary evidence.

It is logical that certain individuals can be capable of sadistic evil. Small gangs of like-minded criminals and thugs can be capable of murder and torture without remorse—but very rarely do entire nations act in a uniformly twisted and barbaric manner. There will be citizens who will be opposed to their group's violent and bigoted methods and those who have loyalties on both sides. For example, in civil wars, though two or more sides are warring against each other, it will be almost impossible that loyalties and burden of blame will be clear-cut. There will be citizens of warring sides who are married and have children with their enemies before the tensions flared. There will be resistance, double agents and protesters.

Tangled loyalties and internal opposition can be expected in almost any conflict, but when propaganda messages imply the opposite, this is a good sign that someone's own hatred and biases are clouding his interpretation of events. It's human nature for people to see themselves as blameless victims, while their enemies are seen as incorrigible villains who have suffered no pain or loss, as the babies and incubators hoax showed.

One defining feature of war propaganda is that it assumes the enemy hasn't a single redeeming characteristic. This one-sided thinking may be a natural offshoot of fear and the survival instinct in the midst of anarchy, but journalists aren't supposed to fall biased lies, as they did at Liege during the First World War.

Just because a weeping individual makes an accusation, it doesn't automatically mean that the accusation has any truth to it, nor does it mean that you should automatically blame the victim and accuse them of lying. But one-sided reporting should always serve as a red flag to you: a person will lie to win a war just as easily as they will shoot, gas or bomb their opponent for the same ends.

2. Eyewitness accounts are too similar (even during mundane events such as bank robberies, different memories, positions, beliefs, visions and locations will generate different responses, sometimes *vastly* different responses).

Ironically, just because several sources recall the same event the same way, it doesn't mean the event happened as described. Some people are so good at misdirecting eyewitnesses that they can manipulate others into seeing misleading distractions while ignoring salient and critical details. Other times, eyewitnesses may be too emotional to remember what happened, can be influenced by loaded questions, be in collusion with other witnesses or conspire to lie. In the Liege and crucifixion hoaxes, while there were those who claimed to have seen or heard of the events in questions, evidence proved wanting. In the Gulf War hoax, there were several identical accounts of events, even though no forensic evidence was found. Even the helmet hoax saw countless media outlets giving identical descriptions of events; however, most reporters got their misinformation from the same British government website.

3. The accounts of alleged atrocities incite immediate anger; questioning the story is seen as cruel.

No one wants to play "bad cop" when there is a sobbing, broken kid who claims big, bad soldiers tore his family to shreds. Our first reaction (which is perfectly normal and humane) would be to protect the child and make certain he feels safe and secure after his traumatic ordeal. It's not supposed to cross our minds that the kid's parents are alive and living more lavishly than we ever will, and that the lying little brat went through media training.

That's the thinking the hoaxer is hoping for when he springs a fake victim in his scheme to gain support for his warmongering. However, if it's your first instinct to feel sadness, fear or outrage, there's a good chance that this is a sign that the story, if not simply an exaggeration, is an all-out hoax. Propaganda is meant to incite; if the tale incites you, then the story has done its job.

Nayirah's story worked only because her macabre details provoked emotion and suppressed common sense (for a detailed discussion on how ridiculous al Sabah's canard actually was and how easily it would be to spot the lies, see Chapter 18). The Liege and cannibalism stories were also meant to invoke a strong reaction in the audience and not give them a chance to reflect on the troubling details of the yarn.

4. Stories have logical or chronological holes in them.

No matter how convincing or emotionally wrenching a horror story may be, if there are logical flaws in the story, the story is false. The storyteller may be crying; he may hold up a picture of a child; he may even purport to have evidence to prove her claims—however, if he gives inconsistent evidence or cannot account for time lapses in his story, the story is most likely false.

Reporters shouldn't just rely on eyewitness accounts: there should be physical evidence to bolster the storyteller's claims of atrocity. In the incubator hoax, while Nayirah claimed to be a witness to an unspeakable horror, her story had serious flaws in it.

5. Stories revolve around overkill, such as cannibalism.

A skilled propagandist is a shameless one, who has no trouble exploiting an audience to gain sympathy and support. To the propagandist, women aren't just raped; they're carted off to be tortured, mutilated and then eaten. Children aren't just killed; they are savaged and devoured by sick people who make Ed Gein look angelic. These war stories will invoke the rape of women and the mutilation of children and infants. The problem with these stories is that the stories of those who truly suffered at enemy hands will seem pale in comparison to the propagandist's embellishments, and real victims may be ignored or disbelieved as a result.

For example, even though cannibalism does exist, it won't likely happen en masse in a region not known for the consumption of humans. It was virtually unknown in the Balkan region. In the case of the babies and incubators hoax, most people recalled Nayirah's hoax, but could probably not name a single genuine atrocity that had occurred in Iraq.

6. News reports imply that one group of people all behave the same way.

There are rebels and hard heads in every bunch; not everyone will follow orders blindly or without question. Many war propagandists try to make a case for their enemy's mass compliance, even though gaining the consensus of millions or even hundreds of people is nearly impossible.

Those who do adhere to the mass compliance theory will use Stanley Milgram's 1963 experiment as proof that people follow orders blindly from anyone in authority. Milgram was a psychologist who had subjects duped into thinking they were giving electric shocks to another subject (in fact, the "subject" getting the "shocks" was not only working with Milgram, but he wasn't getting any shocks at all). The shocks were supposed to be given every time the other "subject" (who was tested in another room, but who could be heard) gave a wrong answer to a learning and punishment experiment, with the real subjects "increasing" the shocks each time their companion got the wrong answer. To add a little spice to the experiment, the real subjects were led to believe that their fellow subject had a heart problem.

As the experiment progressed, Milgram's confederate began to "complain" about the increasing pain; however, the experimenter would tell the real subject to continue giving shocks to the distressed and screaming man, who would refuse to give answers after receiving "300 volts" (the maximum level was 450 volts). Subjects were free to leave and were under no threat from the experimenter to continue giving shocks. To the astonishment of other psychologists, 65% of subjects gave 450 volts to someone who was no longer responding.

While those results are chilling, they shouldn't be mistaken for mass compliance: it should be noted that other subjects did stop at or before 300 volts; furthermore, subsequent experiments showed that subjects wouldn't comply with the experimenter as much when the confederate subject was in the same room as the real subjects.

What this means is clear: even in war, there will be dissenters, or even traitors who, for various reasons, aren't going to play for the home team. But the enemy will nevertheless be portrayed as faceless automatons who follow orders blindly. In the incubator and Liege hoaxes, Iraqi and German soldiers were both portrayed as brutish robots who behaved in the same manner.

7. There is no forensic evidence to support the claim.

Though difficult for a news consumer to determine, it is not impossible to see whether a journalist has offered any proof of a warring side's misdeeds. For example, does the reporter mention any evidence besides the word of a military authority or eyewitness? If there are claims of mass starvation, can the reporter provide images of emaciated victims? If there is a claim that a warring side committed an atrocity at a particular site, was that site visited by the journalist? What did the area look like?

While this does not prove conclusively that the alleged atrocity took place (after all, a warring faction could kill enemies at one site, then later claim that was the site where the enemy attacked them), it does show that the reporter at least attempted to corroborate the claims.

The lack of evidence is a strong indicator that no atrocity took place. In the Liege, Bosnia and Kuwait examples, though there are people who claimed the accounts were true, there was no forensic evidence to support or corroborate the stories. A battalion of frenzied soldiers wreaking havoc and maiming innocents would have left a clear trail, from blood stains to property damage.

8. The target group seem to have superhuman strength and numbers, even though they have a small military.

This red flag is probably the easiest to spot. For example, is it probable that a country of two million lost one million soldiers? During times of war, people are prone to exaggeration. While this may help the propagandist in the short term, it can damage an entire nation's credibility once the allegation is proven false. In the incubator hoax, it was claimed that hundreds of premature babies were killed in this manner in a very short time span, startling given that Kuwait was a country with a population of less than two million people. What was the rate for premature births in Kuwait before Iraq invaded? Without this vital clue, it would be difficult to hazard a guess whether the number of infants was normal or exaggerated.

9. Stories involving an ethnic or racial group are based on a stereotype of the group, not real cultural idiosyncrasies (i.e., how one side thinks the enemy side behaves)—such as garbled slang, emblems and national symbols that are slightly off.

This is easier to spot for people who are familiar with a nation's culture, idioms and customs than it is for the casual observer, but, as outlined in Chapter 9, any exaggerated stereotypes are a strong clue that the enemy side's own prejudices are creeping into their propaganda. In the Gulf War hoax, Nayirah's story seemed plausible to many because they had seen images of Iraqi soldiers in their fatigues and assumed that these imposing soldiers must be guilty of the crime that the delicate and lithe Nayirah accused them of.

10. The lack of forensic evidence of alleged atrocities—no bodies, blood stains or debris—is explained away by the group by claiming that all evidence was destroyed by the enemy.

If a warring side claims that a specific war crime has taken place at a certain location, we would expect some trace of the crime to be present. If not, then the story is likely a hoax; however, the opposing side will likely claim a mass clean up by the enemy, despite the fact that even minute traces of DNA and evidence of staging or clean up would still be amply noticeable to the trained forensic expert. Furthermore, there can be other corroborating evidence, such as satellite pictures or digital tapes.

To kill hundreds or thousands of people is no simple matter: it's messy, it's time-consuming and it leaves traces of the criminal's handiwork. Not every victim is going to go easily, and blood and bone fragments will likely be left behind. Clothing fragments, teeth and hair will also be present, even if there is a thorough clean up. Burning bodies will also leave behind telltale clues. Satellite cameras may be focused in the area to catch the warring side in the act. There will be some evidence left behind, even if there is an attempted cover up. When there is no trace, even after a thorough investigation, it can be assumed that the event did not take place at that location.

Taking the above red flags together, what you are trying to do is to think before you allow your emotions to cloud your judgment. Propaganda works because it invokes the opposite: it requires the audiences to react instead of reflect, and act before they've had the chance to mull over the details. Propaganda would be ineffective if it appealed on an ideological or intellectual level—what if the person has a different ideological bent or educational level? Then these disparities would allow too many people to oppose and expose the propagandist's lies, which is not what the propagandist wants. He or she wants to make sure almost everyone reacts without thinking.

By thinking first and evaluating each claim carefully, you can weed out real atrocities from manipulative lies to feel sympathy for and outrage toward someone who really deserves it.

Chapter **Eleven**

| **The Mistake**

Many types of "twist" stories make reporters drool: a clean-cut politician is caught having an affair with a sordid individual; a prestigious multinational conglomerate's dubious accounting practices finally come to light; a suburban father mows down his nine children; a mild-mannered federal agent turns out to be a turncoat. What these stories have in common is that they all exploit and contort the conventional roles that players are assigned by the press: who we think is the hero really turns out to be the villain (very rarely will a journalistically-deemed villain ever turn out to be a secret hero).

Though these personality transformations seem as if they come out of the blue, what they actually show is that many journalists didn't dig far enough (or at least ignored or suppressed previous damning evidence to make the person fit a certain role) before they declared a certain person or institution to be "good" or at least trustworthy.

Another boffo story in this vein is the surprise detractor: a high-ranking expert or official publicly and suddenly slams his fellow colleagues. Maybe a former Democratic governor lambastes his left-leaning successor for not being true to his blue stripes or a former executive blows the whistle on his company's incompetence. Here, the story is all about an institution's sad decline—even former members of that redoubtable group are getting fed up with their clique's chicanery.

It looked like the *New York Post*'s Brian Blomquist found just that sort of story when his May 16, 1997 article revealed that Robert B. Fiske, the former Whitewater special council, was not too pleased with Kenneth Starr, the current special council. In an exclusive interview with Blomquist, Fiske told the reporter how he really felt about the investigation:

> The first Whitewater independent counsel says he thinks his successor has come up empty in his probe of President Clinton and the First Lady.
>
> "I don't think they have anything," Robert Fiske told the *Post* yesterday in his first public comments on Kenneth Starr's probe.
>
> "I don't think they have any evidence to go forward with the investigation. I don't know what Starr is doing."

> Fiske said it's "highly unlikely" Starr is holding onto sealed indictments issued by the Washington-based Whitewater grand jury that folded last week.
>
> "If he had enough evidence to lay a stick on anyone involved in this matter, I think he would have released it..."

The article made a splash, and it seemed that Blomquist had trumped his colleagues with his biting exclusive; that is, until Robert Fiske called the *Post* to say that he didn't give an interview to Blomquist. In fact, he never spoke to any reporter on the subject or made those sorts of outrageous comments. But Blomquist did speak to a lawyer named Robert Fisk. Problem was, Blomquist just didn't get the right one.

What started as a simple case of mistaken identity spiraled into something more embarrassing. A Robert Fisk (note the spelling), who was a Washington, DC lawyer, decided not to correct Blomquist after fielding several requests by other mistaken journalists. Fisk apparently got sick and tired of reporters confusing him with Fiske and pretended to be Fiske. The *Post* corrected its mistake with the temper tantrum headline "Just a nobody." Blomquist was flown to the *Post*'s New York headquarters for a verbal spanking.

As smirk-inducing as that gaffe was, it wasn't the last mistake to grace the pages of the *Post*. A few years later, the *Post* lamented in an October 17, 2003 editorial that the New York Yankees had lost a critical baseball game:

> Despite holding a 3-2 lead in games over the Boston Red Sox, the Yankees couldn't get the job done at home; their season ended last night in the seventh game of the American League Championship Series.

The editorial went on to gripe that, "In the end, though, the hitting fell short and the bullpen simply didn't deliver. It's a crying shame that Roger Clemens' career had to end on a losing note." The article ended on a philosophically optimistic note: "Wait'll next year!"

If it was the *Post*'s wish for the Yankees to win, then Christmas came a couple of months early for the paper: the Yankees actually won the game. The *Post* simply ran the story before the game was over, assuming the Yankees couldn't reverse their fortunes by the deadline. What the scribes didn't realize is that nothing is certain in life except death, taxes and that attention-starved starlets are willing to sink to any level just to get another five minutes of fame. The *Post* scribe didn't wait until the game was over to write the editorial.

Nor did they wait a few months later when a front page "exclusive" story in their July 6, 2004 edition that carried the headline "Kerry picks Gephardt":

> John Kerry has chosen Rep. Richard Gephardt, the veteran congressman from Missouri, to be his running mate, *The Post* has learned.

> Gephardt, sixty-three, a twenty-eight year veteran of the House of Representatives, could be named by the presumptive Democratic nominee as the party's vice-presidential candidate as soon as today.

The scoop may have been an "exclusive," but it wasn't the least bit accurate about Kerry's choice for veep. The Democratic presidential candidate had, in fact, picked North Carolina Senator John Edwards as his running mate.

But let's not single out the *Post*; after all, it does have its strong points, such as the gossipy "Page Six" which gives much-needed free advertising to passé celebrities. Speaking of celebrity gossip, London's *Daily Mirror* certainly was game for it when Sir Paul McCartney and his wife Heather Mills welcomed their new baby. The *Mirror* seemed to out-scoop its rivals with an October 30, 2003 front-page headline loudly declaring "It's a boy!" The article added "The baby—probably to be called Joseph—was not due until the end of November. A Caesarean had originally been planned in mid-November, two weeks early."

The article itself seemed informative, except that McCartney and his wife welcomed a new girl instead. In the rush to be the first to report the gender of the ex-Beatle's baby, the *Mirror* made an error that was carried on by both Reuters and *AP* before being exposed. At least the *Mirror* had a 50% chance of getting little Beatrice Milly McCartney's gender right.

Declaring the wrong sports team the winner (as the *Tampa Tribune* did in a June 8, 2004 editorial), or getting the gender of a musician's infant wrong are embarrassing, but at least those mistakes aren't inexcusable. On November 3, 1948, when Harry S Truman and Thomas E. Dewey both ran for U.S. president, the *Chicago Daily Tribune* ran with the now infamous front-page headline "Dewey Defeats Truman." Too bad it was Truman who won the election. In the rush to declare the election's winner, the paper made the wrong call and lost face as a result.

Why Journalists Make Mistakes in Their Stories

There is a very simple reason why journalists make errors in their reports: reporters are humans. Just as your waiter can get your order wrong or a college scheduler can accidentally book a class of 200 into a room that has a maximum capacity of forty, reporters too can relay erroneous information as facts. The difference between reporters' mistakes and most everybody else's is that journalists' goofs are more likely to be made in front of an audience.

Take, for instance, the *New York Daily News'* front-page headline in its January 29, 2004 edition that screamed "City Under Siege! Parking tix on pace to break $1B for year." The article told New Yorkers that any parking faux pas was going to be more painful than ever:

Over a four-month period last year, more than 2.7 million parking summons were issued, up 18% from the same period in 2002. The city's ticket blitz is even worse than you thought.

There are so many parking summons being written that the city is on pace to crack $1 billion in revenue from parking fines this fiscal year—a first.

However, the *Daily News'* numbers were off—revenues were projected to be in the ballpark of about $540 million, almost half of what the newspaper reported. While over half a billion dollars is quite a tidy sum for a city to collect from mere parking tickets, it was nowhere near the magical "billion" figure many headline writers love to use. To its credit, the *Daily News* got its math wrong and made a correction on its front page the following day.

But the human tendency to screw up doesn't excuse journalists and editors from all of the mistakes they make. Sometimes the error is a minor one: a magazine's senior editor is misidentified as a managing editor, a person's name is misspelled or a large company's quarterly earnings are wrongly reported by a hundred thousand dollars. No one, no matter how brilliant and careful, has ever gone through his entire life without making a single mistake. Mistakes happen—that's why newspapers have a "Corrections" segment in the front section.

These benign and innocent mistakes don't usually get reporters into trouble, but in Blomquist's case, they did. Sometimes the wrong person is identified as a child molester. A company is falsely accused of wrongdoing based on a miscommunication. These errors happen, not because the reporter sets out to deceive or is being duped by a hoaxer, but because he honestly believes that that's what happened. In the Blomquist case, he thought he had the right Robert Fiske, and the voice on the other end confirmed it. Blomquist simply ignored one glaring problem—that Fisk wasn't a reasonable facsimile of Fiske.

Journalistic mistakes are more likely to happen when reporters are rushed, since there is less time and more pressure to deliver important news. Even before the Internet explosion, reporters were still under pressure to perform on short notice, but there was ample time to double-check information. Now, with all-news channels and Internet news sites, news can come too fast, and neither the news producer or consumer have time to think carefully about the veracity of a source's claims. Snap decisions can be humiliating or even dangerous.

This desperation can lead to normally intelligent journalists believing truly fantastic yarns. Guards are let down, leading to reporters making careless errors in their work. The desire to find a titillating quirk can get reporters into embarrassing trouble, too. The November 12, 2003 edition of the *New York Times* ran an obituary for noted photographer Marvin Smith. Though

Smith was praised for his life's work and the obituary made mention of Smith's close relationship with his twin brother Morgan, the *Times* could not help but add this tidbit:

> The brothers were so close that Marvin never used the pronoun "I," much less claimed credit for a particular photo. After Morgan died of testicular cancer, Marvin had his own testicles removed.
>
> "He continued to say 'we,'" Dr. Willis-Kennedy said.

Surprising, yes; accurate, no. First, Morgan Smith died of prostrate cancer; second, Marvin Smith kept his testicles right where they were. The author of the obit relied on the word of a single source without first verifying the accuracy of this outlandish claim. While the Smith brothers shared a deep fraternal bond, even marrying identical twin sisters, their togetherness stopped there. How much time did the *Times'* writers spend in verifying such a personal claim? In its correction, editors conceded that the writer had heard the allegation from a single source, without finding corroboration— but if the story was true, why publish such a disrespectful and irrelevant factoid in someone's obituary in the first place?

Mistakes can be found everywhere: on television, newspapers and radio, on the front page and at the tail end of a newscast. The news consumer needs ways to spot mistakes. Lead stories are vulnerable to errors, but smaller, straightforward stories are as well.

Getting the Story Before it Happens

Obituaries are a newspaper mainstay: Who died? From what? When? What mark did this person leave in the world? Who grieves over this dearly departed? These are important questions for most of us: there is comfort in knowing that we have left a good impression on those around us when we're gone and since it's highly unlikely we'll ever read our own obits, the next best thing is to read how others are treated in theirs.

Most newspapers carry paid death notices and also obits of people of note: performers, artists, writers, politicians, athletes, researchers, activities, socialites, tycoons and anyone else who has made a public impression. These will be posthumous profiles of who was who. The basic information these obits will tell the reader is:

• Who died?
• When?
• Where?
• How/why the individual died;
• Achievements/claim to fame;

• Memorable quotes from the deceased, if any;
• Possibly quotes from a colleague or high profile individual who knew the deceased;
• Who the deceased leaves behind.

There is very little deviation from this formula. In North America, at least, obituaries are supposed to be a forum to briefly discuss the distinguished life of the individual in as kind and charitable of a way as possible, while still maintaining accurate and relevant information. Obituaries aren't usually the place for a scribe to get creative.

But the rules don't always work out that way. Marvin Smith was accused by the *Times* of having fewer body parts than he did, but could other deviations mean that there is factually suspect material within the obit?

Katherine Sergava was a dancer and actress of some note in the 1930s that went on to teach the craft in her later years. The November 29, 2003 edition of the *London Daily Telegraph* announced her passing on November 11, saddening her admirers and fans alike:

> Kathryn Sergava, who has died aged ninety-four, was the sloe-eyed Russian siren taken up by Metro-Goldwyn-Mayer to replace Greta Garbo when the great actress decided to retire from Hollywood in 1934.

Though the *Telegraph* did not mention the circumstances surrounding the actress' death (you know, those irritatingly minor questions news articles are supposed to answer, such as where, why and how she died), it did make mention of how the attractive actress failed to live up to expectations of becoming the next Garbo. The article did not quote anyone who had known Sergava personally, though in many obits this is not uncommon. The *New York Times* followed up with their own Sergava obit on December 4:

> Katharine Sergava, the dancer and actress who portrayed the dream-ballet version of Laurey, the heroine, in the original production of "Oklahoma!" died on Nov. 11 in Palm Springs, Calif., where she had settled in the mid-1960s.

Various sources gave the year of her birth as 1909 or 1918, and she was also occasionally billed as Kathryn Sergava and Katya Sergeiva.

How Sergava died was still a mystery, but the *Times* had at least nailed the "where." Reports of Sergava's death were reported on *Playbill* magazine's website, as well as the Internet Movie Database, which had carried the news in the "biography" section of Sergava's listing. The obit may not have been overly informative, but it gave the reader a sense of a bygone actress.

There was just one small, annoying problem with the obituary: Sergava was still among the living.

Apparently no one at the *Telegraph* bothered to confirm her death. Furthermore, the *New York Times*, which did not cite the original source for the story, took their cue from the *Telegraph*. As the *Times* itself admitted, "The *Times* was unable to confirm her death independently…" But the *Times* gave her place of death as California, while acquaintances that knew the actress said she wasn't living in Palm Springs, but Manhattan. Both the *Telegraph* and the *Times* couldn't agree to the spelling of Sergava's first name (though Sergava's name has been spelled Katherine, Kathryn, Katharine, Katharina and Katerina), and didn't confirm the actress' death with her family.

In this case, two highly respected newspapers wrote about the death of a woman of note—and no one working for either paper confirmed Sergava's death. If a report of someone's death is missing crucial details, such as the cause, then the journalist hasn't done a thorough job of researching her piece.

Lest you are feeling jealous of the perks associated with fame, even the non-famous can create their very own pre-death obits. Robert Michael Mathison may have gotten himself in some trouble during his time, like getting arrested for theft, assault and faking a heart attack during his arrest, but a short, paid obituary in the *St. Paul Pioneer Press* on July 15, 2003 let readers know that, deep down, he was a good man: "Mathison, Robert M. Age fifty of St. Paul. Died on July 12, 2003. Loved by everyone; loved everyone. Survived by three sons, Shawn, Jeremiah, Ryan and daughter Courtney. Private services."

The obit was also faxed to the judge assigned to Mathison's case. Fortunately, the judge, who was aware of Mathison's history of faking coronaries, thought that it wouldn't be beneath Mathison to try to fake his own death. Mathison was found alive and well and was promptly arrested. However, while a spokeswoman for the Pioneer Press said later that while the paper usually double-checks paid death notices placed by the deceased's family before publication, that somehow Mathison's brief obituary managed to get past editors without being confirmed. Since most paid obits are submitted to the newspaper by the funeral home, an unusually brief obit submitted by someone not affiliated with a home should have been flagged. It wasn't.

But this wasn't the only pseudo-obit to make the rounds. *The Milford Cabinet*, a weekly newspaper in New Hampshire, ran an obit on August 14, 2003 announcing the untimely death of Kathleen M. Connor-Allwarden, complete with a professional-looking photo of the forty-four-year-old who, according to the following obit, died from "undetermined causes":

When she taught figure skating for the N.F.S.A., she discovered that she delighted in children. She earned a bachelor of science in elementary education from Plymouth State College, and then worked at Carpenter Elementary School in Wolfeboro for six years, teaching first and third grades. While living in Wolfeboro, she began a figure skating program for the town, which has grown to be a successful recreational program.

The glowing obit was factually accurate in every way but one: Ms. Connor-Allwarden was still alive. Apparently, someone dropped off the obit at the *Cabinet* offices and the paper ran it without anyone verifying the information. No one was the wiser until Connor-Allwarden's parents phoned the paper to correct the error. *Cabinet* editor Michael Cleveland defended his paper's practice of running submitted obituaries without confirmation in an interview with *Associated Press*: "We never go: 'Prove it!' We still feel we can trust our readers." Though Milford police sent the letter for forensic testing, the sender of the obit was never publicly revealed.

At least it wasn't as bad as Gertrude Thomas' false obituary—the sixty-seven-year-old Wombourn, Britain woman was also the victim of a fake obituary in October 1969, except that her mother had read the obit and promptly died of a heart attack. Newspapers need to show caution before running even paid obituaries.

When Surviving a Lethal Accident in a War-Torn Country Just Isn't Heroic Enough

War heroes almost always make excellent copy: people who agree to risk their lives in dangerous places on behalf of their country are considered by many to be brave and honorable. Second, the more horrific the predicament, the more likely it will grab the attention of the news media, especially since the survivor outwitted both the elements and the enemy. A soldier injured while doing the limbo in a foreign night club just doesn't pass media muster; a soldier who lost a limb while saving his comrades and fighting the savage enemy will find himself getting top billing on every news broadcast in the country. Being a brave altruistic warrior makes you the stuff of legends.

The 2003 U.S.-Iraqi war was controversial and marked by a growing list of deaths and casualties, but there was at least one bright light—Jessica Lynch. Private First Class Lynch was blonde, slender and had a winsome smile. The West Virginia native wanted to be a schoolteacher, but she followed in her brother's footsteps and joined the military, eventually getting deployed to Iraq as a supply clerk. On March 23, 2003, word came in that Lynch had perished along with her comrades in the 507th Maintenance Company when they were ambushed by Iraqi soldiers near Nasiriyah.

There was a happy twist to this bloody saga: it turned out that Lynch didn't die after all. She not only survived the ambush, but was rescued ten days later by her fellow soldiers and saviors, who videotaped the operation. Though she was seriously injured, Americans rejoiced that Lynch had survived.

Then the media frenzy began: who would be the first to report on all the lurid details of Lynch's capture, captivity and rescue? Ultimately, it was the *Washington Post* that first broke the story of Private Lynch's capture, ordeal and rescue.

But to get the "scoop," the *Post* relied only on unnamed "U.S. officials" who, according to the *Post*, claimed that Lynch's initial capture was violent and potentially lethal. Many readers also learned that Private Lynch actually had a streak of Lara Croft to her:

> Pfc. Jessica Lynch, rescued Tuesday from an Iraqi hospital, fought fiercely and shot several enemy soldiers after Iraqi forces ambushed the Army's 507th Ordnance Maintenance Company, firing her weapon until she ran out of ammunition, U.S. officials said yesterday.
>
> Lynch, a nineteen-year-old supply clerk, continued firing at the Iraqis even after she sustained multiple gunshot wounds and watched several other soldiers in her unit die around her in fighting March 23, one official said. The ambush took place after a 507th convoy, supporting the advancing 3rd Infantry Division, took a wrong turn near the southern city of Nasiriyah.
>
> "She was fighting to the death," the official said. "She did not want to be taken alive."
>
> Lynch was also stabbed when Iraqi forces closed in on her position, the official said, noting that initial intelligence reports indicated that she had been stabbed to death. No official gave any indication yesterday, however, that Lynch's wounds had been life-threatening.

Strangely, this front-page story did not include any forensic evidence supporting the official account of Lynch's ordeal, any eyewitness accounts of the events, or even an interview with Lynch herself (though, on this last point, at the time Lynch was most likely too wounded to grant any interviews). The entire account was supported on a single type of source; that is, unnamed officials.

Even then, the identities of the "U.S. officials" in question were also kept secret from *Post* readers: how many officials did the *Post* reporters interview for the story? From which government or military branch(es) did these sources come from? What were their qualifications? How did these sources gather their evidence? Did they speak to Lynch directly or did they get the information third or fourth hand? How reliable have these officials been in the past? Why did these officials demand to remain nameless? Did these reporters try to independently confirm these details with other avenues of evidence? If the events took place as described, why did the State Department refuse to confirm this account of events? Though not one of these questions were answered for *Post* readers, the officials' account of Lynch's ordeal was good enough for *Post* journalists and editors to publish.

Though the editors at the *Post* stood by this account (seeming to have full trust in their sources), their first about-face came one month later, when the paper finally admitted that much of their initial account of Lynch's ordeal was not true, including the claims that Lynch was shot, stabbed and had used a firearm in self defense.

While the revised (and presumably more accurate) account does not detract from Lynch's bravery or ordeal, however, the second telling of the soldier's story paints a vastly different picture than the original article. The first account sounds similar to a combat-themed comic book; the second shows a young and inexperienced person thrust into a complicated ordeal. Later, even the U.S. military's account of events during the rescue was also called into question. In each case, the original accounts made their way into the press without corroboration or resistance.

Had journalists in this case delved into the "official" version of events, they would be more likely to see flaws in the officials' story. For starters, how realistic was it that a critically injured person would be able to fire such a weapon? Were there any credible individuals who could confirm the events in question? How did these officials come to their information? Wouldn't they have a vested interest in portraying Lynch in grander terms than might be physically possible? Couldn't this account be nothing more than war propaganda?

In the second account, the *Post* did rely on forensic evidence and eyewitness accounts, resulting in a story with a far different tone. Many in the media wanted a dramatic story of the mythic heroism of a young soldier valiantly facing down and defeating death: such a story would serve as dramatic fodder for the front pages. When *Post* reporters appealed to authority what they got was a suspenseful, sensational and feel-good tale of heroism; when they relied on multiple sources of information from various sides, the account of events was suddenly tempered and more realistic. Why didn't *Post* reporters attempt to critically reconstruct the story to look for any logical, physical or chronological inconsistencies? Didn't anyone try to independently verify the official account of events?

Some may argue that in times of war, journalists have no choice but to rely on authority for their information, for practical as well as security reasons, but even during times of peace, journalists use the same non-rigorous methods to gather and analyze information. There is an assumption that when quoting information originating from an authority, that authority is above reproach. What is worse, many journalists will rely only on a second or third hand account of an authority figure's opinion, without ever confirming whether what they are being told is the truth. In the Lynch case, the government needed a superhero in a hurry.

Journalists are equally blind and careless when an institution needs a super villain in a pinch, as the next example shows.

From Hero to Villain to Victim

The Olympics are usually reliable to grab audiences, especially if they take place on U.S. soil and/or Americans win lots of awards: it's a canned event loaded with suspense, patriotism, competition, well-built jocks and happy news. Everybody loves a winner, and since the Olympics are all about winning medals and endorsement deals, what else could be as guaranteed of a ratings extravaganza?

Few other events can trump a showcase of ambitious, confident and well-tended athletes—except perhaps the horror of a bomb detonating in a crowded public area. An explosion is newsworthy for the obvious reasons: it's unplanned, unpleasant and unforgiving. Just as the Olympics are all about the celebration of physical persistence and mental focus, a planned bombing shows what happens when those two qualities are mixed with a violent disposition.

But place an exploding bomb in the middle of the Olympics and the merger of two incongruous events has all the elements for a boffo story. On July 27, 1996, the excitement of the Atlanta Summer Games turned into horror when a bomb exploded in Centennial Olympic Park, killing one and injuring 111 others. In this July 30, 1996 article from the *Atlanta Journal and Constitution*, the paper introduced readers to the unassuming man who saved the day:

> He raced against time, but he's not an Olympic sprinter.
>
> Instead, this modest man with an athlete's precision had unknowingly entered a tragic race.
>
> "I ran up into the tower. I got eleven out safely. A few I had to push down the stairs," said Richard Jewell, the security guard who first noticed the suspicious-looking knapsack in Centennial Olympic Park. "We tried to get everyone away from the area. Then, the package exploded." The explosion knocked the stocky Jewell to his hands and knees, but he wasn't seriously hurt.

The article went on to describe Jewell's admirable attributes:

> Although police believe the thirty-three-year-old Jewell saved hundreds of lives with his quick thinking, that hasn't been very comforting.
>
> "I'm feeling bad about the victims that did occur," Jewell said. "If I had one wish, it would be that all the people who were victims were not victims."

One recurring theme in press reports was Jewell's down-to-earth attributes, as this *AJC* article showed:

> Bryant Steele, an AT&T spokesman who met Jewell a few days ago, said, "The action he took saved a number of lives. I think he's a pretty modest fellow about it."

USA Today had come to a similar conclusion in a July 29, 1996 story headlined "Guard's alertness in park makes him an unexpected hero":

> The biggest hero of the Atlanta Olympics is a man of modest height and stocky build, with no sport other than occasional pick-up basketball. He will get no medal and stand on no award platform.
>
> Had early Saturday morning been less eventful, there would have been no reason for anyone to know his name.
>
> But someone planted a bomb in Centennial Olympic Park.
>
> And it was Richard Jewell's fate to be the first one to find it.

Jewell became a media darling: he was a hero deserving of all the praise he received—until he turned into the prime suspect.

Within a day, Jewell seemed to have developed a split personality. The *AJC* suddenly decided that Jewell wasn't all that modest or innocent after all:

> Richard Jewell thought he was going to shake President Clinton's hand for his heroics after the bombing at Centennial Olympic Park.
>
> "Maybe they're going to surprise me," he said when asked by a reporter whether he had been informed of the possible honor. Tuesday, as police kept surveillance outside his house, suspecting him of setting the bomb that killed one and injured more than 100, the chances anyone would be shaking his hand seemed remote, at best.

The *AJC* let readers know how diabolical the Atlanta Park Hero may have been:

> Investigators now say that he may be a hero wannabe who planted the bomb so he could discover it later. While he will talk about his days as a Habersham County deputy sheriff, he did not mention that he left the job under a cloud.

But *AJC* wouldn't let readers know how they got their information. Which investigators talked to Constitution reporters? The article doesn't say. As for the "cloud," again the article didn't specify what specific evidence tainted Jewell's halo, but gave its own psychological profile of the security guard:

Richard Jewell, thirty-three, a former law enforcement officer, fits the profile of the lone bomber. This profile generally includes a frustrated white man who is a former police officer, member of the military or police "wannabe" who seeks to become a hero. Jewell has become a celebrity in the wake of the bombing, making an appearance this morning at the reopened park with Katie Couric on the *Today Show*. He also has approached newspapers, including [t]he *Atlanta Journal-Constitution*, seeking publicity for his actions.

Reporters no longer considered Jewell to be humble or low-key. When Jewell was labeled a "hero" by the *AJC*, the word "modest" came up as a frequent adjective; when suspicion fell on him, he was accused of being a media hound. So was he modest or an attention-seeker? If reporters didn't believe he was unassuming, then why did they portray him as such in the first place? Or had they now decided to downplay his modesty to make him seem like a more believable bad guy?

Other newspaper reporters also seemed eager to take their swipes at Jewell without investigating whether he was a plausible suspect. *USA Today* ran one article with the headline "Guard has been free with interviews." In a July 31 article that openly mused about Jewell's guilt or innocence:

Now he is famous. His image on every television show. His name on the minds of millions in Atlanta.

The reports say he may have planned it all. May have done it to become a hero. A famous man.

May have laid the trap for unsuspecting people to wander into.

I will wait to hear from law enforcement officials. To see if they think the modest man in the parking lot was the one who packed a bag with a pipe bomb and nails, and exploded it upon the world.

Not every media outlet jumped to conclusions, however. "60 Minutes" did a more thorough investigation and decided that Jewell's probable innocence came down to two points: first, Jewell had not been the one who initiated contact with the press, according to his employer's public relations officer, and second, during the time of the mysterious 911 phone call, Jewell was spotted evacuating people from Centennial Park—he simply did not have time to be both the villain and the hero. With this broadcast, plus other skeptical voices, Jewell finally received a reprieve.

The FBI eventually cleared Jewell who then sued various media outlets for defamation, with varying results. Though Eric Robert Rudolph was charged with the bombing in May 2003, even Jewell's obituary will link his name to his undeserved persecution.

Grief, Comfort and the Truth

Violent and explosive teenagers frighten most people: they're young, full of hate and energy, and volatile. They've been known to kill, maim and torture those who are the focus of their anger, and the worst of it is that many of those people have done nothing untoward to these young men. A victim of such brutality will almost always win the public's sympathy, but if the victim can stay valiant even when staring death in face, that too will receive media attention. Stories such of these have elements of both good and evil, and the victim can also play hero.

Littleton, Colorado was witness to such a horror on the morning of April 20, 1999, when Eric Harris and Dylan Klebold, two high school seniors, opened fire in their school, killing thirteen and injuring twenty-three. One of their victims was seventeen-year-old Cassie Bernall, who was killed in the school's library.

Cassie was a troubled teen who had managed to straighten herself out, according to her parents. Her death was noted in the media for one reason, which the *Denver Rocky Mountain News* described in an April 25, 1999 article:

> She will forever be remembered as the girl who died for her faith, the one who looked her killer in the eye and said, "Yes, I believe in God."
>
> She never said another word.
>
> In the days that have followed her death, dozens of young Christians have taken strength from Cassie's strength.

Cassie's death took a life of its own; countless news outlets repeated the story, such as *USA Today* and the *Christian Science Monitor*. ABC's "20/20" also profiled Cassie on September 10, 1999, beginning with anchor Barbara Walters' touching introduction:

> WALTERS: Now, we turn to a story of faith and courage and murder that all came together in one dramatic moment at the shooting at Columbine High. It is about the girl you may remember who died because she was affirming her faith in God. And her shining spirit brought many of us solace as we ourselves struggled to absorb the darkness of Columbine.

Turned into a martyr, Cassie represented goodness and unwavering conviction in the face of death. *Newsweek* labeled her an "evangelical saint." Cassie's parents wrote a book called *She Said Yes: The Unlikely Martyrdom of Cassie Bernall.*

However, by September of that same year, Valeen Schnurr admitted it was she who had uttered similar words when confronted by one of the gunmen. The *Associated Press* reported that another student who had heard the exchange between a female student and a gunman had realized it was Valeen who he heard, not Cassie. Valeen confirmed it. Investigators also doubted that the exchange between Cassie and her killers happened the way it was originally described. However, many reporters were reluctant to set the record straight. As one reporter noted in the October 14, 1999 edition of the *Washington Post*:

> In questions of death and faith, it's the power of the story that counts, the tale that helps the mind grasp the unfathomable. Compared with that comfort, the truth is a trifle.

The words are hardly comfort for a profession that proclaims to be interested in the truth, no matter how ugly or disappointing it may be. What started as an honest error born from fear and chaos turned into a rallying cry for many true believers. It wasn't enough that thirteen lives were taken needlessly, one of the dead had to be more angelic than the rest. The resistance to correct the record stems partly from respecting the feelings of the deceased's parents, but also because in our collective psyche, it is far nobler for a victim to die for his or her beliefs than to survive. Cassie's history was rewritten to make a better story, as if the senseless death of a young girl whose life stopped before it began wasn't moving enough.

Types of Mistakes Journalists Make and How to Spot Them

Just because someone complains about a story's inaccuracy, doesn't mean the story is actually biased or inaccurate, and if no one complains about the truthfulness, it doesn't mean the reporter didn't make a factual error. Silence means nothing. Spotting inaccurate information in a news report takes a little critical thinking and careful listening.

Even though journalists can make a myriad of mistakes, from misspelling a name to fingering a wrong murder suspect, in many cases, it is still possible for you to spot those mistakes on your own if you know what signs to look for in a faulty article. The best way to catch possible mistakes is to look at the type of story you're reading or watching. Certain stories are more vulnerable to serious factual errors than others. The way to spot potential errors is to look for the following trouble spots:

1. Appealing to Authority

Appealing to authority is a common logic error: the phrase simply means that a person bases his knowledge on the word of an expert or official instead of on facts. While there might be comfort in knowing that your doctor thinks that it's only a cold sore, it would be better and more reassuring if he ran some tests to confirm his diagnosis. If you believe that an authority's word has equal weight as research, facts, experimental results and numbers, you might find yourself in trouble later on, especially if your expert has his medical license revoked for being a quack.

Even if he doesn't get in trouble with the American Medical Association, an expert's opinion is still an opinion and cannot be confused with hard, tangible and *verifiable* data. Without support of facts, the person appealing to an authority is simply saying, "this opinion is true since an expert or official believes it's true." However, an expert can be wrong, lying, confused or misinterpreting data.

What we need is evidence, not an opinion, no matter how qualified the authority. We need to know what data the authority based his or her opinion on before we can make an informed decision; otherwise, we're relying on other people to do our thinking for us. There is a reason why appeal to authority is considered to be flawed logic.

Sometimes it feels as if journalists haven't taken many courses in logic or critical thinking: the credibility of many stories strictly hinges on the word of an official or expert. On the one hand, authorities can confirm information that could otherwise not be confirmed elsewhere, but in other cases, the reporter uses an authority's assertion as a substitute for hard data.

Take one example of a *Newsweek* reporter appealing to an authority: "And, while the vast majority of teen prostitutes today are runaways, illegal immigrants and children of poor urban areas, experts say a growing number now come from middle-class homes." In this same article, the reporter states that there is no hard statistical data to support this assertion. As *Slate*'s Jack Shafer pointed out, if there are no statistics kept on the number of middle class teen prostitutes, then how do we know whether the numbers are truly increasing?

Some reporters will quote anonymous officials from another journalist's story without actually trying to independently identify those experts themselves. For example, one *Washington Post* article attributed one piece of information to what an "unnamed official told the Reuters news service." In this case, the *Post* journalist has to be confident that, one, the Reuters reporter is both telling the truth and has his or her facts straight and, two, that the unnamed official is telling the truth, has his or her facts straight and is a credible source of information.

An authority figure (whether it be a government official, scholarly expert or licensed professional) may not be flat out lying: he could be mistaken, misinformed or trying to spin information to make himself or his cause look more favorable. The motivation behind giving reporters information isn't always important—the information may be right, but without other confirming evidence, there is a good chance the information may be inaccurate or misleading.

When the reporter identifies the authority figure by name, the audience can determine for themselves whether the source is credible (e.g., the audience can look up the source's credentials). If the authority agrees to speak only on condition of anonymity, then the audience is asked to assume the nameless source is credible. But now the report has missing information because the journalist has given in to their junior Deep Throat without trying to ask the source to go on record or finding another source who will speak on the record. In a way, this agreement may mean the reporter has confirmed the information that the anonymous source has told them.

For example, one January 9, 2004 *AP* news item stated that "...[P]resident [George W. Bush] wants to aggressively reinvigorate the space program, still reeling from the Columbia tragedy nearly one year ago, said the officials, speaking on condition of anonymity." How many officials said this to the reporter? How would they know? Why wouldn't they say this on the record? Why wouldn't they commit themselves to a seemingly benign statement? Wouldn't they be fired? Reprimanded? Or was the information too tentative?

When reading or listening to a news report that relies on the word of authorities, question the information carefully. Here's a checklist of questions you should ask when listening to an authority figure in a news story:

• How is the source used? To give context or information, or to push an agenda or point of view?

• How credible is the authority? How likely is it that they have access to information?

• Has the authority had a chance to reflect and review information, or is this a breaking story and might the information coming in be sketchy?

• Is the authority giving factual information or offering her opinion?

• Is the authority stating facts outright or qualifying what he says with phrases such as, "I think," "I believe," "it is possible" or "seems to be"?

• What percent of the authority's assertions are based on concrete, provable evidence?

• How much is the reporter relying on the word of an "official source"? How much is the reporter relying on other sources of information, such as documents, eyewitnesses, etc.?

• What assumptions is the authority figure making?

• How specific is the reporter when naming a source? Is the source mentioned by name and title or is he over-relying on secret "high-ranking officials"? Does the journalist use a single anonymous source or several?

• How important is the authority figure in the story? Is the figure a central part of the story? Is the most important information coming from the authority figure? Could the report stand on its own without the official source or expert?

In both the Jewell and Lynch cases, reporters mostly relied on unnamed authority figures for their information. Unless there is corroborating evidence to support what an authority says, don't mistake an official source with an infallible one.

2. Putting a "Face" on a Story

One of the most powerful images to humans is the face: infants as young as two months can recognize faces. People can easily relate to faces—especially if the face is sympathetic and shows emotion (love, pain, fear, anger).

Journalists and editors instinctually know the importance of showing faces in their stories—it is a real way for readers and viewers to relate to a story and feel the same emotions as the person they see or read about. Some of the most powerful and moving news photographs are of people, not scenes of war, buildings or nature. Alan Diaz's photograph captured the moment when armed federal agents raided a Miami home and took a young Cuban boy named Elian Gonzales from his U.S. relatives to return him to his father, and the fear on the boy's face moved many. When a screaming young girl named Kim Phuc ran naked through the streets during a napalm attack during the Viet Nam War, Nick Ut's 1972 photo instantly became part of modern history.

Giving a face to a story goes beyond the visual: it means reporters have to find someone whose life has been directly affected by a current event. Instead of merely talking about crime statistics, a reporter interviews a victim of crime: tears or anger make the dry story come to life. The horrors of war atrocities are better explained if the journalist profiles someone who was tortured in a war-torn country. A story about breast cancer is more powerful if the reporter interviews someone battling the disease rather than showing the audience graphs and charts. Inherently, there is nothing wrong with this practice—we relate to people better than we do to hypothetical constructs. We can talk about welfare reform, but seeing people whose life was impacted by those policies would get the point across.

For news outlets, it's all about the face—the face of a victim, the face of success, the face of terror or the face of a killer—but in the rush to find a "face," many reporters become so desperate to trump their rivals, that any face will do. It may not matter to the reporter if he has used the wrong face; so long as there are visuals to go with the story. Journalists may also find the right face, but in the rush to show the "face" first, they may not get all their facts straight. Of course, most reporters don't consciously think this way—the problem is that they aren't thinking rationally when ratings and bragging rights are in question.

When a major unexpected event happens, reporters look to "humanize" the story; the problem arises when the real "face" is overshadowed by charlatans and con artists who want the limelight for themselves. Also, if both the media and an authoritative institution (law enforcement, government, military) are pressured to find a face quickly, it is here that a news consumer should think whether the person presented to them is the right one and whether information gathered about that person is accurate. Is the face being shown the right one? Did reporters, law enforcement or government have enough time to get all the facts and put them in the right context?

In the case of Richard Jewell, police were under enormous international pressure to find "the villain" quickly. In the Jessica Lynch case, reporters were competing to be the first to talk about the soldier behind the face. The Columbine massacre needed to be personalized, but in the confusion, Cassie Bernall was credited for saying something that she most likely didn't say. When there is a rush to personalize a story, you need to ask whether this is the right person, and—if so—did the reporter have enough time to thoroughly determine exactly what happened?

3. Using a Single Source

This type of shoddy investigation technique comes from the "my mom said so" school of research. If one allegedly credible source makes an assertion, the reporter believes not only that the assertion is right, but that he doesn't need to double check the fact. For example, if a journalist said, "according to an official," what is he actually saying? Simple: he has taken his source at face value and hasn't tried to back his statement. In other words, he is relying on a single source.

North American reporters don't often rely on only one person for their information. Unfortunately, many do tend to fall back on using two sources, as is the case when reporters seek to find "both sides of the story." But if an issue has more than two sides, at least one side is going to be shut out of the story. Some other reporters use the "three-source rule": if the same factoid is confirmed to be true by three independent sources, then the journalist can print or broadcast that piece of information. In the absence of other types of documentation, the three-source rule can be considered thorough. There is an attempt to get to the truth by comparing and contrasting information from a variety of sources.

However, one problem with the three-source rule occurs when all three sources are getting their information from the same unreliable megasource. This comes from the equally problematic "my mom and dad said so" school of research. In this case, multiple sources are giving the reporter false confirmation—maybe mom and dad did say so, but dad asked mom before he answered the question. Since all three sources relied on the same source, the reporter unknowingly has relied on a single source for his information.

In the Jessica Lynch case, multiple "officials" gave Post reporters a valiant but false account of the young soldier's ordeal, but could anyone else corroborate this version of events? In the Richard Jewell case, what specific evidence was there to corroborate the "official" allegations that Jewell may have planted the bomb? There wasn't any forensic evidence, except for his "psychological profile." Profiles can be helpful in finding criminals, but in the case of Jewell, even the profile was wrong. In the Marvin Smith obit, the writer only spoke to one person who made the outrageous claim. With the *New York Times'* Sergava obit, the writer relied on another paper's error. If the reporter is relying on one source only, then believe the story at your own peril.

4. The Rush to Get the "Get"

News outlets only get the glory when they break an important or sensational story first. Unfortunately, when a reporter "breaks" a story, it often leads to him breaking his profession's credibility in the process. Digging, confirming and corroborating information takes time, but if other rivals are nipping at the journalist's heels, he may cut corners to beat the competition. That means accuracy is sacrificed for bragging rights.

When reporters rush, the truth suffers. For example, when Martha Stewart was convicted on all four charges related to selling her Imclone shares on March 5, 2004, both NBC and CNBC reported on the air live that Stewart was found not guilty on some of the charges. In the rush to be the first, the network dropped the ball.

In the Lynch case, the *Washington Post's* drive to be the first outlet to report the details of her capture and rescue led to the paper disseminating false information without questioning its sources. In the Jewell case, the *Atlanta Journal and Constitution* also broke the story that Jewell was a suspect, which led to the persecution of an innocent man. In the Robert Fiske case, the reporter's desire to out-scoop his colleagues with an eye-popping interview led to careless mistakes.

5. The Too Pat "Role"

If the subject of an article seems too good or bad to be true, it is a clear sign that the reporter may have downplayed or overplayed certain facts for the person to "fit" into the designated role. In the Lynch case, she wasn't simply portrayed as a hero, but as a cinematic action hero, valiantly struggling against the forces of evil in order to bring truth, justice and the American Way to the good people of Iraq. Cassie Bernall wasn't portrayed as a typical teenaged girl whose life was cut short by a self-indulgent hoodlum, but as an angelic martyr who seemed to become a casualty in a Holy War.

When Jewell was seen as the good guy, he was portrayed as the modest, aw-shucks hero whose keen senses and bravery saved lives. When he suddenly was deemed the bad guy, Jewell became a publicity-hungry mama's boy who seemed shifty and diabolical. Within a day, Jewell seemed to be afflicted with a sudden personality transplant: from humble and kind to vain and cruel. Either the *AJC* got Jewell's personality traits wrong the first time or the second—was Jewell as good or as bad as the paper claimed? When Jewell was cleared, the damage had already been done.

Lynch was lionized at a crucial time when the US government needed a feel-good war story to maintain public support for the Iraqi invasion. Jewell was demonized to assure international audiences that the U.S.-held Olympics were safe, and that law enforcement could quickly catch their man. When angels or demons make news, it is a good time to question how saintly or sinful the players really are.

When judging a news story, look for all the red flags: time constraints, roles, appeals to authority and shoddy sourcing. If the face is presented in a certain light by a single source—who happens to carry the label "unnamed" or "anonymous" in front of it—it is mostly likely that this person's account of reality will not be the final or accurate version of events. In other words, the first account of a big story is going have to have some serious rewrites.

Section **Three**

Hoaxes

Chapter **Twelve**

| **Reporter as Victim**

Consider the kindness of strangers: just when you think human beings are a rotten and self-indulgent bunch, they do something to restore your faith in them. One minute, a band of heartless teenage thugs strangles a little kid's dog in front of him in a small, obscure town in Alberta; the next minute, hundreds of strangers from around the continent start up a brimming reward fund to help the boy's distraught family bring those despicable young hoods to justice.

But how would those hundreds of good citizens even know about the poor boy's plight? They read it in the paper, saw it on television or even found the chilling tale on the Internet. They saw the boy's sad face, or read these powerful opening paragraphs from the February 4, 2002 edition of the *Ottawa Citizen*:

> A ten-year-old St. Albert boy watched helplessly Saturday afternoon as three jeering teens hanged his pet dog, Sheba, from playground equipment.
>
> The apparently senseless violence shocked even police investigating the case and has caused an outpouring of sympathy.
>
> "I've never dealt with anything like this before in terms of somebody maliciously killing an animal," said Const. Mike Moulds, a fourteen-year veteran officer working at the St. Albert RCMP detachment. "This is quite disturbing to think that people could do this. Very disturbing," said Const. Moulds.

While such unfeigned outpouring of generosity is touching, what's more interesting is that people will give money to strangers without questioning whether the newspaper's account of the event is true. But how could the boy's tale not be true? It's an airtight case: the boy looks sad. He made his story public. Besides, children never lie, or at least they aren't so good as to fool grown-ups. We all know how despicable groups of teens can be to helpless little kids and their pets at playgrounds on weekends. The police are investigating the case. And most important, the media reported the story, and they would not publish or broadcast the information without checking it out first. With all this hard evidence, it stands to reason that the story has to be true.

The trouble is, the three vicious teenagers didn't exist, and the truth behind the dog's grisly fate was less dramatic. So, how did this hoax make headlines throughout North America without any journalists questioning whether the boy would have a motive to lie? By using the same flawed logic outlined above—and not using basic researching skills to find out whether the boy's account was true.

By now, it should be obvious that sad and disturbing stories are likely to cause many people to want to do something to help those in trouble. Journalists and editors should know that by reporting traumatic tales of woe, ordinary citizens would feel compelled to donate their time and money to help a distressed and traumatized youngster who helplessly witnessed the gratuitous torture and murder of his beloved dog.

Yet journalists still publicized such potentially exploitative stories without carefully verifying the truthfulness of those events. But both broadcast and print journalists did not probe further or consider the ramifications if the story were proven false. Ironically, in the same Citizen article, one man summed up why journalists should have been more skeptical:

> "We see things in the paper every day. There are all sorts of injustices, but this just rubs me the wrong way," said Calgary's Clint Undseth, thirty-seven, who is also a dog owner. "This young boy having to watch his dog hanged in front of him, I mean, my God, what's that?"

The job of any good reporter is to unearth accurate and relevant raw information and then process and present that information in an engaging, accessible and easy to understand way, without talking down to the audience. Finding good and new information isn't easy—especially since most people aren't willing to divulge damaging or unflattering information about themselves or their organizations.

Some people shun traditional media, believing that the truth can be found on the World Wide Web. However, the Internet is full of old and repetitive information: there are countless websites discussing the secret identities of obscure super heroes and crop circles, not to mention the countless eyebrow raising number of hoaxes and scams that have come to life through the web. Bad information is everywhere.

Most journalists would defend themselves by correctly pointing out that the Internet isn't policed. Conventional media are supposed to have checks and balances—the process of gate-keeping is supposed to ensure that bad information is not made public, because reporters weed it out and remove it. Journalists would also argue that, unlike Internet sources, media have the training and the resources to find stories that others cannot. Yet new and old media have let a myriad of hoaxers present fraudulent data as real—no matter where you look for information, wading through it requires scrutiny.

How Journalists Get Conned

Journalism and the Olympics share something in common: no one remembers who came in second place. The pressure to come in first with a scoop or interview drives the journalistic machine. Repetition leads to audience boredom and eventual distraction; a new stimulus grabs eyeballs and boosts circulation. What matters in the news world is which newsmagazine or morning show will land the first interview with the victim of the week, not which outlet did a more thorough job.

In the quest to grab attention, journalists are also more likely to run with emotional and sensational events, rather than more mundane issues. An attention-grabbing story needs to make viewers angry, scared or tearful. Unfortunately, there are times when a reporter's hunger to trump his rivals and get the story first leads that same journalist to give a platform to the honesty-impaired. When it comes to dramatic (or more accurately, melodramatic), heart-tugging stories, journalists are the most vulnerable. Any heart-wrenching story that makes the papers must be looked at with a skeptical eye.

An emotionally manipulative story puts good reporters in a bind. A reckless reporter, looking for an audience, unwittingly airs a gut-wrenching hoax that involves a scam artist charading as a victim. If a more skeptical reporter makes his beliefs public, he risks public backlash. For example, those who were real victims may become upset when a fellow survivor's credibility is questioned. Besides, in this society it is considered offensive to blame or question a victim. Strangely enough, bad journalism can discourage good journalists from asking the tough questions. This complicated web gives an uninhibited and unscrupulous hoaxer the upper hand.

This "Catch 22" may explain why journalists get fooled, but why do people deliberately try to fool the press? Some people have deep psychological problems and crave sympathy or attention. Others want to gain support for their group or agenda, and they know that they won't get it unless they pull heartstrings on a mass scale. Still others who scam the media just do it for the money—they know that there is no better way to get people to donate money without question than waterworks.

But other people have less sensational reasons to deceive the press: some people get into a bind and, in a panic, concoct a story to get out of trouble, never thinking the lie will reach a stranger's ear. In the case of young David Barney, he falsely claimed that three teenaged bullies killed his dog to cover up the fact that he was responsible for the dog's death after he accidentally strangled the dog with the leash on a playground slide. He had simply lied to his parents to cover up his mistake: it was his parents who phoned and told police, who then ultimately told the media. Though the truth came out quickly, it didn't come fast enough to stop the flood of outrage and donations from around North America. The story appeared everywhere from the

Ottawa Citizen to the *Drudge Report*. Though the boy lied to prevent parental ire, his lie nevertheless had far-reaching consequences.

If the hoaxer has a more devious or profitable agenda, the damage can be even greater. Many scam artists tell stories that are so well-packaged and rehearsed that any reporter questioning the alleged victim or subject will be seen as brutal, cold, stupid, old-fashioned or even judgmental. What journalist could question a sobbing mother whose two young children were kidnapped or a dying mother whose life savings were stolen? Who could be skeptical of a police officer who said he survived the collapse of the World Trade Center or a man who survived a vicious killing, but witnessed the bloody death of his pregnant wife? If you would feel angry or offended by questioning those who claim to be victims, then you are the ideal pigeon for a scam artist.

A reporter's natural weaknesses can be exploited by cunning hoaxers. A journalist in an unfamiliar foreign country who is at the mercy of translators is an ideal mark for a con artist. Other times, the claim is so sensational, that the reporter wants to be the first to break it and ignores all the obvious red flags. But sometimes it is the very structure of the media story that is ripe for an exploitative mind.

Media Formulas

In journalism, news items are referred to as "stories." The term is no accident: information and events are packaged in a certain way that mimics a narrative. There has to be a beginning, middle and an end. There has to be action, progression and conflict. There also has to be a cast of characters, and each character has a role to play in the telling of the journalistic tale. Some of the common types of characters include the hero, the villain, the victim and the freak.

Certain roles require certain character traits. A victim must be sympathetic. The hero has to do right for the right reasons. The bad guy has to do wrong for the wrong reasons.

But media formulas go further than this: certain events or people have to evoke the right emotions. For example, holidays inevitably will bring stories about charity and helping less fortunate people in need. Christmas, Easter and Thanksgiving are especially ripe for these types of stories.

What this means is that stories and people have to "fit" a certain pattern—oddball or complex people who don't fit the right molds won't make headlines. If those key players do warrant a story, then many journalists will "make" the person "fit" by enhancing or downplaying key details to make the player better suited for the designated role. This may mean omitting important details or interpreting a player's actions in a particular way. For example, many "sweetheart" actresses or singers break onto the public scene with a clean-cut image, but after awhile, their flaws and shortcomings come to light, making it seem as if they were "corrupted" by fame, or at least had a radical personality transplant. It wasn't as though these celebrities never had peccadilloes; journalists simply ignored the starlets' vices at the time to make better copy.

By the same token, an unsympathetic or unlikable underdog is less likely to make the news because the central idea of a victim is an innocent person who is wronged. The victim has to wear a halo. If something "bad" happens to an obnoxious person, then the audience may see the bad event as punishment or comeuppance. Glossing is a subtle tool to package complex events into an understandable "story."

So how does the journalistic story structure make journalists vulnerable to hoaxers? If a scam artist can play the role of victim or hero convincingly enough, reporters are less likely to ask probing questions to try to verify the person's account. If the hoaxer can initially fool police or another authority figure, then that official stamp of approval will reassure reporters enough not to dig any further.

It also helps if the hoaxer has a grabbing, moving and easy to follow story. By using the right types of emotional triggers in the right amounts, a professional fabricator can fool millions of people at once. The story does not have to be logical, but it has to be emotional. A hoaxer doesn't have to worry about contradictions, inconsistencies or logical impossibilities, so long as the account is sensational.

But that doesn't mean that you, as a consumer of news, are helpless against those people who use the press for their own ends. But evaluating news stories may make some people uncomfortable and find questioning the motives of someone who is claiming to be a victim hard to do. This type of skepticism can be difficult: after all, it is considered rude, heartless and politically incorrect to question the truthfulness of someone who has just told you that he has experienced a trauma, especially if the individual seems emotionally distressed.

Unfortunately, it is that kind of thinking that the con artist is banking on. The hoaxer knows that civilized and sensitive people do not shine a critical light on those who claim to be victimized. Isn't the person's gut-wrenching testimony enough?

It was enough for Southbostononline.com and the good people of Boston to believe that a twenty-four-year-old named Kristen Clougherty was dying of ovarian cancer. In 1998, she told friends that she would have to go out of state to receive crucial treatment. One friend helped shave Clougherty's hair; by 1999, others helped raise money for her treatments through a funding raising event, netting her tens of thousands of dollars. Someone contributed this feel-good recap to *South Boston Online*:

> The friends of Kristen Clougherty gathered on Friday, June 4th, to cele-
> brate friendships and to aid Kristen in her battle with cancer. The festivities
> included tributes from local Irish Step dancers and lots of dancing and
> catching up by old friends. The Friends of Kristen Clougherty Committee
> was proud to announce that they well exceeded their fundraising goal, and
> Kristen expressed her deep appreciation for "giving me my life."
>
> Check out our cool pictures of a great night for a great friend!

With the money raised to help her beat cancer, the "great friend" Clougherty got herself a car, liposuction and breast implants. She had neither cancer
nor morals. Before a second fundraiser was to be held, police arrested
Clougherty. She had made up the story to keep a boyfriend in her clutches;
however, the money raised for her treatment simply became a fringe benefit.
It was also discovered that Clougherty tried a pity scam in 1997 when she
covered herself in blood by puncturing her chest with a pin and then claiming to be a victim of a carjacking, later to be proven false. For her deception,
the judge called her "callous," ordered her to repay her ill-gotten gains and
sentenced her to community service.

But not every con artist means to scam the press or the public—the person may have wanted to scam one or two individuals, but then those
suckers were so taken in that they notify the media and the lie suddenly
takes a life of its own: can the deceiver come clean at this point? Can the
hoaxer now plea, "Please don't interview me, I'm just a charlatan trying to
fleece my pigeons for a few hundred bucks," or "I'm just a scared and
trapped person who is too afraid of my family to tell them that I made an
all-too-human mistake"?

Probably not, but that doesn't mean that journalists should not probe
deeper or ask hard questions. Too many times, journalists don't do a thorough job and give hoaxers legitimacy. If heartstrings are being pulled, that's
the right time to think about how probable the person's account is—don't
always rely on journalists to double-check the facts.

Reporters certainly didn't double-check the facts in 1988, when an alternative band called Negativland implicated themselves in a high profile
murder investigation. The murder case in question was the bloody confrontation between sixteen-year-old David Brom and his family; the
Rochester boy took an axe and killed his parents and two siblings. This much
of the story was true.

In February 1988, the *New York Times* ran a story about the Brom case,
suggesting that David and his strict Roman Catholic father argued about the
unwholesome songs the boy was listening to, triggering the boy's violent
streak. No particular song was mentioned in the piece. At this, the band saw
an opportunity for self-promotion.

Through a series of bogus press releases, the band suggested that the fateful song David was listening to was Negativland's "Christianity is Stupid" (a real song they had recorded for their *Escape From Noise* album that was released prior to the murders). The band further hinted that they were asked not to leave town and that a FBI agent named Dick Jordan (a fictitious g-man) was on the "Brom-Negativland" case. To top off their scheme, the band "went into hiding" and suggested that there was a secret tape of the crime.

The hoax was preposterous. Why would the band be implicated, even if "Christianity is Stupid" was the song David and his father argued about? Why would the FBI ask the group not to leave town? On what grounds? Wouldn't a teen's ruthless hacking of his own immediate family prove that other vile and dysfunctional factors were at play, other than normal teenaged rebellion?

Any journalist could have phoned the FBI to request an interview with Special Agent Jordan. Any reporter could have interviewed the prosecutor for Brom's case or have asked to speak with Brom's lawyer to verify this over-the-top account of events. Anyone could have gotten hold of court documents to see what transpired that fateful night.

Journalists could have done any of those things. None did.

The story worked its way up from indie music publications to the *Village Voice* to the *San Francisco Examiner*. In total, over 100 publications carried the story as if it were true, as did radio and television stations. The band was mobbed by the media, until their agent finally came clean in June 1988.

The promise of a big, juicy story is too much for almost any reporter to resist. Gerd Heidemann, a reporter with Germany's *Der Stern* magazine (who was revealed in 2002 to have been a spy for the Stasi, the East German secret police), had told his editors that he had the journalistic scoop of the century: he had found a source who owned Adolf Hitler's diaries and would be willing to sell them to the publication for a hefty fee. The paper paid millions for the diaries and had hired experts to authenticate the series of small notebooks written by the Nazi leader himself. Though not all forensic tests were completed, editors decided to purchase more of the increasingly expensive diaries.

Furthermore, there were some troubling questions about the diaries: how could Hitler's handwriting stay so consistent even for entries written after his right arm was injured (after someone had tried to kill him)? How come the "found" diaries seemed to keep coming out of the woodwork? Why were there so many historical blunders in the entries? Did Hitler have ESP, or how else could his predicting major unexpected events before they happened be explained? Why would Hitler write so much when he was known to prefer to give dictation? Most importantly, who was Heidemann's secret source (the reporter wouldn't divulge his identity, but *Stern* editors didn't press for specifics).

By April, 1983, *Stern* editors were ready to announce their mega-bomb and, not surprisingly, the news made a splash. *Stern* (which is owned by Gruner & Jahr) assured reporters that the diaries had been determined to be genuine. *Newsweek*, the *London Sunday Times* and *Paris-Match* had agreed to buy the rights to the diaries (though *Newsweek* would later print seventeen entries without paying Gruner & Jahr). *Newsweek* devoted two covers to the story. Though some experts doubted the authenticity of the diaries, and one expert reneged his support, most didn't question the diaries—until the final forensic evidence came showing that the diaries were complete fakes.

The diaries were forged by the man who had sold them: Konrad Kujau, an uneducated, uncultivated man who managed to fool an army of reporters and editors with ease. The ink and paper he used were produced long after the end of the Second World War. Both Heidemann (who maintained he did not know the diaries were fakes, though others doubted his claims) and Kujau were given prison time for their deception. Stern and its parent company, who spent millions on the diaries, were left humiliated, as were *Newsweek* and the *Sunday Times*.

Journalists deal with all sorts of people and some of those people lie about anything; for example, the 1999 and 2000 *Toronto Film Festival* were somewhat besieged with web actors pretending to be movie actors to get extra publicity for trailervision.com, a site that spoofs movie trailers.

Some will lie about the weather, their health, their academic qualifications, the number of children they have—even their names. That's what happened to one unsuspecting *Charleston Post and Courier* reporter when he filed this story about a protest outside the Augusta National Golf Club on April 13, 2003:

> Throughout the morning, law enforcement officers stood on the perimeter of the five-acre field. At no point did the protest turn violent, though officers escorted Heywood Jablome away after he held up a sign directly in front of Burk that read "Make me dinner" before shouting "Oprah rules." [emphasis added]

Within moments of the story's publication, readers had let the reporter know that he was scammed by a dirty-minded protester who was in fact a radio DJ who was "protesting" as a stunt.

Speaking of the dirty-minded, stories with sexual elements can also lead reporters straight into trouble. In October 1996, the British tabloid the *Sun* published exclusive photos of a half naked Princess Diana canoodling with her riding instructor, paramour and "love rat" James Hewitt. The *Sun* devoted seven pages to the grainy black-and-white stills, showing the princess enjoying the company of a man other than her husband.

Editors at the *Sun* were given a tape by someone claiming to be an American lawyer, working on the behest of "soldiers or bodyguards." The eighty-second video was taken with a "spy camera" and *Sun* editors maintained they independently verified the five-year-old tape's authenticity. With that ringing endorsement, other media also jumped on the story, including television stations and the *Independent*, which reported on the *Sun*'s scoop on October 8, 1996:

> The footage, showing the Princess in her underwear, is thought to have been shot through a window at Highgrove, the Prince of Wales's country home, near Tetbury, Gloucestershire. It appears to confirm the Princess's fears that she was spied on. The video is thought to be at least five-years-old.
>
> The eighty-second tape appears to show the Princess stripping down to her sports pants and bra, kissing Mr. Hewitt, riding on his back and fighting with pillows. The video, believed to have been stored in a vault in the United States, was offered to the *Sun* during a meeting last Friday in west London.

What newspaper editor can resist a story about a comely member of the royal family prancing around in her underwear? Sadly, the *Sun* editors should have: the pictures weren't of the late Princess and her lover boy, but look-alike actors who impersonated Diana and Hewitt in hopes of getting comedy work. The cameraman, Nick Hedges admitted the tape was his, adding, "Never in a million years would I have thought this would have been taken seriously." It was. The *Sun* was fuming, calling the trick "one of the most elaborate hoaxes of the decade" and claiming editors were "conned by cunning fraudsters."

No media outlet is safe from hoaxes and scams. Eventually, someone will crack the journalist's code and use his or her knowledge against the press. The following case studies show how little investigation many reporters actually do, and how easy it really is to deconstruct a hoaxer's manipulative yarn.

Smells Like Baloney

Sexy dead celebrities make news, especially if they die at the peak of their game. Marilyn Monroe, Elvis Presley, James Dean and River Phoenix got a lot of ink and airtime simply because they stopped breathing. Rigor mortis can be a great way to get media attention.

Religious cults also interest journalists. Cults seem scary: there just seems to be a certain *je ne sais quois* about desperate people getting subjected to brainwashing, strange rituals and kooky leaders with kooky ideas. Whether the cult's followers drink poisoned Kool Aid, get in a bloody confrontation with government agents, wait for the mothership to come or simply run around naked with sacrificed squirrels, the endless possibilities for outré outcomes can make for an intriguing news story.

But couple a dead celebrity with a cult, and media coverage is a shoe-in.

Kurt Cobain was the lead singer of the 1990s group Nirvana, and was revered by his fans. The "Smells Like Teen Spirit" singer had talent, but he also had inner demons that drove him both to musical brilliance and to his suicide on April 5, 1994. Though Cobain was gone, his fans remained loyal to their voice.

Apparently some were so loyal that they decided to worship their fallen hero—literally. As a way for fans to deal with their loss, the Church of Kurt Cobain was founded, according to a May 1996 online edition of *Chart Attack*:

> As if religion wasn't in enough trouble as it is. Now there's a church move-ment growing around dead grunge rock idol Kurt Cobain (Nirvana, of course). Jim Dillon has founded the Church of Kurt Cobain in Portland, Ore. Dillon believes that Cobain's songs held a deeply spiritual message for young people, and that lyrics like "Rape me, my friend, rape me again," essentially mean "Treat me the way you want me to treat you."

The *Village Voice* also wrote about the church, as did the *Associated Press*:

> Smells like teen holy spirit: A fledgling church for disaffected youth has chosen as its patron saint the ultimate symbol of disaffection, the late grunge rocker Kurt Cobain.
>
> Underneath Mr. Cobain's brooding, self-absorbed music is a deeper spiritual message, says Jim Dillon, founder of the Church of Kurt Cobain in Portland, Ore.
>
> "I think there are a lot of people who feel like they are not being talked to in their own language," says Mr. Dillon, who describes himself as the church's de facto pastor. "These so-called Generation X-ers feel disassociat-ed with society at large."

Donations could be made during a Hemlock Society rally (a group that advocates a terminally ill patient's right to die). Reporters from "ABC Evening News" covered the May 28 event but never delved into twenty-nine-year-old Jim Dillon's background; neither did other print media such as the *Oregonian*, which wrote about the church unquestioningly, or many others who fell for the "sorry-looking press release," as one of the reporters who fell for the hoax termed it. The fact that less than a handful of "follow-ers" showed up at the event still didn't get reporters to see that something wasn't quite right about this new "religion."

Interest in the event soon evaporated, until the *Rocket*, an alternative music publication, revealed the hoax in their June 12, 1996 issue. Dillon was in fact thirty-four-year-old "Jerry Ketel," a graphic artist who jammed the media to make a statement about the press' gullibility and penchant for covering sensational stories. Ketel's success in fooling the press was all the more extraordinary given the fact that he had openly told one reporter that the church was "80% ironic." All the red flags were blazing at the event—low turn out, shady characters, dubious claims and smug comments—but the story was just too edgy and bizarre to pass up.

The Mother Who Wanted to Put Everyone Inside Her Heart

Nothing grabs attention like a good story about a mother in trouble. You probably have seen those booming headlines such as, "Mother defends killing intruder," "Mother takes stand," "Shooter kills mother of seven" or "Missing mother found." Those stories are sensational, yet almost all of us can relate to them: in the news media, *mother in peril* is short form for *good, kind nurturer* or *haloed victim*.

It was precisely this type of folksy logic that bamboozled scores of Toronto media outlets, as well as ABC and CNN, with chilling ease. How this hoax so quickly got out of hand (before it crashed and burned with equal speed) shows that when it comes to questioning those in authority, reporters are not as skeptical as they would like to believe.

The hoax is similar to the "Kaycee Nicole" Internet hoax, though the charade lasted days and not months. It was April 3, 1996 when Toronto police let the city's media know that a young single mother on social assistance went to a police station to report that her purse had been snatched by a mugger.

But this was no ordinary purse, and this was no ordinary mother. The purse contained the woman's health card, life savings, pain medication and a one-way bus ticket to Winnipeg, Manitoba. The medication was used to numb the effects of her terminal cancer, and the bus ticket was for her son to be sent to relatives in Winnipeg when his mother succumbed to her illness, as the *Toronto Star*'s front page so boldly declared to its readers on April 6, 1996:

> A purse snatcher who attacked a terminally ill young woman earlier this week has robbed her of more than he realizes.
>
> The twenty-seven-year-old cancer victim lost her medication as well as her money. She also lost her peace of mind as she struggles to secure a future for her seven-year-old son.

At least, that's what the young mother told police at the time. The police took her word at face value—and they also passed the hat at the station that evening, collecting $200 for her groceries. Toronto police, moved by the woman's plight, appealed to the public for help, though at the time they only had the woman's account and no concrete evidence.

And, on the face of things, who could blame them for trusting her? She *looked* sick. Pale, thin and visibly shaken, it was entirely plausible that someone so unhealthily gaunt and bloodless was quickly fading away. She also seemed edgy and shaken, which seemed to further enforce her account of events. As one police officer told the *Star*, "If anybody is down and out, this girl is. She's hit rock bottom."

When the Toronto media picked up the story, they too seemed fairly content with the police's account of events. So content, in fact, that most ran with the story without attribution. "Cancer patient mugged," the local press blared in unison, not "according to police a cancer patient was mugged," nor even, as *Star* columnist Joey Slinger noted in the aftermath, "if her story is true."

A brutalized, down on her luck, dying young mother who, according to one newspaper front page headline, was "robbed of hope"—it was a sad and dramatic story, but one that, despite all the tragic elements, had the potential to have an upbeat ending. Within days, people began to donate money—about $114,000 of it to the woman's son in a special account. Strangers donated twenties, fifties, hundreds of dollars at their local banks and police stations. According to one news report, "bank officials have told police they've never seen so much money collected so quickly for one individual." The fact that the story broke around Easter may have put people in a more charitable and generous mood.

The implications of this unexpected explosion of generosity are intriguing: people were willing to part with five to six hundred dollars based on reading or listening to a single news story. They never met the woman nor knew anything about her, but the story was potent enough to compel at least 18,000 people to donate money and even a few people to offer to adopt the woman's son. As one police officer stated, "This has gone unbelievably wild." According to police, "she was crying over the fact people would go out of their way for her." Another officer agreed. "She's confused. She's overwhelmed. She doesn't know how to say thank you." The power of the press is clear, but during the frenzy, very few questioned whether journalists got their facts straight.

The press claimed that the facts were straight. One newspaper article flat out stated that police had "checked out the woman's tragic story with her doctors," giving the impression that there was an in-depth investigation. The case seemed solid and beyond reproach, since it was claimed the woman's physicians gave her three to six months to live.

But people still wanted to see the woman whose sorry tale sparked such unconditional outpouring. Who was this woman who Fate had abused so callously? There was a natural curiosity on the part of both the public and the press: what did this star-crossed woman look like?

In journalism, very few issues will make it to print or air since there is a fear that "dry" topics won't catch an audience's interest, leading to the journalistic practice of putting a "face" on a story. Thus, there was a natural expectation on the part of the press that people would get a look at the woman who touched so many people's hearts.

Yet even here there was another heartbreaking twist, as the *Toronto Star* described on its front page: the young mother had just left an abusive relationship—she said she was "terrified" that if she made her name and face public, her former partner would hunt her down and hurt her. Even though she had a short time to live, she had to remain anonymous.

However, this condition made verifying the woman's story extremely difficult. But even more grating to reporters was that a story with a faceless apparition in the lead role did not have the same zing as one with a real face. If she looked as ill and morose as police described her, then having her image would help retain audience attention. A compromise between the police and media was reached: the dying woman would be shown in silhouette and her voice would be altered. Her name would not be released, but she would answer reporters' questions by camera hook-up, as she would be in another room.

On April 9, the dying mother gave her first press conference, and an emotional one it was. "I wish that I could put everybody inside my heart so they would know how thankful I am," she said in shadows during the press conference. With her soft and altered voice cracking, she asked that the public stop donating money. She had to regain her composure several times during the conference, which had moved both the media and police. After the conference, a group of *Toronto Star* journalists tried to follow the woman as police drove her home. The police stopped the reporters' car and the chase was off, but it didn't stop the newspaper from reporting on the conference without airing any reservations for the story or woman.

Then, suddenly, a simple Easter saga of kindness and goodwill took a dramatic, dissatisfying turn. Even though the dying mother's name wasn't revealed, her voice was altered and she appeared in darkened silhouette, it didn't stop a lot of people from recognizing her. She had a name—Donna Mercier—but she also had a past—and a secret to boot.

It turned out that Mercier had pleaded guilty to public mischief in 1989 after falsely accusing two men of rape; however, police did not run her name through their databases when she came in to report her purse stolen.

Nor did the police verify her medical condition, as they had originally assured reporters. Had they, they would have discovered that she wasn't dying—or that she never had cancer. She did have one kidney, but she was functioning well with it, even though she was a regular and well-known fixture at her neighborhood doctor's office. She did have trouble at her doctor's office on April 3, when she tried unsuccessfully to get yet another prescription for pain medication. It was after this visit that Mercier went to police to report that her pain medication had been stolen along with her purse. What started as a small time gambit to get more painkillers morphed into a citywide hoax.

The media became outraged at police for not verifying the woman's account, yet they themselves had not verified her story, either. In this case the police didn't lie, they just took a sickly woman's account at face value. True, the police did not run a check on her through their databases, nor did they talk to the woman's doctors about her condition, but journalists ran with the story without verifying a single statement. They just decided it was the police's job to do their dirty work instead.

Just because a tearful, self-proclaimed victim makes an accusation, it doesn't mean that what the alleged victim says is true. But journalists didn't double-check the facts behind the hype. It wasn't until people who knew Donna Mercier recognized her silhouette that the truth was revealed. It was left to news consumers, not the police or the media, to expose the hoax.

There were signs that the story was not on the level—there were too many excuses to explain away the woman's strange behavior. A far simpler explanation was at hand, but it was too unpleasant to consider. Why would-n't she reveal her face? Simple—because she had something to hide.

Mercier was again charged with public mischief, and she again pleaded guilty, though the sympathetic judge gave Mercier a suspended sentence with no jail time. The judge—obviously feeling sorry for a woman who would stoop to lying to police for a second time just to get another little bottle of pills—said that Mercier "has enough problems without me adding to them."

As a footnote, the *Toronto Star* won the 1996 National Newspaper Award for the spot-news reporting category for exposing the hoax it had helped circulate in the first place.

Two Hearts, Two Towers, One Lie

Unusual weddings are almost always guaranteed at least a small mention in most local papers: weddings are an important personal and family milestone, yet the ceremonies themselves are fairly predictable. So when there is a quirky twist to matrimony, journalists tend to take notice.

There are two types of unusual wedding stories: the first are the bizarre ceremonies. Those are the freaky sideshow weddings that are a bride or groom's worst nightmare—two people marry each other by accident; an absurdly expensive wedding culminates in the groom leaving the bride at the altar; the bride and groom get arrested; or either the bride or groom gets cold feet, but is then restrained or forced into the ceremony by their significant other. These stories won't make the front page, but will be used as a "kicker" to make the audience chuckle and feel relieved that their wedding was more mundane.

The other category of wedding story is more tasteful and emotional. These stories are the inspirational ones: despite insurmountable odds, a star-crossed couple exchange vows. Here, either the bride or groom has had a personal tragedy, but in spite of it the couple tie the knot. The bride or the groom (sometimes both) had been victimized by fate or even faced death, but somehow one or both have come back swinging. Against-all-odds weddings are usually the type of human-interest stories that will appear on a Friday or a Sunday to end the week (or at least the work week) on an upbeat note.

It was two owners of a Nevada wedding chapel—Ron Sayed and David Beronio—who suggested a story that the *Tahoe Daily Tribune* couldn't pass up: a New York City police officer and a September 11 survivor would tie the knot at Harveys Wedding Chapel. This type of call was not unusual, since Beronio would call the paper whenever a minor celebrity booked a wedding. Even more heartbreaking, it was discovered, was that the original best man was also the partner of the groom who died at the World Trade Center. One friend and colleague survived the terror attack, the other did not.

A tragic tale with an inspirational ending, though the hero explained to the reporter that he had to first phone "his commander in Brooklyn" to get permission to talk about his tragedy. In the opening paragraphs, *Tribune* readers were introduced to a true American hero:

> As lovely as she is, the most beautiful sight of Daniel McCarthy's life wasn't his bride as she met him Thursday at the altar in Harveys Wedding Chapel.
>
> It was the face of the German shepherd who found him buried under the rubble of the World Trade Center, seventy-nine hours and fourteen minutes after it collapsed.
>
> McCarthy, a New York City policeman who responded to the call on Sept. 11, escaped with second-degree burns across his back from flaming jet fuel. He made it back to the house in Brooklyn he shared with his girlfriend of six months, Eleni Golding. And he grabbed onto the second chance at life he feels God gave him.

An intern reporter named Merlyn Oliver interviewed McCarthy during his stay in Lake Tahoe. The story that ran on Friday July 19, 2002 was unrelenting in its tragic twists:

> [McCarthy] and his partner started up Tower One. On the forty-seventh floor it was so hot from the fire above, that the leather on their gear started to deteriorate. Everywhere people were screaming.
>
> "There was this pregnant woman who couldn't speak any English," McCarthy said. "She kept screaming, 'Please, please, my bambino.' We started bringing her down. I carried her on my back. We made it to the 24th floor."

That's when his partner, Dominick Imperatore, told him to take her out the rest of the way and then come back up.

"I got her out, and then I ran back in," McCarthy said. "I made it up as far as the ninth floor when the building came down. I never saw Dominick again. They never found his body."

The emotional taxation that readers endured was unremitting, but the payoff was just around the corner:

The thirst was unbearable and the pain from his burns was excruciating. He said he saw a vision of his beloved Italian grandmother, long dead, telling him it wasn't his time yet to die.

That he had things still to do. That his dead father was there with her.

Seeing her face over those seventy-nine hours and fourteen minutes kept him going.

It was the wet sensation of a dog licking his face that pulled him out of the underground tomb. Rescue workers were not far behind.

The story was dramatic and full of color. The reader learned about McCarthy's "intense blue eyes," but what about the truthfulness of his story? Here, the reporter's article is short on concrete details or a tangible and verifiable trail. Who could corroborate his account of events? But who needs facts when you have emotion and a great story?

Once the story was published, the response was quick. The *Associated Press* called the newspaper. There was one troubling thing about the story—according to McCarthy he had been pulled out after seventy-nine hours, yet their records clearly show that no one was found alive after September 12. Another newspaper, *New York Newsday*, could not find records for either McCarthy or his alleged partner Imperatore. The New York Police Department dealt the final blow by publicly stating that though they had three Daniel McCarthys on the force, all had left the force long before September 11. McCarthy was a fraud.

The *Tribune* printed a retraction, noting the reporter did nothing to verify McCarthy's melodramatic yarn. In typical journalistic justification, Jeff Munson, then city editor of the *Tribune*, defended the paper by saying, "The personality of Mr. McCarthy... was very intense and believable." In other words, there's an excellent chance a journalist will take your word for it if you have an honest face—or a good enough whopper.

Basic problems plagued the very core of the story: why hadn't other, larger media organizations interviewed McCarthy first? Wouldn't a policeman who survived such a national tragedy be a perfect inspirational "get" for "Good Morning America" or *USA Today*? Wouldn't McCarthy be a symbol of American resilience, primed for presidential praise and media plaudits? How could such a heroic find fall below the media radar? At the very least, there should have been a basic attempt by the reporter to run McCarthy's name into a search engine, or electronic database to see whether his story was mentioned elsewhere.

Beronio had told Oliver that McCarthy did mention to him that the newsmagazine "Dateline NBC" had done a profile on him; however, no such story aired—nor did Oliver attempt to verify this tidbit or locate a transcript.

Had anyone at the *Tribune* conducted basic research, they would have known that there were no survivors found after seventy-nine hours of the towers' collapse—not one. This had been documented. Had anyone at the *Tribune* dug deeper, then it would have been known that McCarthy's story could not be reconciled with the facts.

Even if we assume that the *Tribune* out-scooped the *New York Times*, there are other, more troubling points. First, the only person quoted in Oliver's story is McCarthy himself. Can we then assume the reporter actually verified his account? We can't, since no one else was quoted. Wouldn't it be interesting to know what McCarthy's supervisor thought of one of his or her men? Would his supervisor be proud or saddened? How does this person feel about losing another employee in the line of duty? Even if the story is about McCarthy, a few other voices would be valuable. What does his mother or father think about him?

Second, nowhere in the story does it mention what other corroborating evidence the journalist had found to enhance McCarthy's account. Weaving hard facts with anecdotes would have actually improved the story's potency. Considering the physical toll such an ordeal would take, it would have been of interest to know whether McCarthy made a quicker than expected recovery, or whether his injuries affected his freedom of movement. Asking a medical or burn expert for her analysis may have also given the journalist a better indication of how truthful McCarthy was. Relying only on emotional details is poor journalism.

Finally, though McCarthy's bride Eleni Golding is mentioned (the reporter seems to place her at the interview when she writes that the bride "puts her hand on his arm. It's clear this couple realizes how close they came to not seeing their wedding day") yet does not quote her. Why? Did she actually interview her? Did Golding turn her down? Was she actually not present? What did she think of her alleged hero husband? It's a subtle, but significant omission that raises as many questions as the motives behind McCarthy's hoax. Golding may have been in on the hoax or completely ignorant of her husband's machinations. She could have also been duped, but the reader doesn't get to hear her voice.

Why McCarthy lied is less clear, since he did not profit from his fib, though a week after his hoax was exposed, he was accused of marrying another woman.

Coming to a Small Town Near You?

Incurable diseases may not be pleasant dinner conversation, but those in the news media know they can engage their audiences with the topic, especially if the disease is new, deadly, unpleasant and easily transmitted. Though Severe Acute Respiratory Syndrome (SARS) did not ravage the US in 2003, it had made enough damage to other countries (including neighboring Canada) that the mysterious illness grabbed American headlines. AIDS was another violent illness that ravaged bodies and could be transmitted through blood transfusions, shared needles and sex, and changed the mindset of an entire generation in the late 1980s and early 1990s.

Reporting on any disease in the media requires a strict set of rules and boundaries. City reporters are expected to "localize" the story; that is, a journalist can't discuss an illness in vague terms; he has to find an afflict- ed local resident to interview to "drive the story home." If a local reporter wants to do a story on a rare disease and all 100 sufferers live out of state, that journalist's pitch will be nixed, no matter how fascinating and infor- mative the story would be. While outlets with a national and international mandate may have more leeway (explaining why SARS played more prominently in larger outlets); city-bound journalists face more constraints.

With that formula in mind, the *Mount Pleasant Daily News* in Texas ran a four-part front-page series on AIDS from November 24 to December 15, 1991; though nothing in the first three articles was out of the ordinary (with a local AIDS patient profiled in the third article and local experts inter- viewed for all the others)—it was the final installment that had caught residents in the nearby town of Bogota completely off guard:

> "AIDS is another epidemic that is going to force medical technology to take another couple of steps forward," Dona Spence, an AIDS education spe- cialist for the Ark-Tex Council of Governments said, "and I hope it's soon. AIDS has devastated this country, this state and now this region."
>
> For instance, there are eleven known cases of full-blown AIDS in Titus county and fifty-two HIV infected individuals, Spence reported.

The numbers were sobering, but Spence made no mention of the profile of a typical Titus county patient, but that would soon change. The story picked up national momentum when another revelation from Bogota was made public, courtesy of Spence. As the *Los Angeles Times* reported in its February 14, 1992 edition:

> Six of the 197 students at Rivercrest High School in northeast Texas have tested positive for the human immunodeficiency virus, which causes AIDS,

Supt. Freddy Wade confirmed at a news conference Thursday. That is more than six times the national average infection rate of one in 250 people.

Suddenly, this sleepy little town with a population of just over 1400 was a perfect demonstration of teen promiscuity gone awry. Spence, described as a nurse by many publications, was not only the one who broke the shocking news of the epidemic, but was also a vocal proponent of vigorous intervention and discussion, as the same *Times* article recounted:

> "I am so proud of that school district," said Dona Spence, HIV-AIDS case manager at the Ark-Tex Council of Governments in Texarkana... Spence notified school officials of the cases. "They're really trying to educate their kids. They are living in the real world," she said.

But for Bogota students, the revelations had a traumatizing impact. With media coverage increasing, many of the town's teens were shunned and taunted by out-of-town peers. High school sporting events became strained when opposing teams refused to shake hands with Bogota rivals while chanting put-downs. Students were left wondering how they could be targeted for such cruelty.

The teens' parents had unanswered questions of their own: who were these infected students? How could the identities of six ill teens be unknown to a small, close-knit community? Spence refused to reveal their identities, citing confidentiality. For a while, it seemed that all Dona Kay Spence needed to convince reporters that there was an epidemic in small town Texas was her say-so: stories about her claims still made headlines, though no other source could verify Spence's numbers. Yet Spence's credentials (she claimed to hold a nursing degree and to have served in Viet Nam) seemed credible. As Spence recounted in the February 15, 1992 edition of the *Austin American-Statesman*:

> Spence said Monday that she asked the department to review her files days ago to put to rest the controversy over the figures.
>
> "I wanted them to look through my files so they could see that what we had was legitimate, and I realize that no one wanted to take the responsibility for any of this, and I was going to wind up the scapegoat," she said.

Though people in Bogota openly questioned Spence's assertions, she had implied that she didn't think that rules applied to her. As *USA Today* reported, Spence "ha[d] said she didn't think it was necessary that her claims be verified." It was troubling that Spence, who was in the health care profession, thought she was above having to provide evidence to the public. Why couldn't she find a way of protecting the privacy rights of terminally ill teenagers while still providing evidence of her claims? What had been more unsettling was that Spence was planning to open an AIDS center in the unlikely town of Mt. Pleasant—claiming an epidemic in the area would certainly help Spence secure grants for her project. Suddenly, Spence had a probable motive for exaggerating the numbers.

Then the Texas Department of Health came out with the results of its own investigation—the HIV infected teens did not exist. Spence's claims were a hoax. And that wasn't the only fib Spence told. As People magazine reported, Spence's credentials were also embellished: she attended college, but left without a degree and though she served in the military, she was never in Viet Nam.

Though Spence's scheme was exposed, it didn't do much to help the teens of Mt. Pleasant who were shunned by their peers in neighboring communities. The damage had been done.

iLoo Trouble

Weird news stories may be good for a chuckle, but these are often the most vulnerable to fakery. Some people are desperate to make headlines and are willing to degrade and humiliate themselves to do it. Media whores will sell their souls to the devil if it means getting even a local news outlet to write a sneering local brief about them. If it takes lying to get some press, lie they will.

On the other hand, some weird news items don't come from pathological attention-seekers; sometimes strange events just happen. There is no stunt involved, just someone with a bad idea or the bad fortune to be in the wrong place at the wrong time. Differentiating between a stunt, bad idea or bad circumstances can be nearly impossible at times if the reporter doesn't have enough information.

Despite the pitfalls, reporters still like weird news stories: weird news is easy news that will grab attention, and these stories will most likely fall into the reporter's lap, like this one did for Reuters on May 6, 2003:

> The world's first portable lavatory with Internet access is due to be unveiled in Britain this summer.
>
> The "iLoo" is being built by Microsoft Corp's Internet arm MSN, which aims to showcase its creation at Britain's summer music festivals.
>
> "The Internet is so much a part of everyday life now that surfing on the loo was the next natural step," said MSN marketing manager Tracy Blacher on Tuesday.

The story came from a seemingly credible source—an April 30 press release originating from Microsoft's London office. The story was quickly picked up and debated until the "whatever-will-they-think-of-next" heading. Both the *Associated Press* and the *Seattle Post-Intelligencer* called the company's PR firm, which confirmed the story. As the *Hollywood Reporter* stated on May 12:

> Microsoft's MSN is making another grab for the public's attention by creating portable toilets with Internet access. In a statement leavened with numerous British puns, MSN marketing manager Tracy Blacher said the mobile unit was part of the company's mission to reach Internet users "any time and any place" they happen to be. The idea is to capitalize on the summer season of outdoor music festivals in the United Kingdom by placing an "iLoo" alongside the regular facilities such events require.

The *Rocky Mountain News* also weighed in on the same day:

> No joke: MSN UK (United Kingdom) is creating what Microsoft calls the world's first Internet outhouse, or iLoo. It would have a flat-screen plasma display, wireless keyboard and broadband access.
>
> A spokesman called the portable toilet the first "WWW.C," a reference to W.C., or water closet. "This is another demonstration of Microsoft moving into new product areas to expand its revenue base," IDC analyst Roger Kay told CNET News.com.

But that's when Microsoft's U.S. executives got first wind of the story. Head office quickly dispelled the story, labeling it a hoax, based on their discussions with one of their UK employees. Journalists took MSN at its word and reported their corrections.

That might have been the end of it, except the company reversed itself a day later and then reported that the iLoo wasn't a hoax, but a project from the company's British division who thought the iLoo would be popular with the English. How far along in the planning stages was never reported or discovered. In any case, the head office killed the project for good.

Was iLoo a hoax? It was most likely a stunt gone awry, given the inconsistent stories coming from the British division of the company and the fact that the U.S. head office knew nothing of the project. No diagrams, no prototypes were ever shown as proof: this could mean it was merely in the early stages of development or that there was something else afoot.

In this case, reporters had interviewed the company's hired PR firms instead of the actual project researchers and managers themselves. Had journalists tried to confirm the story with the true architects of the "iLoo," they might have had a better idea of the story's veracity. Once the story became an embarrassment, finding someone who would openly own up to the iLoo project would be all but impossible.

A Huckleberry Huckster

Spunky kids and cute animals can almost always expect to get some form of media coverage. Small community papers are notorious for running imps on their front pages. On the other hand, cute kids usually don't make big news in big city papers, unless the child is ill or has been harmed. As a general rule, serious news outlets don't trouble themselves with the typical antics of children. This unwritten embargo has nothing to do with age discrimination. It's not a news flash that little kids do and say cute things.

Not that kids wouldn't want to try to do the extraordinary: childhood fantasies do revolve around the magical. What boy or girl wouldn't want to travel the world on a pirate ship or fly in the sky like Captain Marvel—all without parental supervision? If only they could pull it off in the real world: plucky, photogenic scamps could expect their exciting adventures to make it to the front page of the newspaper.

But positive front-page press is exactly what thirteen-year-old Edwin Sabillon got for himself when he told New York City police of his extraordinary journey.

On a summer day in 1999, a New York City cab driver came to city police with a teenaged boy who could not find his father at LaGuardia airport—an alarming development, since the boy's father assured him that he would be there. Since the boy had no other relatives in the city, the cabbie took Edwin to Bronx police. The boy could not speak English, but his charming ways endeared him to his new protectors, who decided to go public with the boy's story in an effort to find Edwin's father.

It didn't take long for Edwin's story of innocence, love and determination to quickly make the rounds in Gotham. One June 28, 1999 *New York Times* article co-written by Jayson Blair (later to become known as one of journalism's most notorious prevaricators; see Chapter 14) began with this heart-churning lead:

> Alone in the world but for the father he had never seen, a determined thirteen-year-old boy, equipped with a little money and enough pluck to charm a string of helpful strangers, set out for New York City from his hurricane-devastated village in Honduras last month to find him.
>
> The boy, Edwin Daniel Sabillon, carrying $24 and a paper bag with a change of clothes, his birth certificate and three cookies, arrived on a bus from Miami on Sunday. With the aplomb that carried him through his 3,200-mile journey, he hailed a cab and went looking for his father.

Edwin's mother, brother and grandfather were all killed in mudslides in Honduras, leaving the boy alone. The *Times* revealed the reason why the youngster was headed to Gotham:

[Sabillon's father] instructed the boy to come to New York City. He said he would meet him at the entrance to La Guardia Airport "by the bridge." He gave three rendezvous dates: June 25, 26 and 27. I will be wearing a white shirt, black pants, white sneakers and a black hat, the father wrote, but I will recognize you.

The BBC's website also carried the saga, including a link on its website with a map of "Edwin's incredible journey." The *Associated Press* covered the epic journey, as did CNN; the *New York Daily News* ran the story on its front page. Edwin suddenly became the talk of New York City: a young spunky kid who seemed to embody the American ethic of determination and bravery. He even wanted to be an actor.

There was at least one nagging question. Why hadn't anyone else reported the unsupervised minor to authorities in the last thirty-seven days? No one seemed to have the answer, but there were plenty of analogies to go around, such as one proffered by the *Times*:

The adventures along the way that he recounted to detectives sound like the *Huckleberry Finn* tale in reverse: a stubborn boy sets out on the road to join his father, steals across the borders of three countries, gives the slip to lawmen along the way, loses his possessions and is rescued by a succession of good Samaritans.

The story seemed both incredible and to have come right from a children's fairy tale. It must have been good fortune that the boy was not hurt or killed during his journey. It was a feel good story as the *New York Times* noted:

In many ways, it is also an improbable tale of luck and generosity along a route that most often is paved with hardship and greed.

The story wasn't only improbable, it was a whopper: young Sabillon wasn't looking for his father. He was despondent over his father's death from AIDS eight months earlier. Edwin's mother was still alive in Honduras, but she had abandoned the boy who was living with his aunt in Florida. Though he had journeyed from Florida to New York, parts of Edwin's tale were false. Police had sympathy for the troubled boy, and he was placed in foster care with his mother's blessing. The boy's story was anything but feel-good.

Hunting for Sensationalism and Higher Ratings

Some journalists have a fascination with naked women, especially if those naked women are young, skanky and engaging in bizarre behavior. There's shock, sensationalism and titillation—the typical easy news fodder that can grab a large leering audience without the reporter having to dig or do any research. But find a sordid story like that taking place in the anything-goes state of Nevada, and a national audience will be salivating and demanding to see more.

"Hunting for Bambi" was a raunchy live-action simulation game where men would pay between $5000 to $10,000 to shoot naked women (called "Bambis") with a paintball gun in the desert. Michael Burdick, the "brains" behind the venture, claimed that men from around the country and as far as Australia and Germany had come to play the game. Their souvenir was a tape of their hunt.

KLAS-TV, a CBS affiliate in Las Vegas, shocked their viewers with Burdick's new twist on paint ball. Reporter Luanne Sorrell's three-part series about this new form of kinky fun for predatory men first aired on July 10, 2003:

> It's a new form of adult entertainment, and men are paying thousands of dollars to shoot naked women with paint ball guns. They're coming to Las Vegas to do it. This bizarre new sport has captured the attention of people around the world, but Channel 8 Eyewitness News reporter LuAnne Sorrell is the only person who has interviewed the game's founder.

What kind of men paid for this violent and sexist game? Sorrell spoke to one of Burdick's customers:

> George Evanthes has never been hunting. "Originally I'm from New York. What am I going to hunt? Squirrels? Someone's cats? Someone's dogs? I don't think so," said Evanthes. Now that he's living in Las Vegas, he's finally getting his chance to put on his camouflage, grab a rifle and pull the trigger. But what's in his scope may surprise you. He's not hunting ducks or deer, he's hunting naked women.
>
> "I've done this three times," says Nicole, one of the three women allowing themselves to be shot at. Two other women, Gidget and Skyler, claim they have done this seven times.

The report went on to describe how the paintballs traveled at "200 miles per hour," and could cause bleeding "when they hit bare flesh." If so, then how safe—or legal—was this "game"? The on-the-job hazards seemed disturbing and unsettling.

But media reaction to the story was swift and furious. One typical syndicated opinion piece, published in the *Orlando Sentinel* on July 20, 2003, stated that:

> Things don't get any weirder than "Hunting for Bambi," the new "adult" paint ball game in which men pay large sums of money to hunt naked women who dash about trying to capture flags without getting zapped by a 200 mile-per-hour paint ball pellet.

On the one hand, this feels a little like a summer rerun. They're digging up Hoffa (again) and men are objectifying women (still). Haven't we done this already? Men angry; women stupid. Or vice versa. So what's new?

Another column in the *Seattle Post-Intelligencer* on July 18 pondered where this type of exploitation could lead:

> They're just video games. Geez. No player would go from "offing" an animated prostitute in "Grand Theft Auto" with his game control to doing it for real with a gun.
> Would he?
> Well, this week, we may have edged an uncomfortable inch closer to an answer because, this week we heard about a sick, real-life role-playing game in the scrub brush near Las Vegas.

FOX News also profiled the sport on July 16, interviewing a "Bambi" (who only gave her first name, "Taylor") who assured viewers that the Bambis were "not getting hurt that bad." Burdick also weighed in on his business:

> Despite criticism that the game is sick and barbaric, Burdick said it was all in fun and caters to both male and female fantasies.
> "The majority of women have a deep-seated fantasy of that bad-boy image, to be sought after by a stranger," he told Fox News...

"Hunting for Bambi" became media fodder for days. Reporters looked at many angles: was the game illegal? Was it sexist? Was it dangerous?

But it took the husband and wife team who ran Snopes.com, an urban legend website, to ask "Was it a hoax?" After looking at the website, and noticing that there was no phone number or address, they declared the game to be a joke. How could the women get hit with a paintball without getting bruised or injured? What if the "shooter" missed and hit her in the face?

Other Las Vegas media also questioned the legitimacy of Burdick and his clients, one of whom supposedly paid $10,000 to participate, yet lived in a run down neighborhood. The conclusion was obvious: KLAS was had. After being paid a visit by Las Vegas "officials," Burdick confirmed as much. Burdick wanted publicity for his other equally lewd, but less bizarre videos. Hyping Bambi was the easiest way of getting free publicity for his video company.

The signs of a scam were rampant: paintballs can injure or maim unprotected skin, no contact information was given and the very essence of the scheme went against labor laws. But in the hunt for better ratings, many reporters preferred to act as stenographers for a shady businessman instead of digging a little deeper into his fantastic claims.

Losing Your Credibility

The "Hunting for Bambi" hoax was an undeniable black eye for journalists who were looking to score ratings with a cheap and easy story. If it were the first sexed-up story to fool journalists, then all could be forgiven, since conventional reporters have more experience covering crime and politics than the adult entertainment beat. Unfortunately, the Bambi hoax was not the first time that mainstream reporters flirted with a pornographic story only to find out that they were outwitted by someone with a little more street smarts.

In mid-July, 1998, a company calling itself the Internet Entertainment Group (IEG) (a porn site best known for selling actress Pamela Anderson and Motley Crue drummer Tommy Lee's personal and lurid "home movie," as well as radio personality Dr. Laura Schlessinger's nude pictures) announced via a press release that it would host a website that would chronicle the courtship of Mike and Diane, two eighteen-year-olds who agreed to lose their virginity on the appropriately named website OurFirstTime.com. The site's producer was a previously unknown producer named Oscar Wells.

Mike would woo Diane for eighteen days in July, culminating in their public deflowering on August 4. The story was carried on several newspaper websites, such as the *Philadelphia Inquirer/Daily News*. As the *Wired News* website also reported on July 15, 1998:

> "We're going to do this as tastefully as possible," said Oscar Wells, a web designer based in Los Angeles who says he has no experience with pornography. "I know we're breaking a lot of eggs here."
>
> Though Internet mailing lists and discussion groups are rife with speculation about the site, the teens—known only as "Diane" and "Mike"—and the creator's intentions, Wells said Our First Time is not a commercial venture. Rather, he said, it is an exercise in free speech and a lesson in sex education.
>
> "We're not accepting any kind of advertising, because that would really denigrate what we're trying to do here. It's not a porn site," Wells said.
>
> Wells said his wife is irritated that he's giving away his time and spending their money on the project.

But within a day, Ziff Davis' online news service broke the story that the teens' lawyer and spokesman and Wells were both linked to Ken Tipton, a former video store owner (Tipton had been sued for carrying obscene videos twice by detractors—though he was acquitted, he shut his business down) known for his pro-freedom of speech beliefs. Mark Vega, the lawyer said to be representing Mike and Diane (sometimes written as Dianne), assured reporters that he met with the young couple and that they were real eighteen-year-old virgins. How the lawyer determined they were virgins was not disclosed. While questions swirled as to whether the two virgins would become a mouthpiece for Tipton's First Amendment crusade; the rest wondered aloud whether the stunt was a hoax.

IEG quickly backed out of the agreement, citing its doubts over MyFirstTime.com's legitimacy. Everyone involved confessed that the stunt was a hoax at a press conference held in a condom store. "Mike" was really twenty-three-year-old Ty Taylor, an out-of-work actor, while "Diane" identified herself as Michelle Parma (a twenty-three-year-old former Dallas Cowboys cheerleader who had appeared the year before on the MTV show *Road Rules*, but later died in a 2002 car accident). "Oscar Wells" (as critics noted had to be a nod to Orson Welles and his infamous 1938 radio broadcast of "War of the Worlds") was really Tipton himself, also a bit actor and aspiring independent movie producer, who was the architect of the scheme. Tipton claimed the hoax was supposed to be a "public service announcement" to teach youngsters a "moral lesson" about safe sex (using a porn site that caters to adults to teach teens about safe sex seems illogical, to say the least). The script called for both "Mike and Diane" to change their minds and hold on their virginity at the last second.

Journalists at the press conference were angry at the publicity stunt—calling Tipton a "liar," but all the red flags were there: the website described Mike and Diane as naïve teenagers—ones who looked like well-built models or actors in their twenties. Parma already had television exposure with MTV—wouldn't some pop culture buff scribe (who would have been the most likely candidate to cover a story such as this one) recognize her? What were "Wells'" credentials? Who was he? Who were Diane and Mike? Who knew them? While journalists had oriented themselves to the scam fairly quickly, it didn't prevent some outlets from running with the story before double-checking whether the fantastic tale was true.

Deus Ex Machina

Stalkers are creepy and make good villains for horror movies, but unless the stalker is arrested for harming a celebrity, they don't usually make the news unless they've killed their victim. The idea of one person targeting another individual for daily harassment doesn't seem to make news—unless the stalker can think of an original way to invade his prey's privacy. A stalker named "Sommy" seemed to be that kind of ingenious and innovative predator.

Debbie and Dwayne Tamai were an ordinary couple living in Emeryville, Ontario. Nothing in their background would suggest these two would be victims of a stalker. But what would happen to them in December 1996 would be so unpredictable and frightening, that they would consider moving away. Was the stalker threatening them or leaving dead animals on their driveway? No, this outsider could control the inside of the Tamais' sanctum.

The stalker called himself Sommy, and had a funny sounding voice on the phone. His presence was felt everywhere in the Tamai house. Whenever someone tried to use the phone, Sommy would intercept the call, making belching noises. Appliances and lights would shut themselves off. Sommy, it seemed, was a "cyber stalker," as Reuters recounted in its April 17, 1997 story:

> A Canadian family under siege by a prankster dubbed the "Cyber-Punk" has decided to move rather than fight the electronic invasion any longer.
>
> The Tamai family says an unknown stalker who calls himself "Sommy" has been changing television channels, interrupting telephone conversations and cutting power to their home in Emeryville, a small town about 220 miles west of Toronto.
>
> Ontario police, as well as telephone and electricity utilities, are continuing to investigate the Tamais' claims but remain perplexed as to how an individual could gain complete control of a private residence.
>
> "I certainly haven't heard anything like this before," said police office Deborah Mineau of the Ontario Provincial Police, who has been investigating the case.

The family went to the police for help in January—and that's when the news media around the world descended on the family.

Media outlets from all parts of the United States jumped on the story. The *Tampa Tribune* covered the stalking plight in its April 15 edition:

> The trouble began in December, when puzzled friends told Debbie and Dwayne Tamai their telephone calls to the couple were being waylaid and cut off.
>
> A month later, missed messages and strange clicks seemed minor when a disembodied voice, distorted by computer, interrupted a call to make himself known.

The same story also appeared in the *Philadelphia Inquirer*, the *San Diego Union-Tribune* and the *Seattle Times*. The *Palm Beach Post* also brought news of Sommy, as did the *Daily News of Los Angeles*, the *Rocky Mountain News* and the *St. Petersburg Times*. For months, the Tamais could not live in peace. Experts brought in could not explain how Sommy was controlling the house. In desperation, the family had put their home on the market.

Police were then called in, but couldn't end the stalking. In April 1997, "Dateline NBC" and the Discovery Channel came to the family's home with an "espionage team." They, too, could not solve the Sommy puzzle—but they had suspicions. The manipulations weren't the result of wireless gadgets, they concluded. Whoever was responsible was on the inside, and probably at an age where that sort of practical joking would seem funny. Did anyone in the Tamai house fit the bill?

There was one candidate—the Tamais' fifteen-year-old son Billy. After police had a long talk with Billy, he confessed that he was Sommy. He began playing with the light switches and talking gibberish in a funny voice on the phone extension as a prank, but then it got out of hand. Fearing that his family would disown him if he confessed, he kept silent while continuing the charade.

With the confession, everything fell into place. It was possible that the stalker could control the phone and electricity from the outside—but that would have been difficult and would have required equipment and knowledge on the part of the stalker—as well as motive to invest in such an undertaking (since "Sommy" never blackmailed the family, money was not a motive for the harassment).

On the other hand, an insider playing with the light switches, turning on the electrical switches in the basement and talking on the extension could account for the strange happenings in the house. In news stories with stranger-than-life scenarios, always look for the most mundane explanation—most times, it's the right one.

You Can Take It With You

Despite some people's desire to be known around the world as someone who is original, they soon realize that the news world will immediately force tried-and-true labels on them, regardless of how much of a maverick they believe themselves to be. Are you a hero, victim, villain, official or freak? There are few roles to fill in the news story: if mothers are short-form for kind nurturer (a form of hero) and policemen are short-form for brave protector (a hero or official), then how do other people usually play out in journalistic yarns?

Unless they do something worthy, teenagers and young adults usually are in the news being either abused or abusive. Young attractive entertainers and businessmen are both winners, but the suits also get to be authorities. Foreign leaders knocking the President are seen as villains. Then there are old men.

Some old men have done well for themselves (survived wars or made a fortune) and are seen as wizened sages who can impart advice. These old guys can be honorary authorities. But other elderly gentlemen are too grouchy and paranoid to warrant such a romanticized view of old age; these are the ones who get shown as endearing freaks.

The nutty old man stereotype is well known: he'll be immature, self-indulgent and cantankerous (aren't all old men described as grumpy and cantankerous?), but in his own strange way, his grievances and solution will have a certain logic to them. He's mad as hell and he's not going to take it anymore. He might be rich or, more often in these type of stories, he's poor, lives in a small backwards town and has a funny-sounding name. He's got a beef and, in his declining years, he's trying to right the wrong that has made him so bitter.

He's not going to take it lying down, no sir: he's going to right those wrongs, by gum, even if it kills him. How he ultimately does so won't be the way younger people would: it will be funny, but more importantly, his solution is going to be weird.

In the news world, these old men have to do something out of the ordinary, but not something violent or vile. Unless they set explosives in a government building to protest their tax bills, these old guys won't make the front page: they are the quirky footnotes to a newscast. Their purpose is to make readers or viewers chuckle and shake their collective heads.

It was August 15, 2002 when *Wireless Flash* reported on an old man in Long Island, New York who seemed to know his place in the news world:

> A deceased cattle rancher in Bozeman, Montana, took care of his heirs by installing an automatic teller machine in his tombstone.
>
> Cattle rancher Grover Chestnut died earlier this year at the age of seventy-nine. However, before he cashed in, he installed an ATM at his tombstone and gave ten heirs debit cards, and told them [they] were allowed to withdraw $300 per week from the grave.
>
> Chestnut apparently figured the tombstone ATM was the best way to make sure his grave had regular visitors.

The *San Francisco Chronicle* picked up the story, as did some radio stations, but there were problems with the wire story: for one, why did the story carry a New York byline if it originated from Bozeman, Montana? How logistically plausible would a gravesite ATM be? How often could it be in use? Who'd pay for its installation and maintenance?

Not surprisingly, the story turned out to be a hoax, as the *Bozeman Daily Chronicle* discovered when it could not find records for either Chestnut or an ATM machine installed in a cemetery. *Wireless Flash* has carried several too-good-to-be-true stories on its site. The *Chronicle* published a correction on its website and removed the dubious tale.

Having a Pulse on the Plausible

Finding the right guests for television news shows isn't an easy task. It's not enough for the person to be knowledgeable, they also have to be able to speak in sound bites. A brilliant business analyst who keeps nervously sticking his finger in his ear may be fine for radio and print outlets, but he's not going to get an invite on CNN or the Fox News Channel any time soon. The guest has to have some visual appeal and personality.

So how does a television news researcher or booker determine who the best expert guests to book on a program are? One way is scouring the Internet until the booker finds someone who fits the bill.

Comedian Paula Poundstone found herself in the hot seat in June 2001 when she was arrested on charges of committing lewd acts on children, and for child endangerment for driving under the influence of alcohol with her foster children in the car (she pleaded no contest to "felony child endangerment and misdemeanor infliction of injury on a child" while the other charges were eventually dropped). With a fairly well known comedian in such crude trouble, the news media naturally followed the story for months.

Someone behind the scenes at Fox News looked for a guest who could talk about Poundstone's predicament. The person scoured the Internet and read the following February 25, 2002 article from the online publication *Hollywood Pulse*, with the headline "Poundstone Granted 'Supervised' Child Abuse":

> Paula Poundstone... was granted supervised child abuse privileges by Los Angeles Superior Court Judge Bernard J. Kamins due to her good behavior over the past six months.
>
> While making the point that Poundstone has not yet earned the right to mistreat her kids in private, the judge declared in open court last Friday that the embattled comic had proven herself worthy of earning the opportunity to practice so-called "monitored" abuse.

The article went on to explain the judge's unique reasoning for his "decision":

> "I believe firmly that Miss Poundstone now qualifies to practice poor judgment with her children in the presence of a court-appointed monitor," Judge Kamins noted... "I'm not yet ready to go the next step and permit she and her children private abuse time. But Miss Poundstone's exemplary behavior and positive strides since last summer lead me to believe that she's fully prepared to put her children at risk so long as a professional abuse expert is present at all times."
>
> The monitored abuse privileges allow Poundstone to drive in an inebriated state with her children in the car and to touch them in "naughty places" so long as both are done with the knowledge and approval of the judicial chaperone.

The article reeks of pure bitter sarcasm. The title is a giveaway that the author's intentions are to spoof events, not chronicle them. Coupled with the fact that the website is a celebrity journalism parody, it should stand to reason that any right thinking news producer would chuckle at the piece. Could anyone actually believe that the article was serious?

Yes.

Someone at the Fox News Channel did take it seriously, and *Hollywood Pulse's* cofounder, Ray Richmond, appeared as a guest on the March 1, 2002 edition of the "Fox Report With Shepard Smith." Surprisingly, Richmond did not parlay his gift for satire onto the screen, but gave fairly innocuous comments such as, "Celebrities are not treated as everyone else," and that, "We don't know how it is in jail, but certainly in the courtroom there is always going to be a difference with celebrities."

Richmond was no celebrity expert, but he held his own without FOX producers becoming suspicious. It was only after his television appearance that Richmond clued everyone in on the gag on his website.

That anyone could think that *Hollywood Pulse* was in the same league as the *Hollywood Reporter* shows either producers are unworldly or they do not have a firm grip on reality. How did network brass react when questioned about Shepard's appearance? Embarrassed? Contrite? None of the above: a spokesman for FOX said that Shepard said "nothing satirical," and that, "It's a well-known fact that Ray Richmond is a media whore and this is him trying to extend his five minutes of fame." Yes, thanks to the sleep-walkers over at FOX.

Forget Waldo and Carmen—Where's Milo John Reese?

Everybody loves a good mystery: the suspense, the potential for lurid gossip and the chance to use their armchair detective skills to speculate what happened and who was responsible. Murders may be too macabre for some, but a report of a disappearance can make for interesting gossip and even better news—it can become a serialized drama in a newscast, so long as the person is found safe and sound, but sometimes the person is never found or recovered. In those cases, an unresolved disappearance will also disappear from the headlines.

In the fall of 1999 the town of Reno, Nevada looked like it would be the scene of such a mystery: an anti-porn activist with an unusual past suddenly vanished without a trace. An *Associated Press* story that appeared on November 9, 1999 edition of the *Las Vegas Sun* opened the first scene:

> Washoe County sheriff Lt. Doug Gist said a helicopter search Tuesday near the Old Bridge Ranch brothel turned up no trace of Milo John Reese, director of the group Nevada Against Prostitution.
>
> Reese, fifty-four, of Reno, was last seen by his wife Sunday night when he left for a meeting at the legal bordello located next to the notorious Mustang Ranch brothel, which was confiscated last summer by the federal government.
>
> Reese did not tell his wife what the meeting was about or who he planned to see. Investigators said his car was found Monday about a half-mile from the brothel, but they're unsure whether he reached it.

Things did not look good for fifty-four-year-old Reese, the story went—one of his car windows was shattered by a rock. Worse, traces of blood were found "inside and outside the car, which was left about a quarter-mile from Interstate 80," near two brothels. Not a good sign. It looked certain that Reese had met a gruesome end.

Except that he hadn't. By November 11, sharp-eyed witnesses and a bank security camera saw Reese in California. Reese came out of the woodwork and confessed to staging his disappearance for the benefit of the news media. To bring attention to his "crusade" Reese was willing to fake his own death to gain publicity. It was an expensive stunt: police billed Reese for the search.

This wasn't the last brush with trouble Reese would have: in 2001 Reese was accused of stealing a Cessna after taking five flying lessons, and instead of landing in Miami, he flew to and crashed the plane in Cuba.

How to Spot Fraudulent Stories

If you can get past the emotionally manipulative parts of a hoaxer's sob story, then you'll find that certain logical inconsistencies become obvious. It's hard enough to remember what happened in real life, trying to approximate reality when lying is much harder than most people think. When Anaïs Nin said "We don't see things as they are, we see them as we are," she wasn't joking. Hoaxers are no different in this regard.

People tend to interpret events based on what past knowledge or experience they have. If you were asked to describe a stranger's office, you wouldn't be able to, since you'd have never seen it. However, if you see an office every day, you might come up with a reasonable guess. If you only see one once in awhile, then your description will be more generic and shaky. But in both cases, if someone were to compare your guess with the stranger's actual office, they would know you weren't being honest.

The same logic applies to a hoaxer's story. A liar with little knowledge or experience is going to have more inconsistencies and be less convincing with details than a liar who does. But as we'll see in Chapter 17, a lack of knowledge isn't an impossible barrier the overcome if the hoaxer is emotionally manipulative.

When you listen, watch or read a news story that involves claims of over-the-top cruelty or heartbreak, listen carefully before you react to it, thinking about which parts of the story are playing on your emotions. Then start breaking down the story to its bare bones (considering most news reports aren't heavy on details, this isn't as hard as it sounds). Start by not thinking about the emotional aspects (i.e., happiness, sadness, anger, fear), but by thinking about only the concrete facts mentioned in the piece. Who are the key players? Which ones are actually interviewed and which ones are only mentioned? What happened in what order? What concrete or tangible evidence (witnesses, documents, physical evidence) is mentioned as proof that the story is true? Who are the actual sources of the story?

Sometimes those questions alone will be enough to tell you that the story may be inaccurate or misleading. But if those questions still don't settle your doubts one way or another, then think about who would benefit from publicity and how. Is there a motive to lie? Are reporters relying on hard evidence? Are they just reporting the account of a single person, or the word of an authority figure? Are there holes in the story? Could the person be lying or exaggerating? Could the person be hiding something?

Here are some other signs to look out for when reading or watching a news story:

1. Someone makes a fantastic claim with superlatives, but little proof.

The interviewee may cry and use colorful language, but what are the actual facts of the story? Does this claim make sense from a logical or physical point of view? Are there any eyewitnesses to the event? Is there hard evidence to verify the story? Does this person try to seem "special" or supernaturally unlucky? Did the reporter interview others who knew the interviewee long enough and well enough to make a reasonable judgment about this person? (Neighbor accounts might be helpful, but they aren't bulletproof. There are countless interviews of neighbors of murderers who say "I'm shocked he's a murderer since he always seemed like a nice guy." Yeah, right.)

For example, in the Negativland hoax, all information came from the group itself—no reporter had bothered to telephone the FBI for confirmation.

2. There are more simple and mundane alternate explanations available that can account for the phenomenon. The more complicated the story, the less likely it is to be the correct one.

Many of us feel guilty when we are suspicious of a person who claims to be a victim—even if the alleged victim has holes in his story; so we give the person the benefit of the doubt. But when a subject needs to explain away troubling contradictions to make the story "fit," then we know the truth differs from the subject's account. We may want to believe an average Windsor family could attract a cyber-stalker who can control the phone lines and electricity in the house, but the truth was more simple: the family's teenage son was fooling around with the phone and light switches.

In Donna Mercier's case, every time someone wanted a tangible piece of evidence, she provided yet another reason why it wasn't possible. Yes, it was entirely possible that a terminally ill victim of crime may also fear an abusive partner so much that media glare and police protection will not calm her fears. On the other hand, the more simple explanation—that she was lying, and exposing her identity would give this fact away—turned out to be the correct one.

3. There is too much hype surrounding the event.

With the Donna Kay Spence AIDS hoax, the evidence seemed to indicate that she was trying to drum up enough support to open her own AIDS center, and had made up the small-town epidemic to raise her profile and solicit state funds. When someone's story is so powerful as to attract mass attention, it may be the time to question who or what is behind it—is it a real event or is it merely empty hype? In the Hitler diary hoax, the claim that never-before-seen diaries could easily fall into the lap of a journalist seemed contrived, especially since everything previously known about Hitler's writing habits contradicted the claim.

4. The subject relies on charisma or personal traits rather than on concrete facts, or the subject is emotionally manipulative (i.e., cries, overreacts to a reporter's tough questions).

If the subject has an "aw-shucks" charm or seems to want reporters' pity, there may be a self-preserving reason for it. If a person is weeping during an interview, it can either indicate an interviewee's personal distress or acting ability used to distract the reporter from thinking on a more skeptical level. The reason that Daniel McCarthy's shaky story was printed without any attempt at verification was that he had a "very intense and believable personality."

Similarly, don't let a subject's age, race or gender fool you. Children can lie effectively to adults, as Nayirah al Sabah and David Barney showed.

5. The subject has something to gain by speaking to reporters (not getting arrested, plans to sue for a large sum of money).

No matter why an interviewee agrees to speak to a reporter, ask "what does this person gain by talking to journalists?" Sometimes a hoaxer may want media attention to try to seem "innocent" of criminal activity. In the Pepsi tainted can scare, people spiked their cans, then gave interviews in the hopes of suing the soft drink giant. Other times, an interviewee feels forced to speak with reporters, as in the case of Donna Mercier. Donna Kay Spence wanted attention and money to open her own clinic. Mercier wanted to acquire a previously denied prescription for painkillers. David Barney wanted to get out of trouble for accidentally killing the beloved family dog. Negativland wanted to get publicity.

In rarer cases, the hoaxer who's received media attention has not actually spoken to journalists, as in the case of Nayirah. Finally, the hardest cases of hoaxes for news consumers to detect are the ones when the hoaxer is working behind the scenes with a journalist, who has kept the person's name out of the public forum. Konrad Kujau, the mastermind behind the Hitler diary hoax was only known to the journalist—neither the public nor the editors of Stern knew of Kujau's existence.

6. The subject seems to avoid answering simple and direct questions, or the subject is specific on some points, too vague on others.

Susan Smith's description of her children's kidnapper was too generic. Daniel McCarthy's account was short on specifics, though it was colorful and dramatic, as was the pseudo-saga of the young Honduran runaway. Times, dates, names, locations and other verifiable information is needed—if there is no concrete evidence, the story may be a sham.

7. The subject's story has flaws in it.

Don't excuse or explain away a story's gaping holes—either the journalist did not do his homework, or the person he interviewed is not telling the truth. When Susan Smith described her alleged carjacking ordeal, she did not explain what she was doing as the kidnapper drove away with her children. When Nayirah described soldiers removing Kuwaiti babies from their incubators, she didn't say what the nurses and volunteers did with the infants after the soldiers left.

8. The story conforms to the subject's view of what an event might be like (i.e., what an uneducated mother or father may think a kidnapping might be like if they are trying to cover up the murder of their child), or there are strange elements of brutality and gentleness in an alleged crime.

A person not familiar with another subgroup's lingo will sound false and even ridiculous trying to emulate the group's slang. Many hoaxers who try to "stage" an event or scene to make their accounts more convincing actually give their hoaxes away. For example, in the Charles Stuart hoax, he claimed armed men shot him and killed his pregnant wife. But why would a robber inflict more severe injuries on a pregnant woman when she is a lesser threat than a strong, young man?

In several child murder cases, parents claimed their children were kidnapped by strangers and went to the media to plea for their children's return. When police eventually found the child's body, the remains would be wrapped in a blanket, and a few even had the child's favorite toy next to the body. A stranger would not take these pains—but a guilt-ridden parent would.

Thinking about alternate explanations is an excellent way for a news consumer to determine the accuracy of a report. Hoaxers can be manipulative and winsome; reporters can make their stories seem more researched than they actually are. By ignoring the "trust me's" from both sides and by looking at the heart of the story, a news consumer can make a better judgment about a story's truthfulness—and not part with hard-earned money or rally around a guilty party.

Chapter **Thirteen**

| **Reporter as Hero**

Many scam artists' rumors and hoaxes made headlines because they understood what journalists were looking for in their stories: unusual, yet simple events, charismatic players who fit into easily identifiable roles, and the potential for colorful anecdotes with emotional pull. It's that journalistic tendency to gravitate toward simplistic, sensational stories that can get an unsettling number of reporters into trouble. In most cases covered in this book, the hoaxer's stories were believed without reservation and their lies were disseminated without a single reporter verifying key information.

Yet there are good journalists out there who don't fall for scams and who unearth corruption. Investigative journalism gives its audience information that is useful, truthful, accurate and balanced. If there weren't any accurate stories, there would be no point in watching or reading the news.

Unfortunately, when many people think of good journalism, they think of Watergate. A story that was reported three decades ago isn't exactly a fresh example of stunning journalism. Yet it's important to know the difference between solid and shoddy reporting: by knowing the differences, it can be easier for a news consumer to spot bad or misleading information.

Some people rely on their gut instinct or common sense to differentiate the two, but "intuition" and folksy logic can be easily manipulated and exploited by a con artist. What the hoaxer can't control is critical thinking and a thorough investigation into his background. A fabricator uses tricks to make his story seem true, but even the most elaborate trick has its weaknesses. A good reporter keeps digging until he finds the chinks in the hoaxer's façade.

The Gulf War hoax certainly had enough large holes for even the most mediocre reporter to spot, but the story's emotional pull was blinding most people's judgment. While it was other reporters who exposed the incubator hoax, Harper's publisher John MacArthur was the one who questioned Nayirah's true identity. If the young witness had a reason for concealing her full name, perhaps that secret would explain whether her story was true or false.

As MacArthur revealed on "60 Minutes," he used a parlor trick of his own to find out who the young girl really was:

> I started asking questions. And I finally heard a rumor that Nayirah was the daughter of the Kuwaiti ambassador, so I used an old reporter's trick. I called up the embassy, and I said, "Nayirah did a terrific job at the Human Rights Caucus, and I think her father must be very proud of her. And doesn't she deserve her place in history?" And the ambassador's secretary said to me, "You're not supposed to know that. No one's supposed to know she's the ambassador's daughter."

Though his ruse worked, some would frown on his tactics; however, when it comes to con artists and other fabricators, sometimes the only method of exposing their lies is by giving them a taste of their own medicine. Good journalism sometimes requires outsmarting and outmaneuvering a dishonest and brazen source.

Even though journalism is supposed to give readers and viewers an unvarnished version of events, it hasn't stopped people from complaining that the press is too negative and only covers "depressing news." Positive news is hardly newsworthy. Wars break out; crime destroys lives and unethical power brokers crush their weaker prey; these events have a greater impact on our lives than who won the annual state spelling bee. Nor does a useful news lead start with the sentence, "Jack Strobe, President of Strobe Industries is one of the most brilliant businessmen who ever lived, and the rest of us are blessed with his piercing ideas and insight." Journalism shouldn't be reduced to cheerleading and stenography.

Good journalists ignore an interviewee's hyperbole and egotism to see where the real story lies. William "Chip" Smith was a twenty-eight-year-old high school teacher in North Carolina who had the admiration of his pupils and the respect of his colleagues. By all accounts, Smith was a beloved educator who had won Rock Hill High School's "Teacher of the Year" award. In the spring of 1980, the *Rock Hill Evening Herald* wrote a glowing profile on Smith, stating that he studied at Oxford and that his book, based on his university thesis, would be published. However, the reporter who wrote the story did not verify Smith's biography.

But the *Charlotte Observer*'s Jim Morrill did go beyond the plaudits to find the real Chip Smith, as he revealed in his July 12, 1981 front-page story:

> Colleagues, supervisors and parents agree he's intelligent, an affable and excellent teacher, a tireless worker widely admired by students.
>
> He was an honors graduate and star baseball player at Guilford College in Greensboro, N.C., with such an exceptional record that the college nominated him for a prestigious Rhodes Scholarship. His senior thesis on the Kennedy assassination was outstanding, college instructors say.

But for reasons no one—not even Smith—can clearly explain, embellishments crept into his credentials.

Ask boys on Rock Hill High's baseball team, or their parents, or the school principal, and they'll say Smith played pro baseball for the Kansas City Royals, rooming with star third-baseman George Brett. Fellow teachers and coaches recall hearing about his studies as a Rhodes scholar at Oxford and about royalties from a book he wrote on the assassination.

Morrill's probing led him to discover that:

• Kansas City Royals records showed that Smith never played for the team;

• Officials at McGraw-Hill, the book publisher that Smith claimed had published his book said that they had no record of Smith in their files;

• The North Carolina state secretary for the Rhodes Scholarship Trust denied that Smith was ever a finalist, though he was an applicant;

• Other points of Smith's résumé were either exaggerated or fabricated.

Had Morrill solely relied on the word of Smith's supervisors, colleagues and students, he would have received glowing references and confirmation of Smith's claims; however all these sources got their information from the same source—Smith. Though the checks into Smith's background were "routine," Rock Hill High and another newspaper that interviewed Smith took the teacher at his word.

When confronted with this information, Smith pleaded with the paper not to print the truth and Smith's mother had asked that the truth be suppressed, lest her son commit suicide. The paper exposed Smith's lies; Smith lost his job, but didn't try to kill himself. Unfortunately, the paper received harsh criticism from readers for printing a fabricator's lies, even though Rock Hill's role model won awards because he was lying to his bosses and charges alike.

Morrill wasn't the only journalist who was criticized for revealing the truth. Reporter George Dohrmann also received public criticism when he reported on academic fraud uncovered at the University of Minnesota's men's basketball program in a March 10, 1999 *St. Paul Pioneer Press* story:

At least twenty men's basketball players at the University of Minnesota had research papers, take-home exams or other course work done for them during a five-year period, according to a former office manager in the academic counseling unit who said she did the work.

Four former players, Courtney James, Russ Archambault, Kevin Loge and Darrell Whaley, confirmed that work was prepared for them in possible violation of the student code of conduct and NCAA regulations.

Another former player, Trevor Winter, said he was aware of the practice.

James, Archambault and the office manager, Jan Gangelhoff, said knowledge of the academic fraud was widespread.

[...]Gangelhoff said she "struggled for a long time" whether to disclose the allegations. When asked to prove them, Gangelhoff provided the Pioneer Press with computer files containing more than 225 examples of course work for nineteen players, dating to 1994, that she says she wrote and players turned in. Gangelhoff said she kept only about half her files.

Gangelhoff also provided printed copies of five pieces of course work that she said had been turned in by students. Some of the papers had grades and instructor's comments written on them. All five pieces also appeared in Gangelhoff's computer files.

Though many readers were angry that the *Pioneer Press* dared to disparage the University with the truth, the series would go on to win the 2000 Pulitzer for Best Beat Reporting. In this case, Dohrmann and other *Pioneer Press* journalists didn't just rely on the University's public relations department for fodder nor did they take Gangelhoff at her word: Dohrmann looked to independently verify Gangelhoff's statements and asked her to produce conclusive proof of all her claims. Many people from all sides of the issue were interviewed and the *Pioneer Press'* own analysis showed that the graduation rate for the University's basketball players were less than half than the national average—a strong motive for some at the University to undertake devious methods to retain athletic students.

A good journalist also looks at all information, no matter how mundane or trivial it may seem. In 2002, one newspaper began its investigation of a suspicious land deal between real estate broker Joe Elliott and the Escambia County Commission. Elliot's friend W.D. Childers was a former political legend and senator from Pensacola, Florida who was now chairman of the commission and who, with three other commissioners (Terry Smith, Willie Junior and Mike Bass), voted to buy a soccer complex from Elliott, who had bought the property at a lower price from a bank on the same day (the bank repossessed the complex from the previous owner). As reporter Amie K. Streater asked in her February 3, 2002 article in the *Pensacola News Journal*:

Why spend so much when in December, the county stalled key projects because of a projected $2.4 million revenue shortfall?

Why did Junior have a change of heart about the soccer complex? He voted twice in 1998 against buying it. "We're not working for ourselves, we're working for people who put us in office, and I don't have that many soccer players in my district," he said in 1998. Yet he recommended the purchase four months ago based on Elliott's written sales proposal.

If the purchase was needed, why didn't the county just buy the soccer complex from the bank that foreclosed on it? Prior to peddling it to the county, Elliott got an option on the property. He bought it from the bank for $3.3 million and simultaneously sold it to the county for $3.9 million. Couldn't the county have cut out the middleman and saved $600,000?

[...]Why did Junior make these purchase proposals as late-night, add-on items to the commission agenda? That meant the public had no prior notice that the purchases would be discussed. In spite of that, commissioners W.D. Childers and Mike Bass voted with Junior.

As more details emerged, the land deal seemed to go against Florida's "Sunshine Law" that prohibited politicians from talking about their votes or business in private. As a result of the *News Journal*'s probing and questioning, four of the five country commissioners were arrested and were charged with a variety of offenses from grand theft, extortion, racketeering, bribery and money laundering. Though Childers was considered a political legend, his questionable ways of doing business were exposed because a journalist took notice of a last-minute addition to a commission's agenda. For her efforts, Streater's stories were nominated for the 2003 Pulitzer Prize.

What Separates a Good Story from a Bad One

A reporter needs to convey information and context to the news consumer: it's not enough to simply report the facts as they come, the reporter has to dig, cajole and probe sources until he can answer important questions about a person or event. That kind of journalism takes time, effort, resources, critical thinking and patience; and even then, not all readers or viewers will appreciate the results, simply because they have not grasped one important facet of reality: the truth is ugly and it hurts.

What this means is that a good news story isn't necessarily a feel-good one: just because a news consumer may not like the story's content, doesn't mean that the content is wrong or inaccurate. Yet good news stories do have other elements in common, such as:

Attention to Important and Relevant Detail

It might satisfy some gossips to know how a singer pulls on her false eyelashes, but how much information does that tidbit convey to a news audience? Most people pull on their real or ersatz lashes; it's not a newsworthy piece of information. On the other hand, how an educator of young, impressionable minds embellishes his résumé is extremely important: how wise is it to let an honesty-impaired individual influence students? Would the teacher have been hired if he told the truth?

Important details about a person or company's status should be given in any story. For example, if a struggling company suddenly pulls itself out of massive debt and reports record profits within a single quarter, the audience should know whether that turnaround happened because of pure luck, competent management or dubious smoke-and-mirror tactics. In the basketball fraud case, the reporter investigated each claim by looking for tangible proof and talking to many different sources. In the Chip Smith case, the journalist tried to independently verify each of Smith's claims by interviewing those who would be most qualified to give informed answers.

Solid Color-Data Ratio

A fiction writer has to use disjointed snatches of both fantasy and reality to make his creation sound and look real. A journalist, on the other hand, is already dealing with reality: he just has to translate that reality into something the reader will be able to understand. A highly investigative piece should only use color as an accent; the bulk of the article should be facts, figures, evidence and interviews.

A good news story is not a romantic one—the facts alone should make the story riveting. In the Florida land deal case, the journalist used questions and facts to tell her story. In the Chip Smith case, the reporter contrasted what Smith's admirers believed with what was actually true. In the basketball fraud case, the reporter relied on evidence and facts, not color, to tell his story.

Investigation Over Stenography

The official party line may be both pleasant and convenient for us, but believing lies can hurt us in the long term. A journalist doesn't have to be lazy or naïve to go along with certain hoaxes and lies, he or she may rather print lies than be abused by reality-phobic complainers. This cowardice reduces journalism to stenography; fortunately, good journalism involves reporters listening to someone's story without interruption, and then delving into details to see how well the story stands up.

In the Gulf War hoax, MacArthur decided to uncover the witness' true identity. Morrill decided to look into Smith's background. Dohrmann decided to look into Gangelhoff's accusations, while Streater decided to look at a last minute addition to a commission's agenda. None of these journalists glossed over the details and all questioned the status quo, regardless of the consequences.

Critical Thinking and Questioning Authority

Investigative reporting is impossible without critical thinking: if the reporter believed every story told to him, then he would give all information equal weight, regardless of whether the information was true or false. Questioning authority and thinking about alternative explanations are the keys to a good news story. In the Gulf War hoax, Nayirah was presented one way, and MacArthur considered an alternate explanation as to her identity. In this case, he was right on the money. In the Chip Smith case, he too presented himself in a certain light, but Morrill considered an alternate explanation, which turned out to be the correct one. Streater's article also questioned those in authority, and Streater discovered their back room dealings were not legal. Dohrmann's articles questioned a University administration's behavior and he discovered that they, too, were not acting in good faith.

Forgetting Pleasantries

A good reporter isn't necessarily a polite one. A good journalist will question everyone, demand hard evidence and tell the truth, no matter how unpleasant it may sound. People will complain, but the reporter has done his job well.

In the Gulf War hoax, MacArthur had the nerve to question the credibility of a sobbing fifteen-year-old girl who claimed to have been psychologically traumatized by enemy soldiers, and he used a trick to get information—two impudent, but effective actions that led to the truth. In the Chip Smith case, Jim Morrill questioned a beloved teacher and went against the wishes of the hoaxer's mother to expose Smith's lies.

So far, we have looked at cases where reporters have spread information because they were duped. But sometimes, the reporter knows he has it wrong simply because he's the one who has made the story up from whole cloth.

| **Reporter as Villain**

Where would journalists be without experts? Quoting authorities is simply the reporter's shorthand for letting readers know that he has done his homework. Without the word of authorities, many journalists feel their stories don't have an official seal of approval.

The practice of quoting experts, even for mundane stories, is common enough: experts are supposed to give a story context and depth. It came as no surprise when one *Associated Press* reporter named Christopher Newton quoted two experts for his short September 9, 2002 piece on the changing U.S. crime rate.

Newton first noted that the U.S. government's statistics showed that most categories of crime had been at their lowest levels since 1973—but *why* there was a decline couldn't be gleaned from the numbers alone. Newton took care of the problem by interviewing experts. The first expert discussed why the crime rate was dropping:

> "When people have jobs and poor neighborhoods improve, crime goes down," said Ralph Myers, a criminologist at Stanford University. "Crime also has been impacted by the implementation of tough sentencing laws at the end of the 1980s."

The second expert seemed to agree with his aforementioned colleague:

> The effect of tougher sentencing laws can best be seen in the drop in the rate at which people in the United States are assaulted, said Bruce Fenmore, a criminal statistician at the Institute for Crime and Punishment, a Chicago-based think tank.
>
> "There is overwhelming evidence that people who commit assaults do it as a general course of their affairs," Fenmore said. "Putting those people behind bars drops the rate."

Both Ralph Myers and Bruce Fenmore sounded as if they knew what they were talking about. One was a criminologist and the other a criminal statistician. Both came from important and esteemed institutions. Both discussed data that other media outlets also reported. The quotes seemed informative and impervious to any chicanery—except that neither man exists, and neither does the Institute for Crime and Punishment.

Newspapers from the *Washington Post, Atlanta Journal and Constitution, Sacramento Bee* to the *Buffalo News* ran the story without double-checking Newton's facts. CNN and Court-TV also carried Newton's piece on their websites without worry. The Justice Department had released the figures cited in Newton's piece—what could possibly be wrong with a story that originates from the *Associated Press*?

However, according to *AP*, three crime experts and one *New York Times* reporter did take an interest in Newton's piece: none had heard of nor could find the experts in question. When *AP* took a closer look at the existence of Myers and Fenmore, Newton was fired.

Newton had a habit of quoting from phantom sources in at least forty articles. In all cases, Newton's facts were accurate, but most of his quoted experts were fakes. There was no "Robert Janson" of the "Voice for the Disabled" or "Joanne Fu" of "Across Cultures." Newton had simply been too lazy or unwilling to find real experts to quote for many of the hundreds of stories he wrote for *AP*.

As in the Newton case, sometimes journalists weave truth with fiction. Quotes, people or anecdotes are fabricated to liven up an otherwise boring piece, but some offenses may be more insidious and harder to prove. For example, how do we know that an "unnamed" or "anonymous" source really exists? Was the "official who spoke on the condition of anonymity" real or created by a desperate reporter?

Other times, reporters fake information at the behest of police. The *Eastside Journal* (now known as the *King County Journal*), a Washington state newspaper complied with area police by running a story about a nonexistent arson. Police hoped the story would help catch a killer by having him believe his accomplice carried out his murderous scheme.

It's not as if the business of journalism has corrupted these reporters; even some college interns have gotten in on the act. Eric R. Drudis, a student at Northwestern University's Medill School of Journalism interned at the *San Jose Mercury News* in the summer of 1999. Drudis also wrote stories for Medill's own news service, including this November 15, 2000 story about a twisted teenaged tryst:

> A fifteen-year-old sophomore at Niles North High School in Skokie pleaded guilty Tuesday to beating her eighteen-year-old prom date because he wouldn't kiss her.
>
> Prosecutors said the Skokie girl pummeled her ex-boyfriend at a post-prom party at his house last May.

At first, the girl claimed her ex-boyfriend tried to rape her. But she took back the story after police found no evidence of sexual assault.

She later admitted she made up the rape allegation because the boy rejected her drunken advances.

"I'm sorry I did all of this," the girl said... "I need to learn how to control my temper."

Drudis' fabrications were uncovered over a year later by the *Mercury News*: over thirty sources Drudis claimed to have interviewed could not be found, including the ones in the above story. Drudis was a well-liked and award-winning student who one newspaper editor liked so much, that she did not fact-check his stories. However, the *Mercury News'* investigation came only after Medill's own news service noticed that his sources couldn't be verified.

There are times when reporters fabricate their entire stories—when not just a single quote or scene, but every copy inch of the story is a work of fiction. Problems outlined in the story are nonexistent; people and organizations are merely plot devices for the journalist to spin an eye-popping story. The reporter wasn't duped by a con artist—he or she is the con artist. So how is a news consumer able to spot deliberate frauds in a reporter's work?

Why Journalists Tell Lies In Their Stories

Dishonest reporters don't have any distinguishing outward characteristics. They come in both genders, all ages, races, religions, sexual orientations, educational backgrounds and social classes. "No name" reporters are no more or less honest than "star" reporters. Healthy reporters lie, as do those with various physical ailments. Even the reasons why a journalist will lie will differ: some have psychological problems; others are manipulative and conniving, and still others are desperate or lazy. There is no single reliable profile for a corrupt journalist.

Journalism is a profession where a single individual has access to a large and trusting audience, and that power can lead some reporters to use their position to suit their own ends. In 1917, journalist Henry Louis Mencken wrote an article for the *New York Evening Mail* about the history of the bathtub. Mencken claimed, among other things, that the first American bathtub was installed in Cincinnati, Ohio in 1842 and that doctors thought bathtubs caused illnesses. Finally, the tub gained respectability in 1850 when President Millard Fillmore had one installed in the White House:

But it was the example of President Millard Fillmore that, even more than the grudging medical approval, gave the bathtub recognition and respectability in the United States. While he was still Vice President, in March, 1850, he visited Cincinnati on a stumping tour, and inspected the original Thompson tub. Thompson himself was now dead, but the bathroom was preserved by the gentlemen who had bought his house from the estate. Fillmore was entertained in this house and, according to Chamberlain, his biographer, took a bath in the tub. Experiencing no ill effects, he became an ardent advocate of the new invention, and on succeeding to the presidency at Taylor's death, July 9, 1850, he instructed his secretary of war, Gen. Charles M. Conrad, to invite tenders for the construction of a bathtub in the White House.

For years, journalists and scholars alike used Mencken's account of the bathtub in their books and articles without ever verifying how accurate it was. But nine years later, the journalist came clean, so to speak—he had made up the entire chronicle as a payback to his editors for not running his pro-Germany articles during the First World War. In a way, Mencken got his revenge.

Even though it has been decades since Mencken confessed to lying, some newspapers have still quoted the vindictive Mencken's lies as fact. In 1992, for example, *Washington Times* reporter Tom DiBacco wrote a story about how President Fillmore brought the first tub to the White House. It was a *Times* reader, not an editor, who caught the error.

Mencken wasn't the only well-respected figure who told whoppers in his stories. A story published in 1747 in the *London General Advertiser* recounted a moving speech about "Polly Baker," a young unmarried mother on trial for (obviously) having had premarital sex. Baker's moving speech outlined that she was a good mother, and that men who committed the offense were not punished. Compelled by her stirring speech, the judges not only found the plucky woman not guilty, but one even married Miss Baker the following day. U.S. newspapers also reprinted the story without verification. Thirty years later, Benjamin Franklin admitted Baker did not exist, but that he had created the story to draw attention to the double standard women faced when it came to morality. Strangely enough, many American history textbooks still treated the Baker story as truth even as late as 1917.

But the problem of dishonest journalism is not as uncommon as some believe: journalists such as Julie Amparano, Patricia Smith, Bart Ripp, Michael Marcus, Eric Drudis, Kim Stacy, Stephen Glass, Janet Cooke, Jayson Blair, Jack Kelley, Wendy Bergen, Uli Schmetzer (who changed the name of a single source in one story), Brad Evenson and editor Scott Fletcher (there are more) have all been dismissed for fabricating whole or parts of their stories, making people up or lying to their editors.

Not all reporters mean to deceive their readers: they may be trying their hand at satire and end up assuming that their newspaper or magazine is the appropriate place to do it. Sometimes it *is* the best place to do it if the publication happens to be satirical in nature. In 1996, the defunct satirical magazine *Might* had its own "Tribute to Adam Rich" issue, a touching obit to the former "Eight is Enough" television star who supposedly died at the hands of a mugger. The truth was that Rich was very much alive; the writers were simply spoofing celebrity journalism. However, a few people thought Rich had indeed met his maker and took the cheeky magazine's ersatz obituary as fact.

But other times, the publication is supposed to be a serious one, and then satire becomes harder to detect. For example, in the *New Times Los Angeles*, "Antoine Oman" reported that two teenage kidnapping victims were to host a NBC reality series called "Survive This!" in which the point of the show was to let loose several attractive teenagers in remote areas where they had to escape from sadistic criminals. Oman went on to write how several "experts" saw the show as beneficial to the traumatized would-be hosts:

> Other mental-health professionals told *New Times* that trauma victims don't really need extended private healing time, as psychologists and psychiatrists once believed. All the media exposure, plus the seven-figure deal each of the girls is expected to get from NBC for the reality program, will go a long way toward helping them to feel better, the experts insisted.
>
> "Look, I wouldn't want this to happen to my son or daughter," said UCLA Rape Prevention Services director Martin Finoogian, "but you have to think of how fast Roy D. Ratliff will fade from their minds when these two girls are faced with the pressures of not tanking in the ratings so they can keep those million-dollar paydays coming in."

Though the yarn has the feel of politically incorrect spoof, nevertheless, some reporters called NBC to confirm the story. Even the reporter, Antoine Oman, was a one-shot nom de plume for the culprit, writer Tony Ortega, who later wrote about Oman's "dismissal" from the paper. Though the *Hollywood Reporter* had discovered the story to be a hoax, the *Drudge Report* had linked to the article and at least one major market radio station picked up the story as fact.

But sometimes, the lie defies logic. In the August 2002 edition of *Details* magazine, Inside.com founder and former *Spy* and *New York Magazine* editor Kurt Andersen supposedly wrote an article called "Dudes Who Dish," about men who gossip. However, Andersen had never written the story, nor had any role in it. The story was published—fact-checkers seemed to have not contacted the author and even editor-in-chief Daniel Peres had not been suspicious, though Peres ran with the story without a signed contract. Though he denied writing the piece under Andersen's byline, senior editor Bob Ickes, who had a troubling history with other publications, later resigned from the magazine.

The *New York Times Magazine* was also faced with allegations of journalistic dishonesty in February 1982 when one of its freelance writers, Christopher Jones, wrote an article claiming he had seen dictator Pol Pot through his binoculars while visiting Cambodia. It was discovered that Jones never went to the country and had stolen parts of his work from a novel. Confronted with this deception, Jones conceded that he plagiarized because he "needed a piece of color." Almost twenty years later, in the November 2001 *New York Times Magazine*, a moving and colorful article written by Michael Finkel profiled one "Youssouf Male," a young teenaged Ivory Coast laborer whose hardened existence touched readers. With an eye for detail, Finkel described one leg of the young man's journey:

> Youssouf walked through his village and into the bush. Soon, he was as far from home as he had ever been. He kept walking. Later in the day, he worked for a few hours in a family's fields, in exchange for a meal and a place to sleep. The next morning he walked on. He walked for twelve days. Then he reached a very wide path that looked to be made out of a wonderful kind of rock. He had never seen an asphalt road before. The road was filled with bicycles and mopeds and four-wheeled mopeds and giant four-wheeled mopeds that had rows and rows of seats and even bigger mopeds that carried enough sacks of rice to feed his village for a year. It was a very exciting road.

When one Canadian relief agency noticed the boy in the *Times* picture was not Youssouf Male, Finkel confessed that Male was a "composite" of the Coast's child laborers; in others words, Finkel lied and was fired for his transgression. As the *Washington Post*'s Howard Kurtz noted, Finkel's other articles were also opulent descriptions of cursed foreigners struggling for mere survival—and each of these stories had hard to trace sources.

If there is one generalization to be made about dishonest journalists, it's that print reporters seem more vulnerable to fabricating stories than their television or radio counterparts (though when falling for hoaxes, reporters from all media types seem to be equally lackadaisical). There may be a number of reasons for the apparent discrepancy: first, in this day and age where digital equipment can record interviews with ease, many print reporters still don't tape or digitally record their interviews. Telephone interviews can be as easily recorded as face-to-face interviews, but many print reporters don't record in either setting. What these reporters do is just take notes, which leads to problems if there is a discrepancy between what the reporter wrote and what the interview subject claims he actually said. A tape (audio or video) is hard evidence; notes can be sloppy, illegible, incorrect, misinterpreted, misremembered or even fabricated.

Second, unless the television journalist is also a "videographer," television reporters have at least one other individual (i.e., the camera person) present at the scene, which may help the TV reporter stay more honest. The print reporter is on his own.

Third, there are fewer radio and TV stories, while papers and magazines have more items, many of which may be short items buried in the middle of the newspaper or magazine. The difference means articles are less likely to be noticed or scrutinized. Perhaps these reporters see their work as "filler" and may not see the harm in making up an article that few people are likely to read or examine closely.

Without the proper safeguards, such as skeptical and demanding editors, vigilant fact-checkers and the mandatory taping of interview subjects, an unscrupulous newspaper or magazine reporter can deceive with relative ease. Some journalists are serial fabricators: they have lied to readers for years before getting caught. *USA Today*'s Jack Kelley had more leeway to quote unnamed sources than did the rest of his *USAT* colleagues, nor did it seem that he tape recorded interviews (if he had, he could have given his editors recorded proof of his interviews).

Yet that doesn't mean that a TV or radio reporter hasn't deceived audiences, either. "Dateline NBC" aired a segment on November 17, 1992 about the flammability of General Motors' "side saddled" gas tanks. The program shocked viewers when a 1977 GM truck exploded before their eyes. Who could question a videotaped demonstration of a car's unsafe features? But the demo was rigged by the show's producers, who planted a remote controlled explosive device inside the car. GM sued and NBC settled the suit by admitting that producers had rigged the inferno.

Not every fudging of TV news is as serious. On January 26, 1994, ABC's "World News Tonight" with Peter Jennings aired one segment with Cokie Roberts reporting in her rain coat in front of Capitol Hill during the President's State of the Union address. What viewers didn't learn until later was that Roberts was not in front of the Capitol, but in an ABC studio sound stage, standing in front of a blue screen, with the Capitol image superimposed. Making matters worse, the network's spokesperson had said that Roberts was rushed for time because she had a prior speaking engagement, and to hide her dress, she had put on the coat; however, that story turned out as bogus as the blue screen.

While Roberts' deception was more embarrassing than harmful, there have been worst offenses against broadcast journalism, as the following case study shows.

It's a Dog Eat Dog World—Then Again, Maybe Not

Violence is a trusty staple for television news. Body bags, bright yellow tape, bloody garments and flashing police cars make excellent visuals for local and national news. There's drama, fear, a captivating story and easily identifiable roles: victim, villain and sometimes hero.

Yet violence doesn't have to be limited to homicides. Military visuals can also grab viewers, as long as the scene is not too gory. If you don't have brave soldiers or ruthless criminals, even a couple of rabid pit bulls will do in a pinch.

For four days during the "sweeps period" in May 1991, KCNC, a Denver television station, rocked the city with reporter Wendy Bergen's hard-hitting exposé "Blood Sport," focusing on illegal dogfighting. Apparently, bloody underground dogfights were rampant, springing up in people's basements, to the delight of Denver gamblers.

In television news, it's not good enough to simply tell viewers that Denver dogs are tearing each other to shreds—a reporter needs moving pictures to drive the point home. Bergen had the visuals in the form of an anonymously sent tape of two dogs fighting and training on a treadmill. Faces of gamblers who were interviewed were obscured, and there were anonymous sources quoted. The secrecy and violent footage gained attention for the Emmy-winning reporter.

Unfortunately, the type of attention Bergen received would prove to be her undoing. There were plenty of signs that something wasn't quite right with the home video of the dogfights. For one, it was always the same two dogs that were mauling each other. If dogfights were as prevalent as Bergen claimed, then wouldn't several different dogs be seen on the tape? If betting on dogfights was so rampant in the city, how come there weren't any gamblers—or anyone else watching this dog fight? And why was one of the dogs training on a regular treadmill?

It was a columnist for the *Denver Rocky Mountain News* who reported that the "anonymous tape" Bergen claimed to have received was actually one staged for the reporter's benefit. Bergen denied the allegations—but then law enforcement managed to track down and identify the two dogs on the tape. After one of Bergen's cohorts made an immunity deal with prosecutors, the dogfight was finally revealed to be a hoax.

What began as a search for the truth and smashing ratings morphed into a rather pathetic descent into prevarication. Bergen relied on the word of a telemarketer who claimed that dogfighting was big business in Denver. The source set up a dogfight for the benefit of Bergen and her cameramen, though neither was suspicious that they were the only ones in attendance. Bergen was asked by News Director Marv Rockford to get more footage, specifically of the pit bulls' training. However, Bergen's source wouldn't cooperate.

This time, Bergen took the dogs and had them videotaped at one of the cameraman's homes, working out on his treadmill. But then came another snag: even *watching* a dog fight was a crime. With this revelation, station brass put the series on hold. In response, one of the cameramen offered to reedit a tape of a newly arranged dogfight and dub it on VHS, making it seem as if it were a home movie. He would send the tape to Bergen "anonymously"; but the second dogfight had none of the zing of the first and wasn't usable.

But Bergen, determined to air her story at any cost, said she placed a blank VHS tape in an envelope and claimed to station executives to have received an anonymous tape of the dogfight, though no one asked her to pop the tape in the VCR so that they could view it. Bergen then reedited the original tape to look like an amateur home video, and no one at KCNC recognized the footage—or dogs—as the same they saw only a few months before. Without questioning the source or the veracity of this new "tape," Bergen went ahead with the phony exposé.

As a result, Bergen was not only fired, but was charged and convicted of dog fighting, conspiracy and being an accessory. Bergen left the journalism business, but she isn't the only reporter who started with honest intentions, only to resort to lying to get the story.

Children Under Twelve Get Heroin for Free—Details Inside the *Washington Post*

One of the most infamous episodes of journalistic contrivance, this hoax still haunts the *Washington Post*, though the scandal rocked the paper back in 1981. The reporter in question was Janet Cooke, a young, intelligent and vivacious journalist who worked at the *Post*. Her impressive résumé included a Master's degree in literature, another degree from Vassar and membership in the National Association of Black Journalists.

It took her only eight months into her tenure at the *Post* to make a splash at the paper. On September 28, 1980, Cooke stunned Washington, DC with her controversial front-page article "Jimmy's World," the tale of an eight-year-old heroin addict. Cooke described how the young boy, who was the result of a rape, lived in a house full of drugs.

Though the journalist interviewed high profiled experts for her story, it was Cooke's vivid use of color that chilled readers with its bluntness:

> Jimmy wants to be a good dope dealer. He says that when he is older, "maybe about [eleven]," he would like to "go over to Condon Terrace (notorious for its open selling of drugs and violent way of life) or somewhere else and sell." With the money he says he would buy a German Shepherd dog and bicycle.

Jimmy was a child with "sandy hair, velvety brown eyes and needle marks freckling the baby-smooth skin of his thin brown arms." Cooke went on to describe the drug-dealing stepfather doping up the youngster:

> Ron comes back into the living room, syringe in hand, and calls the little boy over to his chair: "Let me see your arm."
>
> He grabs Jimmy's left arm just above the elbow, his massive hand tightly encircling the child's small limb. The needle slides into the boy's soft skin like a straw pushed into the center of a freshly baked cake. Liquid ebbs out of the syringe, replaced by bright red blood. The blood is then reinjected into the child.

Immediately, a firestorm brewed over the article. Washington mayor Marion Barry and city police openly doubted the story; why would a drug dealer give drugs away for free? Nevertheless, the mayor ordered a citywide search to find and help the boy, demanding that Cooke reveal the identity of the child. Both *Post* editors and Cooke declined, citing confidentiality. Since Cooke claimed that drug dealers threatened her life, her editors did not press her for Jimmy's identity.

Because Cooke used vivid details and spoke to high profile experts, her supporters believed her, even though Jimmy hadn't yet turned up. Executive editor Ben Bradlee and *Metro* editor Bob Woodward (one half of the famous Woodward-Bernstein duo who uncovered Watergate) stood by Cooke, and said reporters shouldn't "have to play cops." The paper fought off subpoenas, citing the First Amendment. Eventually, the glare died down and Cooke continued to write more stories.

Six months later, on April 13, 1981, Cooke won a Pulitzer for her vivid description of a lost little boy. Two days later, her story fell apart: when a routine autobiographical check showed Cooke fudged her academic credentials, allegations that she fabricated Jimmy resurfaced. After failing to show her editors where Jimmy lived, Cooke came clean: Jimmy was a hoax.

Cooke was fired, and the *Post* faced the biggest scandal in its history. Later on, Cooke maintained that she overheard workers at a drug rehab center talk about an eight year-old addict, but since no one at the clinic would later divulge his identity, Cooke resorted to fiction.

How could Cooke have been hired, when she lied on her résumé? How could *Post* editors not press her to reveal the boy's identity before her story went to print? The *Post* was left to explain itself while Cooke left journalism. Almost twenty years later, a *GQ* magazine profile on Cooke revealed she eventually found her way into a $6 an hour retail sales job at a department store; however, these days, fibbing journalists getting their comeuppance may be a thing of the past.

On the Perils of Giving High Fives and Using Color

Janet Cooke managed to hoodwink several seasoned editors at what is supposed to be one of journalism's great institutions. But Cooke had only fabricated a single story, unlike Stephen Glass—a young rising reporter who took pathological lying to a new, disturbing level.

Glass, a former fact-checker, worked at the *New Republic*, though he also wrote for other magazines, from *Policy Review* to *Rolling Stone*. Many journalists were surprised that a charming twenty-five-year-old reporter could manage so many assignments—and find so many oddball characters and situations to write about. His stories were quirky and caught the attention of other editors and reporters.

And Glass was a master at using color in his stories—many times, facts and hard evidence seemed scant. But when it came to describing gullible and homely women, overzealous activists and victimized cab drivers, Glass excelled. He also seemed blessed with the gift of being in the right place at the right time—he could find unusual characters and events that no other reporter could. A computer hacker's conference? Glass got an invite. A convention where lurid Monica Lewinsky memorabilia was sold? He was there. A cab where the driver was robbed in broad daylight? Glass was right inside the taxi when it happened.

But there were signs that this ascending young reporter had serious problems with his larger-than-life tales. In one story, Glass wrote that he was witness to the following scene in an Omni Shoreham Hotel room during a convention of young conservatives:

> The mini bar is open and empty little bottles of booze are scattered on the carpet. On the bed, a Gideon Bible, used earlier in the night to resolve an argument, is open to Exodus. In the bathroom, the tub is filled with ice and the remnants of three cases of Coors Light. The young men pass around a joint, counterclockwise.

In response to the March 31, 1997 article, American Conservative Union Chairman David A. Keene wrote to point out that the hotel did not have a mini bar, nor did he witness the kind of lurid shenanigans that Glass described. Keene also called Glass "quite a fiction writer." However, Glass corrected himself by stating the hotels had mini-refrigerators, but maintained the rest of his article was accurate.

That wasn't the only controversy to dog the young reporter. Glass' articles on the effectiveness of the D.A.R.E. program and righteousness of the Center for Science in the Public Interest were also questioned. But with each complaint, the editors at the *New Republic* stood by Glass, never questioning whether there was more to the vehement denials than guilty parties throwing tantrums.

Was Glass investigated by the magazine or even questioned? The editor at the time, the late Michael Kelly, stood by his young, modest scribe.

"You either trust your writer or you don't," Kelly would later recall in an interview. This black and white logic would haunt the magazine later.

Many others at the *New Republic* had also mentioned that Glass was boyish looking, self-depreciating, modest and worked hard to please. It stood to reason that Glass looked honest and acted honest; therefore, he must be honest. The motivations behind his behavior were never questioned.

Despite the simmering grumbles from those Glass wrote about and others who could not verify parts of Glass' stories, the suspicions didn't detract from Glass's vivid descriptions of flamboyant figures and surreal events. In *Spring Breakdown*, Glass described the young Republican boys who would rather party than listen to politicians. "Shirtless Seth bows and then flexes his biceps over his head as he grunts loudly." After Seth lured a homely girl into his hotel room only to humiliate her, Glass noted that, "Charlie g[ave] Seth a high five. He promise[d] to get the photo developed and duplicated in the morning. The men start[ed] chanting Seth's name over and over."

Glass wrote articles for several other magazines, including *Harper's*, *Rolling Stone* and the April 1998 edition of *George* magazine. The *George* article profiled Washington attorney and former President Bill Clinton's longtime friend Vernon Jordan—at one point accusing Jordan of lecherous behavior. Glass discussed in the magazine's contributor's section how difficult it was to crack open the story:

> "[Jordan] is a very difficult character to write about because everyone relies on him so much that they're reluctant to discuss him... He is part of every Clinton story, but he is the part that no one talks about."

In his last *New Republic* story in May 1998, *Hack Heaven* chronicled the escapades of one Ian Restil, "a fifteen-year-old computer hacker who look[ed] like an even more adolescent version of Bill Gates." Restil, it seemed, was a capitalistically swinish extortionist who would hack into company databases and offer to fix their security glitches—for a hefty fee. This young and self-indulgent one-note wonder was well rehearsed in giving corporate suits his hedonistic demands:

> I want more money. I want a Miata. I want a trip to Disney World. I want *X-Man* [sic] comic [book] number one. I want a lifetime subscription to *Playboy* and throw in *Penthouse*. Show me the money! Show me the money!

How did Ian's mother respond to her child's thuggery? According to Glass, she could not be happier: "We're so proud of him... He's doing such good things, and he's so smart and kind."

Glass claimed to have attended a conference sponsored by the "National Assembly of Hackers" as "teenage hackers and graying corporate executives flocked to Ian, patting him on the back and giving him high-fives," Ian announced he had hacked and sabotaged a new company:

> "And now they're going to show me the money," he said, swirling his hips and shaking his fists. "I want a Miata. I want a trip to Disney World..."

Besides having techno-geeks and suits behaving in the same way as the stoned-out young conservatives in *Spring Breakdown,* Glass mentioned several laws, publications, organizations and even a hacker agent in his article. One online publication, *Forbes Digital Tool* had taken an interest in Glass' piece.

None of the people or organizations Glass mentioned could be located. How could tech-savvy editors be that out of the loop? They weren't, but editors at *Digital Tool* decided to write a piece on Glass' inaccuracies. Perhaps ego more than skepticism drove the editors to pursue the story (Adam L. Penenberg, the *Digital Tool* editor who broke the story of Glass' deceit wrote, "At first it appeared that *Digital Tool* had been scooped by a weekly political publication"), but nevertheless, their investigation led them to contact the *New Republic.*

They and *New Republic* editor Charles Lane discovered that Glass hadn't just fabricated his stories—but also his proof. He fabricated business cards, letterheads, websites and even the notes he handed over to fact checkers for verification, and none of them were the wiser (it seems as if these fact-checkers had relied on the material Glass gave them rather than independently verifying the information themselves).

For *Hack Heaven,* Glass had even asked his younger brother to call the magazine posing as one of the principles in his story. In two and a half years, Glass had fabricated all or part of twenty-seven of his forty-one *New Republic* articles, while his stories for *George, Rolling Stone* and *Harper's* were also suspect. For Glass' fabrication in *George* magazine, editor John F. Kennedy Jr. apologized to Vernon Jordan in the July 1998 issue of the magazine.

Was Glass a good reporter gone bad? In most of his stories, Glass had relied on poor sourcing and had little concrete information. Instead, what he relied on was color—gossipy and minute details about peculiar people who turned out to be phantoms. Even if he had not made up his stories, Glass' articles may have made for an interesting read, but with so little information, they had almost no utility. Glass got away with what he did because he seemed to have a gift for finding and describing trivialities.

Glass seems to have weathered his disgrace with some aplomb. A movie was made of his time at the *New Republic,* called *Shattered Glass.* After graduating from law school and penning the autobiographical fictional book *The Fabulist*, *Rolling Stone* magazine kissed and made up with the man who fabricated parts of an article he wrote for them. In September 2003, Glass wrote an unremarkable story for the magazine about the Canadian decriminalization of marijuana. Seems Glass has become one of the singular characters he fantasized about in his articles.

Tobacco Fields of Dreams

After the Stephen Glass fiasco, one would assume that media outlets would be more vigilant with their reporters; however, Glass is not the last journalist who was caught fabricating his stories, nor was the *New Republic* the last esteemed publication to be fooled. The *New York Times* prides itself as the "paper of record," and many journalists consider reading the *New York Times* as a part of their research for their stories. What happened in 2003 would shake the paper to the core.

Jayson Blair was a young *Times* reporter whose résumé seemed impressive enough: he was a University of Maryland journalism graduate who was editor of the *Diamondback*, the school's newspaper, with later internships at the *Times* and the *Boston Globe* as well as a stint as a part-time stringer for the *Washington Post*. He also had a charming personality and worked hard. On paper and in person, Blair looked good.

But there were plenty of signs that Blair was a time bomb. He had substance abuse problems. He behaved erratically. There were corrections—and lots of them—for the stories Blair wrote: in his four years as a *Times* scribe, he logged almost fifty in total before he was finally exposed. At least one other journalist complained that he lifted her work. Some editors felt uneasy about his writing, but despite the red flags, Blair kept reporting for the *Times*, having many of his stories appear in other newspapers who used the *Times'* wire service. The paper's readers had no clue how troubled Blair was.

Blair was unremarkable as a writer, but he was writing more stories and getting more bylines, becoming a national correspondent and covering high profile assignments such as the Washington, D.C. sniper shootings. He had broken the story that John Lee Malvo, the teenaged partner of the murderous duo, had been the sniper in some of the shootings.

He also wrote about the rescue of Private Jessica Lynch, who was missing in Iraq. In the article, Blair said he had interviewed Lynch's father and described the Lynch family home in a March 27, 2003 article, claiming that Private Lynch's father "choked up as he stood on his porch here overlooking the tobacco fields and cattle pastures, and declared that he remained optimistic."

Blair also covered another U.S. soldier, Sergeant Edward Anguiano, who at the time was missing in Iraq. Blair's April 25, 2003 article began with describing the mother of the slain soldier who lived in Texas:

> Juanita Anguiano points proudly to the pinstriped couches, the tennis
> bracelet in its red case and the Martha Stewart furniture out on the patio.
> She proudly points up to the ceiling fan.

There were two problems with this passage: first, the words weren't Blair's,
but those of Macarena Hernandez, a *San Antonio Express-News* journalist.
Hernandez wrote a near identical passage, but that Anguiano had not taken
the furniture out on the patio:

> So the single mother, a teacher's aide, points to the ceiling fan he installed
> in her small living room... She points to the pinstriped couches, the tennis
> bracelet still in its red velvet case and the Martha Stewart patio furniture,
> all gifts from her first born and only son.

Second, Blair had not been to Texas, nor had he interviewed Anguiano.
Convinced that Blair had lifted her week-old article and had made educated
guesses about Anguiano, Hernandez went back to the Anguiano home to see
what happened to the furniture. As Hernandez wrote in the *Los Angeles
Times*: "The Martha Stewart patio furniture wasn't on the patio: It was in its
box next to the kitchen table. I doubted that Anguiano had found the energy to haul [the furniture] outside after we spoke."

On April 29, 2003, the news of Blair's deception was made public. By
May 1, Blair resigned. But how did Jayson Blair get away with years of public deceit? By accounts, it seems as if he had both devious ingenuity and
supervisors who were either too oblivious or unwilling to deal with him.
With a laptop and cell phone, Blair could pretend to cover the news outside
the office, even though a closer examination of his phone records clearly
showed he rarely left town. Blair studied photographs of places he was supposed to cover to make it seem as if he was there. It seems as if no one at the
Times noticed his expense reports, either. Blair cribbed from other reporters;
he fabricated quotes and scenes. He filed phony expense reports and lied
about his whereabouts. His scoops on the Washington-area sniper case were
also discovered to be fakes.

For four years, Blair scammed with near impunity. As the *Times* noted
in their May 11, 2003, 14,000 word front-page retraction of Blair's chronic
delinquency:

> An article about the decision by the parents of Private Lynch to fly to Ger-
> many to meet her while she was undergoing treatment there carried a
> dateline of Charleston, W.Va., April 5. But the hotels in the area have no
> record of Mr. Blair's checking in. And an editor in the national department
> of the *Times* said he saw Mr. Blair in the newsroom in New York shortly

after 4 that afternoon. The editor, who had been under the impression Mr. Blair was in Charleston when he spoke to him late that morning, asked Mr. Blair how he had returned to New York so quickly. Mr. Blair said he had taken a 2:30 p.m. flight. There does not appear to have been such a flight that day. And there are calls made from his desk extension to towns in West Virginia beginning at 2:20 p.m., phone records indicated.

Didn't the *Times* realize that Blair was the reporter who got the information last, considering he had culled information from other articles? How could they keep a reporter who had permanent real estate in the "Corrections" section of the paper? This, the same reporter whose erratic behavior triggered the now infamous internal memo from Metropolitan Editor Jonathan Landman: "We have to stop Jayson from writing for the *Times*. Right now." Some argued that Blair, who is black, got away with what he did because of the *Times'* affirmative action policies. However, that absurdist argument assumes that out of all minority newspaper reporters, Blair was the only non-white reporter qualified and willing to work at the *Times*.

Furthermore, neither Christopher Newton, Jack Kelley nor Stephen Glass were hired through affirmative action. Many other journalists have been fired in recent years for other journalistic transgressions, most notably plagiarism. To say that affirmative action led to the *Times* humiliation is to ignore that lazy and careless reporting has led to misinformation being disseminated through the press.

There were earlier signs that Blair was trouble. Though he attended the University of Maryland, he never graduated from the journalism program. After Blair's firing from the *Times*, the *Boston Globe* conducted its own investigation into the stories Blair wrote for their paper and also discovered there were serious errors and transgressions committed, but the severity of those offenses did not reach the same levels as his misdeeds at the *Times*.

In a strange twist, many of the people mentioned in Blair's articles knew of the deceptions, but did not complain. One person who Blair claimed to have interviewed (but didn't) did not complain because, as he said in a later interview, "With most reporters, I thought everything got spun around a little bit."

Blair wrote about one injured U.S. soldier in Iraq, Lance Cpl. James Klingel. Blair's front-page story claimed, among other things, that Klingel was permanently disabled and that he had a girlfriend. Though Klingel's mother had read the error-ridden article, she later told the *Los Angeles Times* that "We were laughing about it. I kept asking him, which girl would be thinking that she was the girl mentioned in the story?" The Klingels did not complain to the *Times*.

Blair was fired, but many felt the *Times* did not take full responsibility for allowing such flagrant transgressions to go unnoticed and unpunished.

Howell Raines, the executive editor of the *Times,* and managing editor Gerald Boyd both resigned from the paper shortly after the Blair scandal. But Blair has not merely skulked away from journalism—he was assigned to write an article for the women's fashion magazine *Jane* about stress in the workplace and was supposed to write a movie review for the aforementioned *Shattered Glass* for *Esquire*, though the assignment was later scrapped. David Granger, *Esquire* editor-in-chief, defended his initial decision, claiming "It was intended as a joke that readers would see when they picked up the issue." No one else was laughing. Sadder still, Blair signed a six figure deal with Millennium Press, who published Blair's book about his days at the *Times*, and Showtime decided to make a TV movie about his exploits.

Terminally Lying

Throughout the book, we've seen several people fake terminal illnesses for various reasons. But would a journalist do the same? At least one already has.

In April and May 1999, thirty-three-year-old Kim Stacy was a columnist for the *Owensboro Messenger-Inquirer*, a small newspaper in Kentucky. But she wasn't your run-of-the-mill reporter: she was one on the brink of death, battling the ravages of cancer. As she painfully confessed to readers in her debut column: "I have terminal brain cancer. I was told I had about ten months to a year to live." But it didn't stop her from writing about her ordeal at the request of her editors. No, they didn't ask for verification of her illness—after all, she said she had less than a year left.

Stacy's Sunday columns were blunt and exposed her loneliness, but despite her inevitable death sentence, her writings had tinges of optimism and hope, as her April 4, 1999 piece showed:

> I'd never thought about dying, even though I've always known nothing lasts forever.
>
> I thought about the little things I take for granted each day. The simple joy of riding my bicycle in the morning before heading out to spend my day as a reporter. Those cozy evenings at home with my cat Prissy, where we linger over supper, usually take-out, then curl up on the couch with a good book, a long movie or a favorite CD.
>
> It may be a simple life. But it's a life I enjoy and the way I've always wanted it to be.

Stacy's columns also hinted at the insecurity she said she felt:

> Owensboro was a great job opportunity. I was looking for a change in scenery. I liked the people, and even being a hillbilly. I seemed to fit right in or, at least everybody made a place for me.

In the same column, she noted that she had battled stomach cancer twice (describing how she gave her doctor a high five when he told her she was cancer free after facing stomach cancer a second time) and that despite the chemotherapy and fear, there was a blessing in her first two battles:

> Immediately, coworkers and friends rallied around me, making themselves available for anything I needed, even if it was only to talk. Most surprising was the comfort I received from the community. People who I saw every day as I went about my job—strangers in many ways—would drop by the office to wish me well or call me to see if there was anything I needed.

In a handful of front-page columns, Stacy wrote about her own struggle with "terminal brain cancer." Her columns were vivid in their descriptions of her fear and valiance: "I'm going to die! I'm going to die!" "I can't believe I'm going to die," and "My life may be over in six months, but I'm not going out of this world without a fight." Her columns were descriptive, though Stacy had a tendency to overuse the words "I" and "me" even when she was discussing other people. She also seemed at peace with her fate, as her April 11, 1999 piece revealed:

> Most people think that I'm a little more irrational these days, just a little bit too calm and serene for someone about to play out the last days of her life.
> But I can afford to be irrational and frivolous.
> It doesn't concern me what people might think if I go skipping through mud puddles or stop in the middle of the street to stare up in the sky or eat ice cream at three in the morning while watching Scooby Doo reruns.

The same column also hinted where Stacy's priorities lied:

> [...]I want to go about my usual day doing the things that make me happy and bring peace to my life.
> And for me, that is my job.
> It's the reason I get up in the morning.
> It's why I hurry out the door, anxious to meet people, see what's happening and write it down at the end of the day.
> It's the reason I stay up at night and replay the day's events, wondering how I could have made a story better. Sometimes, I'm too excited about tomorrow's story to go to sleep.
> Sure, there are other things in life—spending time with family, hanging out with friends, crying at a sad movie or reading a good book. I could write a poem, climb a mountain, go see a play or just sit on my front porch with a cup of coffee as the sun comes up.

But those things are life's bonuses. The nuts and bolts of my life is my job, the way in which I have chosen to make my small contribution in the bigger scheme of things.

Stacy also wrote about her fateful encounter with Josh, a terminally ill boy with a sunny disposition. Her April 18, 1999 column detailed her meeting with the brave and selfless young man with the big heart whom she met while she faced her first bout of stomach cancer:

> While waiting for my turn with the doctor and hoping to help time pass a little more quickly, I anxiously looked for an eager individual to strike up a conversation.
>
> A small boy and a woman, who I assumed to be his mother immediately grabbed my attention... I realized by his small, fragile body, pale complexion and bald head, he was wrestling with a terminal illness.
>
> The thing that appealed to me about this little boy was his blue eyes, the prettiest I have ever seen. They reached out to me with a peacefulness and laughter I know I will never feel again.

After describing how she was "mad at God" and mad at her family for seeming to "smother [her] with care and attention," Stacy learned that the boy was battling a rare form of leukemia for the past three years. Josh talked for "thirty minutes" about how he was not afraid to die, that he worried for his parents, about his illness and that "God still sends miracles to those who believe." The boy was not angry, but compassionate, in fact, so compassionate that he asked Stacy if they could exchange addresses. She agreed and then they exchanged letters; sadly, within two weeks, Stacy discovered that Josh had lost his fight.

Many Owensboro residents who themselves faced terminal illnesses took comfort from Stacy's columns and had let editors know their reporter had made their suffering easier to face. Murial Gillim, a *Messenger-Inquirer* reader who met Stacy, wrote a letter to the editor praising Stacy's chronicles that was published on April 18, 1999:

> It is not often, maybe once in a lifetime, that one meets a person who has such courage and convictions in the face of a terminal illness
>
> [...]I am saving all her articles, and I invite others to do the same. Who knows, someday we may be faced with some adversity and will be able to glean substance and hope from her writings.
>
> Way to go, Kim. I feel so fortunate to have met her. My prayers are with her.

But there were others who eyed Stacy's columns, too. Her friends, former coworkers and family also read her columns and noticed what she told her readers wasn't exactly what she had told them. Treatments and symptoms outlined in her columns didn't quite correspond with her verbal accounts of her illness. The publisher of one of the papers where Stacy once worked phoned the *Messenger-Inquirer*.

Confronted by one of her editors with the accusation of dishonest conduct, Stacy dropped her first bombshell: no, she didn't have cancer, but she did have AIDS for the last four years. She said she feared the stigma associated with the disease would be too much for her to endure in her already weakened state; after all, she lived in a small town in the South. As she recounted to the *Associated Press*, "I grew up in a small town atmosphere where you are crucified for having AIDS or being gay." The paper dismissed her on August 20, 1999 for lying about her illness, but questions still lingered as media attention from around the country focused on her revelations.

Two *Messenger-Inquirer* reporters escorted her to a clinic to confirm that Stacy was in fact HIV positive. While the results of that test were never made public, the second bombshell hit: the reporter was afflicted with neither cancer nor AIDS—she was healthy, though her father confirmed that she had diabetes. Why did Stacy lie about being terminally ill? According to Stacy, she simply wanted to "make friends" and playing on the sympathy of others seemed to be her way of connecting to people.

There were other warning signs: Stacy had told coworkers at her former paper as early as 1995 that she had stomach cancer, though that too was a bogus claim. It was through her changing stories that her scam was finally brought to light.

But her columns also revealed another, more subtle clue that would be apparent to more astute readers with a good understanding of psychology. Strangely, while at times Stacy seemed petrified by her "condition," more often than not, she seemed fairly (and at times, inappropriately) unconcerned about her illness and its implications.

Indifference is not so much a sign of bravery in those battling a terminal illness as it is a symptom of another disorder (indifference is not to be confused with putting on a brave face in public; there is a difference between "I'll fight and go on with my life despite the obstacles," versus "I don't care about being sick and the obstacles don't bother me at all"). This lack of distress or concern is known as *la belle indifference* and is a fairly good indicator that the person claiming to be sick may not be sick at all.

For those fighting a disease such as cancer for a second or third time, there may be other psychological scars, such as post-traumatic stress; indifference is associated with conversion disorder (the disorder formerly known as hysteria), meaning the individual has psychological problems, not physical or terminal ones. Sometimes indifference may be present even when the person doesn't have conversion disorder but for a different reason: if someone has to construct a reality from memory, there are going to be points he or she may miss, no matter how good of an actor the person may be.

If someone is trying to guess how a cancer patient thinks and behaves, he might recall someone he knew who had cancer, read books, watch documentaries, even watch movies or use his imagination, but he will never have all of the same nuances or reactions as someone who is actually fighting cancer. At most, he can be a convincing imitator to those who decide to take him at his word, but there will always be elements of his performance that will signal to the skeptical or initiated that his condition isn't authentic. No one can think of every facet.

Stacy got away with her tale for two reasons: one, few of us have the savvy, courage or impudence to question someone who proclaims to be dying and, two, "cancer" is a trigger word that creates fear and encourages us to feel rather than think. But is it fair for anyone to question someone claiming to be a victim of cancer? After all, don't most people who say they have cancer actually have it?

If we listen just a little more carefully to those facing a terminal illness, a pattern emerges. People who are dying truly have to face many of our worse fears all at once: finality, pain, suffering, misplaced guilt, hard work and endurance without reward, disillusionment, loss, rejection, cruelty from insensitive people, pity, financial ruin, sometimes even victimization and abandonment. Will the insurance company refuse to pay for treatments? Who will look after their young children? Why do they have to die so young and in so much pain? Stacy wasn't anywhere near death's door and her writing reflected this crucial difference.

Superficially, her words spoke of trauma, but a more careful reading raised several red flags. When someone is faced with fighting a painful, disfiguring, unpredictable and potentially terminal illness, he is forced to think about certain ugly truths because those truths are part of his continuing reality. For example, not once did Stacy seem even remotely concerned about how her parents would deal with having to bury their own child. (For those of you who argue that each one of us is special and that different people do their own individual thing, think what you would be feeling if a shark bit off your arm. It is unlikely you would be thinking about what movie you wanted to see that evening.)

If Stacy had a brain tumor, didn't she fear that what she felt was her greatest asset (that is, her mind) would be ravaged; thus wrenching her away from her greatest love and livelihood (that is, her career)? She never mentioned it: it's a connection she never made in any of her columns, and for someone who was self-centered (as witnessed by the large number of "I's" and "me's" scattered throughout her columns); it was an odd point to neglect. What's interesting is that Stacy clearly and plainly identified her priorities, but seemed unconcerned about how they would be affected by her illness. Would her illness take away her independence? What would happen to her cat Prissy when she passed on? It was her omissions that gave subtle, yet definite clues that her story was in fact a poorly thought out scam.

As for Murial Gillim, the Owensboro resident who commended Stacy in her letter to the editor, she phoned the paper the following Monday to ask why Stacy's columns were no longer published, according to the *Messenger-Inquirer*. Though she said she was "shocked" when informed of Stacy's deceptions, "I'm still going to pray for her," Gillim told the paper. "She really needs our prayers." Ironically, Stacy's hoax turned out to be prophetic: on March 2, 2004 Stacy passed away at age thirty-eight at St. Francis Hospital Dialysis Unit in Illinois. Stacy was a diabetic and died from kidney failure.

Interviewing Phantoms

Some newspaper reporters are an editor's darling, while others never seem to be able to rise above staff writer. Editors don't like dry writing; straight facts and reportage tend to bore them. While some white-hot scribes have a knack for getting scoops and exclusive interviews, many A-list reporters have another gift—they can use color deftly in their stories to animate their words. Their flair, vibrance and imagination give them star quality in the eyes of their superiors. One of those journalists who could enliven her words was Patricia Smith.

Smith was a poet who also worked as a rotating metro columnist for the *Boston Globe*. Her strength lay squarely in her use of adjectives and fascinating quotes. For example, in her April 24, 1998 article entitled "It all began with betrayal," she started her column this way: "So we've established that Stephen Fagan, he of the forehead-hugging hair, Palm Beach preening and makeshift social status, is the most pathological of pathological liars. First he fibbed to his two young daughters, twisting their young worlds awry at a time when they had no choice but to believe him."

Within the article about a father who was finally arrested after he abducted his two daughters from their mother, Smith quoted one Janine Byrne, a "South End cosmetologist" about her feelings on the case:

> "I got three kids, and I tell you, if they were missing all that time, I'd turn heaven over and shake God out to find them. I don't trust her. In twenty years, I'd either have them back or know they were dead."

Smith, a 1998 Pulitzer Prize finalist, was known for her mastery of the language and finding eloquent people to bring her stories to life. In her April 20, 1998 column about the Boston Marathon headlined, "In the long run, awe is for sale," Smith interviewed one man who was not impressed with the city's athletic tradition:

> On Saturday at noon, as Jim Burke and two other guys hefted a crowd barrier upright and lined it up with all the others, nothing-better-to-do spectators stood and ogled. They were less than twenty feet from the finish line of the Boston Marathon and Jim just kept doing his job, only slightly rattled by the fact that there were two days to go before the running of the thing and already folks were stupefied, staring, fixated on the race's end point as if Ted Kennedy or Julia Child had just jiggled across in first place.
>
> "It's a crazy thing," Jim observed later, between chomps on a Subway sub that simply couldn't hold any more meat or oil. "It's like the line is a tourist attraction. What in the hell do people get out of just standing there staring."

Smith's strengths were writing about the city's smaller, more precious moments, such as a young girl preparing to go to a Baptist church on Easter Sunday, as recounted in the April 13, 1998's "A little girl's rite of passage":

> They'd shopped for weeks for the dress, white with a sheer overlay dotted with violets, cinched with a lacy belt that tied in back. Carolyn's white tights drooped a little around her ankles and, of course, the black patent leather shoes hurt, but only a little. "Seems like that girl's feet grew a size since we bought those," said Carolyn's mom Dorothy Gibson. "You know, when they get a certain age, nothing sits still."
>
> Gibson admitted that the sojourn to Twelfth Baptist was a special occasion for her daughter. "She doesn't go to church every Sunday, but this Sunday is Easter Sunday. In a way, it's for children. You just pray they'll hear something that will guide them."

But sometimes Smith's columns dealt with more melancholy topics. In her May 11, 1998 column called "The cruel truth about cancer," Smith profiled "Claire," a blunt, raw woman grappling with nature's possible death sentence:

> Claire has heard the media furor about the "cure" for the killer, about the mice who had what she has and now they don't. "I'm not proud," she says. "Right away I said 'Rub it on my skin, pop it to me in a pill, shoot me up with it.' If I could find a way to steal it, I would. Hell, if I could get my hands on it, I'd swallow the whole... mouse..."
>
> Nobody knows she has it yet. She's still a slightly chubby 142 pounds, she still has her hair, and her eyes haven't sunk back into her head like the eyes of the people in those pictures she sees, those pictures that look like

death no matter how perky the silk scarf, determined the smile, or well-crafted the makeup... None of her friends know that there is something false and foreign growing inside her, an ogre she imagines chomping.

Smith detailed how Claire (the woman's middle name) found out about her shrouded enemy:

> Claire has been thinking about dying for weeks now, ever since her doctor said the tragic word, ever since she found out why she was so woefully tired all the time. The ogre had found a home in her head and may have settled in for good. There are fine prospects for treatment, her doctor told her. Looks like we found it just in time, he said. Let's schedule that surgery. The tumor is small, but feels so determined. She imagines its jagged teeth.

Despite Claire's fight, she seemed resigned to her fate as Smith recounted:

> "I've gone casket shopping. I've had dreams of lying in one with a big hole in my head that you can see right through. It drives my mother crazy."

Claire's vivid story didn't just upset readers—it upset her editors, too, but for a different reason. There were newsroom whispers that Smith had been faking parts of her stories: her interviewees, to be precise.

These accusations may have been shrugged off as professional jealousy save for two facts: first, while working as a reviewer at the *Chicago Sun-Times* in 1986, Smith was disciplined for reviewing an Elton John concert editors claimed she never attended (it was a charge she denied, though her concert tickets were never redeemed and her review was inconsistent with what had actually taken place), and second, Smith was under investigation in 1995 for making people up in her articles.

The whispers were coupled with the fact that, as one *Globe* editor admitted later, Smith had "named people with incomplete identifiers saying things that in some cases seemed more eloquent than one would expect." In other words, her work didn't ring true before, either. The second investigation revealed that Janine Byrne, Jim Burke, Dorothy Gibson and Claire were all phantasms: people who existed only in Smith's vivid imagination. While parts of her stories may have been true, the people she allegedly interviewed were fake—but could readers have been able to guess that something was amiss?

There were signs—two of which her editors had spotted but somehow chose to ignore. First was her use of shoddy sourcing: where did Janine Byrne work? What exactly was Jim Burke's occupation? Where did Dorothy Gibson work? What did we know about "Claire" other than the fact that she was sick? There was nothing to pin these characters down: maybe Smith was careless or got carried away with her adjectives, but the real reason was that these people simply did not exist.

The second warning sign was how the people in her columns spoke: like Smith herself. Each person spoke like a fictional character—ever ready with a colorful turn of phrase. Though it is possible for a reporter, who comes in contact with countless people, to find characters who speak in rich, showy metaphors, chances are she won't be finding someone like that every day. Her too-good-to-be-true characters really were too good to be true.

There was a third sign as well: the ratio between tangible facts and extravagant details was disturbing. Even in soft news or "slice of life" columns, there should be some meaty facts to go along with the pretty presentation: a newspaper's purpose is to print news. Columnists, though free from having to present dry information in a detached way, are still expected not only to have their own "voice," but are also expected to offer analysis. To analyze, a columnist needs hard data. Smith offered few details and little analysis in her work.

When reporters or columnists replace substance with clever parlor tricks, they are no longer journalists. For example, Smith described the anger of women who had cancer, but not the specifics of their illnesses. Many of her columns were meandering descriptions and, though laden with animated language, lacked a clear journalistic purpose. Where were the facts? Where was the analysis? What would a reader learn from her columns?

After being allowed to write one last column, Smith was out, but a further investigation showed that at least twenty other Smith columns had parts that were fabricated as well.

The White Hot Babe That Wasn't, Part One

Starlets have charmed both reporters and editors alike for decades. These fledgling wannabe stars are desperate to hit it big and tend to be extremely media and camera-friendly. Their names are big enough to gain some sort of recognition with an audience, but not so big as to be inaccessible to the press.

One shimmering starlet that caught the smitten eye of *Esquire* magazine was Allegra Coleman: a hippy-ish, dizzy, yet stunning twenty-two-year-old actress who was on the verge of stardom. The November 1996 cover story boldly declared the comely Ms. Coleman to be a "Dream Girl"; the accompanying shot of the actress displayed the mandatory come hither stare and naked midriff.

Journalist Martha Sherrill had the honor of interviewing the flaky and somewhat difficult actress; Coleman could not decide whether to open up to the scribe. Perhaps because what little Coleman did say was so incoherent that Sherrill decided to rely on over-the-top color instead, such as this passage:

> Allegra Coleman is sitting in her old white bathtub of a car, her old Porsche, older than she is, even older than I am. She is speeding. The road is winding.

The top is down. Her thin white shoulders are shaking. Her hands on the steering wheel are vibrating. The enormous blue sky is overhead, and there are men, middle-aged men, in the cars around her, and it's weird, but suddenly everybody is a man, and everybody is stuck in traffic, two lanes bunched up with new metal and rubber, but she is free, moving ahead, passing the cars on either side, passing the men, one by one, all blurs, all dark suits and dumb-founded expressions. They catch sight of her blond head. They stare like starving dogs. Dogs through the glare of windshields, with tongues and wet noses up against the glass.

The middling interview suddenly took a dramatic turn when Sherrill and a distracted Coleman were involved in a fateful car accident:

> Later on, of course, I heard the rest of it on my tape: the horrible scream-ing of brakes, the rubber. It was as if the tires were laughing at her, laughing at me. The bathtub's final hour. There were metal sounds, then silence. The howling sirens, the terrible drawing nearer of the sirens, louder, louder still, the slamming of doors, so many doors, the voices of our rescuers, the Jaws of Life, then more silence, long, long stretches of no sounds at all. Then the tape runs out.
>
> The jaws of life took me out of the driver's side, says the official police report... When I woke up, I believed whatever they told me. She was miss-ing was all Hollywood wanted to say.

At least one *St. Louis Post-Dispatch* columnist thought Coleman was real, griped about the article in his October 24 column; many agents and talent scouts had inundated *Esquire*, wanting to get their hands on the magazine's heartthrob find. What neither camp noticed was that the story was a spoof of fawning and fluffy celebrity (or more appropriately, starlet-gazing) jour-nalism: there was no Allegra Coleman (except in the mind of Sherrill). Model and actress Ali Larter posed in a series of pictures as Coleman.

The signs were painfully obvious, from the brainless quotes to the liberal use of color, to the dramatic, if satiric ending. The article was choking under the weight of useless "observations"; the article could be nothing else but a hoax. The intensity of the descriptions pointed to overwrought satire, but some readers decided to take *Esquire* at its word, and believed in the existence of the ditzy Allegra.

The White Hot Babe That Wasn't, Part Two

The next best thing to writing a profile about a luscious starlet is writing a profile about a shapely female athlete. The babe factor is about equal, as is the name recognition; the only difference is that the athlete has talent.

One such athlete with a killer body, heavenly looks, unbelievable talent and an improbable name was Simonya Popova, a teenaged Russian tennis player on the verge of stardom, according to a September 2, 2002 article in *Sports Illustrated*. Popova was very much like Allegra Coleman; she was young, beautiful, almost famous and not quite the master of the *bon mot*:

> Popova is a beacon of candor. "I have no secrets," she says... "If women's tennis is all that, how come we still make, like, 40% less than the men at events outside the Grand Slams?" she asks. "Did you know that twenty-six men have won more than $500,000 this year, but only twelve women have?" And don't get her started on Kournikova. "I hear Anna wants to write a biography, but can you publish a book if you don't have a title?" she says. "Seriously, Anna's nice. It's just that she's, like, so jumped the shark."

This color-filled profile also revealed that the young never-before-heard-of athlete had her own diva-like moments:

> Popova has also let it be known that, like Kournikova, she won't lodge at designated tournament hotels. She'll take a suite, preferably at a Ritz, though an Inter-Continental will do. ("And not one of those add-a-desk-and-call-it-a-junior suites," she adds. "I'm talking the claw-foot tub, the polished rocks in the ashtrays, all that stuff.")

The article seemed to concentrate on trivialities, though there were nagging questions. Why hadn't anyone mentioned Simonya anywhere else in the press? How realistic did the story sound, and why was a teenaged girl from Russia talking the way a thirty-something American male would think a teenaged girl speaks? The article sounded like a spoof.

It sounded like a spoof for one reason: it *was* a spoof. In an attempt to parody fawning sports journalism, *SI* decided to create the fictitious Popova, with a model posing as the ersatz tennis diva. The name "Simonya" was simply a nod to the Al Pacino flop *Simone*, a comedy movie about a virtual "actress." While some fell for the hoax, *SI* editors came clean about Simonya shortly after the article's publication.

White Russian Lies

Stories about helpless and exploited children serve as a painful reminder that there are truly despicable people walking among us. This type of news fodder is depressing and disturbing, but there are still ground rules when covering these stories in the Western media: the names and faces of the young victims are not revealed either because of legal or ethical considerations (almost an exercise in futility these days when those familiar with the case can easily post identifying information about the child on a website).

But those same rules don't always extend to children living outside the United States. Here, American reporters have more leeway to provide a more visually brutal and truthful account of events, instead of a sanitized approximation of the child's daily horror, though the children's last names may still be withheld. While the more liberal standards can bring to light the plight of helpless and abused foreign children, the problem is that the differing standards can make it seem as if no Western child is forced into a similar situation.

This bizarre double standard wasn't on the minds of *Time* magazine editors one summer when they decided to investigate the problem of child prostitution around the world. The June 21, 1993 "Sex for Sale" cover story detailed the child sex trade in Asia and Europe and the short, tragic lives of the victims. Some of the child prostitutes were named, such as Armine Sae Li, fourteen-year-old former child prostitute from Thailand who developed HIV as a result of her plight. A few others were also named, including three young boys from Russia:

> Sasha, a scruffy-looking longhaired resident of Moscow, has a lucrative profession. He sells the sexual services of small boys. His base of operations is a garden in front of Moscow's magnificent Bolshoi Theatre, where both local and foreign clients know to seek him out. Sasha pimps for a number of male teenagers who hang out with him near the Bolshoi, but his main "team" consists of three younger boys—Marik, eight, and Volodya and Dima, both nine.

The article described how Marik was sold to Sasha for "a case of vodka." The story was accompanied with six disturbing photos of the young boys dressed up as girls, ready to service their male clients. The pictures were taken by seventeen-year-old Alexey Ostrovskiy, a Russian photographer with an inconsistent reputation. The photos showed the boys in various poses, though the pictures seemed somewhat stilted.

It was the unnatural poses of the boys that caught the attention of one chief photographer with Reuters News Pictures in Moscow, who posted his doubts over the authenticity of Ostrovskiy's pictures on a Compuserve newsgroup. The photographer wrote, among other things, that the pictures were "a set-up, faked by the photographer, who duped the reporter into believing him." Marik's own mother also said that her eleven-year-old son (not eight as the article claimed) lived with her and did not work as a prostitute, though she did not explain how it was that her son, who said he was paid to pose for the pictures, ended up in Ostrovskiy's company.

Time editors stood by the pictures, though they did concede that there was no way to prove whether the pictures were genuine or fakes. However, after the boys in question kept changing their stories Ostrovskiy told the *Washington Post* that he staged the photos and a Moscow police investigation determined that the photos were a fraud, *Time* editors apologized to their readers in the October 11, 1993 issue, writing, in part, that "the boys still insist to us that they were and are engaged in child prostitution, one boy has denied it to others. Had we known this at the time, we would not have run these pictures. We regret the error."

The editors of *Time* complained to the editors at Reuters, who then recalled their photographer from his position and subsequently resigned from Reuters—and sued *Time* for libel. Despite the fact that the Reuters photographer had been one of the first to question the staged pictures, editors at Reuters frowned on his public rebuke of *Time*; as one Reuters spokesman said, "as a policy we do not like to criticize other media publicly." Perhaps the policy stemmed from the fact that the "other media" happened to also be one of Reuters' more important clients, or because *Time* editors complained that the Reuters photographer, along with a translator, tried to coax Sasha (the real or imagined pimp who tape recorded the entire conversation) to recant his story.

How could editors trust a seventeen-year-old with a poor reputation who kept changing his story? Did *Time's* editors notice the stilted poses? In any case, what was at first presented as the unvarnished truth turned out to be a confusing muddle of changed stories and uncertainty.

Fishy Monkey Business

It's cool to know obscure, weird things and even cooler to participate in obscure, weird things, but the coolest thing is to write an article about the obscure, weird things you did. Such was the luck of Jay Forman, who wrote about his experience with monkey-fishing in his "Vice" column: no, it wasn't fisherman's jargon, he told readers of Slate.com, but the sport of fishing for actual monkeys. Apparently monkey-fishing is something the island folk of Lois Key in the Florida Keys like to participate in. Forman got his chance to monkey-fish in 1996, as he recounted in the June 7, 2001 edition of *Slate*:

> Once we found a nice spot, we prepared to fish. Sturdy deep-sea poles were the preferred tackle. I've never heard of anyone landing a monkey on light-weight fly rods, but I suppose it is possible. I have friends who have landed tarpon on them, and tarpon are much bigger than monkeys.

Forman used vivid color to humorously describe the strange Floridian pastime, but make no mistake: monkey-fishing was an ugly, extreme sport. To reel in a monkey took planning and knowing the right bait to use:

Fruits were the bait of choice. Apples were good because they stayed on the hook well. Red Delicious were chosen over Granny Smith for the advantage in contrast. Other baits included kiwis, which were more deceptive, but trickier to cast due to their mushy flesh. Oranges worked well; their rinds combined with their bright coloring made them a natural choice. And after a long day of eating its own feces, what monkey could resist a tasty orange?

Now came the cruel part. Once the bait was on the hook, I watched as the monkey-fisherman cast it onto the island, then waited... The monkeys swarmed round the treat, and when the fisherman felt a strong tug he jerked the pole. I knew he had hooked one by the shriek it made—a primal yowl that set my hair on end. The monkey came flying from the trees, a juicy apple stapled to its palm.

However, the flowery details didn't fool reporters at the *Wall Street Journal* who quickly declared the article a hoax. After the usual "we stand by our story" pledge from *Slate* editors, a more thorough investigation by the *New York Times* proved that monkey-fishing wasn't literal fishing for monkeys, but the illegal practice of using dynamite while fishing to propel the unsuspecting fish to the surface. Foreman's monkey-fishing was a scam. Two weeks after the first questions were raised, *Slate* apologized to readers.

How did this hoax make it to an online publication such as *Slate?* The use of color won over the editors, though editor Michael Kinsley later admitted that while he did not like the story, others at Slate did and he felt compelled to publish the piece. Something as fantastic and as surreal as screeching monkeys flying through the trees was too much for some editors to resist, even if the story made no sense. If it's a choice between publishing a dry, but factually solid story or a colorful, but shoddily sourced story, editors may be loathed to admit it, but the colorful yarn will usually be the one an editor chooses to publish.

How to Spot Fraudulent Stories

Reporters who fabricate stories betray the very essence of their jobs, but smoking them out isn't always easy. Nevertheless, there are signs to look for when reading or watching a news report and in this case, familiarity is the best defense for the news consumer. Here, it's important to know a reporter's body of work: a single reporter is likely to be fooled once (as in the case of reporter James Scott who fell for the "Heywood Jablome" prank); if, on the other hand, the reporter claims he was lied to on numerous occasions, it most likely means the reporter is a fraud.

A reporter who says he has been duped on numerous levels is claiming to be lazy and naïve—but the logistics of such an event would have to hinge on having multiple extraordinary coincidences happen in rapid succession.

For example, in Christopher Newton's case, he claimed he believed he had spoken to Ralph Myers, but was fooled—but then Bruce Fenmore could not be located, either. How likely is it that two completely unrelated men from two different states would choose that precise moment to con the same reporter on the same story? Why would they? Stephen Glass claimed that he was duped by hackers for his final *New Republic* story. Could a reporter be so jinxed as to be fooled by an endless stream of people for months on end? Was Glass implying that there was a hacker conspiracy against him?

Just because smoking out a devious reporter is not always easy, that doesn't mean that there aren't some signals that a reporter is fabricating parts, or all, of his story:

1. All people in the story or report sound alike (i.e., there is no variation in tone, sentence structure or intelligence level).

For the fabricating reporter, his biggest weakness is not being able to vary the speaking style of his phantom sources. Great fiction writers can do this, as did John Kennedy Toole in *A Confederacy of Dunces*. Novelists are in the business of creating characters; on the other hand, fibbing reporters are simply cutting corners in their work; they're less concerned with character development because news articles don't lend themselves easily to this type of writing.

Think about it: does everyone you know speak the same way? Your boss speaks differently than your children. Different people have different idiosyncrasies in their speech patterns and thought processes, depending on their age, geographical background and education. If a Harvard-educated tycoon and a janitor sound alike in the same article, it's a big hint that the reporter is up to no good.

For Janet Cooke, her lack of understanding jive roused suspicions in many readers, who made public their doubts about the veracity of her street smart sources. In one paragraph, Cooke quoted Jimmy's "mother": "I was tired of sleeping with all those different dudes and boosting... at Woodies."

In Stephen Glass' case, his far-out characters all behaved and spoke the same way—cocky, wise and materialistic. Even Jayson Blair's fictitious quotes lacked linguistic variety, as did the eloquent Patricia Smith, whose characters, despite Smith's background in creative writing, seemed every bit as articulate as she. *USA Today*'s Jack Kelley roused suspicion with other reporters because he managed to get powerful and articulate quotes in short order from distressed people whose first language wasn't English.

When reading a news report, pay attention to the individual quotes. Some reporters do clean up quotes for their stories, but if all players speak with the same rhythm and tone, then there is an excellent chance that the quotes were altered or fabricated completely.

2. The stories are too good to be true and have no concrete sourcing.

Lies of this nature are not difficult to spot. Stephen Glass wrote about many strange incidents, yet his sourcing was atrocious—there was no way to prove what Glass alleged was true, since only Glass himself was witness to these bizarre occurrences—he had no other witnesses or concrete proof. How can anyone verify that Glass witnessed an aroused store Santa Claus, drunk conservative men humiliating an ugly girl and a cab mugging? Kim Stacy had written about receiving a letter from a young boy fighting leukemia, yet did not opt to quote the letter specifically. Why not? If he were as articulate and moving as she claimed, then why not quote a line from his own words to give her readers a better sense of who this boy was? The reason for her oversight was exposed when she was discovered to have fabricated her disease. In the monkey-fishing hoax, the story was literally too good to be true, and the main witness to the event was the writer himself.

3. The stories sound similar to urban legends.

Here, the stories will have the same characteristics as outlined in Chapter 6. Some legends are based on real events, but if the story also has logical holes in it, it may be a sign that the reporter has perhaps embellished or fabricated parts of his story for dramatic purposes, such as Jay Forman did with his monkey-fishing story.

4. There are logical or chronological inconsistencies.

Any logical, physical, psychological or chronological inconsistencies should be looked at with a skeptical eye. Journalists may cover people and events that deviate from the norm, but those individuals and incidents still have to conform to what is physically and logically possible. How many hard drugs can a child take before he receives permanent brain damage? Why would a drug dealer give drugs away for free to anyone, let alone a child? Wouldn't it be more logical if the stepfather used Jimmy as a mule or cover?

5. There are numerous clichés and stereotypes permeating throughout the stories.

People covered in news stories all have roles to play—if those roles seem too contrived, it may be a hint that the reporter has altered or fabricated information. The same goes for clichéd scenes—if the scene or person seems too generic or stereotyped, it might indicate a devious reporter's lack of imagination.

In the Stephen Glass debacle, his stories were rife with predictable hypocritical characters (the hedonistic conservatives, the all-too-proper suits—even Ian Restil's "mother" seemed too close to June Cleaver for comfort). For Janet Cooke, the low-life characters she created were predictable in their responses. Though both Cooke and Glass had seemingly stranger than fiction characters, both reporters relied on well-worn stereotypes to animate their phantoms. In the Simonya Popova article, the young "tennis star's" quotes seem clichéd; that is, most young teenaged girls do not talk that way.

The more neat and pat the anecdote, the more likely the messy, real life quirks were downplayed, altered or made up from whole cloth. The same goes for clichéd situations or anecdotes—Jayson Blair setting Private Lynch's family in a tobacco field seemed like a parody, as did Wendy Bergen's money-hungry dogfight gamblers. Kim Stacy's "Josh" was an idealized version of how people think a dying child should behave—compassionate, selfless, serene and wise beyond his years.

6. There is an over-reliance on color rather than hard facts. Small superfluous details overshadow or outnumber the amount of verifiable information, such as dates, eyewitnesses, documents and statistics.

Color seems to be the dishonest journalist's best friend. As noted in chapter three, color is referred to as those superfluous details that can spice up dry information or put a "face" on stories. Many magazine and newspaper editors like details such as quirky anecdotes and how an interview subject lights her cigarette. Good anecdotes and descriptions of people and events sometimes help readers relate to strangers and visualize events.

But some reporters take color too far and substitute hard facts with frills. Many editors do not want only the facts in their stories since straightforward reporting is seen as "mere reportage." While some color may make an article more interesting, for many reporters, it is a form of filler to hide the fact they didn't find much information for their stories. When reading an article, pay close attention to the ratio between hard data and color. Too much color may be an attempt to misdirect the reader. A journalist overly depending on color to tell the story may have a dubious reason for doing so, as Stephen Glass did in his stories. If the reporter has more color than information in any given article, this is a red flag that there may be some real fabrication in the story.

With Patricia Smith's stories, though she was a master at describing and animating minute detail, her sourcing was questionable, as were the number of hard facts in her articles. As interesting as her works were, they were neither useful nor grounded. Her work added nothing concrete to the public discourse. Jay Forman's monkey-fishing article and Martha Sherrill's Allegra Coleman profile were a mastery of whimsical and colorful details—and nothing else.

If the story relies heavily on color, then take a second read at the flowery details—how realistic do those elements sound? Could the reporter prove that the event took place as described? In "Jimmy's World," Cooke's assertion that a drug dealer gave away drugs was a critical key in unmasking her hoax. It may help to imagine the person or event yourself to see if it sounds plausible or possible. As we'll see in Chapter 18, breaking down anecdotes can be an effective tool in spotting fakery. If any clues will send clear signals of journalistic deceit, will be in the reporter's use of color and quotes.

7. The stories have shoddy sourcing and information.

News should be informative—so how informative is the article or broadcast? Did you learn anything? Were there too many gaps or unanswered questions? Are the interviewees mentioned by their full names? Does the reporter give attribution for his evidence or does he make it seem as if he is the only one who could find that information? If you separate the color from the facts, how much information are you left with? This type of omission may not mean that the story is a fake, but combined with other factors mentioned above, it may mean the information given is unreliable—or, at the very least, useless.

8. The story is meant to shock or be emotionally manipulative, but there is not enough information or evidence to warrant a strong reaction.

People can't think as clearly when their emotions are being manipulated. Many con artists know this and take full advantage of it. Emotions are used as a distraction to hide the fact that the reporter doesn't have strong information.

If you watch or read information knowing that someone may use this ploy, it may help you spot fraudulent stories. Just because a story isn't emotional or sensational doesn't mean it's accurate and truthful. Christopher Newton's stories and the fake Kurt Andersen piece don't fit this category, but Kim Stacy, Jayson Blair, Patricia Smith, Jack Kelley and Janet Cooke all played on heartstrings, while Stephen Glass and Wendy Bergen both went for the more lurid aspects of the human condition.

Be skeptical when reading or watching the news: does the story sound plausible or is there something that doesn't sound right? Does everyone the journalist quote sound alike? Does the reporter relay an incident as told to her by another party or does she claim to have witnessed the event in person? Do the story's players sound realistic or seem surreal?

Try to imagine the events as they are described by the reporter—does this scenario sound plausible to you? Make no assumptions and fill in no blanks yourself: if something in a story sounds fishy or is flat out wrong, don't assume you're wrong or jaded, especially if you have been to the event or location in question and it deviates substantially from what you know to be true. The truth may be that the reporter made an honest error, was careless or was duped, but there is also a chance the reporter fabricated some or all of her story.

Chapter **Fifteen**

Academic and Scientific Hoaxes in the News

Contrary to popular opinion, the press doesn't just report on self-absorbed Hollywood starlets and sensational, grisly crime: most mainstream media outlets cover health and science news as well, and these stories can get prominent play if the breakthrough or discovery is exciting enough.

So what type of science news is considered journalistically exciting? Miracle diets or cancer cures will make news, as do stories on gross obesity. Surprisingly, astronomy gets a fair amount of play, whether the coverage is on eclipses, comets or the latest in space travel. Breakthrough drugs can also nab headlines. On the other hand, physics and chemistry don't get as much space as health-related science news. Here, it will be news the audience can relate to and understand: weird, contagious illnesses such as Ebola, flesh-eating bacteria and SARS will get prominent play, while diseases that will make the patient look unattractive won't grab a reporter's attention.

Reporters rely on the word of medical experts in lieu of their own independent investigations, even if sometimes those experts can get bamboozled themselves. Take the case of "Carlo" (no last name) of the Philippines, who made headlines when he claimed to be a hermaphrodite (someone born with both male and female genitalia) who was pregnant, as the May 28, 1992 edition of *USA Today* noted:

> Carlo, the thirty-two-year-old Filipino male nurse, who is six months pregnant, is expecting a boy and says he already feels the baby kicking inside him. "I feel proud that I'm going to be the mother of a baby boy. I'm happy that now I'm really feeling fulfilled like a complete woman," he said.

Carlo appeared on NBC's "Today Show" as the real deal; the morning news show later discovered that "Carlo" was actually Edwin Bayron, who was just a guy with a fake belly under his shirt. What was more embarrassing was that doctors who examined Bayron didn't uncover his not-so-clever ruse. Bayron wanted to bolster his application for a sex change operation in order to marry his boyfriend; hence he hatched his incredible story, and might have succeeded if it wasn't for one semi-thorough doctor who examined him more closely.

Why Reporters Fall for Scientific and Academic Hoaxes and Scams
Those who work in medicine and other sciences have, for the most part, more brains and endurance than journalists. First, most reporters don't have as many letters after their names as a neurologist or biochemist. Second, even though both scientists and reporters are in the information-gathering professions, scientists will take decades to find the answer to their questions; reporters are vexed when they have to wait hours for the answer to theirs. Reporters are on deadlines and have to answer more questions, but it's this difference that makes reporters more vulnerable to hoaxes (however, this doesn't mean the researchers aren't impervious to deception, either). There is a saying among reporters: a journalist's knowledge is thirty miles wide, but only one inch deep.

It's this perpetual shallowness that gets reporters into constant trouble. A newly released study may have major structural flaws that make its results useless, but unless the reporter either interviews experts in the field who are both knowledgeable and savvy, or the reporter himself is versed in the jargon and complexities of scientific research, the journalist will help spread bad science and pseudo-science to the public. Without knowing what separates good science from bad, reporters give credence to researchers whose lax controls can cause long term damage to the public.

On the other hand, those who turn to alternative medicine to solve their ailments are in no safer position, since many studies of alternative therapies have no uniform standards or controls for testing. Yet many true believers don't seem to question the lack of tight controls, claiming traditional medical and scientific methods can't translate to alternative therapies. However, a person who is given any type of treatment can either get better or not (i.e., his condition stays the same or worsens). If someone doesn't stabilize or improve after a treatment has been given, then it's not a good treatment.

Despite the rigors and standards in life science research, fakery and hoaxes have made their way into this profession, too. Mistakes happen, as do poorly conducted studies and outright fabrication of data. Some researchers are also vulnerable to chicanery. Other times, con artists only pose as doctors and researchers while plying their dubious trade firmly outside the boundaries of academia. These people fool the desperate and gullible into believing they are legitimate healers or scholars.

A fake expert doesn't even have to prey on the desperate. On June 3, 2004, the *Associated Press* reported that a possible meteorite fell near Olympia, Washington. The source was one Bradley Hammermaster, who claimed to work at the University of Washington. Hammermaster "estimated that the object was about the size of a small car. He described it as a piece of a larger meteor. [He] told KIRO Radio shortly after 3 a.m. that a team was being assembled to head for the area where the object was believed to have hit near the tiny southwestern Washington community of Chehalis." It was assumed that *AP* had verified Hammermaster's credentials.

It turned out they didn't. Shortly after the story was picked up by several newspapers, it was discovered there was no Bradley Hammermaster nor did "Hammermaster's" report turn out to be true, though other witnesses did see a meteor light up the sky in the vicinity. *AP* was forced to quickly retract their story.

To compound matters, there are some episodes in academia that not even scholars themselves can agree on as to whether they were hoaxes or not. In 1912, Henry Herbert Goddard, a New Jersey psychologist who believed that intelligence was innate and strongly advocated the use of eugenics (i.e., the selective breeding of people who are deemed to have "superior" genetic material while preventing those with less desirable genes from having children).

To bolster his case, Goddard chronicled the path of the Kallikaks. One member of the family married twice: once to a Quaker woman with desirable genes and once to a barmaid who was deemed mentally "feeble." It was this split that interested Goddard, and he made a stunning case for being careful of whom you choose to reproduce with.

His book presented pictures that purported to show both the "good" and "normal" line of the Kallikak family as well as the "bad" line. The good Kallikaks were attractive and seemed bright and intelligent, while the "lower" line of the Kallikaks seemed barbaric and slow-witted. In his account of the "bad" Kallikaks, Goddard wrote that "there are Kallikak families all about us... multiplying at twice the rate of the general population, and not until we recognize this fact... will we begin to solve these social problems."

Of course, Kallikak was not the family's real name, and several decades later something else about Goddard's work didn't seem real, either. The photos of the bad Kallikaks faded, revealing what they really looked like—the depraved eyes and grimaces were gone and they lost their genetically inferior look. Their faces were made that way with photo manipulation.

Were the pictures doctored? In a way, yes. Someone (perhaps the book's editor) had touched up the photo plates; some scholars believe this tinkering was done to make the Kallikaks look more stupid and menacing, while other psychologists maintain that the retouching was done to enhance the quality of the pictures without Goddard's prior knowledge. Yet whether Goddard himself played a role in this embellishing is not known. In any case, the pictures shown did not accurately reflect the family in question.

Which leads us to how journalists fall for bad science: if scholars cannot agree on whether one of their own fabricated data, then how can journalists untangle the mystery? Many reporters covering health, science or medical issues don't have medical training; they are not well versed in the scientific method or in critical thinking. Not every study is a good one and not all scientists are created equal—but for a journalist not initiated in the ways of scientific and scholarly research, these distinctions become difficult to make.

Then there are reporters who just don't bother to double check information. Between 1991 and 1993, various media outlets reported that a March of Dimes study claimed that violence against pregnant women was by far the leading cause of birth defects (read: domestic violence against women). However, writer and professor Christina Hoff Sommers looked into the study, calling the March of Dimes directly and asking to see a copy of it, but the organization never heard of the study it supposedly conducted. Further investigating showed that the study never existed.

But where did reporters get their information? It was a game of telephone wire: one person heard about the study from another and so on until the source of the information, according to Hoff Sommers, conceded that she saw "more [women were] screened for birth defects than they [were] ever screened for domestic battery"—a far cry from a formal study that supposedly proved that domestic violence was the leading cause of birth defects. Yet publications from *Time, Chicago Tribune, Boston Globe* to the *Dallas Morning News* repeated the phantom study as fact.

What this episode showed was clear: none of the journalists located the original study. No one called the March of Dimes to ask for a copy of the report. Journalists had relied on the word of someone not affiliated with the study for their information. If so, then how would they know how accurate, useful, valid and reliable the study was?

One study (with a million dollar grant from the National Institute of Health) involved three researchers from the University of Maryland interviewing inner-city African American teens from Baltimore and determining the effectiveness of a certain sex education program. The study, published in the January 2003 edition of the journal *Pediatrics*, showed that the counseling, coupled with parental guidance, was effective.

Despite the fact that there was no control group (making the results impossible to interpret), there seemingly was no other trouble with the study. However, the U.S. Public Health Service investigated and found that the three part-time researchers, who had worked on the study in 2001, had fabricated their data—in other words, none of the subjects they interviewed existed. The researchers who wrote the study insisted that the fabrications from the three had been caught and excluded before the study was published. But why the fraud was not publicly released for over two years was never explained, nor how one study attracted a whopping three dishonest researchers. How many researchers worked on the study? If three deceitful workers were employed, what kind of standards did the main researchers use to screen applicants? Though the three culprits were discovered before the publication of the report, the fact that they were hired at all is troubling.

At least the fabricators were caught before the results were disseminated. In July 1981, Cornell University researchers had published their breakthrough discovery that there may be a single cause for all types of cancers. The results seemed to prove if researchers could find the cause for the disease, then all cancers could be easily cured. The results were published in the journal *Science*.

The good news was short lived when other researchers could not replicate the results of the experiment. It seemed that the only one who could was twenty-four-year-old Mark Spector, a PhD student at Cornell who had the reputation of being the only person who could make long and complex experiments and processes work and work quickly. Only after one researcher had examined one of Spector's doctored samples were the young man's fabrications brought to light. Though he denied wrongdoing, his doctored credentials and notebooks were also discovered.

But news consumers usually won't be trained in spotting fake scientific data, nor will they likely read the original studies. They will rely on journalists to decipher the jargon and report on the findings, even if the reporter is no savvier in spotting shaky science than the audience. The good news is this isn't a big problem, since the majority of studies aren't fraudulent. The bad news is that many studies aren't reliable for another reason: they are poorly designed and executed. Knowing the difference between a good study and a bad one can help you decide whether to believe in the next big medical breakthrough you hear about in the news.

Bad Science vs. Fraudulent Claims

Researchers engaging in scientific fraud try to pass lies for the truth. These charlatans will publish bogus data for their own ideological or personal reasons, which can lead to harm further down the road. On the other hand, bad research usually means researchers weren't lying, but were careless or lazy— yet the results can be just as damaging. Many highly publicized studies were based on bad research.

When listening to news reports about studies or breakthroughs, pay attention to see if the reporters make mention of how the study was conducted. If so, then look for structural flaws in the study or experiment itself. If one of the following controls wasn't properly adhered to, then there is a good chance that the study was a bad one:

Double blind/placebo. There is a difference between getting better and feeling better. Some people will equate feeling less tired with healing, which isn't necessarily the case. As well, researchers may behave differently to subjects if they know these are the people who get the treatment.

To ensure against subject or researcher bias, controls have to be put in so that neither the researchers nor the subjects know what group the subjects are in. This is what scientists refer to as the "double blind" technique. In one way to make certain no one knows who is in what group, some subjects are given a fake treatment or a placebo. All subjects seem to get the treatment (let's say a pill), but only one or two groups get the real treatment. The rest get a sugar pill. Researcher and subject expectations have been accounted for and controlled.

Randomization. If a researcher decides which group of ill subjects will get a certain experimental treatment, he may try to make his results look better by assigning the subjects who are less sick to the treatment group and giving the sicker patients the placebo. To make sure that doesn't happen, subjects should have an equal chance to be assigned to any group.

Control for outside or irrelevant variables. There is no point in conducting an elaborate study if the results can become contaminated with outside influences. If a psychologist conducts a study on anxiety and has two groups of subjects answer a researcher's questions and one researcher is more intimidating for one group than another researcher, the difference in the researchers' demeanors is an outside variable that will alter the results. What this means is that researchers have to be able to control those outside variables from creeping into the experiment in the first place.

Control groups. Basically, almost all studies are a type of comparison— even a study about a treatment is comparing the difference between the results of the experimental treatment to the conventional treatment or no treatment (placebo).

Good studies compare at least two different variables. "Taking Drug X is better" is useless advice—what does "better" mean here? That Drug X is better compared to what? Not taking any medication or taking some other medication? Comparisons can't just hang out there—there has to be at least another variable to compare to.

Many studies don't compare their results with others. For example, in 2000 one book, *The Unexpected Legacy of Divorce: A 25-Year Landmark Study* chronicled a researcher's twenty-five-year study, which claimed that children from divorced homes were more depressed than those of non-divorced families. How did the researcher come to this conclusion? By interviewing only children from California whose parents were divorced. But what sounded impressive to many was that the researcher interviewed the same group of children over a twenty-five-year span. For this, she got a lot of play in the mainstream press.

Interviewing one group of people over the span of a quarter century may sound thorough at first, but the study itself was worthless because the researcher never bothered to interview children whose parents never divorced.

Perhaps children from divorced families feel blue and insecure about the future at times, but then again, who doesn't? Are these children more or less depressed than children who lost a parent through death? Are children whose parents divorced amiably as depressed as those whose parent divorced because one parent was horrendously abusing the other and threatened to kill him or her? What about a parent who divorces the other because the other parent is physically or sexually abusing the child?

We don't know because the researcher didn't bother to compare her results to children who come from different homes. A ten-year study comparing children from various backgrounds would have given more useful information than a twenty-five-year study that only looks at one side of life. The only thing anyone could really glean from this "study" was that there are some discontent and neurotic white people in California. If that's news to you, then you need to get out more often. But it didn't stop *USA Today*, the *San Francisco Chronicle*, the *Peoria Journal Star* and the *Toronto Star* from reporting on the findings as solid and unquestionable.

Bad research can stem from careless errors, researcher expectations or poor experimental design, while fraud stems from greed and a lack of morals. But both can be promoted as good science by journalists or other researchers, as the following case studies show.

An Unreasonable Facsimile

Scientists are a scary bunch: first, they know more than most of us. Second, they use words that most don't understand, but their most intimidating trait is their ability to trump nature herself. Their words and abilities are not accessible to the average person, begging the question: what happens when a rogue scientist embarks on some dark process or experiment that the rest of us are unable to comprehend, let alone stop? What if scientists end up controlling every facet of our lives? What happens to human beings as we know them?

It's precisely these questions that make a compelling story: a moral populace up against a mad scientist who has no moral compass or inhibition. The scientist who can control nature, his fellow man and even the future seems like a formidable opponent. If cold logic can do one better than Mother Nature, then the rest of us are at his mercy.

It certainly felt that way when the *New York Post* ran the following article in their December 20, 2002 edition:

> A Canadian cult that has set up a human cloning company said yesterday that it will birth the world's first human clone before the end of the month.

The Raelians, a Quebec-based religious sect that believes humans were created by aliens, said the baby girl will be born by Cesarean section at an undisclosed facility.

The baby is the genetic replica of an American woman in her thirties who's unable to have kids with her husband naturally, said Dr. Brigitte Boisselier, the director of the cult's cloning company, Clonaid.

It was bad enough that a scientist could clone a human, but the fact that these scientists belonged to a foreign cult that preached free love and promiscuity was alarming. Though the *Post* did concede that the cult had no evidence of their claim, those at the paper nevertheless seemed to think there must have been some credence to the claim for editors to give ink to the Raelians. Other newspapers and television stations also prominently played up on the Clonaid bombshell. Of course, the *Drudge Report* had references to the story for days.

But this was not the first mention of the cloning story, far from it. Members of Clonaid (who had close ties to the Raelians) had made their desire to clone humans public months before the birth of "Eve," whose parents lived in Florida. For example, Reuters had mentioned the Raelian's quest to ditto humans in a November 26, 2001 story.

[...]Clonaid, which purports to have established a new research laboratory in an undisclosed country, will not be making announcements on its progress in the project, Rael [formerly known as Claude Vorilhon, leader of the Raelians] said.

Reuters weren't the only media outlet to report on the small cult's big plans. The *Las Vegas Review* profiled resident Boisselier in this September 2, 2001 piece:

Raelian scientists are working toward adult cloning, but say they need to perfect the baby model first. Boisselier said that once she perfects the technology, her twenty-two-year-old daughter will be enlisted as the surrogate mother who would give birth to an infant clone. She would carry a cloned egg to term.

The Clonaid website says it will charge "as low as $200,000" for such services.

The idea wasn't farfetched to West Virginia lawyer Mark Hunt, who told the Charleston, S.C., Gazette that he had invested $500,000 in Clonaid before he finally severed ties with the organization. The paper reported Hunt and his wife enlisted Boisselier to clone their ten-month-old son, who died two years ago.

The Raelians also got play on CNN on August 6, 2001 when reporter Leon Harris interviewed Boisselier:

> HARRIS: The last time we spoke with you, perhaps back in March or so, you said that you were going to have a human clone by the month of April and that did not happen. Or did it happen?
>
> BOISSELIER: I never said that it would be by the end of April. I'm very surprised when I hear that on the—or when I read that in articles. I said that we were in the process of doing it and we are; our research is going very nicely, and everything is fine with Clonaid.
>
> Now, I will not reveal exactly when the first clone... is supposed to be born because I don't want to have the FDA into that every day. But everything is going very, very nicely.

Though those at Clonaid got ink and air time for simply announcing their desire to clone humans, once they had announced their success, the news media couldn't get enough. *United Press International* had expressed skepticism over the claim in a December 22, 2002 story, noting the cult had not provided any names or evidence of their claims, but then went on to discuss Clonaid's other endeavors:

> A total of ten human cloning implantations were conducted this year on five different couples, including the American couple plus one other in North America, two in Asia and one in Northern Europe, Boisselier said. Five of those implantations were successful, she said, and the remaining implantations spontaneously aborted.

CNN had interviewed Boisselier (a self-described Raelian "bishop") numerous times and even carried this story on January 1, 2003 on its website:

> A company founded by members of a sect that believes mankind was created by extraterrestrials says the alleged first human clone—an infant girl—returned home Monday and will undergo testing to verify its genetic makeup.
>
> The girl, dubbed "Eve," went home Monday, said Clonaid spokeswoman Nadine Gary. An independent expert will take cell samples from the mother and girl this week and conduct tests to prove they are genetic duplicates, said Brigitte Boisselier, CEO of Clonaid. The company says its scientists produced the child.

Eleven days later, panelists on CNN's "Reliable Sources" (a program focusing on journalism issues) debated whether colleagues should have covered the yarn in the first place. One reporter noted that the Raelians had not one shred of evidence: no names, no records, no DNA samples, no process, no photographs of the alleged cloned infant, not even a published paper in a scientific journal. The Raelians did not even produce a baby.

What tipped off reporters that Eve was just a hoax? While some journalists maintained their skepticism by not writing about the story at all, many others gave the story prominence. Michael Guillen, a freelance journalist and former science editor for ABC News who had a reputation of believing some aspects of astrology and ESP, agreed to examine the claims with other experts, but then backed out, citing the group's lack of proof and candor. By late January, Florida officials could not prove Eve existed. What was worse, was that identical claims of cloning an infant back in March 1978, this time a sixty-eight-year-old man who claimed he cloned himself. Again, the *New York Post* was one of the first papers to announce it in their paper (on the front page, no less).

How did a cult manage to bamboozle the press? They simply provided the news media with a fantastic claim and were willing to be interviewed. Though reporters who covered the story said they were skeptical of the claims, it did not stop newspapers from running with the story on their front pages and TV stations from leading with the Baby Eve saga on their newscasts. The fact that a fringe cult could get two weeks worth of mainstream media coverage with the claim of cloning a baby without actually having so much as a picture of any baby shows how little proof a scam artist needs to pull a hoax.

They Won't Be Having More Fun for Long

Scientific theories about evolution usually don't make the news—these are seen as dry, boring stories with no audience hook, but sometimes even these findings might make it to print or broadcast if the hook is strong enough. In late September 2002, many media outlets reported on a bizarre finding: blondes were on their way out.

One NBC affiliate's website gave a disturbing and clichéd assessment for the evolutionary endurance of those with light hair color:

> They say "blondes have more fun," but new research says their days are numbered.
>
> Blonde hair occurs naturally only in people whose genealogy is from Northern Europe. The gene that causes blonde hair must be present in both parents.
>
> According to the World Health Organization, there are now too few people who carry the gene for it to survive. Scientists expect natural blondes will be extinct within 200 years.

The *New York Post* also could not resist the bad puns or the dire warning in the article "Study is a blonde bombshell," published September 30, 2002:

> Another German academic has research claiming that blondes actually don't have more fun.
>
> Professor Hans Juergens believes men associate blondes with marriage and housekeeping but seek out brunettes for sex.

The *London Daily Star*, BBC, CBS, ABC, CNN and a slew of other outlets also rang their solemn bells that fair-haired humans were evolutionary goners. So how did the press get this kind of little factoid in the first place?

Most had found the story on a British news wire, which in turn got its information from a German news wire. The German news wire service had gotten the information from a two-year-old article in a woman's magazine called *Allegra*.

Soon after, reporters received an advisory from WHO in conjunction with the group's press releases. No, the WHO explained, the study never existed, and they never commissioned one like that, either. In fact, hair and evolution just weren't the kinds of subjects a group calling themselves World Health Organization would trouble themselves with.

No one who originally reported the story bothered to get any confirmation—from the WHO or the German researchers in question. But this isn't new: many phantom studies are reported as real, such as the nonexistent March of Dimes study. Many reporters hear about a study from another source and run with their "scoop" without ever trying to find the original study or the original researchers. While both the Blonde and Dimes studies did not deal with health issues, other fake studies have. Desperate people may lay their hopes on this type of erroneous information—that is why evaluating these types of reports is important.

Lead and Krypton(ite) Aren't Just Bad News for Superman, Either

In the sciences, the race to be the first to create and discover new elements and processes is what drives many researchers to take bold, innovative steps. It isn't just the drive for knowledge, but also the accolades and prestige that give scientists the incentive to find uncharted ground. To be first gives bragging rights, research grants and possible Nobel prizes.

In the 1999 issue of the journal *Physical Review Letters*, scientists at the Lawrence Berkeley National Laboratory in Berkeley, California announced that they had created the impossible: two heavy artificial elements, made by bombarding lead nuclei with a beam of krypton ions. They were dubbed superheavy elements 116 and 118 by the Russian physicist team who created the new element in an "atom smasher." Other scientists called the discovery of the newest and heaviest element in the periodic table a "surprise," but, predictably, news spread quickly into the mainstream press, such as the September 13, 1999 edition of the *Dallas Morning News*:

> Some of the world's most advanced laboratories are practicing the ancient art of alchemy.
>
> Rather than turning lead into gold, modern alchemists have turned lead into something more amazing—a chemical element that even Mother Nature couldn't make.
>
> Element 118, made from lead and krypton, has joined two other new members of chemistry's best-known club, the periodic table of the elements. These new elements are substances never before seen, and their creation only recently imagined. They are the heaviest elements ever made, packing 114, 116 and 118 protons into their nuclei. Their very existence suggests that chemists are close to a fabled goal—making a relatively stable "superheavy" element.

Dr. Victor Ninov, one of the group's researchers, was also interviewed for the *Morning News* story:

> Scientists have to be pretty lucky to see the element they created, Dr. Ninov says. He compares the confirmation of new elements with playing the lottery.
>
> "You can play once and win right away, but the statistical fluctuations are really terrible," he says.

The new elements made news in the *Contra Costa Times* (which began its June 8, 1999 story with "Better open up another page for the periodic table. Scientists at Lawrence Berkeley Laboratory have created two never-before-seen elements using a theory that could lead to a quick discovery of even more, researchers say"), the Scripps Howard News Service (which complained that the element's names were given "unromantic" names), the *Kansas City Star* (dubbing the find "Shangri-la"), the *Denver Post*, the *Baton Rouge Advocate*, the *Pittsburgh Post-Gazette* and the *Cleveland Plain-Dealer*. The elements could last as long as thirty seconds, a long and promising period of time, which gave hope for better things to come.

Eventually, a serious problem was uncovered by other researchers: they couldn't replicate the findings. By 2002, a review of the data showed that the results were fabricated, and Dr. Ninov was fired. Superheavy element 118 did not exist, and researchers were forced to withdraw their findings. If other scientists aren't able to duplicate the experiment and its results, then it is a troubling sign that the results are either a fluke or that someone has fudged them. In this case, other team researchers hadn't carefully verified Ninov's data, nor were any proficient in the computer software used in recording the results of the experiments, making it easy for him—or anyone else—to doctor the results.

Finding an Animal as Probable as the Unicorn

The job of many scientists is to unlock the secrets of the past and future: what happened and how? Where did life begin? How do we think? How do diseases start and what can stop them?

These mysteries revolve around our everyday lives. Many scientists investigate these cases, but sometimes they also try to answer questions to new problems. These are tough puzzles to solve, since there are few leads or knowledgeable experts. To find a problem or phenomenon that no other researcher has ever discovered before is fairly rare; however, if the problem has ancient origins, the task becomes that much more intriguing and romantic for both scientists and journalists.

Pseudonovibos spiralis was one of these startling mysteries. The animal's strange-looking and elaborate horns were discovered in 1993 in parts of Cambodia and Viet Nam. Even though no other part of the animal was ever discovered, that didn't stop scientists from speculating about the creature's bleak origins. Was the animal an extinct goat or ox? Where did it come from? What did it look like? Why did it vanish? By the following year, German researchers made their findings public.

The newly discovered and endangered creature made its way into the mainstream press and reporters, too, speculated about the mysterious animal. The July 17, 1999 edition of the *London Independent* also weighed in on the matter:

> In the century's most astonishing series of wildlife discoveries, Vietnam is yielding up its hidden animals.
>
> A country closed to scientific examination by nearly four decades of savage warfare involving the Japanese, the French and then the Americans has, during the 1990s, produced at least six large mammals previously unknown to science—a rhinoceros, at least four species of deer and antelope, and a particular type of primate. And some scientists consider these finds [to] represent only the beginning.

The article went on to describe the origins of the discovery:

> More mysterious has been an antelope given the scientific name *Pseudonovibos spiralis*, which has been known since 1994 from its horns, which turn up in markets, but has not yet been seen by scientists as a whole animal, alive or dead.

Pseudonovibos spiralis also made its was into the in the November 1, 1999 edition of the *Sarasota Herald-Tribune*:

> Kansas scientists suspect the head from a virtually unknown type of Asian ox may be tucked away in a box or a closet in Southwest Florida—and they want its DNA. "It's a real mystery about a new mammal that scientists are trying to unravel," said Robert Timm, curator of mammals at the Natural History Museum at the University of Kansas. "No scientists have ever seen this animal, so it would be very valuable to see this mount."

By 1991, researchers finally took a closer look at the horns. The horns weren't the remains of some endangered and exotic animal, but came from common cows. The horns had been heated, twisted, carved and otherwise manipulated by human hands to look as if they had come from a rare animal. What was even more embarrassing was that DNA tests conducted on the horns found that they were a perfect match for Vietnamese cattle. *Pseudonovibos spiralis* was a fraud based on researcher's naïveté and Vietnamese folklore.

How did the hoax endure for eight years? Scientists made assumptions based on too little evidence: relying on horns, not questioning why other parts of the animal could not be found and not comparing the DNA of the horns with other area animals right away. With proper confirmation, scientists were too taken with the prospect of discovering a previously unheard of animal to ask the right skeptical questions.

The Double Cross

The press has a fascination with multiple births—from the McCaughey sextuplets to the Dionne quintuplets right down to the Olsen twins. Yet of all of the multiple birth possibilities, twins still have that magic allure. Are the twins alike or different? Did they have their own special language as toddlers? Do they run impressive capitalistic empires together or do they just find themselves identical twins of the opposite sex to marry? But one of the more intriguing twin stories are the ones where the identical twins were separated at birth and then reunited, especially if the twins end up following the same route in life. If they both took up carpentry, were neat freaks and married women named Gloria, the reunited siblings can expect some play in the local press.

Psychologists and geneticists have a fascination with separated identical twins, too, but it has nothing to do with the curiosity factor, particularly if the twins were reared in vastly different environments. These sibling rarities can tell researchers how much of their personality and intelligence was inherited and how much was shaped by outside forces. Studying these twins can give valuable clues as to how much instruction and parental rearing can actually influence a person's moral and intellectual development.

Sir Cyril Burt was a highly regarded British psychologist who advocated the claim that intelligence was three quarters hereditary. His findings and arguments influenced the educational system in post-war Britain and, to a lesser extent, the U.S. Since intelligence was seen as fixed at birth, young children were given exams, which determined the quality of education they received; for students who scored high on the exam, this meant receiving better education than those who scored poorly. There was no point in trying to get poorer scoring students to improve; after all, they did not possess the innate intelligence to do any better.

Twenty-five years later, many people questioned this restrictive educational model. To silence his critics, Burt finally published a series of papers of the ingenious experiments he conducted decades earlier (updated, as he duly noted, with the help of his assistants Miss Margaret Howard and Miss Jane Conway). Large samples of identical twins that were separated at birth and then raised in radically different environments were given IQ tests. The results were clear: the twins performed nearly identically on their tests. Intelligence was innate, accounting for 80% of scores.

Burt's studies were covered in U.S. newspapers, from the *Washington Post* to the *Daily Oklahoman*. In the May 30, 1957 edition of the *Washington Post*, one reporter discussed Burt's "confirmed" theories:

> [...]Sir Cyril [Burt] said [his research] supported the theory that... differences of brain capacity are the results of differences of brain structure, this capacity, like other physical differences, could be largely dependent on heredity.
>
> This is confirmed, Sir Cyril reported, by surveys of children brought up from birth in London orphanages, and by studies of identical twins reared in widely different home surroundings.

When Burt died in 1971, U.S. psychologist Leon Kamin began to look into Burt's work and noticed serious flaws. Details about the sample and testing conditions were too vague, and the results were identical for every study. What was even more troubling was that in twenty years, Burt had supposedly tested over a hundred pairs of British separated identical twins, a highly dubious claim.

Others who looked into Burt's studies couldn't track down Miss Howard or Miss Conway. Burt's data was also sparse. The conclusion was simple: Burt's studies were based on nonexistent data.

To this day, there are psychologists who vehemently defend Burt and maintain his studies were real. However, this doesn't answer basic questions about his work. One defender wrote that he found someone who may have remembered one of Burt's assistants. Others contend that Burt did not use his assistants' real names in his papers, but why would a psychologist have the need to hide the identities of his assistants? Why wouldn't these assistants set the record straight when news of his possible chicanery became public?

There are other questions: have any of the twins who were part of Burt's experiments spoken up and confirmed that they had participated in this study by now? How did Burt come across and gain access to over one hundred separated identical twins? What happened to the paper trail, or to those who had contact with the psychologist? Someone, anyone in the academic community who had assisted or participated in these studies would have come forward to confirm that some part of Burt's studies was genuine. The silence is telling.

Others claimed that Burt had lost the papers from his crucial experiments during the Second World War, found some of them, but then never had the chance to put them in order; however, even fragments of these studies could have confirmed that he did in fact conduct these experiments.

With Burt's defenders still justifying his behavior thirty years later, their convoluted explanations ironically violate one of science's most important tenets. The rule of Occam's Razor states that the simplest explanation is most likely the correct explanation. Their explanations of the lost twins, assistants and documentation are anything but simple.

How to Spot Fake and Bad Science in the News

Assuming that reporters haven't misinterpreted a study, it is possible for a news consumer to determine whether the study is real or accurate. Does the study make sense? How are other researchers in a similar field reacting to the study? There are several cues as to how reliable a new piece of research is.

1. There is no control group for the study.

In any good study, a control group should be used, if possible. A control group is an important tool for researchers—it gives them an anchor, a reference point and, most importantly, a context. We can't make judgments unless we compare a group who experienced a particular treatment or action to a group who did not.

Suppose a researcher believes that nagging cures colds. In his government-funded study at a prestigious university, he has his highly trained grad school assistants relentlessly nag test subjects who have colds—and, lo and behold, the researcher finds that eventually all his subjects stop showing signs of illness. Do his results prove that he's onto something with his "nagging cure"?

Obviously not. The marquee value of the scientist's name, sponsor, institution or assistants means nothing. The subjects got better, but who's to say they wouldn't have gotten better without the nagging? He can tout his findings all he wants, but it's doubtful that *Lancet* or the *New England Journal of Medicine* will publish his paper.

To prove that his unconventional treatment works, at the very least, the researcher would need another group of sick subjects who didn't get nagged while they were nursing their colds. Chances are, those subjects will get over their illness at the same time as the nagged group (or even, perhaps, faster, since they wouldn't be under the same stress).

However, most journalists aren't schooled in the scientific method—they aren't looking for good studies, but for shocking, surprising or sexy results: how those results came to be is less important. If the study was poorly done, then the answers are inaccurate.

What this means is simple: the next time a scientific study on the news interests you, determine whether the report mentions the results were compared to a control group. Even if there is a control group, it's not a guarantee that the study is a good one—but you can be sure a study without one is not worth your time.

2. No one can find the original study or the original researchers.

In the Blonde Extinction and March of Dimes hoaxes, no one could track down the original researchers. If you can't find the names of those involved in a study using a search engine, then it's a pretty good sign the study and the researchers don't exist. If a study seems relevant to your medical condition, the best route is simply doing the legwork yourself: an Internet search should take you directly to the university or institution that produced the study, and it will be here where you may find details on the study. Even if the study exists, reporters may have exaggerated or misinterpreted the findings. This may be the best way to get the information you need.

3. The researcher has the same correlation coefficient through his various studies.

If you flip a coin ten times, it's not guaranteed that you will land five heads. There will be some variation in your results. In other words, no matter how many studies a particular group of researchers conduct, their results come out the exact same every time. In the Cyril Burt case, his studies always came out identical—to three decimal places, quite a feat considering the number of subjects in his experiments were different each time. Even if intelligence was 100% hereditary, we would still expect some variation in the data. Subjects have off days, misinterpret questions or answer questions correctly by accident.

4. The results are too clean, or the researcher is the only one who can "make" the results happen.

Nobody is so special that he is the only person on the planet who can get the right answer. In the Mark Spector case, only he could speed up slow processes and get certain biological reactions. No one is that gifted, no matter what his mother tells him. The lone genius may sound romantic and exciting in fiction, but in real life, it's a sign that someone is fudging data.

5. Other researchers cannot replicate results.

This point is related to the above red flag: the purpose of a study is to produce particular results and treatment procedures so that other scientists can take those findings and apply them to their professions. There would be little point finding a drug to cure AIDS that no one else in the world could produce.

Replication is important for two reasons. First, the results need to be replicated so that others can benefit from the discovery. Second, replication is needed to make certain that the result wasn't just a fluke.

If other scientists can't replicate the results, then either the original researcher has left out key details of his experiments or he simply has lied about conducting the experiment in the first place. If the researcher is making excuses as to why he is the only one with the magic touch, there is a good chance the researcher faked his data.

6. A researcher with poor credentials or dubious connections makes a fantastic claim or claims to be able to produce a result no other mainstream researcher can.

Academic cred, just like street cred, matters. A "scientist" or "doctor" who bought his PhD at a diploma mill is a quack, and a quack cannot cure diabetes, infertility, impotence, AIDS or cancer. These people may seem authoritative; they may be polite and nice to patients; and they may even stand up to the Establishment, but they cannot cure and they cannot conduct a valid experiment. In the Clonaid case, "researchers" were affiliated with a cult and refused to publish their findings or provide any proof of their claims.

Finding a cure for a terminal or debilitating disease takes decades: researchers have to go through slow and complicated processes many times over before they can reach a sound conclusion. Some processes can take years. But in a world of drive-thrus, microwaves and instant messaging, patience seems to be anything but a virtue, especially when you've been diagnosed with a terminal disease. People want results instantly, even if one isn't coming for the next thirty years.

The desperation and the drive to live are understandable. The problem is that con artists look for the weakest and most desperate people to prey on. No matter how appealing a treatment or breakthrough may seem, a fake treatment won't work.

Section **Four**

How to Spot Rumors and Hoaxes

Chapter **Sixteen**

| **Sources and Investigation**

Anniversaries of national tragedies are guaranteed a spot in any media form: remembering the horror and the helplessness seems to be a cathartic exercise for both victims and their onlookers. Anniversaries give enough time between the victims and the tragedy to give a calmer account of what happened and how fate changed their very souls. One anniversary to be commemorated for years to come will be September 11.

Scott Fletcher was a managing editor for the *Barre Times-Argus*, a newspaper in Barre, Vermont. On the first anniversary of the collapse of the World Trade Center, he managed to find one Martha Harris, a quiet woman whose nephew had perished in one of the towers. The event changed her life, as recounted in the September 11, 2002 edition of the *Times-Argus*:

> On the morning of Sept. 11 [2001], Martha Harris was, like most of us, at work when events began to unfold. She watched the video just once, watched the second jet hit the second tower as the first tower smoldered. That was enough. She never saw the towers fall, never saw the now-famous images of New Yorkers fleeing what would become ground zero with huge plumes of smoke and debris billowing behind them.
>
> She saw the jet hit the tower and concluded the world was coming apart. Her first thoughts were of a nephew, the last of her family, who worked in Tower Two. She left work, she teaches creative writing—check that—she taught creative writing at schools in Vermont and New Hampshire, and headed for home. The news of the tower's collapse was delivered by car radio. She spent the rest of that day and the next on the phone trying to reach her nephew.
>
> He was unreachable. He died in Tower Two, as a co-worker of her nephew finally responded to Martha's frantic calls to the company's message service.
>
> That was it. Martha was done with life here.

According to Fletcher, Martha sold her house, cashed in her savings, and retreated to a hunting camp without electricity, telephone or even plumbing. The story went into detail about how Martha now lived her simple life.

What the story didn't mention was her nephew's name, what company he worked for, or even the name of the school where she taught (whether she taught grade school, high school or post secondary isn't mentioned). The details to reassure the reader that the color-laden story was true weren't there. Several *Times-Argus* readers did try to pin down a Martha Harris, as described in the story, but had no luck. In fact, Mrs. Harris did not exist— she was nothing more than a figment brought to life by Fletcher.

Information does not magically fall into a reporter's lap: all data has to come from a source known to the reporter. Yet reporters need to extend a simple courtesy to their audiences; namely, that they give identifying information about their sources whenever possible. There are times when identifying a source isn't possible; especially if the source needs shielding for professional or personal security reasons, but when there is no reason why the reporter can't divulge the specifics, then it's time to wonder why information is being withheld from the reader or viewer.

Fletcher never mentioned why Harris' nephew's name, occupation and place of employment weren't disclosed (i.e., did Harris decline to give the specifics, or did the editor consider such important details to be frivolous?) There would be no reason why these important facts would be denied to the reader. Yet this was neither the first nor last article from Fletcher that would rely on sketchy details about the people he interviewed. This was a warning sign that something was wrong with the editor's work.

Shoddy sourcing and sketchy details are not the only red flags to watch for when reading or watching the news. Rosie Ruiz didn't look all that sweaty or exhausted for a woman who just ran the Boston marathon. Everyone in Stephen Glass' articles seemed to talk in the same voice and offer the same pieces of pithy wisdom. Wendy Bergen's dogfight tape merely showed the same two dogs fighting over and over again. Kim Stacy seemed too composed and carefree for someone who had a time bomb ticking in her brain. But what if there weren't any obvious signs of deception? How can we tell if a source or reporter is a credible and reliable one?

Most times we can't be entirely certain about an interviewee's believability since we can't (or wouldn't want to) conduct a background check on him or her. Yet sometimes it pays to take a closer look at someone who, for whatever reason, isn't making sense or may have a motive to lie. Who is making the claim, and what does he get if he is believed? In the fake lotto winner scam, Battle had a motive to lie: if someone else later (rightfully) claimed the winnings, perhaps she could have tried to sue the person for a portion of the winnings. Donna Mercier wanted more pills. Charles Stuart and Susan Smith had motives to lie: they both wanted to give themselves an alibi to avoid a lengthy prison sentence. What we are looking for are any clues that a source or reporter is being less than straightforward with us.

Finding the Motive

Everything comes down to motive: why is this person talking to reporters? Publicity hounds crave attention. Murder suspects want to influence a potential jury pool into believing their proclamations of innocence. Business executives want free advertising. Victims want to avenge their suffering. A con artist wants to scam the public for personal gain.

Many fabricators unintentionally give themselves away with their stories. For example, in Donna Mercier's case, she emphasized that her medication was stolen, meaning that she may have had some reason for wanting another prescription or at least was trying to account for why she was missing her painkillers.

In Kim Stacy's case, she claimed that her motive for lying was to "make friends," and her assertion may not be implausible. In her debut column, she made reference to her secret motive for fabricating her illness:

> Immediately [after they were told about the cancer diagnosis], co-workers and friends rallied around me, making themselves available for anything I needed, even if it was only to talk. Most surprisingly was the comfort and concern I received from the community. People who I saw every day as I went about my job—strangers in many ways—would drop by the office to wish me well or call me to see if there was anything I needed.

Finding alternate motives means reading or watching a news story in a different way; instead of focusing on the emotional or logical elements, you are trying to consider several reasons why someone in that position would talk to the press, then trying to decide which motive seems the most plausible, given the context and angle of the story, coupled with the information given by the source.

Types of Sources

Figuring out a source's motive may depend on determining what kind of source he is. Is he a leaker? Is he maintaining his innocence? Each of these sources have their good sides and their red flags.

The unnamed source. The news consumer doesn't have the chance to decide how credible the source is, but some reporters may give more defining information about the secret source than others. The question for the audience is, why is this person insisting on being unnamed in a story? Does he fear retribution? Is he trying to silently right a wrong? On the other hand, the person may be exaggerating, skewing facts or lying in order to further his own agenda or to hurt someone else's credibility. What's more, sometimes the anonymous source does not exist—the reporter has made up a source to lend credibility to a factually shaky story.

If the story hinges on unnamed sources, read it with caution. If the reporter relies on only first names, it may be to protect innocent parties, bolster sources with low credibility or hide the fact that these sources don't exist at all. Anonymous sources aren't necessarily fraudulent, but they may have an agenda and a reason for keeping their name out of the news, especially if they are leaking information.

The publicity hound. This person doesn't care why the cameras are rolling, just so long as he's standing in front of them when they do. Some want the publicity to further a career, while others crave pity. When someone who has a fantastic story suddenly makes the rounds on every major news outlet, it might be good to question whether he made up the story, or is at least exaggerating elements for his own benefit.

However, some people don't know how to turn down media requests, or may be giving interviews since their company's public relations department is actively encouraging it. If the person is consistently soliciting media interviews, then it is more likely that the person is an attention-seeker, and most good reporters will let their audiences know if this is the case. In the Eagle hoax, the dog's owner was the one who initiated media contact, but many articles did not clue readers on to this.

The slagger. This source may be making serious accusations against another person or company or may be gossiping about others. This negative focus may be because the other party richly deserves it, but it also may be because the source has a vested interest in belittling his rival or obstacle (he may wish to sue the other person or remove the competition).

If the story relies on a negative source alone (without any corroborating evidence), it may mean the reporter hasn't independently verified the person's allegations. Look for all the evidence the reporter provides to confirm or refute the slagger's claim.

The rent-a-quote. A thoroughly worthless source, the rent-a-quote is filler. Pithy or clever quotes that add nothing to the story mean the reporter is trying to stretch out a story—or that the editor or producer are trying to add a "just folks" touch to the piece.

Verifying the Source

In their rush for time and their drive for scoops, some reporters don't always run background checks on their sources. In 2003, the "Slammer" computer virus had made its rounds, but one *Computerworld* magazine reporter seemed to scoop his rivals by insisting that the virus had been created by terrorists. The story appeared on *Computerworld*'s website on February 5, 2003:

A radical Islamic group that is on the U.S. State Department's list of designated terrorist organizations has claimed responsibility for the release of the Slammer worm late last month.

In an exclusive exchange of e-mails with Computerworld spanning two weeks, Abu Mujahid, a spokesman for Harkat-ul-Mujahideen (HUM), a self-proclaimed radical Islamic jihadist organization, said the group released the Slammer worm as part of a "cyber jihad" aimed at creating fear and uncertainty on the Internet.

"[...]Do not underestimate our abilities to create fear and chaos on the Internet, using programs we find and modify to our purposes," said Mujahid. "We do not need to attack the infrastructure to terrorize the Kufars," he said, referring to non-Muslims. "We use the Internet to spread misinformation and confusion."

If the journalist relied on "an exclusive exchange of e-mails," then how did he know that the person writing those e-mails was in fact Abu Muhahid? Did he see him? How did he confirm the man's identity?

He didn't; the e-mail exchange was a hoax. A New Hampshire freelance reporter duped the *Computerworld* reporter into thinking he was someone else, meaning that the entire article was based on lies. Without confirming evidence, the reporter's story fell apart. Some reporters still don't double check who they are speaking to over the phone (as in the case of Brian Blomquist when he interviewed the wrong Robert Fisk[e]) or corresponding with over the Internet. In this case, knowing that the exchange happened strictly through e-mail messages helps the news consumer know that the "exclusive" might not be genuine.

Looking for Hard Evidence

While Mike Barnicle's fateful column was touching, it was interesting for one other fact: how did Barnicle get his hands on the letter that was purportedly written by the parents whose child survived? His column made it seem as if he had read the letter or had heard it from the parents themselves (how would he know how the letter was composed, unless the senders or receivers told him?) In fact, Barnicle hadn't seen any letter—and his columns never made reference as to how he knew about the contents of the note.

Accurate news stories show the reporter's trail and report the evidence by name. Had Barnicle received the note from a credible source, he would have said so in his column. Keeping that piece of the puzzle hidden meant that revealing it would expose a deficiency in his reportage. Shoddy sourcing is a reliable sign of shoddy reporting.

Some people are aware of this journalistic deficiency and take full advantage of it. Joey Skaggs is a jammer; i.e., a professional media hoaxer. Over the years, he has presented fraudulent and ridiculous stories to the press and has taken on various aliases in his quest to pull one over reporters.

And he keeps fooling the media over and over again.

In the December 11, 1999 edition of the *Washington Times*, one of Skaggs' scams made it into the paper without raising questions:

> Investors Real Estate Development in Cranford, N.J., is hoping to revolu-
> tionize the way we think about death with the Final Curtain, a memorial
> theme park where artists design their own tombs and tourists pay admis-
> sion to see them.
>
> The Final Curtain has received "tons of requests" to purchase plots at
> its cemeteries in Paris, London, Sydney, Australia, California and Ten-
> nessee, said assistant marketing director Paul Carey. Also popular is the
> Final Curtain's timeshare plan, which lets its deceased customers spend a
> season in another cemetery.

How could a body be moved to "another cemetery" for a period of time and then be returned to its original plot? Why would someone want to do this? How economically feasible would this game of musical plots be for the cemetery? But it wasn't the only questionable passage in the article:

> Mr. Carey says this concept "really solves a lot of the needs people have."
> Some of those needs apparently include being cremated and inserted into
> an Etch-a-Sketch. Another customer wants to be interred in a glass box
> with a crane attached so observers can turn him over in his grave.
>
> Yet another wants her ashes spread across an ant farm.

The story was ridiculous and the sources weren't properly vetted, yet the story ran as if it were true.

Hoaxes such as the Final Curtain yarn aren't just limited to the imagination of Skaggs. One reporter also tried his hand at jamming with positive results in the November 20, 2003 edition of the *New Times Broward Palm Beach*:

> Anarchists plan a massive infiltration of a Republican governors meeting that
> begins Thursday, November 20, in Boca Raton. Dozens of members of a rad-
> ical organization will attempt to disrupt the three-day gathering hosted by
> Gov. Jeb Bush by disguising themselves as reporters and aides. The scheme is
> meant to cause widespread disturbances that will unravel the event.
>
> The plans began, of all places, in a West Palm Beach building on
> Belvedere Road that once housed a Taco Bell restaurant. In October, a
> group that calls itself Anarchists for a Better State (anarchistsforabetter-
> state.4t.com) rented the space and began making plans for protests at

FTAA and at an annual meeting of the Republican Governors Association, which runs through Saturday, November 22, at the posh Boca Raton Resort & Club.

Readers who take comfort in relying only on search engines and websites also would have been thwarted by the author, who mentioned a bogus, but active, link in his piece that led to a website that seemed to confirm the group's existence. The article went on to describe the group's leader:

> The group's top organizer is Michael Bakunin, a plumber with a heavy New England accent from Plymouth, Massachusetts. A tall slender man in his thirties who other members say once played college basketball and majored in physics, he speaks mostly in parables about government theory and the downfall of the ruling class. "When you speak of the ancestors of our cause and then you speak of what we are doing today, you speak of what we are giving the cause for tomorrow," he told about 75 anarchists during a meeting three days before the conference. "This week, we begin the ascent of activism and the descent of our government."

The telltale clue left by the author was the name of the organizer Michael Bakunin. Bakunin was an anarchist all right, but one from Europe, who was alive in the 1800s.

Whether it is confirming a source's name or pinpointing where a piece of information came from, the less specific information you are given, the more likely the story has structural or factual flaws. The trick is determining what is evidence and what is fluff.

In print, finding the fluff can be difficult, since color and dialogue often seem important, informative and truthful. In January 1999, *Philadelphia* magazine ran a story called "The Boys in the String Band," about "Neil" (not his real or full name as the reporter helpfully pointed out), a Mummer who was in the closet about his homosexuality, but relished his involvement in the New Year's celebration since he could "be himself" one day a year. The story was short on specifics, but had relied mostly on color and colorful quotes.

According to the writer, Neil assumed that his fellow Mummers were oblivious to the truth, but his friends were fully aware of Neil's true leanings:

> [Neil and George] embrace, sending feathers and sequins flying. It's hard to tell where one Mummer ends and the other begins.
>
> I steal a glance at Robby [one of Neil's friends], who has the strangest look in his face. "Look at that," he says, a bit of disgust in his voice.
>
> "What do you mean?" I ask, playing dumb. But I can't help but think: *My God, does Robby know the truth?*

"They're the two biggest closet cases in the parade," Robby says.

What?

"You mean—you know?" I splutter.

Robby looks at me. "What, do I know they're fags? Of course I know. Everybody knows. You think we were born yesterday? You'd be surprised how many of 'em there are in the parade. There's Chuck D., Frankie, Joey, Jackie B.—look, you ain't reporting nothing new, buddy."

It was later revealed that the article was a complete work of fiction and a poor attempt at satire and humor, but how could news consumers know this?

The reader may not have been entirely certain of the hoax, but there were plenty of warning signs. Poor sourcing, few tangible facts, the over-the-top ending and the fact that there was hardly any variation in the speaking styles of any of the sources—or even the writer himself.

Finding Shoddy and Dubious Sources in Articles

Poor sourcing is a reliable red flag that an article may be a hoax. Scott Fletcher, the *Times-Argus* managing editor who wrote about Martha Harris, also wrote a story about DeeDee, a sixteen-year-old heroin addict living in Vermont. Her sad tale was featured in the September 15, 2002 edition of the *Argus*:

> She is sitting near Montpelier's pocket park, near Christ Church on State Street in Montpelier, in the shadow of the state capital building.
>
> Her arms are spread wide along the top of the bench, her face hidden behind an expensive pair of sunglasses. She is wearing a very tight white tank top and a very short, black miniskirt, both of which appear to be too small for her. A pair of black heels completes the day's ensemble.

The article ended with DeeDee driving off into the sunset for a night of paid debauchery:

> It is after 6 p.m. on State Street in Montpelier and what is left of the Vermont capital's mini rush hour is long gone.
>
> DeeDee is still here. The sun is dipping behind the hills but the golden dome of the capital is aglow. DeeDee is removing her sunglasses when a gleaming SUV pulls up to the curb. A well-dressed man is behind the wheel and DeeDee alights from the bench and speaks to him through the passenger window.
>
> She gets in and the SUV roars away and darkness descends on the city.

While this anecdote sandwiched an otherwise accurate article about drug use, it's interesting to note that those facts were detached from the proof of

DeeDee's existence. The information about drug use in Vermont was on the level, but it was the use of color that was fabricated.

For many media outlets, their source is another media outlet, regardless of whether the information seems suspect or not. Such was the case in a March 5, 2004 wire story from *Wireless Flash*:

> The metrosexual movement may have gone too far—now, straight guys are trying to dance with each other instead of women.
>
> According to the upcoming issue of *Stuff* magazine, the hottest dance trend in New York clubs is "gancing," a term for when guys boogie oogie oogie together.
>
> One popular "gance step" features one guy pretending to be a shark while his pal runs away in fright. Another manly move has the guys pretending to be kangaroos complete with pouches and Fosters beer.

Wireless Flash's source wasn't a single nightclub owner or participant, but the lad magazine *Stuff*, purveyors of augmented B-list bosoms. The original April 2004 article described this latest guy trend:

> Drew Lerner is having the time of his life. The twenty-six-year-old travel agent is in a hip New York City bar, his favorite song is playing, and he's dancing like a madman… with another man. And neither of them is gay.
>
> Welcome to the formerly hidden world of gancing (aka, guy-on-guy dancing). While a woman hoofing it with a member of the same sex has never been an eyebrow raiser, the idea of two straight men following suit has historically been frowned upon. You know, like when you see a dog wearing a sweater? It's not normal, so you frown.
>
> But as far as Drew is concerned, it's as simple as a love of shaking his groove thing versus a lack of receptive skirts. "I couldn't get any girls to dance with me, so I decided, I'll just dance with this dude," recalls Lerner. "But it works on other levels. When I'm doing moves like the Dog with a buddy, girls at the club not only form circles around us, but they actually want to join in."

One of the alleged "gance moves" was called the "Diana Ross" and was described in this way:

> Gancer No. 1 pretends to be drunk-driving across the dance floor, while gancer No. 2 runs away from him so as not to be the victim in DUI Diana's soon-to-be vehicular homicide. As the song ends, gancer No. 1 runs over gancer No. 2 and then flees the scene of the crime. Note: Only to be performed during the playing of any Supremes song, ideally "Stop! In the Name of Love."

Several web logs cited *Stuff* as their source, never questioning how reliable an April issue of a men's magazine can really be. Despite the tongue-in-cheek writing style, very few people who cited *Stuff* realized that the article was an April Fool's joke and the invention of the magazine's editor, as was *Esquire's* "Freewheelz" article.

For the most part, the above examples dealt with previously unknown and untested sources; however, sometimes someone who has been truthful in the past may decide it's more advantageous to lie.

The Problems With Believing Previously Credible Sources

The "favorite son" (or daughter) is blessed with an audience who believes him (or her). And why not? This is a person who has proven himself to his community in the past. His talent and abilities are documented; he has given reliable information in the past, and it may even be to his detriment to lie. Even with a clear track record, it's still important to analyze his story—you never know when he will decide to take a gamble with his credibility.

At times, there may be very little that can be done to smoke out a person's bogus tale. In 1982, the *Welland Tribune's* sports editor Wayne Redshaw received a press release announcing that a nineteen-year-old Western Michigan University freshman and former Welland resident named Victor Notaro would be playing at a World Junior Cup soccer tournament in Australia. The press release looked legitimate and Notaro confirmed to Redshaw that he would be playing in the tournament. This wasn't surprising since the young man played soccer in Welland, and had won a soccer scholarship.

During the cup, Notaro phoned Redshaw to give him details of the previous game. One of those games was mentioned in the March 1, 1982 edition of the *Welland Tribune*:

> Victor Notaro of Welland was the hero for Canada here Monday (Sunday Welland time).
>
> Notaro scored Canada's only goal as they defeated the Soviet Union 1-0 in the finals of the World Junior Cup under-21 soccer championship.

Redshaw also interviewed Notaro's coach, who had called the editor to give him an interview:

> Canadian coach Paul Piak of Vancouver told the *Tribune* in a telephone interview "the club is over ecstatic. I just can't explain it," said Piak minutes after the victory.
>
> "The club played superb," added Piak, who said he was mentally drained and also physically suffering from a heart ailment.

Piak also noted that defense was the key to Canada's victory as they didn't allow a single goal en route to the championship... "The West German game took the toll on our players with fatigue and injuries," added Piak.

Redshaw's story about a local boy moving up in the world was relayed on a wire service, and other media outlets across Canada picked up the story.

Unfortunately for Redshaw, the tournament did not exist, as the Canadian Soccer Association informed the public, nor was Notaro in Australia. The young man called the editor from Kalamazoo and had apparently recruited a confederate to pose as his soccer coach. Without Internet or call display, Redshaw did not have the same means of confirming Notaro's story.

Not that Redshaw didn't talk to Notaro's old Welland coaches to confirm the story. "They were a bit surprised since he was a below average house league player," says Redshaw about the twenty-two-year-old hoaxer. "[Notaro] always called me at my house in the evening hours to let me know how the game went," he adds.

Notaro didn't just lie to Redshaw—he had even told his parents about the tournament and they had believed their son. What was there to question? The young man was a soccer player who was on his college's soccer team (this was confirmed by the university's soccer coach). The Notaros were a well-liked family in their town, and they too could confirm their son's story since their son had also phoned them to report on his progress. Notaro had no previous record of lying. Since Notaro knew the sport intimately, his lies would be more convincing. The press release was created by Notaro to give credence to his premeditated fabrication. "The release looked legitimate," Redshaw recalls.

What motive did Notaro have for lying? He was vying for the Welland Sport Council male athlete of the year award, and "winning" the "Junior World Cup" gave him enough of an edge to beat his opponents. What Notaro didn't bank on was Redshaw informing other media outlets about the game. Though he had initially won the award, news of the hoax changed matters; Notaro withdrew his name and the award went to someone else.

Keeping vigilant (without being paranoid) can be helpful in smoking out scams, but the best method of determining a story's veracity is using logic over emotion, as the next chapter shows.

Chapter Seventeen

Logic Versus Emotion

Despite the abundance of news outlets, getting media access is not as easy as it seems: with so many media-savvy interests or newsworthy events all competing for attention, not every event makes news. There may be countless robberies and muggings happening every day, yet not all of these crimes will get even a small mention in a paper's "news briefs" section. Editors and reporters have to be discriminating and pick events that will both spark audience interest and be culturally important to them. If a con artist can figure out a scheme that seems to meet both these criteria, it can mean his hoax may displace a real news event.

At times you can't even blame the press for buying a scam artist's story: sometimes it's better to believe a suspect story than to dismiss a real story that has serious ramifications. When someone's life may be in danger, there may not be time to question the story's veracity. Threats toward children would fall into this category. Is it better to check out a parent's credibility before reporting on a missing child, or is it better to report first and ask questions later? Most people would agree that valuable time would be wasted if reporters were fixated on a distressed parent's trustworthiness rather than on publicizing the plight of an abducted child.

It was that kind of harrowing morning on November 6, 2003 when Katrelle Regina Henry phoned Washington, DC police to report that her car had been stolen—along with her infant child, who was inside the vehicle at the time of the robbery. A stolen car by itself is not a media event, but a stolen car with a missing baby inside makes news.

An "Amber Alert" was immediately issued by police, and Henry made a public appeal for the return of her child. WRC-TV in Washington aired Henry's pleas on both its newscast and its website:

A three-month-old child is safe at home, after a dramatic morning.

The baby was missing for more than two hours after the car he was placed in was stolen.

The baby's mother, Kutrell [sic] Henry, put the boy in the car outside her home in the 1200 block of Eaton Road, Southeast at 8:40 this morning.

She started the car, then went back into the home to get her one-year-old girl niece. When she came outside, the woman says the car and the baby were gone.

Most people would have considered the reunion a happy ending, except that police discovered that Henry's young son was never missing in the first place. Henry's car was stolen, but to ensure that jaded and overworked Washington police would actually look for her car, she also claimed that her son was abducted (the child was staying with a neighbor the entire time). In this case, there was no reason for journalists to initially suspect the woman's claims; her lie made news because it was better to play it safe than to risk the life of a young child.

What makes this hoax interesting is that Henry understood something that most reporters covering the case missed; that is, nothing works to get attention and credibility faster than using an emotional trigger. Our minds take a back seat to our hearts: when we hear that a helpless baby is in the power of a criminal, we don't stand back to question whether the claim is true. We react as if the claim were fact. Fabricators know this and simply use our naïveté and benevolence to their advantage.

Many rumors and hoaxes deliberately play on our emotions; most hoaxers rely on some form of emotional manipulation, such as invoking anger, fear, superiority, greed, pity, insecurity or sadness to make absurd claims sound plausible.

Fortunately, since these types of stories rely on emotions and not facts, they are filled with shoddy logic and can be easily uncovered as hoaxes. There are ways we can inoculate ourselves from overreacting to these whoppers. By recognizing and spotting emotional triggers, we can learn to separate fact from emotional appeal, such as pain or fear, to look for confirming evidence instead.

Most news items are packaged as "stories" and these stories have a beginning, middle and end. There are a cast of characters, developments and even twists. Both real and fake news stories need these elements to bring their stories to life; the only difference is that real stories rely more on facts and fake news stories rely on fictional tricks and techniques. Knowing how to spot the difference can go a long way in separating legitimate stories from fraudulent ones.

Fictional stories need sympathetic characters, an attention-grabbing beginning, emotional pull, an exciting turn of events and closure. Real life doesn't always lend itself to these conveniences, but many reporters may try to shade information or enhance or downplay certain events or characteristics to present unfolding events in this way. Other times, the added frills aren't entirely relevant to the story. For example, a victim of a tragedy may be described as "beloved," "beautiful" and "popular" even though those qualities had nothing to do with the person's tragedy: "[The victim of a hit and run accident] was a woman whose recent ordination as a... minister was a culmination of all her many gifts, a close friend said..." These glowing descriptions are supposed to underline the tragic turn of events, but they can also imply that homely and grouchy outcasts deserve less sympathy.

A hoaxer's story will have more logical holes and be more dependent on story structure than a genuine news story. The bigger and more elaborate the lie, the fewer bases a liar can cover. No hoaxer can think of everything.

Many times hoaxers don't need to think of everything: logical holes can be glossed over if the scammer uses the right cues to cover up any deficiencies his story has. If his story sparks fear and outrage, as did Katrelle Henry's story, reporters and the audience aren't as likely to question the account. Whether the reader is meant to feel anger (as they did when Nayirah claimed Iraqi soldiers murdered little babies) or patriotism (as they did when they read about Jessica Lynch's fight with another group of Iraqi soldiers) emotionally manipulative hoaxes make sure the audience is too worked up to question the story. Emotional triggers help con artists to get away with lies. Most hoaxes are weak and full of plot holes, but if the audience is distracted enough, they won't notice that they are being lied to.

Watching or reading the news takes a different approach than reading a novel or watching a movie: in fiction, we are supposed to let go of our skepticism and bond with the characters. Unless we suspend our belief and let our feelings color our judgment, the exercise becomes ridiculous and unfulfilling. Romeo and Juliet would be reduced to two unstable and melodramatic brats, Sherlock Holmes would become an obnoxious and arrogant cokehead and Darth Vader would be a lunatic running around with a plastic helmet obscuring his vision.

Watching or reading the news takes a different mindset to appreciate: processing information takes active listening and critical thinking since information can be wrong, misleading or fraudulent. No matter how stirring a news story may be, if it doesn't make sense, the story is a fraud.

How to Spot Emotional Manipulation

Emotions, intuition and gut reactions tend to play a bigger role in our decisions than critical thinking or logic do. How we "feel" about someone is more important than what we "think" about them. Though "vibes" never helped anyone pass a history exam, people still use emotions to make important decisions in their lives. One of those important decisions is whether to trust someone. Judging trustworthiness isn't always based on what the person said, but on his facial expressions, gestures and body language. Several studies have shown that people will use behavioral cues to determine a person's trustworthiness. Untrustworthy people are said to have shifty eyes, profuse sweating, poor posture and antsy feet. Credible people are believed to have good eye contact, a warm personality, a friendly smile and a calm, cool demeanor.

Of course, all these "signs" are worthless—a good liar is a practiced one and will work hard on his delivery. He will make a concerted effort to make eye contact with his audience, he will suppress any physical tics, he will make himself seem sympathetic and trustworthy and he will feign shock, hurt and outrage when confronted with inconsistencies in order to throw the heat off him. He has a lie to dress up, and if he decides to lie in front of a large audience, he is going to concentrate on his delivery.

Yet most people still use these physical cues to judge someone's credibility. Con artists know this: it's what many bank on to gain credibility. Their stories might not make one ounce of sense, but if they can perfect the "lost puppy" stare and fake a warm personality, they can dupe the softhearted with relative ease. An experienced fabricator has a good feel for how people make judgments—on their initial feelings. For good measure, they may try to scare us, sadden us, shock us or even anger us, but that manipulation has the same underlying motive: they want us to do everything but think about the truthfulness of their stories.

Ironically, the types of emotional stories that make news are the same ones that many fabricators use to gain credibility. Katrelle Henry, Charles Stuart, Kristen Clougherty, Daniel McCarthy, Dona Spence, Aikaz Akopyan, Susan Smith, Heinz Braun and Nayirah al Sabah all used strong emotional triggers in their hoaxes, from danger to patriotism. Listeners were manipulated into sympathizing and caring for the fabricator, and millions of people gladly complied.

Emotionally exploiting the masses isn't confined to interviewees. Reporters such as Patricia Smith, Kim Stacy, Stephen Glass, Michael Finkel, Jack Kelley, Wendy Bergen and Mike Barnicle have on at least one occasion used emotion to prop up their questionable stories. Readers learn to care about poor, abused homely girls mistreated at the hands of drunken Republican punks or for helpless dogs who are forced to maul each other. These "reporters" don't want their audiences to question the inconsistencies that their moving stories may have.

If emotional manipulation is part of a fabricator's repertoire, then one way to inoculate yourself from falling for these lies is to know which stories lend themselves to these types of journalistic abuses. While every story type has the potential to be perverted, some stories seem to attract more hoaxers than others.

Stories Vulnerable to Emotional Manipulation

Popular hoaxes range from false heroics to false victimization. These stories have their advantages: the roles are clearly defined and the audience will have a built-in sympathy or reverence. These hoaxes rely on trust. Because it can be hard to prove whether an event happened, people tend to give the storyteller the benefit of the doubt, especially if the hoaxer can provide "proof" of her claims (why would anyone risk publicly compromising and humiliating themselves?) Any type of story that does not lend itself to scrutiny is one that a news consumer has to view with a good dose of skepticism.

War stories need to be looked at with a critical eye: while many stories of war atrocities are true, many others are simply propaganda yarns used to incite hatred or cultivate support. Amid numerous stories of human rights violations, a fabricator can easily slip in his or her hoax without detection; unfortunately, it is these hoaxes that are usually the most inciting, over-the-top and sadistic, painting an enemy in an unrealistic light, which in turn prolongs the hatred, suffering, atrocities and body count.

Abused women can also be exploited toward a hoaxer's ends. Donna Mercier claimed that a mean mugger and abusive ex-partner had it in for her. Susan Smith claimed that a heartless carjacker ripped her babies away from her. Belgian officials accused German soldiers of ravishing their young women. Tawana Brawley also claimed to be an exploited female. This type of hoax is particularly infuriating: while a liar initially gets sympathy, his or her hoax not only overshadows true instances of abuse, but also casts suspicion on real cases that lack the same level of brutality or clarity of roles.

Finally, stories about cancer and AIDS are common ones for hoaxers. Journalists such as Kim Stacy, Patricia Smith and Mike Barnicle all falsely used an illness for emotional effect. Non-journalists such as Debbie Swenson, Donna Mercier and Kristen Clougherty also played the cancer card to fool the press, while Dona Spence and various "C.J.'s" invoked the fear of contracting AIDS to arouse people's sympathies. Oddly enough, con artists do not usually invoke other fatal or painful diseases, most likely because no other diseases are as well known or evoke as powerful of emotions as cancer and AIDS do.

How to Evaluate an Interviewee

An emotionally driven story alone can't guarantee that the audience will believe the story—what brings the story to life is the people who share their experiences with the news media, and ultimately with the public. For many people, making themselves vulnerable to mass criticism by speaking openly with the press can be a traumatic experience. These people may be shy and introverted by nature, but to have to interact with a potentially hostile press and public (who may notice and ridicule every real or perceived mistake) may mean that the individual will stutter, tremble and misspeak. These interviewees may have already gone through some sort of trial by fire (such as a war or an assault), only to find that they have no time to regroup.

Then there are those people who seem to be the perfect victim or hero. They cry on cue, speak in useful sound bites and act just a little more wounded or intrepid than most of the others who make it on the news. What reporters see are compelling, media-friendly characters who have an equally compelling and moving story to tell. What the public sees is a distressed or heroic person in need of protection or praise—but neither side may have a clue that the well-packaged interviewee is nothing more than a fabricator. Fortunately, there are ways for you as a viewer and reader to weed out the fakes from the rest by asking yourself a few simple questions:

1. What are the stakes for the person telling the story?

This question is a crucial one to answer, but it's not always obvious what a person has to gain by lying publicly. Is this person trying to convince the audience of his innocence or to save himself from imprisonment? Is he planning to sue someone for negligence? Is he trying to cover up a crime? Is he trying to protect someone from harm? Is he trying to protect his reputation?

The interviewee may not be lying, but by focusing on the person's motives, you may see he is exaggerating, leaving out important information or repackaging information to his own benefit. While it's not possible to discover the truth by pondering this question alone, thinking about ulterior motives helps you focus on a story's shortcomings.

2. How well is this person trained in media relations?

Interviewees who can think in terms of sound bites and camera angles can also be trained in holding back unfavorable or important information. They know what stories play well in the press, and they know how to say things without saying anything. What this means is that the reader or viewer is getting prepackaged and filtered information.

The purpose of media training is to make people look better than they do in real life. This training instructs clients how to present themselves, what to say, how to say it, how not to flub one's lines and how to handle a hostile press. In one way, a media trainer is a lot like an acting coach. Media training is used by not only many corporate executives and politicians in a bid to snag positive publicity or fawning headlines, but by those who have ruined their own reputations and are desperate to rehabilitate their image without having to actually work on their own moral lapses.

Clients are grilled in the ways of the press and are shown how to use those ways to their advantage. As one business magazine article that touted the benefits of using media training dutifully stated, "All journalists, print and broadcast, pay attention to details of setting and appearance, looking for what they call 'color.' Choose the interview setting, if you can, and make sure it says the right thing about the story you want to get across. If necessary, bring in props such as simple charts and graphs." In other words, clients are taught that reporters are a shallow, malleable bunch that can be beguiled by flow charts.

Media training can lead to getting better media access. Imagine two people on opposing sides of an issue who are both asked to state their position in a five-minute TV debate. One person has no media training, while the other one does. Whose five minutes on the air will go further? Media training can make otherwise equal sides suddenly become unequal.

Media training also means you, as a news consumer, aren't necessarily getting an accurate picture of a person or an issue. Knowing some of the tricks media trainers use can help you determine how "processed" an interviewee's answer is. Does the person seem guarded? Are his answers too vague? Have you heard those same answers from other people during other unrelated interviews? Is he always putting a positive spin on negative events? If so, then chances are the individual has learned how to avoid answering unpleasant questions and is primarily concerned with his own image, and not telling the complete truth.

There are other signs that an interviewee has gone through professional media training:

• The person may suddenly dress more demurely and conservatively;

• The interviewee uses the first name of the reporter more than once during the interview;

• The person seems to mimic the reporter's body language and posture;

• The person speaks in sound bites;

• The person's answers are a form of "bridging." Bridging simply means the interviewee avoids answering a reporter's tough question by connecting the content of the question with a more positive irrelevant subject the interviewee wants to talk about. Not only does the interviewee avoid answering the reporter's question, but he gets to plug his own image and agenda at the reporter's expense without looking evasive. Some common phrases of the media-trained include the following:

> "Our hearts go out to the families that have been impacted."
> "We are cooperating fully with investigators."
> "It's too early to gauge the full extent of the problem."
> "The lawsuit is entirely without merit."

By spotting media training, you will be better able to judge how much information you are really getting from an interviewee and better guess whether the person is giving real information or merely spin. Sometimes, though, it's not the interviewee who is trying to exploit the reader's feelings, but the reporter.

3. If I remove all the emotional triggers from the person's story, what am I left with?

An accurate story will still make sense, even if all the emotional elements are removed. If it doesn't, the interviewee is most likely lying, omitting key details or exaggerating. In the Charles Stuart case, if the attacker wasn't menacing and the murder victim wasn't an upper-middle class professional who was about to become a mother, would it make logical sense that a killer would use more force on the less threatening victim, especially since Charles Stuart's cell phone would lead the criminal to "believe" that Stuart was a police officer? Wouldn't the robber fear the "cop" would be armed?

4. How much information is this person actually giving?

Presumably, a reporter interviews someone to get information. The interviewee knows this: reporters will explain the reasons why the person was asked to be interviewed in the first place. If the interviewee provides little or no information, then there is the possibility that the person is either self-obsessed, biased or not a credible source for information. Is the person mugging for the camera? Is the person obsessed with his own feelings to the point of ignoring the reporter's repeated requests for information? What did you learn after listening to the person?

5. Is this person qualified to give that information?

Is this an eyewitness who saw the event happen or who only viewed the aftermath? Is this expert qualified to discuss the topic? If someone isn't knowledgeable on a topic, person or event, then the news consumer is getting an earful of useless or inaccurate information.

6. Is the person using parlor tricks during the interview?

Attention starved actors are professional emotional exploiters and frequently use the media to gain attention, particularly during interviews with reporters. They will smoke a cigarette during an interview, they will come on to or cruelly insult the reporter or burst into tears at odd moments.

These stunts are no accident, nor are they any mirror of the actor's "real" personality: these are calculated moves used to not only gain strategic publicity and to manipulate the scribe, but also to cultivate a marketable persona. These over-the-top performances are parlor tricks used to make certain the reporter either relays the piece of "color" to the readers, or at least describes the actor in the way the actor wants to be covered.

People who are trying to portray themselves as victims will cry a little for the camera (with a tissue conveniently handy), hunch over slightly forward, frown and give little doe-eyed glances at the reporter. They will dress conservatively and may even sport helmet hair. A bad reporter will sympathize with his interviewee and ask questions that seem to validate the person's victim status.

A good reporter will endure irate letters from easily offended viewers and firmly question the interviewee's claims of victimhood. If the interviewee is a fraud, he will quickly lose his composure and throw an angry tantrum. Unfortunately, not all reporters throw down their weight on the weepy interviewee since they don't want to be accused of being insensitive.

But as a news consumer, you aren't bound by civility. When watching an interview, pay close attention to the person's movements and facial expressions: is a person feigning happiness by maintaining a frozen smile (or grimace) throughout the interview? Does a "brave" or "tough" winner or hero swagger or emphasize his own prowess? Does an allegedly prim and moral interviewee get serially offended by the slightest utterance? Look for signs of insincere behavior—a person who is too busy maintaining a persona will have less concentration for keeping his lies or exaggerations straight.

7. Does this person answer the reporter's questions directly or is he being evasive, angry or irrelevant?

A great way to misdirect and distract a questioner is by throwing a fit during an interview. Anger and outrage are popular reactions for people who want to distract and confuse someone who is probing too deep. Many fabricators in a criminal setting will resort to fake fury when trying to convince a police officer or DA that they are innocent. Tears are also a popular distraction, as are jokes and witty comebacks. Listen to an interviewee's answers; if he is evasive or gives answers that have little to do with the question, that means the interviewee is hiding something from the reporter and the public.

How to Determine When a Reporter is Emotionally Manipulative

Many print reporters rely on color to tell their stories: some use it as an effective way to give readers a richer, more vivid description of people and their surroundings. However, others use color for less productive reasons: some use it to hide the fact they haven't done thorough research; others do it to bolster weak arguments, while others do it to manipulate readers' opinions or to cover up the fact that they made their stories up. While not all reporters use color for deceptive reasons, descriptions of this nature are a good starting point when evaluating a news story.

The next time you read a positive profile in a magazine about a winner you are not familiar with, skip over any emotional descriptions. Any passage that is riddled with positive adjectives or colorful anecdotes should be ignored. Read only the sentences or fragments that offer factual information.

Note the ratio between read and unread passages. How much filler was there? After reading the edited profile, make a note of your impressions of the person's profile. Do you feel that this type of coverage was justified? What did you learn about the person? How much filler was there? What's your impression of the person once the color and empty praise have been removed? Should this article have been written in the first place?

If the story relies heavily on a victim-villain or hero-villain dichotomy, it doesn't mean the story is inaccurate, but it may mean that the reporter has consciously or unconsciously taken sides between two parties. Does the information rely on factual information to make the case, or does the reporter rely more on emotional descriptions? Is the hero's humble personality or bravery the sole focus of the article? Is the victim's attractiveness and personality more important to the journalist than the chronology of the tragic turn of events? Do the deemed villain's character flaws overshadow the reporter's proof that this person is worthy of derision? Does the reporter provide any corroborating evidence to back up his position? If not, it's time to question how much evidence the reporter had before he ran with the story. Too many adjectives in a single story is a clear sign of emotional manipulation. So is the misuse of interviewees.

Some people are interviewed because they have certain knowledge, but others because they have certain feelings the reporter wants to convey in their story. These interviewees may be eyewitnesses, relatives of heroes, villains or victims, or may be streeters who are asked for their opinions. They won't enlighten you with their profound knowledge, but may be reliable to provide any of the following handy quotes:

"I was angry."
"I was scared."
"I was grateful."
"I was sad."

These quotes are useless, but they may be included because it was emotions, and not information, that the reporter wanted to emphasize.

However, prime-time news programs aren't immune to manipulation, since many liberally use melodramatic music to emphasize segments of stories. Dramatic music means something bad and scary is up ahead: hard-edge music may mean a young person has fallen in with a bad crowd, broken the law or turned to drugs and prostitution and whispering piano tells the reader a sad or sensitive moment is coming up.

Close-ups and camera angles can also be used for manipulative purposes: does the person look attractive or unattractive on camera? Does the person's attractiveness reflect their role in the reporter's story? The pretty ones are supposed to be the heroes or victims, and the villains are just ugly looking and harsh.

Speaking of visuals, which ones are presented by the reporter? Are they directly related to the story or merely stock footage? A medical story may include footage of a no-name scientist working in a lab, but the footage may be of scientists working on an unrelated experiment and have been provided by a public relations firm (meaning the station or network did not go out in the field to take the footage themselves).

News magazines can use footage of a real or fake victim walking in a rose garden or playing the piano, while an anointed winner may be mountain climbing or puttering around in his hot air balloon. In these cases, the background footage may be used as a way to direct viewers as to how they should feel about an interviewee. Does the action seem natural or staged? Does the action reflect the role the interviewee seems to play? Have the visuals given more tangible information or helped further your understanding? If not, then the reporter may be lying or have been duped, but it does raise the possibility that the reporter is telling you what you ought to think about that person—which is fine so long as the reporter provides evidence that justifies his use of footage.

What conclusion should a viewer or reader draw based on the evidence the reporter provided? Is an abattoir selling dead stock? Did a suspect's investment plan turn out to be a pyramid scheme? Was a foreign leader guilty of war crimes? While the journalist has to rely on others for the information to answer the above questions, he should still present his proof in a logical and clear way.

But some argument problems can creep into the news product. A personal attack occurs when someone's character or personality is denigrated rather than their arguments or, in the following cases, their culpability. In the Richard Jewell case, the former Atlanta security guard was attacked in the press for his alleged character flaws, but at no point did a single journalist present information that showed that Jewell was responsible for setting off a bomb during the Olympics.

Appeals to authority mistake an expert's opinion or views for actual fact. While *Washington Post* reporters relied on unnamed military officials for their information about Jessica Lynch's capture, they had not corroborated the account with other sources, which later proved to be a mistake.

There are other argument mistakes—sink or swim reasoning, the straw man fallacy and circular reasoning—and these too have been used to bolster a weak or flawed news story. If a reporter fails to show how one or more factors caused a certain event, then it's possible to use that weakness to determine how accurate or truthful the news item actually is.

Accounting for Parlor Tricks

Some people are naturals at using sneaky parlor tricks to their advantage: they work quietly behind the scenes to achieve an important goal, then publicly announce that they intend to achieve a certain difficult goal after they have already snagged it. The more gullible will express doubt that the goal can be reached and will be impressed when the person reaches their goal quickly and effortlessly. It's a classic trick that shows that not everything in the public record is as it appears. If events fall together too neatly into place it may be because the events didn't happen as described. If an event seems impossible or too good to be true, consider whether there were some behind-the-scene machinations or at least a subtle con.

Magician James Randi wrote in his book *Flim-Flam!* on the subject of Linda Anderson, a fifteen year-old girl who could allegedly see while blindfolded (a gift that first appeared during a church service, according to the girl's father). The experimenters who believed the girl conducted tests by having her read the *New York Times* while blindfolded. She seemed to be able to read the text through her covering.

But Randi noticed that the girl had a concave nose, making a small gap between her face and the blindfold. Suspecting that Anderson was able to peek through this gap, he reapplied her mask in such a way as to close the secret gap. Suddenly, Anderson could no longer "read" with a blindfold. A simple parlor trick made the girl seem superhuman. Her distinct nose gave her an edge to outfox trained experimenters with—but not someone who was in the business of using parlor tricks.

By removing the emotional and romantic elements of the story and accounting for possible parlor tricks, you can see flaws and fabrications that journalists, academics and other professionals miss. Look for the "concave nose" to spot manipulation and find the truth.

When Interviewees Have Psychological Problems

So far we have assumed that the fabricator is essentially psychologically intact and is lying for personal or financial profit. However, someone may give inaccurate or biased information because he has a psychological problem which colors the way he sees the world.

What some personality disorders have in common is that they can color or even impair the way the person sees his surroundings. This doesn't mean the person is insane, or that someone with these types of problems cannot tell the truth or be trusted. What it does mean is that under stress or other situations, the person gives inaccurate information because his disorder drives him to think that way.

The following descriptions won't make you a psychologist or even a reasonable facsimile of one, but they will help you keep in mind that many interviewees and even reporters do have psychological problems, and these disorders may color what the person believes:

People diagnosed with histrionic personality disorder have strong attention-seeking drives, and they have some or all of the following symptoms, according to the *Diagnostic and Statistical Manual, Fourth Edition (DSM-IV)*:

• Can't function well unless they are the center of attention and will do anything to draw attention to themselves;

• Go through shallow, but mercurial mood swings;

• Are melodramatic and exaggerate their emotions.

What this may mean is that someone with this disorder may seek out the press to get attention, and if it takes over-blowing emotions or grabbing pity to do it, then so be it. We might expect the person to play the role of a hero, winner or even victim just to get praise and attention. Some people will do or say anything for media attention (known in many circles as being a "media whore"). These people may overstate how badly they were victimized or how much they achieved.

In a similar vein, people who have a narcissistic personality disorder have no sympathy for others, have a superiority complex and seek not only attention, but praise (not pity, thank you). According to *DSM-IV*, they also:

• Firmly believe that they are more talented, beautiful, great and important than they really are;

• Are convinced they are "special"; hence only other "special" people can understand them and they are entitled to anything they want;

• Are arrogant, jealous and insensitive to the feelings of people around them.

They may cast themselves as better business professionals than they actually are. They may unnecessarily belittle others and may insult reporters for whom they have little respect.

Borderline personality disorder means that those who suffer from it are impulsive and have an unstable self-concept, but they also:

• Have a poor and shaky self-image and believe people they care for will leave or abandon them;

• Vacillate between idolizing and demonizing their relationships, which tend to be "intense";

• Have mood swings, tempers and impulsive and destructive behavior patterns.

Their insecurities may taint their judgment about themselves and move them to downplay their own role in positive affairs. Their evaluation of others may swing from one extreme to another, meaning that their positive impressions of others are exaggerated, as are their negative assessments of their real or imagined enemies. Their objectivity may also be impaired, making their praise or complaints of others suspect. Since reporters may go with an interviewee who gives the strongest impression of others, that account may not be the most accurate. Finally, the mood swings may mean that if two reporters interview the person at different times, they both may give vastly different descriptions of the person, with both being only partly right.

One of the better-known disorders is the paranoid personality disorder. Obviously, someone suffering from this problem:

• Is distrustful and suspicious of the people around them, believing others are exploiting them or lying to them;

• Questions the loyalty of their loved ones and doesn't confide in these people, either;

• Holds grudges and misinterprets benign comments and gestures as insults.

People with paranoid personalities may honestly believe some conspiracy is afoot when there is none; however, many whistle blowers or activists may be too easily dismissed as "paranoid." After all, if there aren't conspiracies afoot, then why are they a criminal offense? Last, someone with this disorder may distrust the media and refuse to be interviewed by reporters, meaning that important information that he alone may hold will not get disseminated to the public.

Finally, people with an antisocial personality disorder do not believe rules, morals, ethics or laws apply to them, but also:

• They repeatedly break the law, since they see no reason to conform to society's conventions;

• They have a disregard for the trutht—they will lie about their names, health and just about anything else for personal or financial gain;

• They do not plan ahead and are irresponsible, aggressive, impetuous and lack remorse for their actions (that is, the only reason they are sorry is that they got caught).

Someone with this disorder may make up stories and use the press for his own personal benefit. Not all hoaxers are afflicted with an antisocial personality, but it's not uncommon, either.

Someone's personal demons can color their world-view: they may even have the right information, but their interpretation of what those facts and events mean may be wrong. Other times, a person's disorder may lead them to lie for profit or to get pity. Be aware that some people's personality defects will naturally attract media attention: reporters look for people and events that deviate from the norm, and some people will do anything to oblige. The media and a person with psychological problems can be a treacherous combination, particularly if the person is under stress (an intense media spotlight can be extremely stressful).

There are two more psychological conditions worth noting—malingering and conversion disorder. In both cases, these are people who aren't sick but still claim that they have an illness.

People who suffer from conversion disorder truly think they are sick. They may show symptoms, but when examined by a doctor, are perfectly healthy. The symptoms may be stress-induced, but the person has no underlying physical disorder. Those suffering from conversion disorder are vulnerable to quacks. Many people who have been "cured" by a controversial treatment were never sick in the first place. The "cure" is simply the quack calming down and reassuring his "patient." The less sophisticated the patient, the more crude and illogical their symptoms will be. The problem is that people who suffer from the disorder don't think their illness "is all in their heads"—after all, they feel pain and have other ailments. But a confident person with conversion disorder is still a person with conversion disorder.

On the other hand, malingerers know there is physically nothing wrong with them. They lie to sue someone or to get attention. True malingerers fake illness or disability for profit—whether to gain insurance money or to file a lawsuit, their "illness" is merely a means to an end. If this person is followed when he does not expect it, he will suddenly show himself to be perfectly healthy. Many reporters don't catch malingerers simply because they do not spend time watching the person from a safe distance to verify the person's claims.

One rare type of malingering condition is known as Munchausen syndrome. People who have this disorder aren't physically sick; they will simply make up illnesses and self-induce physical symptoms so they can go to the hospital. Some people with Munchausen's will go from hospital to hospital and endure tests and even operations, though there is nothing physically wrong with them. They will deliberately take drugs to make themselves sick. They will complain of stomach pains, dizziness, fainting spells, nausea, rashes, fevers, bleeding and even lupus, all in the hopes of getting admitted to a hospital. People with this disorder will induce the symptoms and will present a melodramatic tale of their illness. The symptoms will be vague and, at times, logically impossible. They ask for a lot of painkillers, but they don't get too many visitors. If caught, they will go across the state, country or even world just to go hospital jumping.

Some people who play upon a journalist's emotions are doing so because it is their nature to do so. If it takes blubbering and screaming in front of cameras to get what they want, they will do it. They don't know the meaning of shame or restraint. Unfortunately, most journalists have no training in psychology and may not have the tools to be able to make those judgments.

People will use the media in creative ways to get what they want. Others may have problems, which will inevitably lead them to misinterpret events; yet others will put their reputation on the line and lie in a public forum just so that they will be liked or envied by a few more people. But regardless of why people choose to lie to the media, there are other ways a news consumer can uncover these hoaxes without even having inside information or specialized knowledge.

Chapter **Eighteen**

Deconstructing News Stories

With so many hoaxes, scams, urban legends, mistakes and outright lies making their way into the news, it's surprising that most media outlets haven't taken more drastic steps to improve their vulnerable areas, such as double-checking wire copy and having uniform standards for fact-checkers. Sham companies have been portrayed as blue chip performers, charlatans were made over as scientists and homicidal mothers were presented as traumatized victims: so why do news consumers still believe the dubious stories spun by con artists and deceitful reporters?

Most of us don't pay as close of attention to the information we hear as we think we do. We skim the papers or listen to or watch the news while doing other chores. When a story does grab our attention, it's usually one with lurid details or with elements of danger. Though many of us would loathe to admit it, it takes sensational claims to grab a large audience—from macabre crimes to war. In the ruthless battle for circulation or viewership, many media outlets sacrificed thoroughness for parlor tricks. News consumers don't think of demanding better news coverage or rewarding more diligent outlets with their patronage.

The news media lost much of its credibility by reporting frauds as fact, but some people are either still easily fooled by media hoaxes or they believe nothing at all. Some people don't listen to or read the news, either.

Yet none of these extremes are smart options. It's true that too much false information makes news, but there is still useful and important information that media outlets disseminate every day. Believing everything you read can get you in trouble, but ignorance isn't bliss, either. There is still a great deal of news that can be useful to us, but how can we separate the good information from the bad?

One way not to judge a news report's veracity is by assuming one type of outlet is more truthful than another. Scams and hoaxes thrive in radio, television, newspaper, magazine and Internet outlets. With convergence becoming a permanent media reality, hoaxers have a bigger chance of carpeting many different outlets at once, giving the false impression that many journalists covered an event when in fact only one journalist actually wrote the story. Besides, all media outlets quote and rely on each other for their information. Esteemed journalistic institutions have been conned, as have small local outlets.

Nor does a particular type of news story shield news consumers from lies and deceit. Some reporters lied about major events of importance, such as when Jack Kelley claimed that he found a smoking gun diary in Kosovo—but then other journalists have lied about more trivial points, as did *Sacramento Bee* sports writer Jim Van Vliet when he claimed to have filed a story live from a stadium, though he had only watched a San Francisco Giants game on television.

People fabricate stories for many reasons—from lying about their religion and home situation to immigrate to another country to lying about their sexual experiences to boost a career. But just because a person may make up some parts of their story, it doesn't mean that everything he says is false; for example, an interviewee may lie about some parts of his account to protect his reputation or safety.

With so many hoaxes making their way into the news, it seems as if weeding out lies is hopeless—if reporters and editors can't spot a fraud, then how can a news consumer? News consumers have a great power to evaluate information—and to judge each story on its merit. With careful listening and knowing what red flags to look for, it is a fairly simple task to judge which stories are real and which ones may be fakes.

It is even possible to refute someone's claim without any outside information or knowledge; many times it can be done by carefully listening to and reading the information presented. By knowing how news stories are constructed and packaged, it is possible to spot fraudulent information and hoaxes.

It is important for news consumers to analyze information they hear or read, because bad information can be harmful. What if you invested your life savings in Homestake Oil or Enron? What if the company you worked for went bankrupt because of false rumors? What if you sent money to Donna Mercier or Dona Kay Spence out of pity or fear? What if the police or angry neighbors believed you were responsible for the disappearance of Susan Smith's sons or the Olympic Park bombing in Atlanta? What if you placed your life in the hands of a charlatan because you heard a glowing news story about him on television?

Taking control of the information you receive can help you ignore the junk and find the real information. Breaking down a story can help you better understand the chronology of events and see whether there are holes or inconsistencies in the story. It can also help you understand what you hear or read better than passively listening to a news item. Deconstructing news reports can help you to focus on action and the plausibility and chronology of each part of the story—and help you remove emotion to understand what the story is about. Nothing can be more frustrating than believing you understood what you've heard or read, only to find out from someone else that the story made no sense.

Some stories seem more convincing than others, but even the most convoluted yarns have been accepted without question by millions. No matter how plausible a story may be, it's still possible to reveal frauds without the benefit of any outside knowledge. By retracing someone else's steps, many times we can prevent ourselves from believing lies.

This system isn't unusual or even untested—police departments use these same techniques to evaluate eyewitness' or suspects' accounts of crimes. Witnesses may be asked to play out their accounts on camera at the crime scene so that police can see whether the story is plausible. You, as a news consumer, can also deconstruct events mentally by breaking stories into "cells": assigning one cell per action to ignore the emotional or racial contents of a story. Deconstructing the news gives you control and the freedom to judge each story objectively: given the information in the news report, does this story make sense?

Understanding a Story

To break down a news story, it helps if we know how a journalist puts it together in the first place. With any good story, all the individual parts have to be placed in the right order, and those parts have to interact with each other in a logical and coherent way. If any of those parts are out of place, or if two or more parts contradict each other, then it means there is something fishy with the story.

If someone claims that he was robbed and tied up, then he can't claim he ran to the phone afterwards to call the police, unless he accounts for how he freed himself from the ropes. Each action of a story narrows down the range of possible outcomes for the next action.

When we hear someone's story, we may think we understand what we hear, but many hoaxes and frauds that make little sense still make it to print or onto the airwaves. When listening to an interviewee's account of events, understand what the story is about in terms of the real world. Is it a story about one person victimizing another? Is it a story of a careless person paying for a mistake? Is it a story about someone breaking legal or social laws?

News stories are simple beasts: they have a beginning, middle and end—and some action deviating from the mundane to grab the audience's attention. A story starting with the sentence "A school bus drove all the child passengers home safely and without incident" just doesn't make news.

Each story has an opening scene: real-life events happen in real places. Participants may be lost, intoxicated or kidnapped and not know where a series of events took place, nevertheless, the events occurred in an exact location. A story also contains a series of actions, and each action serves a purpose: a person flashing a gun is signaling he is in control and is about to make extraordinary demands. A person climbing out on a ledge is obviously wishing to end his own life (these actions will be referred to as the control action, since it controls the direction in which the action is heading). Sometimes an action shocks the listener, who is more likely to react without thinking about consequences; other times an action is used to misdirect our attention (something we'll talk about in the next chapter).

Finally, stories have characters, and those characters have a role to play. In news stories, these are confined to hero, victim, villain and oddball.

Taken together, what we are looking for is any discrepancy or inconsistency in a news item. Is the claim too good or too bad to be true? Are problems downplayed? Does someone's motivation sound strange? Are there logical holes in the story? What is each link in the chain of events? What is the relationship between links? Do any links seem to be missing? Do some links not fit properly? Why not? Many hoaxes could have been debunked immediately if the right questions were asked. Here are some logical holes that have come across in different news stories:

• A stranger who supposedly kidnaps and kills a child, leaves the body in a "gentle state" (i.e., wrapped in a blanket, well dressed, with a favorite toy);

• A criminal leaves the strongest victim (who would be the greatest threat) unharmed or minimally scathed, but kills weaker victims, such as children or a pregnant woman;

• Someone in the story does not disclose approximate time lapses, though the source should know;

• There are elements of overkill in the story, though it is not necessary on a physical or psychological level;

• A physically weak individual is credited with great strength.

Sometimes you can get clues from pictures or videos as to whether a reporter is lying, or at least exaggerating. If the reporter makes claims about the dire conditions of a particular place, then the visuals should fit the scene. If there has been a prolonged water shortage and cold weather, then we wouldn't expect to see thriving plants in the background. If we do, then at the very least the reporter is exaggerating or has been fooled.

How to Break Down a News Story

Most news reports have very little information: the five W's, a quote or two and possibly some background information. Many newspapers and magazines, in a bid to attract younger readers, are now publishing even shorter articles—the shorter the article, the less information it has. Television and radio reports have even less information than print articles, since long-winded stories confuse and turn off listeners. What this means is that there isn't an overload of information, making deconstruction easy. Short stories are easier to break down than longer ones, meaning that there are few links in the chain of events to examine. There will be few players to identify. The beginning, middle and end will be in close proximity to each other.

How do you break down news stories? First, ignore any emotional or sensational parts of the story. Second, identify each of the players involved in the story and their relationship to each other. Finally, break down the sequence of events and then look at all the parts separately, then again as a whole. Do all the parts fit? Does the story make sense? Are there any unanswered questions? Is there something in the story that doesn't make sense?

Now, let's take the theory of deconstruction and apply it to an example we've seen earlier: the incubator hoax of the Gulf War.

Example One: Nayirah

In Chapter 10, we saw how Nayirah al Sabah's story about her alleged witnessing of Kuwaiti babies being forcibly removed from incubators proved to be a hoax, and how her story fooled journalists and academics alike. Her "testimony" seemed to be true because it was told in what appeared to be a public forum, she was a weepy young girl who appeared to have nothing to gain by lying and she did not look old or wise enough to outfox adults. However, several reporters, including ABC's John Martin and *Harper's* writer John MacArthur, blew open the fraud by digging deeper into her claims.

Would it have been possible to unravel her deception without vigorous investigation? Surprisingly, it would have been possible for any news consumer to dismiss her story by deconstructing what she said.

Nayirah's credibility hinged on three key points: one, the story was told by a crying teenaged girl, two, it was an emotional story about the death of babies and, three, Americans were already suspicious of Iraqi soldiers. Yet what are we left with if we remove the crying girl, the emotions and the ethnic designations? Let's take out all the distracting parts of the story and look for any logical or chronological holes. The following description is a crude, but accurate breakdown of Nayirah's story.

Let's set up our scene: we are in a hospital's maternity ward with nurses, volunteers and infants in incubators. So far there is nothing in her story that should set off suspicion. We would expect to see nurses and volunteers in the hospital and infants in incubators, so this part seems perfectly plausible and gives us little clue as to what could happen next. A maternity ward can lead to any number of story outcomes: from a birth to complications during a delivery. But this scene takes place in an invaded country; we suspect the story will involve danger, though we do not know yet if the result will be victory or tragedy.

The next part of her story is the control action: the range of possibilities is narrowed down and the story takes a turn in a frightening direction. What has changed is that soldiers have stormed the hospital. We know nothing of the hospital security measures, but it is probable that armed enemy soldiers with a plan would have no trouble gaining access to a maternity ward, though at this point we don't know what the soldiers' intentions are, except that they plan on doing something negative toward those in the maternity ward. The second action is dramatic and dictates how we should feel (outraged, frightened). The new event encourages emotion over skepticism; we are not asked to think, but to feel and to sympathize. We aren't asked to reflect, but to react.

At this point, we might ask ourselves some questions that we hope the journalist will answer. Which hospital did this incident occur in? Who are the other witnesses? Who is investigating this incident? Which troops were ordered to the hospital? Unfortunately, Nayirah al Sabah did not recount her story to reporters, since her account was given to news outlets through a Video News Release (VNR); meaning that none of the outlets that aired her tale bothered to verify her claims. This point of the story raises important questions, but her truthfulness still isn't suspect.

The next action continues the extraordinary account. Now the infants have been removed from the incubators and placed on the floor, and the exiting soldiers have taken the incubators. This time, there are gaps the story does not answer: how were the babies removed from the incubators (i.e., did the soldiers bend down to place the infants on the floor or did they throw them to the ground)? Did anyone in the hospital try to flee from, plead to or confront the soldiers? Why did the soldiers take the incubators and not other equipment, such as surgical instruments or generators, which would be more important to an army?

Now a logical inconsistency dogs this sorry tale: how did the soldiers remove the infants? If babies were taken out gently, then this poses a problem: why would soldiers carefully remove the infants (to whom they do not have any emotional attachment) from the incubators if their purpose is to kill them? This is a not a realistic scenario.

If the soldiers threw the newborns onto the floor during the process of removal, then the infants would most likely die from blunt force trauma. But if the removal happened in that way, Nayirah would have said so. After all, her story was recounted amid a stream of tears, underlying the cruelty of an army capable of murdering helpless babies. The purpose of Nayirah's testimony was to underscore the heartlessness of enemy soldiers.

However, there is something else troubling about the story: this part of the story is meant to misdirect and control what the listener hears to draw attention away from the logical flaws and toward the more sensational claims of the story. The misdirection in this case is the armed soldiers taking helpless infants out of the warmth and security of their incubators. Who could argue or question such a vile, straightforward claim? Yet the claim has a blaring logical flaw—its relationship to the last part of the saga.

The next part of the story is underplayed, but is a critical point we need to add since it is part of Nayirah's testimony. According to the girl, the soldiers left the ward or the hospital, and the babies were "left on the cold floor to die." But what information is left out? The critical time line that would tell us how long it took the soldiers to place the infants on the floor to the time of the babies' deaths. This is the part of her story that is so problematic that everything falls apart.

According to Nayirah, the soldiers left the infants on the floor to die, but she didn't say how long this took, nor what the hospital staff did during this critical period. Did they just stand around, were they arrested (unlikely since this isn't mentioned), physically bound (also unlikely since she doesn't say so), beaten (again unlikely) or did they take the babies from the floor to give them safety and warmth? What was Nayirah doing? Why would soldiers kill infants who posed no threat, but leave the stronger eyewitnesses alive? What seemed an unimportant development in the story suddenly becomes crucial.

The final scene wraps up the young girl's yarn: the infants died on the floor. But we now know that there are other unaccounted for obstacles in her story. Why didn't the nurses or volunteers instantly pick up the infants from the floor? Nowhere in the story did the girl state that the soldiers incapacitated, kidnapped or murdered the hospital staff; logically, they would be able to save the babies.

What are we left with? Putting the cells together reveals some serious flaws, and it now becomes obvious that if the story isn't a complete fabrication then, at the very least, it did not happen as the girl recounted. Would soldiers storm a hospital, take infants out of incubators, place the infants on the floor, leave the hospital staff unharmed and so frightened or confused as to leave the infants to die on the floor? It's doubtful. Once racial and emotional factors are removed from consideration, we are free to judge the story on merit.

When we analyze a story, flaws or missing information become obvious if we carefully digest the story one action at a time. The story becomes so ridiculous, that it's a wonder that it ever made it to the press in the first place—yet it did, and most who heard it never questioned it.

Nayirah's story and many others like it get published and swallowed because reporters, editors and news consumers don't always catch fraudulent information, no matter how ridiculous it sounds. We look at the unimportant parts, such as drama, sympathetic characters and the scapegoat. If we learn to ignore those parts and look at the story structure itself, it is possible to smoke out the lies and exaggerations. To analyze a news story, here are a few questions to ask yourself when listening to a report:

• What is the sequence of events? What are the opening action, the critical actions and the climax?

• What is the rough time frame? Hours or seconds? How long do key events take place, and where are the key players during these events?

• Who are the players involved? Who are the implied victims, witnesses, bystanders, villains, cohorts and/or heroes?

• Does each individual action make sense?

• Does the sequence of events make sense?

• Is each part of the story logically plausible?

• Do the individual actions contradict each other?

• Are there any gaps in the story?

• Does the entire story (with the individual actions interacting with each other) make sense?

• Taken together, is the entire story logical and physically possible?

The more you analyze news stories, the easier deconstructing the news becomes. If Nayirah's story had been looked at through a critical eye, it's doubtful it would have been aired or published. But could deconstruction work on more domestic stories? Let's look at another example: Susan Smith.

Example Two: Susan Smith

In Chapter 9, we saw how Susan Smith gripped the nation with the story of the carjacking and kidnapping of her two young sons. Smith had claimed a generic-looking black man stole her red Mazda with her two sons inside, but in fact, it was Smith who murdered her children, to make herself more desirable to her ex-boyfriend. Though it took police nine days to finagle a confession from Smith, could news consumers have been able to find flaws with her story with deconstruction alone? Let's look at a new way to analyze Smith's story.

It is our opening action that sets the scene: a mother is driving her two small children in her vehicle. The scene is generic and does nothing to arouse our suspicions: nothing indicates which direction our story is going: maybe the mother stops to help a stranded motorist or injured animal or a drunk driver hits her vehicle, but for now, the realm of possibilities is vast.

The next event controls the action: now the range of outcomes is narrowed. A man with a gun appears in front of the car. It is a shocker: we would not expect to see a carjacker in the middle of the road. Though there is nothing impossible about the new event, it does give us the opportunity to begin to think critically and ask questions. Why did the carjacker pick this stretch of road in the daytime? Where is this area? Were there any witnesses? Have there been similar carjackings in the area?

The second action furthers the story: the mother has stopped the car. Now we can begin to look at the mother's behavior. Why would she stop the car? Why didn't she swerve, speed up or even drive her vehicle into the carjacker to protect herself and her children? Why has she been so compliant? Though this may be a perfectly natural reaction under extreme circumstances, we still have to understand each player's motives.

Though each of us reacts differently in a traumatic situation, we may have questions: has anyone interviewed Smith or the police? Is this behavior typical or probable in this situation? As news consumers, do we need to be understanding, or do we want to simply understand?

The third action is meant to shock the listener or reader and elicit sympathy and emotional outrage. The mother has been ordered out of the car, with her children still inside. At this point, mother and children are separated, but we aren't told how Smith reacted to this dangerous situation. Did she struggle? She doesn't relate this in her story; so it is likely she did not.

This scene leads to further unresolved problems. The carjacker is getting inside the vehicle. How is the mother reacting to the carjacker? Would a mother leave her children to fend for themselves with an armed criminal, knowing her two children would face certain death? Again, there are problems with our story. Though the scene is meant to frighten, several holes confuse more than outrage. Would the carjacker even want two small children in the car? Would a mother be so compliant as to ensure her own safety, but not that of her children?

Our closing scene has the carjacker leaving the adult behind while driving off in the car with two small children inside. This is Smith's explanation for her missing vehicle and children. Yet there are other unanswered questions. What was Smith doing? Was she pleading with the carjacker to save her sons? Did she try to grab them from the back seat? Did she run after the car, screaming, trying to draw attention to her plight? Though the story seems complete, unanswered questions tell us that Smith might be lying.

While deconstructing a news story can't completely confirm or refute the truthfulness of a report, it can show any flaws, and where the real story lies—and it may be one that is very different than the original story. We can also begin looking for alternative explanations. A grown woman, who would be a greater threat to a criminal, is left completely unharmed in a confrontation, yet her two sons were taken. She does not fight to protect her children. Maybe she is too scared, too stunned or even too selfish. Did the mother take her purse out of the car? Was there anyone nearby at the time of the carjacking?

Deconstructing Smith's story could even lead to focusing on the right suspect. The story was originally about a young mother and her two kidnapped children. Once police began to investigate, they discovered the real story was of a mother covering up the act of the double murder of her two sons.

Understanding Why People Talk to the Media

When getting into character, actors always ask "What's my motivation?" The same question can also apply to a person who chooses to speak with journalists: what's her motivation for agreeing to speak in front of a microphone? Is it to gain sympathy or support for a person or cause? Is it to persuade an audience, police or a kidnapper? Is it to protect her reputation or cover up her guilt? Is it to solicit legislative change or to encourage the audience to open their wallets? Is it to guilt or punish another party or to seek publicity? In the case of Nayirah, it was to encourage foreign intervention. In the case of Susan Smith, it was to cover up her crime.

Once you get a handle on an interviewee's agenda, you may be able to figure out what really happened. Sometimes the key to exposing a hoax rests upon finding why a person went out of her way to gain a reporter's attention.

When someone is trying to gain an emotional reaction during an interview, ask yourself two questions: one, why does this person or company want to be seen as sympathetic or victimized and, two, if this person is casting himself as the victim, am I to assume there is a villain in this scenario? The more dramatic the claim, the higher the stakes.

Ask yourself: what is the person's advantage if she speaks to the press? A cover of innocence? Free publicity? The chance to slander a competitor? Is she helping in stirring up public outrage? Winning a war? Spreading stereotypes? It all goes back to motive: why are you being tapped on the shoulder?

Remember, not all motives are bad: many times, the motives are to right a wrong, help others, encourage legislative change, increase one's feeling of safety or to close a painful chapter in a person's life. But understanding why someone is agreeing to speak in an intense public forum can go a long way towards finding the truth.

Deconstructing More Complicated Stories

In the Susan Smith and Nayirah al Sabah stories, both women gave simple accounts of a one-time event, but could deconstruction help with more complicated tales? Critical thinking can help unravel complicated stories, and though it may not prove conclusively that a story is a fake, it can show the story's weaknesses and contradictions.

In the case of "Hack Heaven," though Stephen Glass described the bogus antics of a fifteen-year-old boy's domination of a large computer company, deconstruction could still work. How likely is it for a multi-million dollar company not to press charges against their extortionist, blackmailer and saboteur, when this act would encourage other young hackers to follow suit? Why would the company speak to a reporter and admit to giving into blackmail—which is against the law? Why would any company publicize such embarrassing information?

In the Donna Mercier case, there was always a reason why she could not be seen in public—first illness, then fear of an ex-partner. In this case, deconstruction shows an alternative explanation for Mercier's odd behavior, one that is simpler than her convoluted reasons for not wanting to reveal her identity: that she has a history of making dramatic and false claims.

Even in the Sommy saga, deconstruction can lead the news consumer down the right path. Why does this family's phone and lights go haywire only when their teenaged son is in the room? How could someone break in to both the phone and electrical systems? What's the motive? Is it easier to control the phone and lights with gizmos—or for someone inside the house to pick up the extension and fool around with the light switches?

Deconstructing news stories is best for eyewitness or participant accounts of an event. It is an easy way to place yourself in an unrepeatable situation. Deconstruction is the next best thing to being there. Sometimes a person may make up part of her story to make herself appear more heroic or cover the fact that she was behaving less than angelic. An interviewee who was attacked in a bad neighborhood may tell the reporter she was there because she was lost but, in fact, she was there to buy drugs.

Thinking critically, looking for problems and finding alternative explanations are powerful tools for the news consumer. Changing the way we listen to stories can help us separate lies from the truth. But sometimes the smarter hoaxer will trick us with sneaky red herrings, also known as misdirection, which the next chapter shows us how to detect.

Chapter **Nineteen**

| Misdirection

Suppose you are standing in a convenience store line with several other people. There may be people standing by the front door, and in various parts throughout the store. You're not paying attention to anyone in particular, when the next instant two male assailants with shotguns burst through the store and proceed to clean out the till. The robbery lasts only minutes, but now police ask you to give a description of the two bandits. How easy would it be for you and your fellow eyewitnesses to give that description?

The usefulness of your description would partly depend on how clever and premeditated the culprits were with distracting their victims. If the men made no attempts at hiding their faces, then we'd expect fairly accurate descriptions. If the men wore masks, the descriptions would be less useful, but the robber's height, weight and build could still be described accurately.

Yet what if the men wore rainbow clown wigs and red rubber noses, but made no attempts to disguise their eyes and mouths? Do you think you could remember their facial features, or would you just focus on and remember the clown hair and nose? If so, you would have absorbed a useless piece of information: the wig and nose are items the robbers could easily discard without being recognized. On the other hand, no robber can get rid of his facial features as easily.

Many robbers know how easily distracted people can be, especially if they are under stress and had no prior knowledge that the event would take place. It's the same reason why some getaway cars place colorful but easily removed items on the car: they know witnesses will remember the distracting item but forget the color, make and model of the car. Unusual and eye-catching extras are used to try to misdirect any potential witnesses.

Some criminals go one step further: they make all eyewitnesses strip naked. Besides embarrassing witnesses and preventing them from pursuing their attackers, robbers know that the shock of this unrelated demand will impair how well witnesses will be able to describe the criminals.

This technique is called misdirection, and it's used by other professionals, too, such as magicians who use it so audiences look away from the real and unimpressive trick and toward the more dazzling but irrelevant "magic."

It's probably a magician's most important device to distract audiences so that they can't figure out how the trick was really done.

Con artists and other fabricators use misdirection as well, though many probably aren't consciously aware of it. Since lies are based on imagination, the fabricator has to rely on irrelevant, but powerful details to misdirect the pigeon's attention away from the logical plot holes and toward the more dazzling details. In this case, misdirection is a form of lying.

The problem is that reporters tend to look for those dazzling details to spice up their stories. Why look at logic when there are eye-grabbing, or at least heartstring-tugging, details being offered?

In the news world, Christmastime begs for stories about compassion and giving to the downtrodden. If there was anyone who was downtrodden at Christmas, it was a twelve-year-old boy who was forced to make his way into the cold world alone—at least according to a December 23, 1995 article in the *Deseret News*:

> The parents of a young boy whose birthday falls on Christmas Day abandoned him last week at the Salt Lake bus station.
>
> The boy, twelve, roamed the streets of the city for six days before walking into a state youth services office Wednesday. He asked for a place to live and then threw a letter toward workers.
>
> The note, apparently written in his mother's hand, broke the hearts of officials from the state Division of Family Services:
>
> "To whom it may concern," it began. "I am writing this letter to tell you we can no longer care for our son, Mark. He's my stepson, and he's almost thirteen-years-old. My husband (the boy's natural father) just found out he's dying from AIDS and he doesn't want Mark around, and I can't care for Mark alone. His natural mother died shortly after his birth. We give our permission for you to do whatever you think is best, but it will be a waste of time to look for us because we're leaving the country."

While newspapers across the country wrote about the little boy lost, very few journalists bothered to question the strange nature of the letter, try to interview Mark, or take a good look at the child who looked more like a grown woman. The story was tragic, but had hints of the typical upbeat Christmas story—even Mark's birthday landed on Christmas.

When "Mark" refused to be physically examined, it was discovered that the boy was actually a twenty-seven-year-old woman named Birdie Jo Hoaks who had scammed other citizens with the same sob story. In February 2004, Hoaks, now thirty-three, used the same scheme again—though this time she was caught before the media got wind of the story.

Hoaks' emotional misdirection initially worked: by claiming to be a help-less and lonely orphan, she had managed to gain sympathy, even though, despite her diminutive stature, she hardly looked like a preteen boy. Though Hoaks' story was too neatly packaged, it was also too much for some media outlets to resist.

Misdirection works because the storyteller has the advantage: he knows all the twists of the story as well as the ending, while the audience can only guess. Trying to figure out which elements of the story are important is guesswork for the listeners, who can get easily sidetracked by trivialities or red herrings, such as humor or emotional triggers. The listener can forget about the holes in a story if the hoaxer can misdirect their attention toward more interesting details. Misdirection is used to deceive and distract an audience.

One of the more powerful distractions is emotional misdirection; that is, a hoax's believability is bolstered by injecting emotional details into the story. War propaganda almost exclusively hinges on emotional manipulation. However, even many peacetime hoaxes and lies relied on emotional misdi-rection, as in the case of Birdie Jo Hoaks. When Jayson Blair placed Private Jessica Lynch's father in a tobacco field in one of his fraudulent stories, he was pulling on readers' heartstrings, most likely so that they wouldn't notice his shoddy and nonexistent reportage.

Fear, sadness and anger are the distracting emotions of choice of the hoaxer, though humor can also be used to disarm the audience. Stephen Glass' yarns were funny enough that many people failed to notice that the events could not have happened as Glass described. The ATM tombstone hoax also relied on humor as a misdirection: most who heard the story of the old curmudgeon laughed at his oddball antics and didn't question the feasi-bility of having an automated teller in a cemetery.

Physical misdirection uses sleight of hand to get an audience to look away from telltale signs of manipulation and toward irrelevant details. This misdirection is popularly used by quacks that make their sham treatments look mystical, and by others who are tying to hide their parlor tricks from the public. When Edwin Bayron claimed to be a pregnant hermaphrodite, he simply strapped on a fake belly: had anyone physically examined him, his ruse would have been immediately discovered. When Susan Smith claimed to have been car jacked, her car was missing, lending credence to her story: what financially limited person would sacrifice her car? The same one who'd sacrifice her children as well. Charles Stuart's self-inflicted gun shot wound was also a form of physical misdirection.

Verbal misdirection is the parsing of words so that the audience hears one message, but the speaker is saying something different. One place where verbal misdirection thrives is in crisis communications. One public relations firm's website entitled "Crisis Rules" instructed potential clients to "take responsibility" for the crisis, but noted that this was not the same as "accepting blame."

When you hear that someone has "accepted responsibility" for a crisis, do you also think that the individual also accepted blame for it? While it seems as if the phrases are interchangeable, the truth is that accepting responsibility is very different from accepting blame, yet many people aren't aware of the difference. Information consumers need to be aware of verbal misdirection. In this case, this misdirection is meant to placate the public with some sort of statement of contrition without the offending party actually having to be contrite.

Finally, factual misdirection uses false information that supposedly bolsters a hoax's veracity. In other words, a lie or mistake is used to prove a hoax is real. For example, when Senator John Kerry began to emerge as the Democratic presidential front runner during the 2004 primaries, one rumor posted on the *Drudge Report* in February claimed that Kerry was linked to a young woman, and that the woman's unnamed "friend" claimed "fantastic stories— stories that now threaten[ed] to turn the race for the presidency on its head!" The woman "linked to Kerry" was later revealed to be one Alexandra Polier.

Though there had not been any proof about the nature of the affair, a February 16, 2004 wire story from Talon wire service seemed to have the scoop on the next best thing:

> [A] source at one of the major television networks said they are specifically forbidden to talk about this story on the air until one of the other major television networks reports on it first.
>
> However, Polier taped an interview with one of the major television networks at Christmas substantiating the alleged affair. The television network is trying to gather more proof of the charges made by Polier before airing what would be potentially damaging to the Kerry presidential campaign.

Both Kerry and the woman denied any relationship and, to this day, the "taped interview" still hasn't turned up. Who told Talon about the tape was never disclosed; however, the rumored tape seemed to have implicated Kerry—that is, before the denials and the lack of evidence. As for the unnamed friend, the person has never made a public appearance.

The Rule of Occam's Razor

Simple explanations tend to be the best ones. The more direct the explanation, the more likely it is to be the correct one. Convoluted and complicated accounts of events are more likely to be justifications or excuses, rather than the truth.

Hoaxers rely on special cases to make their stories work. Donna Mercier's stories were full of special cases: she was mugged, she was dying, she was hiding from an abusive partner. These were public reasons for reporting her purse stolen and then refusing to make her face and name public.

This explanation is too cumbersome—could there be a simpler explanation to cover all the facts? Yes, that she was conning police and revealing her identity would expose her ruse is a much simpler and more accurate description of events.

Hoaxers love to invoke special cases; many fabricators claim they can't reveal their identities in fear of reprisals. Yet, when their identities become known, their stories quickly unravel. Again, it is probably wiser to go with the simple explanation. A source hiding his identity may be hiding from the enemy but, then again, he might have less noble reasons for his secrecy.

Occam's Razor is a helpful mental tool to use to smoke out fishy stories, since misdirections require that the fabricator appeal to special cases. By adding a wrinkle to a story, the fabricator adds an extra layer of protection from skeptical listeners.

One popular violation of Occam's Razor is the "it was here, but now it's been destroyed by my enemy" explanation. Popular during wartime, this pat little explanation tries to explain to a pigeon why damning evidence against an enemy is missing. One warring faction may claim their enemy killed thousands of civilians or soldiers, but when independent inspectors come to look for the remains, none exist. The "victim" will claim that the bodies were there, but that the enemy somehow managed to dispose of all of them, even if the rival wouldn't have the means to do so.

The 2003 U.S.-Iraq war was sparked by the insistence that Iraq was hiding "weapons of mass destruction"—however, once inside the country, those same weapons didn't materialize, even months after U.S. forces overtook the country.

So where were these weapons? Why didn't the Iraqis use these weapons to defend themselves? Why couldn't inspectors or soldiers find them? The reason one reporter gave appeared in the April 21, 2003 edition of the *New York Times*:

> A scientist who claims to have worked in Iraq's chemical weapons program for more than a decade has told an American military team that Iraq destroyed chemical weapons and biological warfare equipment only days before the war began, members of the team said.
>
> [...T]he scientist led Americans to a supply of material that proved to be the building blocks of illegal weapons, which he claimed to have buried as evidence of Iraq's illicit weapons programs.

The scientist... [claimed that] Iraq had secretly sent unconventional weapons and technology to Syria, starting in the mid-1990s, and that more recently Iraq was cooperating with Al Qaeda, the military officials said.

The Americans said the scientist told them that President Saddam Hussein's government had destroyed some stockpiles of deadly agents as early as the mid-1990s, transferred others to Syria, and had recently focused its efforts instead on research and development projects that are virtually impervious to detection by international inspectors...

An American military team hunting for unconventional weapons in Iraq... MET... which found the scientist, declined to identify him, saying they feared he might be subject to reprisals. But... they considered him credible and that the material unearthed over the last three days at sites to which he led them had proved to be precursors for a toxic agent that is banned by chemical weapons treaties.

This explanation of the vanishing arsenal seemed to satisfy the *Times* journalist:

The officials' accounts also provided an explanation for why United States forces had not yet turned up banned weapons in Iraq. The failure to find such weapons has become a political issue in Washington.

Under the terms of her accreditation to report on the activities of MET Alpha, this reporter was not permitted to interview the scientist or visit his home. Nor was she permitted to write about the discovery of the scientist for three days, and the copy was then submitted for a check by military officials.

If the informant existed, it is highly unlikely he was being honest with his American allies: how did the Iraqis dispose of the weapons? Who else could corroborate this explanation? Why wasn't the journalist allowed access to this informant? It is possible that an informant who would know such highly classified information about his country's weapons program would also know that these same weapons were destroyed. It's also possible that this person would have to not only protect his identity, but be barred from talking to a sympathetic reporter; however, the rule of Occam's Razor would lead us to dismiss this explanation as too cumbersome—there had to be a simpler explanation. By May 30, 2004, the *Times'* public editor Daniel Okrent also questioned Miller's story.

Finding Lies and Misdirection in News Stories

Lies make it into the news every day: from factual errors to outright hoaxes and scams; however, these lies are easier to uncover when you know what to look for. Misdirection is a distraction: what you are looking for is ways that a fabricator can try to shift attention away from his story's faults. The way he will try to distract you is by complicating his story and making it harder to understand than it really is.

Looking for a simpler explanation doesn't mean looking for the most polite one; while we don't assume everyone is lying to us, we don't assume everyone is telling the truth either. By listening to a story with an open mind, we can weed out lies from the facts.

Finding lies requires attention to detail; sometimes a single word may mean the difference between swallowing a hoax and exposing a charlatan. The following warning signs can help you smoke out suspect news stories:

Statement Analysis

How people use language can give you valuable clues as to their truthfulness. Changes in pronouns or verb tense can be red flags that someone is lying. If a mother claims her child was kidnapped, but then says "My child was so beautiful and innocent," this would be a red flag that the mother may have had a hand in her child's disappearance and death: why did she refer to the child in the past tense unless she knew the child was no longer alive?

"There are so many different ways to say the same thing—why a person chooses a particular way to say it could very well have some meaning," notes Dr. Michael McGrath, a forensic psychiatrist and clinical assistant professor of psychiatry at the University of Rochester School of Medicine and Dentistry in Rochester, New York and President of the Academy of Behavioral Profiling. "People would rather lie by omission than lie outright," he adds.

McGrath gives an example of a wife coming to a police station to report her husband missing. If she is asked to write out a report explaining what happened, she may write: "The last time I saw my husband John was eight in the morning when he left for work."

"Here, she has given you the person's title, the relationship to her, and his name all in the first sentence, which is what you would expect," says McGrath. "Now if she says, 'I last saw him at 8 a.m.,' that's a rude introduction; she's already distancing herself from this guy."

McGrath suggests practicing statement analysis on celebrity interviews. "Someone is asked a question and the answer is obviously 'yes' or 'no' but they give this convoluted answer that begins with 'I believe this or that...'"

Temporal Cues

Constructing a lie and then having to answer probing questions based on false answers will take longer than answering truthfully. For example, if you gave someone a false age, but then were suddenly asked what year you were born, it would take you a lot longer to answer than if you told the truth from the start, notes Jeffrey J. Walczyk, a psychology professor at Louisiana Tech University. Reaction time may be a better indicator of lying than physical anxiety (or lack of it). "How long after someone hears a question does it take a person to answer it?" he asks. "Consistency or contradiction are one cue to deception."

"There's many different ways in which people can prevaricate, and sometimes people don't think they're lying; they think they're just using hyperbole," adds Walczyk.

Illogical Scenarios

If a sequence of events doesn't make logical or psychological sense, it's a good sign the storyteller is lying or has been duped. If a victim of an attack claims to have been abducted at a busy intersection in broad daylight by a masked assailant, questions about the victim's claims can be raised: where are the witnesses? Why did the attacker wear a mask in a crowded, lit place if he didn't want to draw attention to himself?

Fillers in Color

"The use of filler can be another cue," says Walczyk. "Most people, when things happen, what they recall if they are a witness is probably the central important actions. In a crime scene, they'll remember that someone shot someone else but the details usually are poorly remembered [as to] what they wore. If people have extremely vivid collections of details when they purportedly witnessed something, that to me could be a sign that there may be lying going on, or at least imaginative embellishment."

Pointless details clutter an article or report, and eat valuable time and space in a story. If the reporter has chosen to add frilly details at the expense of factual information, it is a good sign that the reporter, one, has come up with only sketchy details and is trying to stretch a short piece into a feature; two, is oblivious to his job's mandate, since he is too in love with his writing style or looks (in the case of TV); or, three, is making up the story and is using color as a distraction.

Choreographed Avoidance

If a victim of a crime begins to cry during key interview questions in lieu of answering them, it is likely that he is trying to avoid giving potentially damaging answers while maintaining his role as victim. "The person may try to steer you away from asking about certain things. If you are starting to ask questions and they realize that they're in trouble, they may start crying or may start attacking you because they hope you'll back down," notes McGrath.

If you can detect when someone is trying to misdirect your attention, it will go a long way to protecting yourself from being fooled by hoaxers. By keeping yourself focused on facts and logic, you can avoid the traps that have ensnared many other news consumers—and journalists.

Chapter **Twenty**

Eyewitness Testimony and Testimonials

Eyewitnesses are compelling evidence: these are the people who saw an event for themselves and can confirm what, how and where it happened. Because witnesses have seen the explosions, the gunfire and the inhumanity up close, many journalists like to use witness accounts to add both drama and credibility to their stories. After all, why would eyewitnesses lie? How could an entire group of witnesses be mistaken? With time constraints, it's tempting for many journalists to accept a witness' statement without reservation. If twenty eyewitness accounts sound alike, then it seems there is no reason to question their stories; afterward, it's strength in numbers—or at least strength in innocence.

One online newspaper, Vallejonews.com, reported frightening news about an abducted California girl on its website on November 5, 2003:

> Police say the girl was walking along the 300 block of McGrue Avenue when a late-model black pickup with a covered bed and tinted windows pulled up alongside her. The driver was wearing a ski mask, police say, and the girl was forced into the truck as it drove away.

How did the police know the events took place as described? An eyewitness came forward and told them so, according to an article in the November 6, 2003 edition of the *Contra Costa Times*:

> A twelve-year-old boy told police he was walking home from school about 1:30 p.m. when he saw a black truck stop in the area of Christopher Way and Borges Lane. A man got out, opened the passenger door and forced a girl of about thirteen or fourteen to get inside, Lt. Eric Mortenson said.

As it stood, the boy's accord seemed solid and beyond question: the description seemed accurate and, besides, why would anyone, let alone a twelve-year-old, lie about seeing an abduction?

Still, there were nagging questions. It may have been strange that no one reported the young girl missing—after all, by the boy's accounts, he made it seem as if she was well-tended and cared for. But then again, perhaps her parents hadn't noticed she was missing, or they may have left town and left her on her own. Since the boy was the only witness to the crime, there was no way of comparing his description of events with other witnesses.

After the police came up empty-handed and began to question the young man about his story's inconsistencies, the boy finally recanted his story: no girl was kidnapped, no masked man menaced the streets. What started as an attention-seeking ploy ended up a media hoax.

Yet the young boy wasn't the first kid to pull a stunt like this: in March 2000, in Arlington, Virginia, four frantic, screaming young men reported to their teachers that they saw a masked kidnapper drag a young girl away. The search was on to save the young girl, but with no one filing a missing persons report, and after the inconsistencies in their story were noticed, the boys confessed that the story was a hoax.

Eyewitness testimony is hardly tamper- or hoax-proof: Nayirah was allegedly an eyewitness to an atrocity but, in fact, events could not have happened as she claimed. During World War II, though many had claimed they witnessed German soldiers cannibalizing victims, the story turned out to be an effective piece of war propaganda. Susan Smith was an alleged eyewitness to her children's abduction. It's not uncommon for people to lie about witnessing atrocities, even if their fabrication costs innocent people their lives. Other eyewitness hoaxers simply want to gain attention, and don't know how else to do it.

Despite these and other problems with witnesses and even testimonials, journalists still rely on witness descriptions for breaking news. A compelling witness is a powerful and credible short cut to tracking down documents and interviewing less-than-forthcoming public officials. Witnesses put a face on an event and bring a story to life. Unfortunately, while eyewitness testimony can be reliable and forceful, it's far from foolproof.

Problems with Eyewitness Testimony

Loaded language. Contrary to what some people may believe, memory is not a tape recorder. Memories can be influenced by a number of factors, and one of those factors can be loaded questions that an interviewer asks an eyewitness. Subtle words and phrases can determine how someone remembers a past event.

One classic experiment showed how malleable memory can be: psychologists had two groups of first year university students watch the same video of a two-car accident. For both groups, the same tape was running at the same speed. After viewing the tape, the students were separated into groups and given a questionnaire. One group was asked:

How fast were the cars going when they collided?

The second group of students was asked a slightly different question:

How fast were the cars going when they crashed?

Despite the one-word difference between the two sentences, the results were definitive: the group who read the word "collided" gave slower speed estimates than the students who read the word "crashed." Both groups saw the same video, yet a single word influenced the subjects' memories.

In another experiment, different groups of people watched another video of a car accident. People who were asked "Did you see the broken headlight?" were more likely to remember seeing a broken headlight than those who were asked, "Did you see a broken headlight?" regardless of whether the movie showed a broken headlight or not.

If our memory can be influenced by subtle outside forces, then a reporter's questioning can greatly influence what the person remembers, especially if the reporter asks loaded questions. When listening to a media interview, pay attention to the types of questions a reporter asks. Are the questions loaded or leading? Do they make assumptions about the event? If yes, then consider that the witness may not be giving accurate answers to the reporter.

Personal prejudices. Those people who were not their parents' favorite child can attest to this one: if we hold certain biases against certain groups of people, we are more likely to blame them for certain events. As Amy Bradfield, an assistant psychology professor at Bates College in Lewiston, Maine notes, "Identification [of criminals] is more difficult for white witnesses if the culprit is black. There's a phenomena known as 'cross race identification bias' which states that people are better able to identify members of their own race than members of another race. This bias is much stronger for white witnesses than it is for black witnesses, although it still exists for black witnesses."

If we associate certain types of events with certain people, we may misremember what we witnessed. On April 19, 1995, Oklahoma City was rocked when a car bomb exploded in front of the Alfred P. Murrah Building, killing 168 people. Though initial eyewitness reports stated that three bearded men of "Middle Eastern appearance" were seen driving away from the area in a pickup truck at the time, the actual culprits were clean-shaven white men. But the initial accounts were so persuasive that one reporter's April 20, 1995 article began with this lead: "The massive car bomb that devastated a federal building in Oklahoma City points the finger of suspicion at Islamic fundamentalist groups set on waging a war of terror within the United States."

Trauma or fear. This factor should not be overlooked. Eyewitnesses may remember events as being more savage, dangerous or spectacular than they actually were. Exaggerations or stress-induced memory errors can point fingers at the wrong people or make the situation seem worse than it was.

Time elapses. The longer the span between an event and the eyewitness interview, the less accurate the recollection is going to be. Memories will be altered by time and other outside influences, though the witness may not think that this is the case. He may forget how the suspect really looked, and give an incorrect description. If a spouse can forget how a loved one looked after twenty years, how will a stranger remember how an assailant looked after the same long passage of time? (See Chapter 21)

Deliberate manipulation. A skilled bank robber knows that memories can be altered by directing eyewitness attention away from important features and towards the useless ones. If all eyewitnesses recall an outré feature of a crime or event, there is a good chance that the thief deliberately distracted his audience. Identical descriptions of events don't guarantee that the witnesses got their information right; in fact, we would expect some discrepancies in descriptions. If all witnesses gave identical accounts of events, then witnesses were either duped or in collusion with one another.

Then there is the problem of "weapon focus," notes Bradfield, "If there is a weapon used to commit a crime, people are more likely to focus on the weapon rather than a perpetrator's face, because they're more concerned about where the gun is pointing."

A good journalist will try to interview eyewitnesses without the distracting influences—if a witness is interviewed in front of a group of peers, the witness may feel pressured to give exaggerated or inaccurate answers. A sensitive reporter knows this, and will try to interview eyewitnesses separately.

Even that tactic may not be enough to determine if an eyewitness has been manipulated, especially if the witness hasn't seen the entire event unfold. On November 4, 2003, the *Poughkeepsie Journal* reported that Clinton Knoll, an assistant principal at Franklin D. Roosevelt High School, was stabbed in the washroom in the morning. One witness was a teenaged boy who saw the crime scene himself:

> Justin Krzeminski, seventeen, a senior at the school, had just left his second-period class when he and a friend walked into the bathroom where Knoll was attacked.
>
> "When we walked in, I saw Mr. Knoll," he said, adding that Knoll rolled over and blood, a cell phone and a pocket knife were visible on the

bathroom floor. "I thought he had been stabbed in the face because he was holding his head."

In fact, Knoll inflicted the wound on himself. The witness was honest, but he did not see the actual event first hand. He was a snippet witness—a person who has seen only a part of an event. Even though these witnesses can be helpful, the snippet witness can be unintentionally misleading and lead us to the wrong conclusion.

Witnesses may feel pressured to misremember details by reporters or authority figures. In one experiment conducted by psychologists Gary Wells and Amy Bradfield, subjects watched a grainy video of a "bank robbery" and were then asked to identify the robber from a series of photographs—none of whom were in the video. When subjects heard a casual comment from the line up administrator saying, "Oh, you identified the suspect," it dramatically distorted not only the person's confidence about picking out the right suspect, but their memory of how confident they were at identifying the suspect at the time of watching the video, as well as their memories of their view and attention.

"One of the major problems with face recognition is that people assume that confidence is associated with accuracy; so they assumed a confident eyewitness is accurate. But it turns out that through lots of experiments we can manipulate confidence without manipulating accuracy," notes Bradfield. "In general, people's memory for events is fallible and is malleable, which are two major problems. People don't understand how quickly and easily their memories can be altered by subsequent experience or a question someone asks them."

With so many factors, how can we be sure that an eyewitness is honest and credible? If an eyewitness account is vague, inconsistent or logically impossible, then the eyewitness may not be forthcoming with the truth, but there are other ways to judge someone's recollection of events.

How to Evaluate Eyewitness Testimony in News Stories

The best line of defense is to listen to both the witness and, where possible, the reporter. The witness can best describe their interpretation of events, while the reporter's line of questioning will determine how much information the news consumer will receive. Leading or loaded questions lead to inaccurate answers. A passive or uncritical interviewer allows fraudulent witnesses to air their lies unchallenged. It's important to listen to both the reporter's questions and the witness' answers.

What questions a reporter asks are important to consider, but also when and where he asks his questions. Is the interview taking place on the street where an event just took place, or in a studio where time has elapsed from the event in question? Does the witness seem "trained" and give measured answers? Could this eyewitness have spoken to a lawyer? Does his demeanor suggest that he has hired an image consultant or public relations specialist? Has this person signed a book or movie deal? If the eyewitness has a management team in place, it is very likely his answers have been filtered and finessed to his advantage. He may want to present himself in the most sympathetic light (known as the "halo effect").

However, you should also pay equal attention to the types of questions the journalist asks eyewitnesses, too. A good reporter will encourage a witness to give accurate and objective answers and determine whether the witness is lying, exaggerating or mistaken. If a witness is confused or biased, it's the reporter's job to navigate through those answers to get to the truth. Simply asking "What happened?" isn't enough.

There are other cues to look out for: is the reporter trying to manipulate or badger the interview subject? Is he asking loaded and leading questions? Does it seem as if the reporter is glossing over important points or cutting off the eyewitness? Is he not following up on interesting, contradictory or suspicious answers? Is he ignoring red flags or key points?

A good eyewitness interview will establish important facts and give a timeline of events, where was the gunman at the time of the shooting? Where was the witness? Were there other eyewitnesses present? What happened in what order?

Many reporters have the problem of asking bad questions; that is, they don't ask questions that are more likely to generate useful information. Listening to a reporter's line of questioning should give you an idea of how much quality information the reporter is going to get from the eyewitness. Here are some types of bad questions:

1. **Long-winded questions.** Some reporters ask long-winded questions because they aren't focused, but others simply are competing with the interviewee for airtime and want to mug in front of the camera or microphone. Regardless of the motives, the longer the question, the more likely the eyewitness will misinterpret the question or forget what the reporter asked him in the first place. Long questions eat up airtime, meaning that the eyewitness will have less time to talk about the event itself.

2. **Speculative questions.** A big time-waster, these questions ask the witness to play futurist or mind reader instead of asking the person about something they know. "Why do you think the gunman went on a killing spree?" is a speculative question that asks the witness to guess rather than give information she knows to be true. A better question would be, "Did the gunman say or do anything that hinted toward his violent actions before today?"

3. Two part questions. Any question with more than one part leads people to forget to answer the first part of the question.

4. "What went through your mind?" questions. Another no-brainer; instead of asking how a person felt during an unexpected and frightening ordeal, it would be better to ask what happened and when. If the reporter asks, "What went through your mind when your plane was crashing in the water?" does he expect the person to say, "It was kind of a bummer, but I was cool about it," or "Man, it was a total rush?"

5. Loaded and leading questions. Some reporters want certain answers, and will try to lead the interviewee to give those answers. "How long have you been an alcoholic?" is a loaded question that makes assumptions about the person's behavior. A leading question would ask "Is it better to give free drug rehabilitation for addicts or just let them run around on the streets addicted and committing crimes?" We know the answer the reporter expects, and an interviewee may give an answer to please or placate the reporter instead of giving the truthful one.

6. Closed-ended questions. These are the questions that will elicit a "yes" or "no" answer:

> REPORTER: "Did you witness the explosion?"
> WITNESS: "Yes."
> REPORTER: "Were you afraid?"
> WITNESS: "Yes."
> REPORTER: "Did you see any casualties?"
> WITNESS: "No."
> REPORTER: "Have you ever seen anything like this before?"
> WITNESS: "Not really."

While closed questions have their place in journalism, the problem is that eyewitnesses have a distinctive role in news stories—they are the ones who tell us what happened, and bring an important event to life. These are the interviewees who paint a picture for the ones who weren't present. It's hard to determine an eyewitness' credibility with restrictive questions.

7. Irrelevant questions. Obviously, the reporter is uninformed and does not have the savvy to handle the interview. You are being denied valuable information about an event when the reporter doesn't ask the right questions.

8. Unfocused questions. "Tell us what happened," is an unfocused (and indirect) question that doesn't probe or demand that the interviewee give details. A hazy interviewer is going to get hazy replies in return.

Television and (particularly) radio interviews are ideal for evaluating eyewitness testimony: you can watch or hear the eyewitness and gain additional clues about the setting and the interviewee's demeanor and response to questions. In print, however, unless it's a "question and answer" format, you won't be able to make the same judgments about the reporter's questions; instead you should concentrate more on the eyewitness' answers.

What Information is Important in Eyewitness Accounts

First, we want to know how this person became an eyewitness in the first place. We should also find out where the eyewitness was at the time of the event, and whether he saw the entire event, or just a part of it. In the Clinton Knoll case, knowing that the witness was not present at the time of the stabbing can allow us to consider that the stabbing may have not resulted from an altercation with a student.

An eyewitness should also be asked what they were they doing at the time of the event: in the Charles Stuart, Susan Smith and Nayirah al Sabah cases, knowing this critical detail may have exposed their hoaxes sooner.

Detailed descriptions of assailants, victims and other players can help us determine whether the eyewitness is accurate and truthful or if he had been duped (or is trying to dupe us).

Testimonials

Similar to eyewitness testimony is the testimonial—those statements from people who have direct experience with a person or procedure and now have a positive opinion about their experiences. From a character reference to an endorsement, the testimonial is a popular tool used by advertisers to get people to buy their products or services. Journalists sometimes rely on testimonials, too, either to bolster a glowing profile of an individual, or to "give the other side" of a controversial figure. Many news stories use patient testimonials for practitioners of medical "miracles."

For example, from 1916 to 1930, John Romulus Brinkley, better known as the "Goat Gland Doctor" of Milford, Connecticut had been allegedly "replacing" the testicles of impotent men with those of goats (an autopsy on one of Brinkley's patients showed that no human parts were ever removed). While the American Medical Association showed that Brinkley's quackery was ineffective and even dangerous, there was no shortage of men whose glowing testimonials made Brinkley seem like a miracle worker. There may have been a change in these men, but it was all psychological. Relying on testimonials alone would give a vastly different conclusion than the physical proofs.

What to Look for in Testimonials

A testimonial may be meaningless, unless there is concrete evidence supporting the praiser's claims. With six billion people on this planet, you can find hundreds of people to support just about anything. Numbers and passion mean nothing unless there is substance to support the praise.

One of the first questions to consider when listening to a testimonial is whether the person merely "feels better" or is physically better. The placebo effect may be taking place: since the person feels as if he is doing something for his problem, he will feel less stress and therefore will "feel" better. What we want to know is whether the person has been cured and, more importantly, were they actually sick in the first place (i.e., was the person a hypochondriac, misdiagnosed or simply lying about being ill?)

The interviewee's use of superlatives should also be considered. If praise is heaped on, but few details are provided, there is a good chance the testimonial is based on subjective feelings rather than objective criteria.

Take note if the interviewee appeals to authority or uses "sink or swim" reasoning. If the person is trying to please his healer, or if he insists that if he hadn't turned to his particular healer, he would have gotten worse, then, again, the subjective feelings of the interviewee have overtaken his sense of objective reality.

When it comes to crime news, glowing character references shouldn't distract you from the facts of a story. On March 28, 2004, the *Wisconsin State Journal* reported that twenty-year-old Audrey Seiler, a sophomore honors student at Wisconsin University had vanished the day before. As media outlets from around the country reported on the disappearance, other chilling details soon emerged: Seiler was seen on her apartment's surveillance camera leaving her apartment without a coat, purse, cell phone, wallet or keys; her car wasn't taken and her apartment door was left open.

But the strangest detail to emerge was that this was the second attack on the young woman, as a March 30, 2004 article on ABCNews.com reported:

> But there may be one clue. Seiler was assaulted last month in an unusual incident that police have still not solved.
>
> On Feb. 1, Seiler was walking near her residence when she was struck from behind by an unknown assailant and knocked unconscious, police said. She was then moved about a block or so from where she was attacked.
>
> She was not sexually assaulted and nothing was taken from her. She was treated at a hospital and released.
>
> But Seiler told police she had no idea who might have wanted to hurt her, and they are not sure if the two incidents can be connected.

The first attack was indeed bizarre: what would anyone's motive be to attack the young woman and take pains to drag her to a further location, if their purpose was not to attack or rob the victim? It seemed as if Seiler's attacker wasn't very practical—but by all accounts, Seiler was. The "straight-A" (according to her family) student was described in only the most positive terms by those who knew her:

• "'Audrey's a wonderful young woman,' [Scott Charlesworth-Seiler, Seiler's uncle] said. 'She's intelligent, personable, mature and very sensible… It's totally unlike Audrey to be in the middle of anything this unusual.'" (April 29, *Wisconsin State Journal*)

• "'She wasn't the type to wander off,' Seiler's father, Keith Seiler, said Sunday. 'She is a great kid.'" (March 30, *Badger Herald*)

• "After the February 1 attack, Audrey '…wouldn't walk anywhere alone since then,' [said] Adam Morris, the roommate of Seiler's boyfriend… Morris, however, described Seiler as outgoing, straightforward and unlikely to leave home without a word… 'She was really shaken for a few weeks,' Morris said. 'She couldn't sleep well.'"

• "Audrey also became guarded and always let someone know her whereabouts. 'She would always call people and tell them where she was going,' Morris said." (March 31, *Capital Times*)

• "[Audrey's mother Stephanie Seiler] said her daughter is a straight-A student and is not given to flighty behavior. 'I know that Audrey always thinks things through before she does them.'" (March 31, *Capital Times*)

• "'It's just very unusual behavior for her,' said Madison Police Officer Jennifer Krueger. She said Seiler's family, friends and officials are all very concerned. Police do not believe she went somewhere on her own without telling anyone." (March 29, *Milwaukee Journal Sentinel*)

• "'I want people to know that this is not typical behavior from Audrey,' her father, Keith Seiler, said in an interview on Monday night. 'That's why police jumped on it so fast.'" (March 30, *Star Tribune*)

• "[A] neighbor, Monica Mendez, who has known Audrey since she was a toddler, said the past few days have been hard on the whole town. 'We're all a bit in shock,' Mendez said. 'It's not like Audrey to do anything out of the ordinary. This is out of character for her.'" (March 30, *Star Tribune*)

Seiler's employer and former high school principal also had high praise for her. Everyone who knew the outgoing and amiable student spoke of her countless wonderful attributes, making the apparent attack and subsequent abduction even more despicable.

But good news was on its way. After four and a half days of silence, Audrey was found near a marsh—bruised, cold, but otherwise unharmed. Police searched the area for the kidnapper, but all they found was a rope, a knife and duct tape. Audrey was found alive, and the story had a happy ending—or, rather, would have had a happy ending, except for a few troubling facts.

Why would someone who had been senselessly attacked leave her apartment without a coat or cell phone? If she had "always" told others when she left her apartment, why didn't she tell anyone she was leaving on the night of the abduction?

After police interviewed the young woman, her story began to unravel. First she told police she was abducted outside her apartment, but then later stated she was abducted elsewhere. Two witnesses saw Seiler walking freely on the street before her "rescue." Someone had been using her computer during the time she was supposed to be in captivity. Her hard drive stored maps of wooded areas and weather reports. Finally, store surveillance cameras showed Seiler purchasing the knife, tape and rope she claimed her kidnapper used. The abduction was a hoax, and Seiler was hospitalized and later charged.

Even though Seiler was a well-liked and studious young woman who received positive testimonials from those who knew her, it didn't make her story accurate. Her story seemed implausible because it was. Why would anyone abduct another person without causing personal injury or demanding a ransom from the victim's family? Testimonials can't override evidence, especially if all evidence points to a scam.

Eyewitness Quality Control

Taking control of the information you receive means thinking about the news in a different way. Looking for clues that an eyewitness is lying or was manipulated is an effective way of evaluating information. One effective way of evaluating eyewitness testimony or a testimonial is to determine if the reporter asked the right questions.

Did this person see the event for himself? How close was he to the incident? Were there any obstacles obstructing his view? Did he see the event from the beginning or did he come after the fact? Was he alone or with friends? Does he turn around during the interview, looking for guidance from his peers? Was he descriptive in his answers? Was he emotionally upset? Was he exaggerating? Was he smirking and mugging for the camera? Was he taking his cues from the reporter?

If you were a lawyer in a court case and you needed to bolster your case (either as a defense lawyer or prosecutor), would you want this witness to testify on behalf of your client? Would he be useful? Why or why not?

By keeping the following points in mind, you should be better able to separate useful eyewitness testimony and testimonials from the lies:

1. Since different eyewitnesses have different memories, vantage points, beliefs and attention spans, their accounts of an event should differ. If not, there may be collusion (the witnesses got together to "get their stories straight"); fraud (the event never took place) or the perpetrator misdirected the audience.

2. For testimonials, if a subject claims to have been cured by dubious treatments, it is possible that the person is lying, is experiencing the placebo effect, was misdiagnosed or just "feels better," but is not cured.

3. Accounts can be tainted by witnesses pleasing the reporter.

4. Differing eyewitness accounts are normal.

5. Some people who are traumatized during an event may not remember all details right away and may be vague. Testimony can be influenced by age, beliefs and past experiences.

6. Just because several witnesses positively identify one suspect, doesn't make their testimony any more compelling than if a single person made the identification—especially if we don't know how many witnesses fingered a different person.

Chapter **Twenty-One**

Forensic and Other Evidence

If any one institution is the premier purveyor of fine feel-good trivia, it is the news media. Factoids flash across the news screen at steady intervals, surveys and polls for obscure topics regularly make it onto radio newscasts and even movie and sports trivia grace the pages of newspapers and magazines—and that's not counting the endless websites that carry those empty calories of wisdom. If you need a piece of knowledge that has no use in the real world, briefly exposing yourself to a news outlet will give you a quick fix.

William Coates was one such piece of living trivia: at 114 years of age, the Clinton, Maryland man was known around the country as being the oldest living man in the United States. It was an unofficial title he had held for the past several years, as was mentioned in the June 2, 1999 edition of the *Washington Post*:

> When the American Association of Retired Persons released a study that said most adults didn't want to live to age 100, nobody asked the swinging centenarians at the Evelyn Cole Senior Center for their opinion.
>
> The study's authors should have dropped by Friday for a big party in honor of Prince George's County residents who are 100 years of age or older [where] the honorees were gobbling down cake, singing solos and fending off prospective dates. It didn't matter that William Coates was 110. He still is a player, dressed in a purple shirt and silver tie and attracting a number of ladies...
>
> "I'm married," yelled Coates, who was one of thirty-three people honored at the county's Celebration of Centenarians...

Sadly, Coates passed away in February 2004. A mention of his death was made in a February 25 *Associated Press* story disseminated by hundreds of media outlets:

> William Coates was a ladies' man to the end.
>
> Coates, believed to be America's oldest man, died Monday at age 114 with two of his children and a granddaughter at his side.

Even at the age of 110, Coates was still charming the ladies during Prince George's annual celebration of centenarians.

"He really lit up every single party and event that we had for the seniors," said Irving Smith, director of the Evelyn Cole Senior Center in Seat Pleasant, who has done extensive research on centenarians.

Coates was born June 2, 1889, and according to Smith, he was the oldest man in America. At one time he was believed to be the second-oldest man in the world, although he didn't have a birth certificate to prove it.

That last sentence should have set off some sort of alarm bells for both reporters and news consumers. While it was not uncommon for those in the 1800s to not have a birth certificate, it certainly was a stretch to consider someone to be the country's eldest citizen in absence of one. By early March, it was revealed that a copy of a 1930 U.S. Census form showed that Coates was listed as being eighteen years old, making him 92, not 114, at the time of his death. Yet even then, some who knew Coates remained firm in their beliefs, as shown in the March 2, 2004 edition of the Maryland *Gazette*:

[Dr. Irving] Smith [a gerontologist who knew Coates for seven years] said he determined Coates' age through extensive interviews with family members and a call to the Social Security Administration, where officials confirmed Coates' birth date of June 2, 1889.

It was noted in some articles that none of Coates' relatives maintained that he was 114 years old, either. With the census form clearly showing a discrepancy, the little factoid turned out to be false. Newspapers and newscasts across the country had no trouble running the story without independent verification. It was on the word of those around Coates that reassured reporters that it was safe to name Coates as America's oldest man, even though he must have looked exceptionally good for a 114-year-old.

Assuming that all reporters have double-checked their facts, or have seen credible evidence, will lead a news consumer to take hoaxes, lies and mistakes as fact. It's important to listen to or read stories carefully, making sure that tangible evidence is used to prove a reporter's assertions. News consumers should remember two words when hearing claims made by a reporter in a story: prove it.

Looking for Proof in News Stories

In the Coates case, even though the man lacked a birth certificate, most editors who ran the story took Coates' supporters at their word, which proved to be a mistake days later. By the same token, a good news story offers the consumer evidence that a certain chain of events actually happened as described.

Real evidence is a crucial component of most arguments, though there are those people who can pretend to show evidence. Some people are masters of bluffing during arguments. They are the ones who, when trying to prove a point, will confidently say that "Studies prove that [fill in the person's opinion here] is right!" That parlor trick alone is enough to make many people back down or not challenge someone's flawed argument.

But if those same objectors asked a few simple questions, they would see how flimsy the arguments were. What studies? How were these studies conducted? Who conducted these studies? How do we know these studies are sound? Has any knowledgeable researcher found contradictory evidence or flaws with the original studies?

Many times, just asking for proof up front is enough to show that the evidence may not exist at all; people who fight dirty are known to claim to have evidence that doesn't exist. But you don't need a degree in the sciences to ask, "How good are the studies you cite? What's the proof that these studies even exist?"

Finding evidence in news stories can be difficult, but not impossible: what you are looking for is documents or items that can either confirm or refute someone's claims. If a crime victim claims to have been punched in the face, then of course you'd expect to see the telltale bruises and welts—and those bruises should be consistent with a sharp blow to the face. If a journalist is reporting from a war zone and claims that there are detention camps, then news consumers should expect to see some filmed or documented evidence of these camps. There has to be evidence that a chain of events occurred in the way described—someone's word alone cannot be enough.

A good news report presents evidence to the reader, listener or viewer that the facts are most likely true, but the evidence should also be carefully examined to make sure that it wasn't misrepresented or manufactured. Though pundits and columnists may grab audiences with their "world according to me" spin, they should still back up their well-packaged opinions with evidence. If, for example, someone claims to have been the victim of a hate crime, does the evidence (e.g., vandalized property or threatening notes) seem to support the person's claim or does the evidence seem fraudulent?

As we saw in Chapter 9, a defaced vehicle isn't always conclusive proof of ethnically or racially motivated attacks. For example, one Pitzer College professor's disturbing plight was recounted in a March 11, 2004 *Associated Press* story:

Students at Pitzer College proposed canceling classes and holding teach-ins
to encourage students to discuss diversity issues every March 9, college
spokeswoman Susan Andrews said Thursday.

The date would fall on the day that a professor's car was spray-painted with racial slurs. The incident prompted some 2,000 students and faculty members to rally Wednesday to show they won't tolerate racism.

[...]Professors canceled classes as the group of seven campuses sprouted with sit-ins, teach-ins and forums as hundreds of students, faculty and trustees discussed their bitterness and what to do next.

The colleges were galvanized after Kerri F. Dunn's car was vandalized and covered in racist, anti-Semitic and sexist epithets Tuesday night. The words "Shut Up" were also written on her car.

Thousands of college students in the area protested in anger over the latest hate crime, but days later, police and FBI had begun to rethink their position on the case; as of this writing, law enforcement officials believed that the crime was staged by Dunn herself. While a vandalized car seemed to make the case conclusive, testimony from two eyewitnesses and inconsistent accounts by the victim given during two separate interviews pointed to a different conclusion. In this case, photos of the vandalized car may also help news consumers decide whether the graffiti was genuine or not. A single piece of evidence isn't enough to make a judgment about a person or event: it takes several pieces to help make a case.

A reporter's story is supposed to answer the "5 Ws," but there are five other questions that also need to be answered: Is there proof? How much? Is it real? Is it credible? Is it conclusive? If the journalist hasn't answered those questions, then the story may not be as conclusive as it seems.

But how does a news consumer find and analyze evidence in a story? First, by paying attention to what information is presented by the reporter, and second (if the story has a personal importance), what the consumer can possibly find by himself. Even though a news story may downplay certain information or even be ideologically slanted, it is still possible to wade through the information given and decide how reliable and accurate the evidence is.

What Isn't Reliable Evidence

Some evidence isn't as air tight as it seems. As we saw in Chapter 20, eyewitness testimony can be prone to mistakes or deception, but there are other less-than-impressive proofs. One of those shaky pieces of evidence is the lie detector. People who are used to lying or have no anxiety over telling falsehoods will pass the test, while nervous truth tellers can give false positives. Anyone who has gone through more than one lie detector test will become adjusted to the procedure and will be able to pass the test, even if he is lying.

Another dubious piece of evidence is the website. Since a license isn't necessary to start up a website, anyone can make up a bogus site in an attempt to gain credibility. The Kaycee Nicole and Anarchists for a Better State hoaxes hinged on faked web pages.

Videos aren't always foolproof either. Wendy Bergman's staged dogfights didn't prove the illegal fights existed, but did prove that they most likely didn't. If dogfights were as prevalent in Denver as the former TV reporter claimed, then why were the same two dogs mauling each other on tape? Why was one dog training on a regular treadmill? When watching "video" evidence, it doesn't hurt to look for any signs of staging.

Then there are other red flags: generic descriptions and sketchy timelines also hint at fakery. Susan Smith's description of her children's abductor was vague in details, making her story suspect. Fortunately, there are more reliable proofs that a news consumer can look for when reading or watching the news.

A Few Types of Evidence

1. The name check. A complete news story will give as much supporting evidence as possible, but the most basic check should be whether the interviewee who gives his name really is who he says he is.

In 2002, Slate.com found itself hoaxed when it printed journal entries from a writer who called himself "Robert Klinger," a "car executive" in Europe. Slate readers did something that editors failed to do: they "Googled" Klinger's name and came up empty-handed.

Yet many editors and reporters still think that if it's on the web, then it must be true. A year later, some Canadian reporters received a press kit, announcing a website for an upcoming magazine for slacker men called *Stu*. When some curious journos had a look at the site, they saw the following preview for the premier edition:

RELATIONSHIPS
No-Maintenance: The *Stu* guide to dating the hot girl's less-hot friend

CAREER
The Kings of Medical Research: Meet four guinea pigs who quit the rat race to become full-time test subjects

SEX
"The Pasha," "The Three-Toed Sloth," "The Mr. Belvedere" and five other low-impact, high-pleasure positions that let you gratify her without breaking a sweat

TRAVEL
Travel is work. Why leave town? Vacationing in your local motel

A magazine industry publication called *Masthead* informed their readers about the new magazine in their September 2003 online edition:

> Calling itself the magazine "for the adequate man" and aimed at men eighteen to thirty-five living a "Stu-ish lifestyle," *Stu* is set for a national launch at the end of October. Named and largely fashioned after publisher and editor Stuart Neihardt, the magazine is a reaction to the fantasy and glamour of the so-called "lad magazines," such as *Maxim*. "This is something that I thought about upon perusing the newsstands and seeing nothing that represented me or the guys I knew," says the twenty-seven-year-old rookie publisher, who has worked in shipping as a tracker for FedEx.

Though *Masthead* was the magazine industry bible, editors hadn't heard of Neihardt before—but his lack of experience didn't phase them. Nor did it phase one newspaper journalist, whose pompous column also made mention of the neophyte publisher. That column ran in the September 24, 2003 edition of the *National Post*:

> There's a new twenty-eight-year-old available on the single market named Stuart Neihardt. Maybe you'd be interested in dating him? At his last job, as a tracker in the shipping department of FedEx, he earned $28,000 a year. He earns less now. He drives a 1990 Honda Civic. He sometimes will "drive out of the city," but will never go on an exotic vacation because it's a "pain in the ass." He believes a man can successfully woo a woman on a date for under $15. He's not looking for a "very attractive girl," either. He went that route once and says, "It was a full-time job to keep up with the relationship. She expected me to be constantly thankful for being with her."
>
> [...]So, gals, is this what you've always looked for in a man? Neihardt is banking on there being many men like him out there with the launch next month of *Stu*, "the magazine for the adequate man."
>
> When asked if he's an "adequate" man, Neihardt answers, "I think so. I hope so." He says there are many *Stu* men out there. "Just look around on the bus."

There was one little question that didn't cross some reporter's minds, despite the nifty looking website, press kit and chit chat with Neihardt—who was this man? If journalists had cared to run his name into a simple search engine, they would have discovered that Stu Neihardt didn't exist, and neither did his magazine—the magazine was a hoax and the man who posed as Neihardt was a journalist with apparently too much free time on his hands.

Don't assume an interviewee's name has been run through a search engine; sometimes all it takes is a simple Google search to see if a person exists. In the Christopher Newton and Stephen Glass cases, running their bogus "expert" or "interviewee" names through an engine would have easily exposed the reporters' games.

2. Forensic evidence. Though it's hard for a news consumer to judge with complete certainty, forensic evidence can be helpful in determining how accurate a news story is. While it is highly unlikely that a journalist would find this evidence himself, he would rely on the word of certain official and nonofficial sources (such as defense lawyers) that it exists. While a reader or viewer cannot examine the evidence first hand, she can look for signs as to the evidence's reliability.

Forensic evidence may be blood splatters, vandalized property, even a detention camp; it is any tangible evidence which may leave clues as to the sequence of events. While forensic evidence can be valuable to a news consumer, two points need to be kept in mind: evidence can be doctored and evidence may be incomplete, thus giving a wrong impression.

In 1984, Benjamin LaGuer was convicted in the rape of a Massachusetts woman. Throughout the trial and over the next twenty years, LaGuer vehemently maintained his innocence. During his years in prison, LaGuer attracted a growing number of prominent supporters, many of whom were journalists. With his charming personality and the forcefulness of his protestations of innocence, many reporters looked into his case and found some flaws with the police investigation and trial. Over the years, LaGuer's innocence seemed a virtual certainty.

At least, many reporters thought so, as did one whose article appeared in the December 12, 2001 edition of the *Worcester Telegram and Gazette*:

> "They left me to die in a trap of shame like an animal," Mr. LaGuer said in an interview from Norfolk State Prison. "Somebody should go to jail. What these people did I wouldn't do to a dog."

LaGuer's plight had become so well known and the case for his innocence seemed so certain that new DNA tests were conducted to see if the convicted man's DNA matched DNA found at the crime scene. But the test seemed almost unnecessary as an article in the January 17, 2002 edition of the *Boston Herald* seemed to show:

> LaGuer, who is serving a life term for the 1983 rape of a fifty-nine-year-old Leominster woman, is appealing his case and was back in court last week in Worcester seeking a new trial. A report that surfaced in November showed that four fingerprints found on the victim's telephone did not match LaGuer. The rapist tore the phone cord out of the phone to tie up the victim.

The fingerprint evidence was never disclosed at trial. The report was found in Devens by state police in a bin of documents slated for destruction. Worcester Superior Court Judge Timothy Hillman last week ordered the state to have all the case files at the next hearing.

When the final DNA results finally came in, the samples found at the crime did not exonerate LaGuer, but in fact matched his DNA—the evidence that should have freed LaGuer damned him instead.

The news shocked those reporters who had rallied to his cause. In one *Associated Press* article, many reporters' views of the evidence were made clear. One freelance journalist who covered the LaGuer case for sixteen years was described as so depressed over the positive DNA tests that he "couldn't get out of bed the day he found out." However, the same reporter said that, though he was "skeptical of everything having to do with this case"—including LaGuer himself—and was "still trying to digest the meaning of the DNA report," he still believed that "LaGuer could still be innocent, and was willing to give LaGuer one more shot."

"There's no doubt in my mind that it was a bad investigation, a bad jury and a bad trial," he added. "The irony may be that, for all that, it was a good result." An editor was also on side with LaGuer, and had this to say: "Obviously, it's pretty damning," he said. "But I still like the guy, and I will continue to accept his phone calls."

3. Omissions. It's important to look for missing evidence: if someone claimed to be chained by the leg and starved for weeks, then we would expect to not only see chafe marks around the person's ankle, but we would also expect to see someone look considerably thinner than they did prior to their confinement. If either of these signs are missing, then we know the person is lying.

In 1971, media outlets in the U.S. reported that a mysterious new tribe in the Philippines had been discovered—one that was childlike and peaceful in its ways. One July 9, 1971 *Associated Press* article described the finding this way:

> The discovery of a tribe of people living in the style of the Stone Age and cut off from the outside world for hundreds of years was announced Thursday by a Philippine government agency.
>
> The tribe promises to provide "one of the most fascinating chapters in the study of primitive man," says [Manuel Elizalde Jr.], the man who found it.
>
> The timid lost tribe, which may total no more than 100 persons was located in the rugged mountains forests... in the Southern Philippines.

As time progressed, the West learned more about the baffling Tasaday from Elizalde. The tribe had no word for war, enemy, rivalries or hatred (apparently the perils of inbreeding had no ill effect on them). The shy tribe only knew peace, happiness and love. They did not have a leader, and concepts such as oceans, drawings, afterlife, meat-eating and salt were foreign to them. As one June 29, 1992 *Associated Press* article recounted:

> The Tasaday man squatted at the mouth of his cave home and talked through an interpreter with members of a scientific expedition to the home of the Stone Age-style people.
>
> A question about what he disliked about his fellow men brought a puzzled frown to the cave-dweller. It was as though such a thought had never before occurred to him. "There is nothing we say is bad about anyone," he replied.

Reporters and scientists flocked to see the Tasaday tribe—but the tribe would only mingle with strangers in the presence of Elizalde. Worse, access to the tribe was only given under certain conditions, and one of those conditions translated to hefty entrance fees. Few questioned the veracity of this simple tribe, though some people did question Elizalde's materialistic streak—the Tasaday mania was making him a wealthy man.

Then, in 1986, after the country had faced internal turmoil, one Swiss reporter who came to see the tribe without a chaperone noticed that not only were the caves devoid of garbage or debris, but that the caves themselves were deserted. When the tribe members were found wearing clothes, the colossal hoax had finally been uncovered. The Tasaday had been created for various financial benefits.

Despite the fact that, to this day, there are those who maintain that the Tasaday tribe was never a hoax, it is interesting to note that the "tribe" lacked garbage and wasn't present when strangers came without warning. Those posing as tribesmen weren't the naïve and naked cave dwellers that were first reported, but were area farmers who wore clothes like billions of other people, and had admitted as much to reporters. The romanticism did not exist, and the residents had been misrepresented to the public.

4. Doctoring. Evidence can be faked, and it is important to look for any signs of tampering or doctoring. Fights can be staged, cars can be deliberately wrecked and bruises can be self-inflicted. Whenever evidence is presented to you in a new report, look for any signs of forgery.

It's not always easy to spot fabrications, especially if you want to believe the evidence is true. That certainly was the case in 1991, when modern photos surfaced purporting to show U.S. soldiers who had disappeared during the Viet Nam war. The appearance of the pictures made national headlines (*Newsweek* had used one of the black and white pictures on its cover). As an article in the July 17, 1991 edition of the *Watertown Daily News* noted:

Government analysts are studying a mysterious photo that according to relatives shows three American pilots who never returned after they were shot down over Southeast Asia during the Vietnam War. "In coordination with the State Department, we are undertaking urgent activities to follow up on this report," Defense Department spokesman Gregg Hartung said Tuesday. The grainy, poorly resolved picture shows three men holding a sign with a strange message.

The men in the picture were reported to be Colonel John Leighton Robertson, Lt. Larry James Stevens and Major Albro Lynn Lundy, Jr. and they seemed to be holding a sign that read "May 25, 1990." However, another picture surfaced, purporting to be that of Captain Donald Gene Carr. Though the men looked to be in excellent physical condition—even after twenty years of captivity—their families had all positively identified their missing loved ones as the men in the pictures.

After examining the pictures, the U.S. government determined that the photos were fakes (the photos also originated from a dubious source). In fact, the man identified as Carr was positively identified as a German man named Gunther Dittrich. Lundy's remains were returned from Laos in 1997, and were positively identified in 2002.

Videos can also be faked easily. One August 7, 2004 *Associated Press* article gave chilling details about one grainy video purported to be of an American civilian who was slaughtered on camera by his Iraqi captors:

There's no confirmation yet of the authenticity of a video on an Islamic militant website showing the beheading of a man identifying himself as an American from California.

The man, who identifies himself as Benjamin Vanderford of San Francisco, tells U.S. troops to stop the occupation of Iraq, just before he's killed [...]The man says he had been offered for exchange with prisoners in Iraq.

The video then showed the American lying on his left side, a knife cutting at his neck. No militants were seen on the footage, unlike in previous videos of hostage killings.

There was no confirmation of the death, no militants seen on the video and no record of a Benjamin Vanderford ever entering Iraq, but the Internet-based film seemed convincing enough; there was plenty of blood oozing from the hostage's neck. Unfortunately for *AP*, Vanderford was alive, in the U.S. and had created his own pseudo-beheading video for reasons only truly known to him. As for the blood, it was, like the rest of scene, completely fake.

Though the *AP* report described the scene as a beheading, the enacted scene merely showed one of the hoaxer's "sawing" Vanderford's neck with a knife. The poor quality video was deliberately edited that way by the twenty-two-year-old hoaxer who claimed he wanted attention and to make a social commentary. Even worse for *AP*, Vanderford's macabre vanity project had already been floating in cyberspace since May, before the news agency got wind of the tale.

But fakery can be much more simple. On September 8, 2004, "60 Minutes" (the Wednesday edition) ran with a story about President George W. Bush's time in the National Guard, and whether or not the future American President had received preferential treatment. The segment purported that never-before-released typewritten memos written thirty years ago by Bush's then-squadron commander, Col. Jerry Killian, showed that Bush was demanding and receiving special treatment. Though Killian died in 1984, "60 Minutes" obtained a handwriting analyst who claimed that the documents were genuine.

But the memos weren't originals; they were photocopies, and how "60 Minutes'" source had access to these previously secret documents wasn't revealed on the program. Nor did the newsmagazine claim that a forensic expert could verify that the typewritten portion of the memos were authentic. Finally, no one who was directly associated with Killian (family, secretary) was interviewed on air to verify whether Killian had or was likely to have written the memos.

Immediately after the broadcast, the memos' authenticity was called into question by several people, including Killian's family (who maintained that the former commander did not write the memos) and anonymous bloggers. (However, one blogger, who used the one-letter-away-from-sounding-dirty handle "Buckhead," later turned out to be a prominent Republican lawyer who pushed for former President Bill Clinton's disbarment). The newsmagazine stood by its story, and later interviewed Killian's former secretary, who said that while the sentiments in the documents seemed genuine, the memos themselves were not. The memos were printed in a type of font that was not available in the early 1970s. The newsmagazine's main source for the story was also less than pristine, and later admitted that he misled producers. Experts retained by "60 Minutes" warned the newsmagazine that the memos might not be genuine. A week later, the venerable newsmagazine admitted it was had. Finding the original documents—if they ever truly existed—was key, but the newsmagazine seemed content with unreasonable facsimiles.

When you are reading or watching a news story, look for any tangible proof a reporter offers to bolster his story. Videos, photos, graffiti, documents and even bomb fragments can tell a story, but if the evidence is incomplete or fraudulent, their value is reduced to nothing.

Chapter **Twenty-Two**

| **Getting All Sides**

Newspapers and magazines can't rely on moving visuals the same way as television; so many print journalists like to open their stories with a vivid anecdote to set the scene of their story. Yet the opening act should be quirky, humorous, accessible and feel like a scene out of a movie. On November 27, 2003 President George W. Bush secretly flew to Iraq to meet with U.S. troops for Thanksgiving dinner. The trip caught most Americans, including reporters, by surprise. The White House decided only a select few reporters would be notified of the event.

It was the *Washington Post*'s Mike Allen who would serve as pool reporter (meaning other competing media outlets were dependent on Allen for their information). For the Bush Administration, it was a public relations coup: a war time president sacrificing a Thanksgiving dinner with his own family to spend the day with his nation's troops was a feel-good story that didn't need any more shine to its sleek exterior.

However, to drive the point home that President Bush's trip was sub rosa and extraordinary, there was one piece of color offered to journalists that was so tempting that almost none could resist. As an article in the November 28, 2003 *Washington Post* began:

> As Air Force One headed under a false call sign for its unannounced landing in Iraq on Thursday, the Boeing 747 passed within sight of a British Airways pilot who radioed, "Did I just see Air Force One?"
>
> "Gulfstream 5," replied Bush's pilot, Col. Mark Tillman. As one of Bush's aides recounted, the British Airways pilot seemed to sense that he was in on a secret and replied archly, "Oh."

Newspapers from the *New York Newsday* to *Los Angeles Times* to the *Times of London* reported on the droll exchange. *AP*'s White House correspondent Terence Hunt (who was described as being "on board Air Force One") wrote that "Bush had warned that if his secret had got out then he would have called the whole thing off" (Hunt also began his story by noting that the British Airways pilot had "almost let the cat out of the bag over US President

George Bush's secret visit to Baghdad"). Though Allen gave some attribution as to where he heard the story (though he did not name the individual), most reporters did not. Knight-Ridder's Ron Hutcheson had also recounted the pilot angle but he noted that the flyboy was "stunned" and that he responded only after "a long silence."

Hunt wrote that "[t]he anxious moment passed and was not raised again, allowing Bush to complete his astonishing visit to have Thanksgiving dinner with his troops in total secrecy." The *Washington Times* reported, "the entire ruse was nearly undone when an observant pilot of a British Airways jetliner spotted the plane," meaning that he, in the President's own words, "was fully prepared to turn this baby around, come home."

Reporters covering the event using the above piece of color had relayed the message, but where did they get their information? As some recounted, it was Bush's own aides who told the story "with excitement." Within a day, enterprising vendors were selling "Did I just see Air Force One?" pins on the street. Almost no reporter at this point found or interviewed the unknown pilot to ask what his thoughts were when he made his fateful discovery. But who cared about a no-name pilot when the situation had a comedy movie feel to it?

While the anecdote made excellent copy, the problem was that no one had bothered to confirm the incident with British Airways before they ran with the story. It was a reporter at Reuters who first tried to ascertain the name of the pilot for a follow up piece, but came up empty-handed—British Airways stated that none of their pilots ever made contact with Air Force One at the time. There were two pilots in the area, but neither captain had radioed in any report of seeing Air Force One nor had they heard anything about the matter on their radio. The White House backtracked on the story, saying the communication happened between the pilot and a London control tower, not the pilot of Air Force One; however, the alleged mystery pilot has never been found or stepped forward.

Reporters don't always interview or account for all players in a story, even if the story seems complete. If one side seems credible, then many journalists will rely on a single account of an event without verification. If that single source is unreliable, prone to exaggeration or is simply mistaken, the accuracy of the story disappears. What you have to do when reading or listening to a news item is to try to determine whether all sides are truly accounted for and, if not, then what relevant sides haven't been given a voice in the story.

We've seen how relying on only one side of the story can lead to journalists spreading lies: Nayirah's false testimonial became credible at a crucial time, Heinz Braun looked like a cunning hero, Kerry McDermott looked like a preternaturally talented and lucky violinist, Adelaide Abankwah received a reprieve based on a hoax and Sir Cyril Burt's nonexistent studies affected the lives of countless children. Both Jessica Lynch and Richard Jewell's public images were forever changed because a media outlet published information given to them by a single source without looking for corroboration.

That's why it's important to look for explicit signs that the reporter has actually tried to double-check information not only by interviewing more than one source, but also more than one type of source. Understanding the news is more than just noting information, but also thinking about the amount of data and where it came from. Sometimes that can be difficult to judge when the reporter liberally uses anonymous sources; other times, we don't think about multiple sources when the story is of a personal nature—and has depressing undertones.

Or even uplifting ones. Juanita Smith, an eighty-six-year-old director of the Topeka, Kansas YWCA Teen Pregnancy Prevention Program, was also a prisoner of war during World War Two, as briefly recounted in both a February 14, 1996 *Witchita Eagle* article as well as this September 24, 2000 profile in the *Topeka Capital-Journal*:

> [...]Served as a Navy nurse in the Pacific theater in World War II and was captured as a prisoner of war on the Bataan Peninsula in 1943. She survived the Bataan Death March and was released in 1945. It was a defining, but still sensitive, time of her life.

So defining, in fact, that Smith said that it was the impetus for her devoting her life to helping teens. Almost four years later, Smith's time in captivity was the subject of a May 2, 2004 *Capital-Journal* feature article:

> [...T]he eighty-six-year-old director of the Topeka YWCA Teen Pregnancy Prevention Program rarely talks about her World War II service as a Navy nurse and the years she spent as a Japanese prisoner of war in the Philippines after the Bataan Death March.
>
> "Although that was a dreadful experience and one that I don't recall with joy, certainly, it was helpful to me," Smith said solemnly. "When I returned to this country I thought, 'I must have been saved for something because so many weren't.' So I have been working with youth."

Smith's lost days had a profound impact on her and her family:

> "It's just not easy to talk about," Smith said, tears welling in her eyes. "It's not so much that I felt so mistreated. We all were and there were certainly men who were tortured more than I was. But we were not permitted to help others who were being mistreated. It tears me up to think about it."
>
> Juanita Robley's parents were told she was missing in action and presumed dead in 1944. They had a funeral service for her...

Smith also stated that she was not forced into sexual relations with her Japanese captors since they saw that she would not give in to the advances of her fellow American prisoners. The *Capital-Journal* couldn't get enough of the story, since the paper ran another article about Smith two days later, on May 4:

> Someone who survived the horrors of the Bataan Death March and imprisonment by the Japanese in World War II might be justified in returning to the United States and feeling they had done enough for their country.
>
> Fortunately for Topeka, Juanita Smith took a different approach. Grateful for having survived, she has dedicated her life to helping others.

Any pretense of detached reporting was thrown out in lieu of emphasizing the bravery and resolve of the "noble" Smith:

> [...]Smith has begun doing something especially courageous again. She is beginning to tell of her experiences as a Navy nurse in World War II, her experiences as a prisoner of war and of the nurturing family that enveloped her in a love that made those experiences survivable.
>
> In previous years she has declined requests to speak publicly of that experience. She just couldn't face up to talking about it.
>
> But it's a story that needs to be heard by all of us. It's a story of incredible cruelty by humans against humans. The worst, she says, wasn't anything that was done to her personally, although there are hints she did suffer personally. The worst was seeing other prisoners being mistreated and not being able to do anything to help.
>
> [...]Because it's so emotionally draining, it's doubtful that Smith will be hitting the speaking circuit with her message. Our community should just be grateful that she's willing to talk about it at all.

How did reporters verify Smith's account of events? Since Smith was the only person interviewed about her time as a war prisoner, did any reporter take any pains to find other corroborating documentation?

No. But parts of her story didn't sit well with some readers, who e-mailed *Capital-Journal* editors. It was only then that they decided to take a deeper look, and then discovered several unsettling facts, including that the U.S. Navy's chief medical historian could find no record of Smith having served in the military, let alone appearing on any POW lists. Other research unearthed that Smith did not graduate from Stanford University as she claimed.

Smith admitted that her story was a lie and vowed to resign from her position with the YWCA. In the fallout, one *Capital-Journal* editor also resigned. In late June 2004, Smith made headlines again for lying when police found her unconscious in her home—along with the decomposing body of her thirty-nine-year-old daughter. Smith had led neighbors to believe that her daughter had moved away from home in March.

So why lie about being a POW? Smith claimed that she used the story in a desperate bid to find employment. Smith was reluctant to go public with her story, not because of trauma, but because she feared that her story would be exposed as a lie. Journalists simply misinterpreted Smith's reticence.

Role Playing

The next time you read or watch a story, focus on one that has an interview with two opposing sides of an issue. Try to find a news story you haven't encountered before and one where you have no emotional or ideological investment and which you would not normally care about.

As you are watching or reading the story, make a note of all the key players and decide what role they play. Are they portrayed as the hero, victim, villain or freak? Don't base your decision on what you think the roles are, but what the reporter thinks those roles are.

Now think about how you came to your conclusions. Was it the way the person behaved that made them seem heroic or freakish? Was it their words that made them seem villainous? Was it the way the reporter interviewed or described the individuals that made them seem as if they were victims? If there are visuals, did they support the person's role? Did a newspaper photograph show the victim looking sad while holding an object that was the cause of her sadness? On a news show, was the villain ambushed by the reporter or was the hero smiling while surrounded by admirers?

Do you agree with the reporter's assessment of the players? Did you feel someone was really a complete victim? Was the villain really at fault? Was the hero heroic? Do you feel any information was missing from the story or that some facts were downplayed? Were the roles too pat? What new information would make you feel differently about each person?

When Woe is Them

There are only a handful of roles in news stories: the good guy, the bad guy, the victim or the freak. Some of these roles have subcategories; a winner can also be a good guy and a spoiler can be seen as a villain or a freak. The role of the victim is fairly limited: a victim is someone who has been overpowered, bested, abused, exploited, scammed, conned, mistreated or imprisoned, but in any case, a victim has not only lost control over his own destiny, but usually something of value was snatched away from him. The element of weakness is associated with victims, even if they rally and eventually triumph: it's that one moment of vulnerability that most of us think about and sympathize with. More sensitive people do not wish to re-victim-ize a victim by confronting or questioning them.

But there is a caveat: the victim needs to appear credible and sympa-thetic: if either of these conditions are missing, the person is no longer seen as a victim, but as a villain, trying to entrap someone else. If the victim lacks a look of vulnerability or has had a past, the aura of victimhood vanishes. Merely being overpowered by a predator or villain is not enough; the person has to look, sound and act like a victim, too. If someone can provide a plau-sible story and behave appropriately, they will find it easier for others to believe their story without corroborating evidence; after all, it is considered rude to question someone who is distraught.

Some scam artists, manipulators and exaggerators instinctively know (either consciously or unconsciously) that a convincing victim will be given more slack; many fabricators choose to play the role of the victim. They will gain credibility, a sympathetic audience and may even receive financial rewards from strangers. If the victim's account is supported by an authority or esteemed organization, the victim is more likely to be believed—never mind that the institution may not have tried to fully confirm the victim's account. Donna Mercier, Tawana Brawley, Charles Stuart and Adelaide Abankwah all played the victim card with initial success. Mercier, Brawley and Stuart all had the backing of police to support their claims.

A victim does not even have to be a victim of a crime to gain media attention; the practice of believing a victim whose story is corroborated by officials, such as police, is nothing new. It was late summer in 1953 when Oklahoma City residents opened their hearts to Roy Edwards, a handsome teenager from Oregon who told Oklahoma City police he "had no home" and no place to go after his mother died in a car accident. City police found young Roy "sitting on the courtroom steps."

He seemed so distressed that police at first were convinced that the boy had suffered from amnesia. The police immediately took the "muscular" boy (who weighed 185 pounds) in, and one of the deputies became his unofficial guardian—but there were at least 75 other folks in town who wanted to take the young man in, as the August 21, 1953 edition of the *Daily Oklahoman* recounted:

> An Oklahoma couple Thursday was seriously considering asking a seven-teen-year-old Eugene, Ore., boy to take the place of their son who was one of twenty-five University of Oklahoma students killed last month in a Florida plane crash.
>
> "I think maybe we could do something for him and he could do some-thing for us," the husband said Thursday afternoon as he and his wife sat nervously in the county sheriff's office waiting to meet Roy Edwards.

The same article also recounted how police verified Roy's background:

> [Chief Criminal Deputy Ross] Biggers checked on Roy Thursday with Eugene authorities and learned the youth had a good record and was an excellent football center and baseball catcher for Coburg Consolidated school, eight miles west of Eugene.

Other newspapers across the country reported on the young man, who received offers of clothes, food, money and shelter from the good people of Oklahoma.

Then, the next day, the other shoe dropped.

The "Oregon Orphan" wasn't quite what he appeared. For one, his name wasn't Roy Edwards, but Milton Mowdy, a "husky" paratrooper stationed in Fort Campbell Kentucky who went AWOL. Police in Oklahoma promptly arrested the young man, whose mother hadn't died after all—she was alive and well, and remarried. She had read about her son in the paper in Oregon.

Mowdy had clashed with his stepfather and enlisted in the army. Soon, the young man regretted his decision and left for Oklahoma, where his father lived. Though Mowdy seemed both attractive and vulnerable, and police assured reporters they had verified his story, the truth was still obscured. Mowdy may have simply given the name of someone he knew back home. People like Birdie Jo Hoaks have managed similar stunts, almost a half-century later.

Though many scammers are superficially convincing at playing the role of the victim, there may be subtle red flags that their performances aren't genuine. Since the faux victim's feelings aren't genuine, he has to guess what a truly victimized or heroic person looks, sounds and feels like—that means that some of his performance won't be on the mark. Since the fake victim has to guess, he most likely won't err on the side of caution—the spectacle will usually be an over-the-top performance. In short, the con artist will overdo it.

Self-centered people only think about themselves and how events relate to them. How family or friends are coping may not be a consideration. In fact, the fake victim may refuse to allow reporters access to his family simply because relatives are aware of the person's true state or devious nature and would give these facts away.

Some hoaxers are truly distressed—but not for the reasons they express. Milton Mowdy was found in an agitated state, yet his agitation didn't stem from being orphaned or homeless, but rather because he had deserted his post and was now surrounded by police. Feeling the heat, he may have believed he was discovered and was about to be arrested. His hoax was meant to save himself from discovery and arrest as well as account for his bizarre behavior. He was a young man who was scared and in over his head; he simply played his last card the only way he knew how.

The more con artists have to gain by lying, the more they will emphasize how an event has hurt them personally (i.e., how the event has impacted on their inner circle is glossed over or ignored entirely). We can expect melodrama from the fake victim: easy tears, puppy dog eyes, exaggerated frowns, self-pity and overreaction to even the slightest probing question. This act is the "hard sell": the person might not feel confident enough that a soft sell can work with his logically dubious story. The overwrought emotions are a form of window dressing.

But it's more than that—exaggerated emotions are a form of emotional misdirection meant to trigger feelings of pity in the gullible, and feelings of shame in the skeptical. How can you question the sobbing pleas of a victim? He's already suffered enough pain—why would anyone want to compound his misery?

An exception to the overkill happens when the fabricator pretends to be suffering from a painful or terminal disease. The fabricator may go to the other extreme: he may declare that he is better off for having the disease, seem indifferent to his alleged plight, or be obsessed with trivial points instead of worrying about the real consequences of being ill (known as *la belle indifference*). In Kim Stacy's case, her articles dwelled on trivial points of life—had she been truly sick, she would have been worried for more serious matters, such as whether her insurance company would cover her treatments during her time of illness or how she was going to face going through new rounds of chemotherapy, radiation or other painful medical procedures. Would she be able to afford expensive drugs? How would she continue working if her brain was under attack by a relentless disease?

When it comes to determining the credibility of a victim, people tend to fall into two extreme categories:

1. Each one of us is a complete individual and thus each of us behaves in our own unique way; therefore, you cannot make judgments about a person's idiosyncratic response to trauma. If you believe this, then you are a scammer's dream pigeon. Appealing to special cases and excusing suspicious behavior simply allows fabricators to lie without being questioned. It's a constricted way of thinking that stifles skepticism and critical thinking. We can't question anyone since everyone behaves differently. What this means is that a con artist's bad acting is merely seen as his own special way of dealing with his pain.

This egalitarian thinking also goes against what we know about human behavior: people do behave similarly in similar situations. A hand on a hot stove produces certain biological, neurological, physical and psychological reactions. The extreme heat hurts us: it burns our flesh, it sends signals to

our brain that we are being damaged, we become distressed and we promptly remove our hand from the stove. These behaviors are self-preserving, not
a statement of traditional values. People who would stick around to get bar-
becued aren't likely to survive and pass their defective genes to their
offspring. Those who do remove themselves from the danger, on the other
hand, are likely to survive long enough to ensure the next generation.

There is predictability in human behavior: psychologists couldn't conduct experiments and advertisers couldn't sell if there wasn't. There may be
some variation, depending on the person's background and hidden motives.
Any deviation in behavior usually signals that some other unknown factor
is influencing the person's reactions.

2. Everyone behaves alike. Any deviations clearly show a person is lying or
is somehow deficient and cannot be trusted. This, too, stifles thinking and
doesn't consider that there is a story behind the unexplained behavior. We
may accuse someone who owes the city money for services to be irresponsible, but without knowing the person's background, we can't be certain
that our negative impression is the right one. The person may be poverty-
stricken, incapacitated or did not receive adequate service and is
withholding payment until the service is adequately rendered. We need
information before we can jump to any conclusion—we need a news story
to explain why a victim is behaving in a particular way.

When we judge a victim's behavior, what we need to do is strike a balance between the two: people generally behave alike (not identically) and
any deviation from our expectations means that there are hidden motives or
events causing the unexpected behavior. A good news report will try to find
those hidden factors for the news consumer.

We need to do more than to study the behavior of those claiming to be
victims—we need concrete proof of their plight. While police may initially
claim the victim's story checks out, this is no guarantee that the story is true.
In news reports, a victim's story should be corroborated with witnesses, documents and any other evidence that confirms the person's version of events.

It's also helpful if we know something about the victim's track record:
has he made similar claims in the past? Are there troubling behaviors in his
biography? Is his family willing to talk about his character and situation?
We knew nothing about Nayirah, Milton Mowdy or Birdie Jo Hoaks: in
two cases, a false name was given, and in another, the last name was withheld. The complicated stories of hardship and trauma would fall apart if the
real or full names were given. If real names are given, and you feel as if you
want to donate money or services to the victim, a simple search engine
check might give you more information—but remember, there's no guarantee that a clean check means the person is telling the truth.

When One of the Sides Isn't Reliable

Oddball characters in the news pose an interesting ethical dilemma: although their eccentricities are newsworthy, they may not be reliable or credible, and the very media glare they seek may prove to be their undoing. Oddballs are an easy mark for reporters, but many times reporters tend to be an easy mark for oddballs, too. When reading or watching a news story about an oddball character, think about whether the person is lying or delusional—in either case, the story may not be in the least bit accurate.

In January 1970, several media outlets began reporting on the extraordinary saga of Michael James Brody, a young New York State man who inherited a substantial sum of money from his grandfather John F. Jelke—"the oleomargarine magnate," as various newspaper accounts called him (this part of the story was true).

Brody wasted no time: he gave a peculiar press conference, as recounted in the January 17, 1970 edition of the *Washington Post*:

> Michael James Brody Jr., a freshly minted twenty-one-year-old millionaire, is out to make people happy by giving away his fortune. He found no shortage of takers today.
>
> [...]Brody and his bride of eleven days, Renee, told a news conference in New York City last night that he would give a piece of his inheritance, which he [gave out as] $26 million, to any worthy person.

However, the same article noted that Brody's stepfather was quoted as saying that Brody's inheritance was three million, but Brody maintained that the final tally was $26 million "and growing." No one had bothered to double check the numbers or question why a twenty-one-year-old would give his money away in such a cavalier and public fashion.

It didn't matter: hundreds of people heard that there was free money for the asking and promptly descended to Brody's residence where he wrote scores of checks for anyone who asked. They left happily with their check in hand—that is, until all of Brody's checks bounced (though it was reported that he had given money to strangers before his decision to make his "donations" public).

By January 19, Brody claimed that he was "tripped out on drugs," when he decided to give away his fortune, and also said "What a joke I've pulled on the world." He was also quoted as saying, "I have 500 jets on standby around the world to bring [U.S. soldiers in Vietnam] home," but then added that he "may be the greatest con man in the world." By this point, Brody's relatives estimated that his fortune was in the one million dollar range. During the hoopla surrounding Brody, someone else would claim to be the oleo heir. A seventeen-year-old boy from Maryland declared he was Brody on a

747 in New York, leading reporters on a wild goose chase to Britain, before the teen came clean about his real identity.

In his quest to maintain the spotlight, Brody then claimed he ended the Viet Nam war, and unsuccessfully tried to see President Richard Nixon. However, with a couple of months, Brody was committed to a mental hospital (though he would later be declared sane). He was arrested for both burning down a house and for threatening the life of President Nixon. He and his wife Renee separated. Sadly, nearly three years later, Brody would violently take his own life, at the age of twenty-four.

In this case, reporters only looked at one side of the story—Brody's—yet the troubled young man was hardly a credible source. If Brody said he was going to give all his money away, then who else would the reporter need to interview? It would have to be someone who would know whether Brody had the funds and the mental stability to do so. If he was broke or unbalanced, then did he deserve the media frenzy he received? By judging Brody's behavior, it could be argued that Brody's psychological problems probably made him less than credible, meaning that the story needed more corroboration and skepticism than it received.

Finding All the Sides of the Story

Sometimes we may even be fooled into thinking that there is even a single side, when in fact the reporter found *no* sides of the story (which is a charitable way of saying the reporter made the whole yarn up). A reporter who relies heavily on color, poor sourcing, few facts, melodrama, confined roles and stereotypes is a reporter whose credibility should be questioned.

USA Today's Jack Kelley filed this moving story about a small group of Cubans who risked their lives to escape their homeland on March 10, 2000:

> Guided by the dim light of a crescent moon, nine people, one pregnant and one carrying a young child, crept from a grove of mangrove trees bordering a deserted beach and walked quickly toward shore.

The focus of the article was "Yacqueline," a young Cuban mother whose photograph was published alongside the article:

> Four nights before Yacqueline was to leave for a new life in America, the small, two-bedroom house that she and her son, Ulices, shared with her mother was abuzz [sic].
>
> Six girlfriends were crammed into the eight-by-eight-foot kitchen, sipping rum and helping Yacqueline wash clothes so she could sell them on the black market. She needed the money, she said, to rent a room in Florida when she and her son got there.

Yacqueline's last name wasn't given, but Kelley's mastery of color seemed to have more than made up for the story's factual deficiencies. After recounting how her father died and how Communist officials would help her in exchange for sexual favors, Kelley recounted her fateful attempt at an escape:

> Eight hours after the boat left carrying Yacqueline, Ulices [Yacqueline's fifteen-month old son], [and others], Ayleen was still on the shore, praying.
> "If they make it safely, I will do whatever you ask," she told God.

The story, which was reprinted in *Reader's Digest* took a sad and shocking turn:

> Seconds later, another wave hit the boat, knocking Ignacio, Yacqueline and Ulices into the water. Ignacio struggled to stay afloat and to keep the child's head above water, Silvia said. Yacqueline, who didn't know how to swim, flailed her arms as if trying to climb out of the water. She opened her mouth to scream but swallowed seawater instead. She never saw Ulices in the water behind her.
> Then, "they all disappeared," [a fellow passenger named] Silvia said.

Yacqueline's tragic end was marked by her heartbroken mother, as Kelley recounted:

> Yacqueline's mother, Ayleen, laid a small wreath decorated with mementos of the dead on the water. There were handkerchiefs, plastic crosses and a baby pacifier that had belonged to Ulices.
> As they watched the wreath drift out to sea, Ayleen told the small group how her daughter had dreamed of drowning only days before the trip. Yacqueline had said that if that happened, her mother could take solace in the fact that she'd be "out of Castro's grip."
> "Sleep peacefully, my child," Ayleen said tearfully as the wreath disappeared from sight. "You're finally free."

Readers were greatly touched by the story. One letter, published on March 14, 2000, read:

> It's easy to take for granted what we have in the United States. *USA Today* reporter Jack Kelley's front-page article gave me a new perspective on just how good we have it here in the USA...
> The article is now taped on a wall in my house in a prominent place so that my kids and I can look at it often.

Another letter published on the same day mentioned the doomed Yacqueline by name:

I'm afraid that many more Cubans like the young woman mentioned in the article—Yacqueline, along with her fifteen-month-old baby—will have to die before the U.S. government finally puts its foot down and stops playing to Fidel Castro's beat.

Congratulations to *USA Today* for having the courage to expose the truth.

USA Today would have the courage to expose the truth again—this time in 2004, after the paper discovered that Kelley apparently fabricated this story as well—the woman in the photo was alive and had never tried to escape her country illegally. *USA Today* editors had tracked down the woman who had legally emigrated from Cuba to the U.S. Her name was not Yacqueline, but Yamilet Fernandez, a hotel worker whose picture Kelley snapped to add a patina of credibility to his colorful story.

What's interesting to note is that Kelley heavily relied on "eyewitness testimony" and "anonymous officials" in his articles—two red flag sources that should signal to the reader that the article may not be as accurate or truthful as it first appears. In Kelley's piece, his description of both the moon and weather were impossible, since the moon did not appear in the area on the date given. Moreover, Kelley claimed that there was a storm the day of the attempted escape, when there was none. Here, again, color could have led a news consumer to the truth.

Sometimes a simple Internet search can expose a hoax or joke. Readers were in for a surprise when they read the November 25, 1991 edition of *Forbes FYI*:

> It has come to our attention through private channels that the Soviet government is preparing to make a very unusual, indeed, unprecedented, offering: the embalmed remains of V.I. Lenin.
>
> With its ruined economy fast approaching crisis point, and a severe winter food shortage looming, the Russian government is being forced to undertake some very drastic measures in an attempt to bring in desperately needed hard currency. Last summer, cosmonauts aboard the Soviet space station Mir, circling 240 miles above the earth, were reduced to earning money for the ailing national space effort by sipping Coca-Cola in an experiment for the company.

The article went on to note that "[b]ids should be addressed to... Gennady Barannikov, Minister of the Interior" in Moscow.

This extraordinary announcement was then reported on ABC's "World News Tonight," using the *Forbes* article as its only source. *USA Today* then ran the story, using ABC News as its single source. Too bad the original *Forbes FYI* article was a joke.

A simple search would have revealed that Gennady Barannikov wasn't the Minister of the Interior—besides, why hadn't the network tried to get in contact with Mr. Barannikov to verify the story and interview him? Mr. Barannikov's real name was Viktor and he had said nothing about selling Lenin's tomb. In this case, two major media outlets ran a story without interviewing a single person allegedly connected to the story. If the source is another media outlet, then there is a good chance that any of the lies and mistakes in the original story will be passed along to subsequent ones.

But business news stories are vulnerable to inadvertent one-sided reporting; who knows a company's goings-on better than those who work there? Some reporters and editors thought that way when one headline screamed "N.Y. investor eyes Northwest, Pan Am," in the *Twin Cities Star Tribune* on May 24, 1989:

> In a bizarre twist to the Northwest Airlines takeover, a virtually unknown investor with unidentified financial backing announced a possible bid Tuesday to acquire both Northwest and Pan Am airlines for a total of $4.92 billion. But questions immediately arose about the credibility and financial wherewithal of the investor, Michael Stern of New York, and his group, Trans Global Holdings Inc. Analysts expressed little confidence that Stern could pull off the deal.

If "analysts" expressed doubt about Stern's abilities and capital, then why run with it in the first place, especially since Stern wouldn't even divulge information about his background or his company? Yet it didn't stop the *New Jersey Record*, the *Chicago Sun-Times*, Reuters, *St. Paul Pioneer Press* and *St. Louis Dispatch* from reporting the news, even though all had voiced doubt about Stern and his company. Needless to say, Trans Global did not cinch the deal.

It was not the only time a company named "Trans Global Holdings" would send out a bogus press release. Ten years later, on July 22, 1999, *Business Wire* disseminated this press release:

> Trans-Global Holdings, Inc. announces that it is currently negotiating the purchase of various companies involved in the computer networking, software and Internet business sectors. While continuing it's [sic] activities in the Vacation Ownership Industry, TGHI recognizes the undying potential of the computer industry and intends to continue to diversify its holdings.
>
> John LaMonica, CEO of TGHI, states "We have uncovered some terrific opportunities within the computer and Internet industries. These will greatly increase TGHI's shareholder value and present us with unlimited potential."

There were four other press releases issued by the company. The contact on the release was *leaderboardinc@home.com*, a rather unprofessional e-mail address for a large corporation. Again, the release was bogus, though the lead players were different. SEC investigated, resulting in the company agreeing to a cease and desist order without admitting to the SEC's fraud charges.

Accounting for all the sides of a news story can help you decide whether information is missing from an article. Good journalists try to interview many credible, knowledgeable and relevant people for their stories—it's those nuances and differences that help the reader or viewer get a better grasp and understand about an event or issue; however, other reporters settle on getting their information from a single side, even if that side is less than credible. By looking for how many sides to a story a reporter presents, you will be in a better position to decide how accurate the story really is.

Chapter Twenty-Three

Being a Savvy News Consumer

Former *Times of London* owner Lord Northcliffe said that news is "what somebody somewhere wants to suppress. All the rest is advertising." How right he was: news should be the dissemination of important and relevant information, regardless of whether the raw truth is unpleasant and inconveniences the cowardly or the sheltered. News is needed to negotiate through a world where con artists and other liars can plunder and destroy without detection for years. More infuriating is that many of these same people stole and scammed while maintaining a stellar reputation thanks to a docile and compliant media: how many corporate demigods have been the recipients of glowing articles and profiles even though their financial wizardry was a sham?

A journalist isn't supposed to validate our worldview or enable our delusions; he's supposed to tell the rest of us where danger or trouble lurks and who can be trusted, even if that same news runs counter to our beliefs that justice always prevails or that every tragedy must have closure. Reporters who adhere to this method of reporting are often criticized for being too negative and ignoring happy news. Some of the more sensitive viewers and readers ask, "Where is the emphasis on heroes or winners? Why are you being so critical toward so many newsmakers?"

They aren't the only ones making that complaint and pushing for happy news stories: people caught in gauche, unethical or illegal activities also wish that news be reduced to sunny chronicles, no matter how dark the truth happens to be. Sadly, window dressing has become an invaluable commodity.

In 2003, the National Zoo in Washington, DC lost its full accreditation after an audit found crumbling conditions and a string of animal deaths. Why didn't the zoo's administration or veterinarians state with solemn dignity that they had not lived up to their duties and then announce their collective resignation? Because zoo brass hired Hill and Knowlton to rehabilitate their tarnished image.

In 1984, when Nestle was facing boycotts for giving free infant formula to hospitals for nursing mothers in Third World countries (which discouraged breast-feeding, thereby contributing to higher infant morality rates), did the company curb the practice that would lead to infant malnutrition? No, they hired the advertising firm of Ogilvy and Mather, whose leaked confidential report suggested that Nestlé monitor its critics and distract consumers with feel-good "public service campaigns" that were completely irrelevant to the accusations. In both cases, good news was used as a shield to protect those engaging in odious behaviors. Who would believe accusations levied against people who get showered with positive press? Lord Northcliffe knew exactly what he was talking about.

Corporations fight for good press even in the most hideous circumstances. One increasingly important specialty in public relations is crisis communications: it is the delicate art of rehabilitating the images of people or companies whose bungling, selfishness, laziness or viciousness have led to a public scandal. Some of the more well-known steps to "effective" crisis communications include the following:

• Responding publicly to the crisis immediately;

• Taking responsibility for the situation;

• Reassuring everyone that steps are being taken to rectify the matter;

• Showing sympathy to the victims and bystanders of the company's negligence and incompetence, alluding to the fact that the company was neither.

It's a well-worn formula that's worked well for businesses and newsmakers alike, but where does journalism fit in? As one well-known PR firm advised potential clients on its website:

> Treat the media as conduits, not enemies. Again, they've got a job to do. You can do one of two things. You can hunker in the bunker and let them use other sources, hostile third parties, people with axes to grind, bones to pick, people who have an interest in giving you trouble—or you can deal forthrightly with the media yourself. We advise the latter.

Three points become clear from this pearl of PR wisdom: first, journalists are seen as potential stenographers for corporate interests; second, it assumes that critics don't have a legitimate grievance and are merely crackpots and kooks who have nothing better to do than disparage a company in public (perhaps those PR professionals may be projecting their own feelings on critics since many in the business are former and failed journalists who may have a bone to pick with the profession). But there is something else we can glean from the above psychopathic passage: the press won't do any further digging if one side gives their side of the story first. The assumption that the white-collar set are above being called on the carpet for their incompetence is chilling.

Hard-hitting stories are going to be the ones that make an unscrupulous or indolent company's public relations department shift into overdrive to try to make the accusations sound groundless and godless. Who needs shame or contrition when almost any loathsome action can be justified and its perpetrator's image can be rehabilitated? Journalists are not supposed to regurgitate a propagandist's likely story; they are supposed to present information in a truthful and accurate way, no matter how painful, upsetting or ugly that truth may be.

A savvy news consumer knows this, but there are plenty of people who hate bad news and will try to avoid it at all costs. They don't know what's going on around them; they are perfectly happy with drinking contaminated water and feeding dangerous meat culled from dead stock to their own children. They will yell at reporters who tell them a health center run by a charming doctor may be a dangerous place for the sick. They are the ones who will think they don't need to hear any bad news in the first place since they believe that things will work themselves out in the end.

The problem with avoiding bad news is that you can't have truly good news in your life unless you confront the bad. Cancer spreads, bullies gain control, wars worsen, swindlers get richer. A journalist is simply informing his audience that something specific is not working properly and that, by knowing what's wrong and where the problem lies, viewers may be able to see the ways to correct it.

But con artists know human nature better than anyone: they know what people want to hear and can exploit those fears and desires to their own ends. Many people don't see obvious hoaxes and lies simply because they don't want to see them. If you're holding stock in or working for a company whose CEO has been accused of fudging the books, but you're still seeing decent returns, then why question the honesty of someone whose financial prowess has lined your coffers? What if the company was accused of exposing its workers and community to dangerous chemicals? Is it better to support a business that keeps the town's economy humming or is it better to demand change, regardless of the consequences?

Do we really want to imagine a world where fifteen-year-old girls can see through blindfolds or where child geniuses who send all their homework through e-mail are trustworthy? How can we not trust innocent-looking teenagers who say they've seen firsthand the evil of enemy soldiers or plucky boys who bravely travel alone across a vast, foreign country to be reunited with their fathers?

We could hold on to those fantasies and ignore that this is a world where there are mothers who will stoop to infanticide just to indulge themselves in a fleeting moment of public pity, and there are well-heeled suits who would ruin the lives of hundreds of investors just so they can buy one more Mercedes.

Believing the wrong news stories can effect our lives and influence the decisions that we make. If crime statistics are over-exaggerated, or if a fabricator claims to be the victim of a particularly heinous assault, we may support a political candidate whose sole platform is "getting tough on criminals." But if a city's fiscal health is a bigger problem than its crime rate, the opponent who has a better economic platform may be ignored by voters.

Evaluating the news is about looking for symptoms: does the story make sense? Have the pictures been altered? Are eyewitnesses telling the truth? Could the chain of events happen as described? Questioning information takes practice; the more information you examine, the faster and easier it becomes to separate lies from truth.

Not all news reports are lies or scams: in fact, more times than not, journalists get it right. Tuning out the news can be as unwise as believing every story you hear: it's no time to become a paranoid conspiracy theorist. By actively listening to the news, you'll be able to spot lies, omissions and exaggerations. To get the most out of the news, here are twenty ways to help you think critically about the information you receive:

1. Get your information from multiple sources.

In an age of media convergence, this isn't as easy as it sounds. Your local radio station, newspaper and national circulated magazine may have all gotten their story from the same wire service, such as *AP* or Reuters. With media concentration and convergence creating bigger and more harmonized media powerhouses, those same outlets most likely have the same owner and the same management team making sure that editors, producers and reporters follow the same format that adheres to the company's "fit," "point of view" and "voice." With fewer independently owned, financially sound media outlets, there may be a seemingly endless stream of media out there, but they are owned by a surprisingly and disturbingly small number of people. The trick is to get your information from outlets that have different owners.

Even if you do get your information from two or more independent sources, they may not be as divergent as you might think. If two reporters from rival media outlets work on the same beat, they may rely on the same sources and press releases for their information. Many reporters do tend to crib from each other shamelessly: for example, the *New York Times* relied on the *London Daily Telegraph* for information about the "death" of Katharine Sergava. Even today, many journalists quote anonymous sources cited by other reporters. The news media constantly look over each other's shoulders to determine what is and isn't news.

Getting your facts from multiple news sources should also mean reading left- and right-leaning sources, as well as foreign publications and broadcasts. While you may not agree with a magazine's interpretation of events, there is nothing to say that the facts used are wrong. Foreign sources will also have access to different information and points of view. The more sources you read, the easier it becomes to notice missing or fraudulent information, especially if one outlet's information directly contradicts another's.

2. Look for the obvious explanation.

In an age where there is an emphasis on understanding, sensitivity and the drive for individuality, we tend to look for convoluted and complex explanations as to why a person has behaved in a certain way. Fabricators like to appeal to special cases when telling their stories; however, motivation for behavior isn't as varied as we may think. Greed, fear, anger and jealousy can account for a significant number of seemingly inexplicable behaviors. Why would Donna Mercier refuse to release her name and image to the public? The same reason most people who shun the spotlight do so—they have something to lose (most notably their credibility) if their name and face become public knowledge. It's the same reason why "C.J." and "Cindy from San Francisco" would not give their full names to the media: if they did, something about their pasts or current situation would show they were lying.

When we listen to interviewees telling their stories, what we are looking for is the simplest explanation that can account for their actions. Remember Occam's Razor: the simplest explanation is most likely the most correct one. The same principle should be applied when watching the news: is the interviewee or journalist using tangled and elaborate excuses explaining why events happened? What damaging information is the person trying to hide?

Obvious explanations also tend to sound the rudest. Polite thinking may be fine for a dinner party, but it's useless when you're trying to get at the truth. If a woman who claims her missing children were kidnapped is weeping in front of cameras, she may not be crying because she fears for them—she may be fearing that the police are closing in on her.

3. Listen to all sides with an open mind.

Court trials would be very interesting if only the defense or the prosecution alone laid out its case: everyone would either look totally innocent or totally guilty. There is a good reason why a judge and jury get to hear from all relevant parties, from eyewitnesses, experts, victims and defendants; it's the best chance of finding out the truth. Even if one side seems to have more credibility than the others, listen to what they have to say before making any value judgments. It also helps to remember that issues and events rarely ever have only two sides. In the babies and incubators hoax, the scam flourished since no contradicting evidence was presented—many assumed the hoax was true. Very few people questioned why journalists would present only one side of the story.

4. Think about information that is missing.

We tend to make assumptions when we are given incomplete information. When Susan Smith claimed a carjacker kidnapped her children, many people didn't think about what Smith was doing while her children were allegedly being driven away by a gun-wielding carjacker: they simply filled in the blanks for her by assuming that she must have put up some sort of resistance or was too stunned to react, never realizing that their assumptions could be helping a killer get away with her crime.

In the babies and incubator hoax, Nayirah never said what happened to the infants between the time Iraqi soldiers allegedly took the infants out of the incubators and the time the babies died. We can assume the infants slowly died of hypothermia, but that assumption doesn't explain why hospital staff didn't try to rescue the infants or why the soldiers would place infants gently on the floor instead of tossing them out and grabbing the incubators for themselves (or simply save time by just taking the incubators with the infants inside and then disposing of the children later at their own convenience).

Next time you read or watch the news, think about what information was excluded. Did eyewitnesses actually say they saw the event as it happened or did they come during the aftermath? One tiny detail can make the difference between believing the truth and believing a hoax.

5. Make time for the news.

These days, it is in vogue to be "too busy" to spend time with our family and friends and too busy to sit down and read a newspaper. Of course, our ancestors had time to kill after having to walk miles to their destinations, build their own houses, make their meals from scratch and everything else without so much as electricity. These same people had time to read a newspaper (often more than one) and stay informed. If you have time to watch trashy serialized game shows, wait in long lines at drive-thrus, download illegal music and read movie spoilers, you have time.

Besides, it doesn't take very long to read or watch the news. Waiting for your burger at the drive-thru? Listen to the news on the radio; otherwise, you'll be dependent on word of mouth for your information. Con artists take advantage of people's ignorance and mental laziness; many quacks manage to ply their trade with ease for years without having to change their names, even if they had been exposed as charlatans—they simply can lure suckers who haven't been paying attention. You might have been too busy to keep up with news about Enron, but if you bought shares in the company, you might be too busy trying to save yourself from filing for bankruptcy protection later on.

6. Don't be satisfied with snippets.

With news available on electronic billboards and on cell phones, many people can fool themselves into thinking they're informed news junkies. A headline or news brief doesn't tell you very much, and if that information is incorrect to begin with, you're filling your head with useless information.

You can't evaluate the news without some concrete information. If you simply rely on headlines as a substitute for real news, almost all hoaxes will sound legitimate. Headlines may seemingly be convenient, but you don't have enough to evaluate their truthfulness or accuracy. Short news articles may be faster to digest, but that's like saying that cyanide pills are easier to digest than a steak.

7. Pay close attention to the speaking cadences of people interviewed in a print article.

It's not only what people say, but the way that they say it that can reveal a lot about the person. Even the quotes themselves may have been fudged or fabricated entirely. Does a janitor from a third world country who dropped out of grade school sound as articulate as a native-born citizen with a PhD in English? Does a sheltered dilettante sound as if she has the same street cred as a gang member? Does everyone in an article sound alike, regardless of their age, life experience, upbringing and education? If so, the journalist concocted those quotes. Open-mindedness is one thing; being insensitive to the natural consequences of class disparities or cultural differences is quite another.

8. Look for logical or chronological problems.

If the story has logical holes, then the reporter got her facts wrong, didn't do enough research to give a full account of events, was duped or made the story up himself. The problem with many news stories is the lack of investigative rigors: the accounts are based on the say-so of officials, rather than scouring for original sources and players. Since most reporters aren't well versed in psychology, linguistics, anthropology or forensics, it is difficult for many to actually compare an eyewitness or official's account of events with what is possible. Try to imagine the story as you hear or read it—do the individual events fit together in a logical way? As we saw in Chapter 18, stories that may seem plausible actually fall apart once you begin to imagine the events for yourself.

9. Note the color-fact ratio.

Lush details about a person's living room may satisfy your inner Gladys Kravtiz, but unless the description is directly relevant to the story, the article loses its usefulness. Good reporters use both color and facts to tell a story and give information, but only if the color supports the facts, not the other way around. Once fact becomes overshadowed by color, the reporter is no longer doing her job: she is merely using filler to hide the fact that she hasn't done her work. Too much color can mean the reporter was either too lazy to go out and find information, or simply made the story up.

Even if the reporter is on the level, too many irrelevant descriptions may indicate that a writer is obsessed with minutiae and is more impressed with his own writing prowess than with what's going on around him. What's the point of knowing how a victim straightened up a tablecloth if she is a con woman lying about her story in the first place?

The next time you find yourself reading a news magazine, read the first paragraph of a hard news story and look away. Without looking back at the article, think about the information you learned from the opening paragraph. Was it factual in nature or descriptive? Is that tidbit likely to stick with you for a day or a week? Could you make use of that information?

Read the next paragraph and repeat the exercise. Did you learn anything new? If so, what was the nature of the information? Now read the entire article. How much color is there? How many facts? Is color supporting the facts or are facts supporting color? If someone asked you, "What did you learn today?" would anything in that article cross your mind?

Color is also important in determining if the reporter is fabricating his story. Do the details make sense? Are there facts or points that rouse your suspicion? If so, you may be dealing with an article that has no facts because it is a work of fiction.

10. Note the standard format of different print and broadcast outlets and look how these outlets could be vulnerable to potential hoaxes.
People magazine's human interest stories follow the same format: usually the first paragraph will be a colorful personal anecdote that will segue into the main article and you can expect at least one interview with someone who is a friend or colleague of the subject who has something nice to say about the person. ABC's "20/20" uses stock background music to reflect the tone of the story, while CBS's "60 Minutes" does not. Some outlets use anonymous sources, while others never do.

Many fabricators have the gift of finding and exploiting a person or institution's weaknesses; Stephen Glass and Jayson Blair both knew the system failures of their publications and used them to spread their lies. In the Emulex hoax, it was a former employee of the Internet Wire Service who knew the inner workings of the service and fully took advantage of his knowledge. Con artists also have some ability to uncover a reporter's intellectual flaws so that they can take advantage of them.

You should also become familiar with a reporter's or outlet's weaknesses—but not because you should try to pull one over them. If you were to try to hoax a particular outlet, how would you do it? In what ways are they vulnerable? In what ways are they effective? Are they too ideologically or politically biased? Are reporters and anchors too in love with themselves to see the world around them? Do they rely on color or sensationalism? Do they look for freaks, heroes or victims? Do they use anonymous sources? Does it seem as if they rely on press releases and VNRs for their information?

Trying to find holes in an outlet's armor can help you determine if someone already has or is now trying to fool you, too.

11. Know the difference between legitimate news and "advertorials."

Advertorials aren't articles: they're ads disguised as articles. Some third party has paid for that positive wording. Travel and health shows are prime sources for a station's advertorial dollars. Bridal, real estate and automobiles sections account for much of a newspaper's advertorial revenue. On a similar vein, "magalogues" are advertising masquerading as news. One side is presented and it is always positive.

A glowing news story may not be an actual fuzzy bunny, but there may be a good chance the reporter relied on a VNR or press release in lieu of research. A genuine news article interviews many people with different expertise and points of view and usually will not hawk products, services or designer bridesmaids gowns.

12. Don't automatically dismiss information that doesn't fit in with your world view.

Prejudices, biases and misconceptions can blind you to important information. Dismissing inconvenient or troubling facts can lead you down the wrong path and hurt your own credibility in the long run. You may not want to believe that some people lie about being victimized or that blue chip executives climbed the corporate ladder by scamming others, but not considering alternatives could lead you to convict innocent people or losing your life savings in a swindle.

On a similar note, don't make judgments on a news story's accuracy or objectiveness before you've read or watched the entire story. Don't assume the article or segment is true or false until you've thought about the information you've read. You may not agree with a reporter's interpretation of facts, but the information may be complete and accurate. Think critically about the story before making up your mind.

13. Don't give anyone the benefit of the doubt, especially the people you agree with.

We can accept that people will lie about being sexually assaulted, using drugs and being faithful, but we still have a hard time believing that people will lie about their children being kidnapped or that they are billionaires. Yet they do lie—and we have to decide whether the person flickering on the television screen is lying or telling the truth.

But prejudices still cloud our judgments. Some people believe a woman would never lie about being sexually assaulted, while others believe that children do not have the cunning to tell elaborate lies without getting caught and still others think that clean-cut, attractive middle-aged men in three piece suits can be trusted.

People lie about being robbed. People lie about the existence of a tribe. People lie about having cancer. We may tend to believe people with whom we feel a certain kinship. Someone who is claiming to be a cancer patient may find a gullible audience with those who have the disease for real. Someone claiming that his child was kidnapped may be able to convince those people whose children were truly abducted.

Even defenders of beleaguered colleagues may have an agenda. Just because an interviewee seems unbiased, it doesn't mean there isn't some back room dealing or closed door choreography going on. As one well-known PR firm advises on its website to potential clients who may be experiencing a public corporate crisis:

> Recruit and use third parties to speak on your behalf. Third parties are becoming critically important. Given the landscape that shows lack of trust on the part of large institutions like big business, it is very important to have other people, hopefully friends, saying the things you want to say about yourself. They are more credible than you are.

If this parlor trick is common during crisis management and communications, then how do you know the defender of a scandal-tainted company or person isn't really a mouthpiece for the damaged party? The defender may truly believe the company is innocent of wrongdoing, but unless the news consumer has more information, it can be hard to believe public support of a besieged person.

Yet this blind trust can lead to cancer patients denying donations to someone who is truly ill so that they can raise funds to a perfectly healthy liar or to victimized parents supporting a child murderer. Make no assumptions about a person's truthfulness—just pay attention to their words, put aside your emotions and think about whether his story makes sense.

14. Forget your manners and stop being so offended.

Some people just love to morally masturbate in public: they are the ones who oppose any unflattering information in a person's obituary or complain about front-page pictures of someone committing suicide. Graphic pictures of murder victims or undercover investigations compel these souls to complain bitterly to editors about privacy and fair play, never once questioning whether they actually live in a fair society.

The demand for sterilized and happy news adds a layer of protection to fabricators who know how to exploit the situation. People such as Donna Mercier and Daniel McCarthy all knowingly or unknowingly took advantage of people's political correctness. Jessica Lynch and Richard Jewell were victims of misplaced politeness: instead of questioning government and police sources, reporters simply reported what they were told.

To get to the truth, privacy will be invaded, authorities will be questioned, images will be raw and audiences will be insulted. It's the only way to shake people out of their slumber. The best reporters are probably seen as the rudest ones: conventions don't stop them from asking the hard questions, yet those who lie and scam may be seen as perfectly polite by audiences. Just because you feel uncomfortable at a reporter's line of questioning doesn't mean that the reporter is wrong.

15. Don't be afraid to write or call a media outlet to ask for more information.

If something about a news report doesn't sit well with you, call, write or e-mail the outlet and ask for more information. If what the reporter disseminated is true, then the journalist should be able to tell you how he came to his conclusions.

16. Don't tune out.

If you're not satisfied with the amount of information coming from a news outlet, don't just drop the publication or turn the channel. The fewer people who tune in or subscribe, the more likely the media outlet will be forced to cut down on its work force—and the more likely the quality and quantity of news will suffer.

Make demands. Ask for more investigative pieces. Ask for more news. It's the only way producers, publishers, editors and reporters will know what they need to do to reconnect with disenfranchised news consumers, and the bigger their audience, the better quality their news stories will be.

17. Know your own biases.

Just because a news story doesn't jive with your own point of view, doesn't mean the story is a lie or a hoax. What are your own political and ideological leanings? Why do you think that way? Knowing your own personal biases can also prevent you from assuming a truthful story is a hoax.

18. Forget folksy logic.

Using logic and critical thinking can tell us if event A caused event B or if one action can follow another. On the other hand, folksy logic dictates that anyone—even an unsupervised child—in a foreign country can, with a little pluck and elbow grease reach their goal without a single negative incident, regardless of the odds and circumstances.

Folksy logic appeals to our idealistic senses; it dictates that anyone with a little ingenuity and impish charm can overcome any odds, no matter how bleak the situation. This pseudo-logic assumes that anything is possible and that this is a just world (or at least a just country) and that everyone gets his just rewards.

Fabricators must love this flaw in our thinking, since they appeal to it so often. Edwin Sabillon certainly used it, as did Victor Notaro, Donna Mercier and, to an extent, Birdie Jo Hoaks. Jayson Blair relied on it when he placed Jessica Lynch's father in a tobacco field. Kim Stacy also used it when she wrote about "Josh."

Journalists such as Mike Barnicle have been caught using bogus information and folksy logic in their fateful columns. Whenever an article relies on folksy logic, it is a red flag that the story is either a complete hoax or at least has been greatly exaggerated.

19. Don't appeal to authority.

Your parents aren't always right, and neither is anyone else, even if they wear a lab coat, have stars on their lapels or work in the Oval Office. What evidence does this person have to prove this piece of information is true? How good is the evidence? Is it used in the proper context? Could there be alternate explanations as to why certain events are unfolding? If not, then don't take their word as gospel.

20. Ask the two most important questions—*why* and *how*.

How are these series of events possible? Why is this person agreeing to a media interview? If those questions aren't answered in a news report, try to think of the various reasons why these particular people chose to make their story public, or how it is possible for this incredible turn of events to have happened in the way described. If you can't come up with reasonable answers, it may be because the reporter didn't provide critical details or because the story is a hoax.

Putting It Together

Keeping informed is a key not only to succeeding, but also to survival. We have to rely on others for fresh information, but those people may be careless, gullible, lazy or simply devious. Information has to be processed with a healthy dose of skepticism, but becoming overly suspicious of every piece of information can become maddening: sooner or later you have to trust that some piece of information you hear or read is true. By learning to actively digest information and think about what's missing and what's impossible, you can become an informed news consumer who can separate useful information from inaccuracies and hoaxes.

Good news evaluation requires that you ask questions. What's the point of this story? To warn about danger? To promote a business venture? To attract a younger audience to the publication? Are all questions answered? Are all claims proven?

There is a wealth of accurate, balanced, useful and relevant information to be found on the news. Journalists do expose frauds, hoaxes and liars. Tuning out won't make your life less stressful—it will simply make it less vivid and more limited. Evaluating the news can open your eyes and your mind, and you can uncover a con artist's scheme and prevent him or her from causing further damage and suffering in your life.

Manual of Rumors and Hoaxes

Section One: Rumors and Urban Legends

1. Is the rumor inflammatory or slanderous?

2. Would someone have something to gain by spreading this rumor?

3. Is there any evidence to back those claims?

4. Could this rumor permanently ruin a company's livelihood or someone's career?

5. Does the target of the rumor have known enemies who have made accusations in the past?

6. Can the origin of the rumor be found?

7. Are key details missing?

8. Can where the rumor started be pinned down?

9. Was the rumor reportedly heard on a talk show or newsmagazine? Can the sighting be confirmed?

10. Was a "friend of a friend" the origin of the rumor?

11. Is the wrong location given?

12. Is a specific date or location given?

13. Does the rumor sound like a story?

14. Is the ending too neatly wrapped up?

15. Is the ending overly just?

16. Is the story too complicated?

17. Does the story use dark humor?

18. Could someone have misunderstood the original source of the story?

19. Is this story about an overnight sensation?

20. Does the story sound like a prank?

21. Have you heard a similar rumor elsewhere?

Section Two: Hoaxes and Mistakes

1. Is the story breaking news?

2. Is the story about a racially motivated attack?

3. Is the journalist reporting the story from a foreign country? Is the reporter likely to be fluent in the language of the country?

4. Does the story rely on unnamed sources?

5. Does the story rely on authorities or officials for information?

6. Does the story rely on unnamed authorities?

7. Does the reporter use color to describe events?

8. How well is the story sourced?

9. Do all people interviewed sound alike in the story?

10. Is it likely the reporter made an effort to interview all key players?

11. Are eyewitnesses interviewed? Do they give similar accounts?

12. Do the timelines given make sense?

13. Is the report about a medical, scientific or health breakthrough or study?

14. Does the study have proper controls (randomization, double blind placebo)?

15. Does the study have a control group?

16. Do the researchers have reputable credentials?

17. Have the original researchers been interviewed?

18. Do the researcher's results seem too perfect?

19. Does the researcher get identical (not similar) results every time?

20. Can other researchers replicate the results, or is the original researcher the only person who can make the results happen?

21. Does the story make serious allegations?

22. Is there proof that the allegations are true?

23. Does the story rely on frightening the audience?

24. Are there more simple or mundane explanations that can account for the turn of events?

25. Would someone have something to gain by lying to the media?

26. Is the story over-hyped?

27. Does the person interviewed seem credible?

28. What makes the interview subject qualified to speak about the subject?

29. Does the interview subject rely on charisma?

30. Does the interview subject rely on emotional manipulation?

31. Does this interview subject have something to gain by lying?

32. Is the interview subject vague on some points?

33. Does the interview subject avoid answering questions?

34. Does the interview subject appear to have undergone media training?

35. Does the interview subject's story have flaws or inconsistencies?

36. Does the interview subject's story have logical problems?

37. How many sources did the reporter use?

38. Is the person being interviewed the "face" of the story?

39. Is the person being interviewed considered a "get"?

40. Do the interview subjects seem to "fit" their "role" too perfectly?

41. Is the person who is the focus of the story claiming to be a hero or winner?

42. Is there any proof that this person's claim is true?

43. Does the person claim to be able to do something no one else can do?

44. Are there alternative explanations that can explain the person's uncanny abilities?

45. Can the person's claims be refuted or confirmed?

46. Are reporters too deferential in their reporting?

47. Does the reporter rely on emotional manipulation to tell the story?

48. Is the story shocking?

49. How well is the story sourced?

50. Does the reporter rely on clichés and stereotypes?

51. Does the story conform to racial, ethnic, regional or gender stereotypes?

52. Are the eyewitnesses the reporter interviews reliable?

53. Does the reporter ask leading or loaded questions?

54. Does the reporter or interview subject rely on grand scale conspiracy theories to explain away logical flaws in their story?

55. Does the interview subject or reporter rely on misdirection?

56. Does the reporter rely on eyewitness testimony?

57. Are eyewitness accounts too similar, even in phrasing?

58. Is it likely that at least one person or group has hired a public relations firm?

59. Does the anecdote seem too cutesy or perfect?

60. Does the person use canned phrases?

Section Three: Propaganda

1. Is this story reported from a war zone?

2. Is the reporter likely to have been censored by government or military officials?

3. Does the reporter rely on interpreters from one of the warring sides?

4. Does the story demonize one warring side while supporting its enemy?

5. Does the story rely on prejudice and stereotyping?

6. Are eyewitness accounts too similar, even in phrasing?

7. Does a story of atrocities spark immediate anger?

8. Do the reporter or eyewitnesses rely on overkill to tell the story?

9. Is one side portrayed as a faceless enemy?

10. Is one side portrayed as ruthless killing machines that all behave in the same way?

11. Do the stories have chronological or logical holes?

12. Is there any forensic evidence to support the claims?

13. Does one side rely on a conspiracy theory to explain the lack of evidence?

14. Does one side get credited with having superhuman strength?

15. Do the cultural or ethnic idiosyncrasies seem plausible?

16. Does the story encourage reaction over reflection?

17. Do the stories appeal to survival fears, such as fear of cold, hunger, torture or death?

18. Is one side seen as reproducing and expanding at the detriment of the opposing side?

19. Are women used to both sexually arouse and invoke pity on the part of the audience?

20. Is the enemy of a small nation portrayed as someone who is bent on world domination?

21. Does one of the warring sides seem to have media training or have hired a public relations firm?

References

Chapter One: Introduction

"ABC World News This Morning" (1998). "Columnist Mike Barnicle Resigns." ABC Television, broadcast transcript, August 20.

Anonymous, (falsely credited to Andersen, K.) (2002). "Dudes Who Dish." *Details*, August.

Anonymous. (2002). "Apology and Retraction." *Daily Evergreen*, October 4, www.dailyevergreen.com.

Anonymous. (2002). "Filipino American History Month Ideas." Pinoylife.com, September 25, www.pinoylife.com.

Anonymous. (2002). "The Big Ass Spanish Boat." Pinoylife.com, October 7, pinoylife.com.

Anonymous. (2003). "Free Reign for Drug Ads?" *Consumer Reports: Publisher's Edition* including supplemental guides, February 68, 2, pages 33-37.

Anonymous. (2003). "Kids need civics lessons, Senate decides:$100 million measure to boost knowledge of history, government passes unanimously." *Charleston Post and Courier*, June 21, www.charleston.net.

Associated Press and *Boston Globe Staff.* (1998). "Barnicle resigns from *Globe*: Fabrications found in 1995 column." *Boston Globe*, August 19.

Associated Press. (2003). "Survey Reveals Misinformed Investors." *Wichita Eagle*, December 1, www.kansas.com.

Barnicle, M. (1995). "Through pain, a common bond." *Boston Globe*, October 8, www.boston.com.

Barnicle, M. (1998). "I was just thinking..." *Boston Globe*, August 2.

Bender, B. (2003). "Army halts media campaign: Form letters called abuse of program." *Boston Globe*, October 15, www.boston.com.

Campbell, D. (1999). "When disaster strikes." *American Journalism Review*, December, 21, 10, page 22.

Cohall, A., Kassotis, J., Parks, R., Vaughan, R., Bannister, M., and Northridge, M. (2001). "Adolescents in the age of AIDS: Myths, misconceptions, and misunderstandings regarding sexually transmitted diseases." *Journal of the National Medical Association*, February, 93, 2, pages 64-69.

Donald, B. (2003). "CNN Admits Planting Question in Debate." *Associated Press*, November 11, www.bayarea.com.

Dumenco, S. (2002). "The Glossies: Would the Real Kurt Andersen..." *Folio*, October 4, foliomag.com.

Dunick, L. (2003). "Horizon scandal should not affect local paper." *Thunder Bay's Source*, November 28, www.tbsource.com.

Dunne, S. (2001). "The short life of Kaycee Nicole." *The Guardian*, May 28, www.guardian.co.uk.

Ebert, R. (2004). "*Sun-Times* will weather the circulation storm." *Chicago Sun-Times*, June 20.

Grueser, S.M. (2003). "'The Rock' does fine in Kirkuk: The majority welcomes us with open arms." *Charleston Daily Mail*, September 10, www.dailymail.com.

Hachey, K. (2003). "Pot and PCs: Presidential candidates debate." *Brown Daily Herald*, November 5, browndailyherald.com.

Henry, T. (2002). "Kids get 'abysmal' grade in history." *USA Today*, May 10, page 1A.

Johnson, P. (2003). "CNN says it 'regrets' scripted debate query." *USA Today*, November 12, www.usatoday.com.

Kelly, K.J. (2002). "The Devil in the Details." *New York Post*, August 23, nypost.com.

King, L. (2003). "Many soldiers, same letter: Newspapers around U.S. get identical missives from Iraq." *The Olympian*, October 11, www.theolympian.com.

Kurtz, H. (2003). "'Light' Not Quite Right for This Forum." *Washington Post*, November 11, A4.

Lowe, P. and Brennan, C. (2003). "Woman wrongly ID'd in Bryant Case." *Rocky Mountain News*, July 24, page 6A.

Marshall, R. (2002). "Front-page blunder teaches hard lessons: Web-site joke gets WSU newspaper in trouble." *Seattle Times*, October 9, seattletimes.nwsource.com.

McKenna, (2003). "Soldiers' letters questioned." *Globe and Mail*, October 14, globeandmail.com.

Mikkelson, B. and Mikkelson, D.P. (2003). "Hunting for Bambi." Snopes.com, July 28, www.snopes.com.

Miller, L. (1995). "Boston columnist resigns after suspicions of fabrication." *Associated Press*, August 20.

Na, K. (2002). "October focuses on Filipino-American culture." *Daily Evergreen*, October 3, www.dailyevergreen.com.

Raddatz, M. (2003). "Letters Home: Soldiers' Glowing Accounts of Success in Iraq Success Were Written by Commander." ABCNews.com, October, 13, abcnews.go.com.

Sorrell, L. (2003). "Bizarre Game Targets Women: Hunting for Bambi." KLAS-TV, July 10, www.klas-tv.com.

Squires, M. and Lake, R. (2003). "Officials: 'Bambi' an elaborate hoax: But man behind videos continues to tell media outlets that hunts are real." *Las Vegas Review-Journal*, July 25, www.reviewjournal.com.

Steinberg, J. (2003). "Form Letters From G.I.'s to the Editors." *New York Times*, October 14, www.nytimes.com.

Storin, M.V. (1998). "Statement of Matthew V. Storin, Editor of the *Boston Globe*." *Boston Globe*, August 19.

Trustman, A. (2003). "Don't shoot the messenger." *Brown Daily Herald*, November 10, browndailyherald.com.

Tuohy , D. (2003). "Challengers clobber Dean for comment." *Eagle Tribune*, November 5, www.eagletribune.com.

Zitner, A. (2003). "Troops' Letters Not What They Seem: Several U.S. newspapers print identical messages from Iraq, not realizing that they aren't original." *Los Angeles Times*, October 14, www.latimes.com.

Chapter Two: Definitions

Anonymous. (2002). "Authorities Say 8 Women Ran $12 Million Pyramid Scheme." *New York Times*, October 27, page 1.31.

Biagi, S. (1992). *Interviews that Work*. Belmont: Wadsworth.

Charles, R.B. (1994). "Video News Releases: News or Advertising?" *World and I*, September, 9, page 96.

Dery, M. (1993). "Culture Jamming: Hacking, Slashing and Sniping in the Empire of Signs." *Open Magazine Pamphlet Series* (Pamphlet #25).

Kennedy Jr., J.F. (1996). "Women's Work." George, September, page 122-127152-153.

Kingston, A. (1998). "Money for nothing: as pyramid schemes once again come into vogue, Anne Kingston warns: buyer beware." *Flare*, June, pages 34, 38.

Kitty, A. (1998). "Objectivity in Journalism: Should we be skeptical?" *Skeptic*, Vol. 6, No. 1, pages 54-61.

Mikkelson, B. and Mikkelson, D.P. (undated). "Glossary." Snopes.com, www.snopes.com/info/glossary.asp.

Sanchez, E. (2003). "Scam Alert Column." *San Francisco Bee*, October 21.

Sifakis, C. (1993). *Hoaxes and Scams: A Compendium of Deceptions, Ruses, and Swindles*. London: Michael O'Mara Books.

Chapter Three: How News is Created

Kitty, A. (2001). "Sales, Canadian-Style: Campaigns romance the young as the single-copy category grows." *Presstime*, May, pages 39-45.

Manoff, R.K. and Schudson, M. (eds.) (1986). *Reading the News*. New York: Pantheon.

McLuhan, M. (1964). *Understanding Media: The Extensions of Man*. New York: Mentor.

Chapter Four: Media Realities

Anonymous. (2001). "What Are You Doing About the Youth Market?" MORI Research Group, May, www.moriresearch.com.

Bagdikian, B.H. (1983). *The Media Monopoly*. Boston: Beacon.

Carr, D. (2003). "To Sell the Ads, Eager Magazines Write the Copy." *New York Times*, September 8, C1.

Geewax, M. (2003). "Move outrages foes of media concentration." *Atlanta Journal and Constitution*, November 26, page C3.

Houpt, S. (2002). "Gotcha!" Globe and Mail, August 13, www.theglobeandmail.com.

Jenkins, H. (2001). "Convergence? I diverge." *Technology Review*, June, 104, 5, page 93.

Kerbel, M.R. (2000). *If It Bleeds, It Leads: An Anatomy of Television News*. Boulder: Westview Press.

Layton, C. (2004). "News Blackout." *American Journalism Review*, December/January, ajr.org.

Simon, R. (2004). "Lawmakers Review Media Ownership Caps, This Time in Name of Decency: Senators ask whether consolidation leads to more complaints. Panel OKs delay of FCC rules." *Los Angeles Times*, March 13, www.latimes.com.

Parish Perkins, K. (2003). "It's all about 'The Get'—got it?" *Dallas-Fort Worth Star-Telegram*, November 7, www.dfw.com.

Terry, C. (2000). "Grading the J-Schools." *Presstime*, September, pages 41-46.

Chapter Five: Breakdowns

Anderson, C. (2003). "Warning Given on Hidden Weapons." *Boston Globe*, August 7, page A24.

Anonymous. (2004). "Channel 2 News at Noon." WBRZ-TV, transcript, January 23, www.2theadvocate.com.

Anonymous. (2004). "The Actuary and the Actor." *New York Times*, March 16, nytimes.com.

Anonymous. (2002). "NY party cocks a snook at fear." *The Australian*, January 2, page 7.

Barnes, B. (2003). "In the Dangerous World of Toys, A 'Guru' Watching Out for Children." *Washington Post*, November 16, C4.

Barrett, D. (2003). "Hillary Clinton launches media blitz to promote memoirs detailing White House life." *Associated Press*, June 9.

Bone, J. (2003). "Clinton fans line up to ask the $64,000 question." *Times of London*, June 10, page 17.

Carter, R. (2001). "Voting 'Irregularities' Rears Its Head at Shea." *New York Newsday*, June 17, page C18.

Coulter, A. (2003). "I could hardly breathe." *Human Events*, June 16, page 1.

Cuza, B. (2002). "Jedi Return, And So Does the Mania." *New York Newsday*, May 16, page A3.

D'Arcy. J. (2002). "The Public wants majesty at Twin Tower Site." *Hartford Courant*, July 21, page A1.

Dobnik, V. (2001). "'Disturbing but wonderful': New platform allows view of World Trade Center." *Associated Press*, December 31.

Eltman, F. (2003). "N.Y. Highway Worker Chases Celebrity." *Associated Press*, June 17.

Feuer, A. (2003). "Long Island Everyman Masters the Sound Bite." *New York Times*, June 15, www.nytimes.com.

Goldstein, A. (2204). "Probe Starts in Medicare Drug Cost Estimates." *Washington Post*, March 17, page A1.

Hacaoglu, S. and Stanley, B. (2003). "Iraq Resumes Pumping Oil from Northern Oil Fields through Turkish Pipeline." *National Post*, August 13, www.canada.com.

Johnson, P (2004). "Panel to review former *USA Today* reporter's work." *USA Today*, January 29, www.usatoday.com.

Kelley, J. (1999). "U.N.: Records link Serbs to war crimes." *USA Today*, July 14, page 1A.

Kemper, V. (2004). "Medicare Ads Set Off Debate: Democrats say White House 'video news releases' mislead. The GAO will investigate." *Los Angeles Times*, March 16, www.latimes.com.

Kurtz, H. (2004). "Reporter 'Panicked' In Probe: *USA Today*'s Kelley Admits a Deception." *Washington Post*, January 11, page A1.

Kurtz, H. (2004). "Kelley story gets new scrutiny." *Washington Post*, January 14, page C12.

Kurtz, H. (2004). "Kelley's Serbian Source Doesn't Recall Meeting Him." *Washington Post*, January 16, page C3.

Landay, J.S. (2002). "CIA report reveals analysts' split over extent of Iraqi nuclear threat." Knight-Ridder News Services, October 4, www.realcities.com.

Logan, T. (2002). "NY Fans Like Sosa Rumors." *New York Newsday*, June 12, page A46.

Milner, M. (2003). "Pioneer Press Aims at Foot, Fires." *Chicago Reader*, September 5, www.chireader.com.

Manuel, M. (2004). "Bogus 'news release' criticized; Federal agency hired PR firm to produce Bush-friendly video." *Seattle Post-Intelligencer*, March 18, seattlepi.nwsource.com.

Matthews, K (2003). "N.Y. Boosts Security for St. Patrick's." *Associated Press*, March 17.

McCarthy, S. (2003). "For Media, This Man Is a Walking Sound Bite." *New York Newsday*, June 27, page A20.

Morrison, B. "*USA TODAY* reporter resigns after deception." *USA Today*, January 13, www.usatoday.com.

Mundy, A. (1992). "Is the press any match for powerhouse PR?: Check out the new and improved devices the big Washington firms have come up with for controlling the agenda." *Columbia Journalism Review*, September/October, archives.cjr.org.

O'Donnell, N., Roth, S., and Klein, M. (2003). "Clinton fans flock to book signing: 1,000-plus show; not all admirers." *USA Today*. June 10, page A8.

Pear, R. (2004) "U.S. Videos, for TV News, Come Under Scrutiny." *New York Times*, March 15, www.nytimes.com.

Pedulla, T. (2002). "Knicks throw curveball; Unpopular pick sent to Nuggets." *USA Today*, June 27, C09.

Rice, H. (2004). "A War story I wish I'd written." *Houston Chronicle*, March 13, www.chron.com.

Roig-Franzia, M. and Ly, P. (2001). "A Long Wait With No Handshake; Many Chilled White House Tourists Disappointed to Miss the New Occupants." *Washington Post*, January 22, page B7.

Rose, M. (2003). "Long Island Man Sows His Platitudes Widely." *Wall Street Journal*, June 16, online.wsj.com.

Roth, Z. (2004). "Spin Buster." *Columbia Journalism Review*, March 16, www.campaigndesk.org.

Roth, Z. (2004). "Distortion." *Columbia Journalism Review*, March 18, www.campaigndesk.org.

Roth, Z. (2004). "Fact Check." *Columbia Journalism Review*, March 22, www.campaigndesk.org.

Sherman, W. (2003). "So-Called Consumer Advocate Gets Paid for Television Toy Pitches." *New York Daily News*, December 18.

Sobieraj, S. (2001). "Bush welcomes guests to White House." *Associated Press*, January 22.

Steinberg, J. (2004). "Ascent of *USA Today* Reporter Stumbled on Colleagues' Doubts." *New York Times*, January 19, www.nytimes.com.

Steinberg, J. (2004). "Source for *USA Today* Reporter Disputes Details of Kosovo Article." *New York Times*, January 26, www.nytimes.com.

Ryan, K. (2004). "Checking Facts Basic to Good Journalism." *Television Week*, March 29, www.tvweek.com.

Usborne, D. (2003). "Crowds camp out overnight for Hillary Clinton book tour." *The Independent*, June 10, page 9.

Vincent, S., Tayler, L., and Kowal, J. (1995). "The Pope in America: They came, they saw, they prayed." *New York Newsday*, October 6, page A5.

Wlazelek, A. (2003). "J. city celebrates its Cinderella: Zora Andrich of 'Joe Millionaire' fame gets the royal treatment." *Allentown Morning Call*, March 30, page B3.

WNYC. (2004). "Man on the Street." *On the Media*, Transcript, May 28.

Chapter Six: Rumors and Common Knowledge

Andrews, A.R. (1981). "Names and Faces." *Boston Globe*, October 15.

Anonymous (2001). "eBay." *Silicon Valley Daily*, January 3, svdaily.com.

Anonymous. (1987). "Around the nation." *Miami Herald*, January 6, page 11A.

Anonymous (attributed to *Union-Tribune* News Services). (2003). "Revenge of nerds: Keeper for Keady." *San Diego Union-Tribune*, December 18.

Anonymous. (2004). "Mocking Macaw: Winston Churchill's Former Foul-Mouthed Parrot Found Alive at 104." ABCNews.com, January 20, abcnews.go.com.

Anonymous. (2003). "Parody site dupes the pros." Cyberjournalist.net, December 29, www.cyberjournalist.net.

Anonymous. (2004). "Daughter scotches Churchill parrot claim." BBC.uk.co, January 21, news.bbc.co.uk.

Associated Press. (1981). "Millionaire Admits Mystery Violinist Hoax for Publicity." *Daily Oklahoman*, October 16.

Associated Press. (2002). "Streisand Wrongly Attributes Quote." Associated Press, October 1.

Barber, C. (1995). "Paul Prudhomme: Don't call him Cajun; The same old story." *Dallas Morning News*, November 15.

Bingham, J. (2004). "Parrot swears he was once Churchill's." *The Scotsman*, January 21, news.scotsman.com.

Borrows, B. (2004). "F*** THE NAZIS, SAYS CHURCHILL'S PARROT." *The Mirror*, January 19, www.mirror.co.uk.

Bremmer, F. (1998). "Quirky little business makes eBay a big buy." *USA Today*, October 28, page 3B.

Carroll, J. (2001). "The sad yet untrue story of Kaycee." *San Francisco Chronicle*, June 5, B10.

Cassel, D. (2001). "'Gorgeous Guy' is San Francisco's new cybercelebrity." *San Francisco Bay Guardian*, May 30, www.sfbg.com.

"CBC Newsworld." (1995). Morning news program (Weather and teaser for Monday's program), broadcast October 27.

Cohen, A. (2002). *The Perfect Store: Inside eBay*. New York: Little Brown and Company.

Cook, M.E. "'Beware the leader who bangs the drums of war...'" (2002). *Sierra Times*. July 2, www.sierratimes.com.

"CNN Live this Morning." (2001). "Violating an Internet Hunk's privacy." CNN, broadcast transcript, July 3.

Drudge, M. (2002). "Now Barbra's in Shakespeare hoax; singer used phony Internet quotes in war cry." *Drudge Report*, October 1, www.drudgereport.com.

Dunne, S. (2001). "The short life of Kaycee Nicole," *The Guardian*, May 28, www.guardian.co.uk.

Fass, A. (2000). "Wacky, fake websites grab attention, while only slyly referring to their sponsors." *New York Times*, August 14, page C8.

Fishman, T.C. (2000). "There are no Free Wheels." *Esquire*, April, 133, 4, pages 58-60.

Graham, L. (2004). "Passions rise over parrots." *Shropshire Star*, January 23, www.shropshirestar.com.

Granatstein, L. (2000). "The URLy bird gets the worm." *Media Week*, June 5, 10, 23, page 65.

Guernsey, L. (2002). "For the New College B.M.O.C., 'M' is for 'Machine.'" *New York Times*, August 10, page G7.

Hafner, K. (2001). "A Beautiful Life, an Early Death, a Fraud Exposed." *New York Times*, May 31, page G1.

Hattori, J. (2001). "Internet plucks San Francisco man from obscurity." CNN.com, July 7, www.cnn.com.

Hazlewood, S. (1998). "IPO (initial Pez offering) sparked eBay launch," *San Jose Business Journal*, November 13, sanjose.bcentral.com.

Hobbs, L. (2003). "Ex-Palm Beacher arrested in S.C." *Palm Beach Post*, June 14, page 3B.

Hoffmann, B. (2004). "Churchill's parrot still squawking at 104." *New York Post*, January 20, www.nypost.com.

Kirchner, P. (1995). *Everything You Know is Wrong*. Los Angeles: General Publishing Group.

Kornblum, J. (2001). "His life was nice and private, then he became 'Gorgeous Guy'." *USA Today*, June 19, page D3.

Kornblum, J. (2001). "Tangled Web snares S.F.'s 'gorgeous guy'." *USA Today*, July 11, page D3.

Lareau, S. (2001). "Kaycee Nicole." Hill Top Design, April 24, Personal web log, www.hilltopdesign.com.

Leslie, R. (2003). "Purdue signs wrong Jason Smith to basketball letter of intent." Hoosiergazette.com, www.hoosiergazette.com.

Lubrano, G. (2003). "An Urban legend invades Sports section." *San Diego Union-Tribune*, December 22, www.signonsandiego.coml.

Lynch, D. (2001). "Not Dead: Beautiful Cancer 'Victim' Only in Mind's Eye." ABCNews.com, May 30, abcnews.go.com.

Macaleavy, T. (1998). "Managing the stress of the season." *Bergen County Record*, December 14, page H2.

Marshall, S. (1991). "Dallas AIDS avenger was teen's fabrication." *USA Today*, October 22, page 3A.

Muhmmad, D.E. (2002). "A man for these times: Julius Caesar." *Allentown Morning Call*, Letter to the Editor, August 7, page A14.

Roeper, R. (2001). "The sad story of Kaycee, cancer and compassion." *Chicago Sun-Times*, June 1, page 11.

Shreve, J. (2001). "They Think They Feel Your Pain." *Wired*, June 6, www.wired.com.

Smillie, D. (2002). "EBay Tale Garners Merit." *Forbes*, July 12, www.forbes.com.

Sutel, S. (2000). "Too funny to be true? Not in the Internet world." *Toronto Star*, June 19.

Rayner, B. (1998). "Clubs suffer as needle rumour persists." *Toronto Star*, August 17.

Redmon, J. (1999). "Fear of needles needless; Officials debunk rumors of hidden tainted syringes." *Washington Times*, March 18, page C3.

Reuters. (2004). "You'll never guess who's still alive." January 20, www.reuters.com.

Tamarkin, B. (1993). *Rumor Has It: A Curio of Lies, Hoaxes, and Hearsay*. New York: Prentice Hall General Reference.

United Press International. (1987). "Slice of finger found in bowl of menudo; store removes cans." *San Diego Tribune*, January 5, page A11.

United Press International. (2004). "Churchill's spirit lives on in his parrot." January 19.

Wallace, L.S. (1991). "Her Deadly Mission Is To Infect Dallas Men With Aids." *Seattle Times*, September 25, archives.seattletimes.nwsource.com.

Ware, P. (2002). "Greet the drumbeat for war with wariness." *Roanoke Times & World News*, Letter to the Editor, October 14, page A8.

Waters, T. (1987). "Mexican Food Firm Works to Undo Effect of False Report." *Los Angeles Times*. January 26, Business, page 12.

Waters, T. (1987). "Firm Says Reports of Finger in Soup Cost It $1 Million." *Los Angeles Times*. May 7, Business, page 1.

Waters, T. (1987). "Azusa Rejects Claim Filed After Reports of Finger in Soup." *Los Angeles Times*, May 14, Business, page 1.

Whitcomb, D. (2002). "Alas, poor Shakespeare; bard misquoted by Streisand." Reuters, October 1.

Chapter Seven: The Competitor's Myth

Alters, D. (1989). "Shhhhh... Some firms are busy spying on the nation's social activists, environmentalists, animal-rights workers and skeptics of biotechnology are targets of a lucrative trade." *Boston Globe*, July 9.

Anonymous. (1993). "Claims of syringes in Pepsi pouring in." *Plain Dealer*, June 17, page A13.

Anonymous. (1993). "Pepsi's nightmare." *St. Louis Post-Dispatch*, June 18, page 2B.

Anonymous. (1993). "The Pepsi scare." *USA Today*, June 18, 12A.

Anonymous. (1993). "Pepsi can warning." *New York Newsday*, June 14, page 14.

Anonymous. (1993). "Syringe sealed in Pepsi can." *Seattle Times*, June 12.

Anonymous. (1993). "Syringe case still open." *Seattle Times*, October 8.

Anonymous. (1993). "Woman responsible for Pepsi hoax fired." *Milwaukee Sentinel*, June 22.

Anonymous. (2000). "Fake news spurs stock stampede Panicked sellers lose billions before trading halt, showing vulnerability of high-speed market." *Atlantic Journal and Constitution*, August 26, page A1.

Anonymous. (2004). "Lottery Loser's shady past: Ohio woman has fraud, assault convictions, uses aliases." Thesmokinggun.com, January 6.

Associated Press. (1993). "Two Ohio women convicted in case of Pepsi tampering." *New York Times*, December 26, page A22.

Associated Press. (2000). "Stock hoax suspect had motive." Wired.com, August 31, www.wired.com/news/politics/0,1283,38552,00.html.

Berenson, A. (2000). "On Hair-Trigger Wall Street, A Stock Plunges on Fake News." *New York Times*, August 26, page A1.

Associated Press. (2004). "Woman claims $162M lottery ticket lost." January 5.

Associated Press. (2004). "Ohio Woman Claims $162M Lottery Jackpot." January 6.

Associated Press. (2004). "Ohio woman admits lying in lotto case." January 8.

Bergsman, J. (1993). "Syringe found In 2nd cola can—FDA investigates tampering." *Associated Press*, June 13.

Birkland, D. (1993). "Couple Say They Found Used Needle In Pepsi." *Seattle Times*, June 11.

Broom, J. (1993). "Arrests Pile Up In Tampering Hoax—At Least 24 Face Charges In Pepsi Cases Nationwide." *Seattle Times*, June 24.

Carlson, P. (2004). "Losers Weepers: The 'Winning' Ticket That Got Away." *Washington Post*, January 7, page C1.

Cox, J. (1987). "Corona importer puts a cap on rumor." *USA Today*, July 30, page 6B.

Cramer, J.J. (2000). "The Anatomy of a bogus press release." Thestreet.com, August 25.

Cramer, J.J. (2000). "Cramer Rewrites 'A Maelstrom of Confusion Over Emulex'." Thestreet.com, August 26.

Davis, R. (1993). "Arrest in Pepsi syringe claim." *USA Today*, June 16, page 1A.

Decker, S. (2000). "More financial news, more financial fakes." *Bloomberg News*, August 26.

Gentile, G. (2000). "Suspect in hoax that cost billions is student, 23." *Associated Press*, September 1.

Janofsky, M. (1993). "Reports of needles in soda cans climb." *New York Times*, June 16, page A16.

Kassler, H. "Data in the corporate universe: It's a dangerous world out there." *Searcher*, 9, 3, March 1, page 16.

Kessler, G. (1993). "A Coincidence? Or copycats? Feds say no viable link in Pepsi syringe cases." *New York Newsday*, June 16, page 7.

Kessler, G. (1993). "Arrest in Pepsi claim: Pa. man charged as reports spread; form takes offensive." *New York Newsday*, June 17, page 4.

Kessler, G. (1993). "Standing by needle story." *New York Newsday*, June 19, page 9.

Kessler, G. and Spencer, T. (1993). "How the media put the fizz into the Pepsi scare story." *New York Newsday*, June 20, page 69.

Knox, N. (2000). "SEC again takes aim at Internet stock fraud 11 lawsuits target con artists who made more than $10 million." *USA Today*, September 7, page 2B.

Krantz, M. (2000). "Hoax sends Emulex stock plummeting—temporarily." *USA Today*, August 28, page 5B.

Marshall, S. (1993). "Diet Pepsi drinkers warned of debris." *USA Today*, June 14, page 3A.

Marshall, S. and Sanchez, S. (1993). "More people report needles in soda cans." *USA Today*, June 15, 3A.

Milicia, J. (2004). "Woman wins $162M Mega Millions jackpot." *Associated Press*, January 6.

Mulligan, T.S. (2000). "Hoax burns Emulex, investors." *Seattle Times*, August 26.

Peterson, J. (1987). "Brewer Will Battle False Rumor About Its Product." *Los Angeles Times*, July 28, page D1.

Pols, M.F. and Harrison, L. (1993). "Pepsi Boss '99.99%' Sure—Syringes Can't Be Getting Into Cans At Plants, He Argues." *Seattle Times*, June 16.

Whitely, P. (1993). "Pop Cans Nearly Tamper-Proof—Bottling Engineer Casts Doubt On Syringe Reports." *Seattle Times*, June 17.

Wills, R. (1999). "Mexican Lager Corona Makes Headway against Domestic Brews in U.S." *Milwaukee Journal Sentinel*, December 27.

Wuerl, K. (1993). "She saw syringe and screamed." *Milwaukee Sentinel*, June 17.

Chapter Eight: The Winner

Anonymous. (1980). "Ruiz steadfastly insists she won the marathon." *Boston Globe*, April 22.

Anonymous. (1986). "World: World notes; Great escape dummies on both sides." *Time*, August 11, page 33.

Anonymous. (1989). "Soviet Union: A little too true?" *Time*, January 23, page 40.

Anonymous. (2000). "From Kindergarten to campus: Justin Chapman gets his university books ready." BBC.co.uk, February 16.

Anonymous. (2000). "The energetic messiah." *The Economist*, June 3, 335.

Anonymous. (2001). "Business 'journalism' deservedly under fire." *Toronto Star*, February 20.

Anonymous. (2001). "Search for Kutz gets special help; Mich. expert, dog seek body." *Wisconsin State Journal*, July 24, page 4A.

Anonymous. (2001). "Finger bone discovered in search by dog." *Milwaukee Journal Sentinel*, July 26, 2B.

Associated Press. (1980). "Ruiz: 2d saddest day of my life." April 30.

Associated Press. (1984). "Pipe bomb found on Olympic bus, Police remove device, athletes escape injury." August 14.

Associated Press. (1984). "LA bomb's hoax 'hero' cop says." August 14.

Associated Press. (1984). "'Hero admits bomb a hoax; Armenian terrorists also claim responsibility." August 15.

Associated Press. (2000). "When college is kid stuff." February 16.

Associated Press. (2001). "Expert, dog find bone but it's likely not Kutz's." *Wisconsin State Journal*, July 25, page 3A.

Associated Press. (2002). "Mom faked son's genius scores ; Helped boy get 298 on IQ test; now she faces neglect trial." March 4.

Astor, D. (2000). "Six-year-old signs as a weekly columnist." *Editor and Publisher*, May 22, page 23.

Audi, T. (2003). "The case of the crime dog: Canine ace's handler faces accusations." *Seattle Times*, July 20.

Bary, A. (2002). "Out of tricks." *Barron's*, July 1, 82, page 14.

Byrne, H.S. (2000). "Hello, new economy." *Barron's*, March 27, 80, 13, page 25.

CNBC/Dow Jones Business Video. (2000). "Enron—CEO—Interview." CNBC, October 27, broadcast transcript.

Connor, M. (1997). "WorldCom takeover plays set by ex-basketball coach." *Reuters Business Report*, October 1.

Cornwall, R. (2004). "Kenneth Lay indicted in $67bn Enron scandal." *The Independent*, July 8, news.independent.co.uk.

Fennell, T. (1996). "The privates' progress: the role of business in health care is growing." *Maclean's*, December 2, 109, page 54.

Fenton, B. (2000). "Boy, 6, enrolls on university course." *Daily Telegraph*, February 16.

Goode, E. (2002). "Boy genius? Mother says she faked tests." *New York Times*, March 2, page A1.

Green, M. (1989). "6 Survive 35 days in quake rubble." *USA Today*, January 13, page 4A.

Greenwald, J. and Gill, D. (1997). "WorldCom: Quiet conqueror." *Time*, September 22, page 50.

Hale, B. (2002). "Kenneth Lay: A fallen Hero." BBC.co.uk, January 24.

Her Majesty the Queen v. Koval and Koval. March 27, 2001.

Horn, R. (1997). "Thais sought hero; got con man instead." *Associated Press*, October 6.

Johnston, C. (1997). "Toronto centre hopes to cash in on growing demand for private health services." CMAJ, February 15, 156, 4, pages 557-9.

Jones, J. (2002). "Dog finds bone parts: Authorities collect burned bone fragments that a cadaver dog sniffed out in the search for a child's remains" *St. Petersburg Times*, February 26, www.sptimes.com.

Jones, J. (2002). "Bones are human, but not little girl's: The bones found in February were suspected to be those of a 3-year-old who disappeared in 1991." *St. Petersburg Times*, October 4, www.sptimes.com.

Kagan, J. (1997). "Who is Bernard Ebbers and why does he want to buy MCI?" *Internet Business Week*, October 6, page 175.

Kanell, M.E. (2000). "Ebbers building a WorldCom: Fearless CEO not expected to let up on acquisitions, a key to firms stunning success." *Atlanta Journal and Constitution*, May 21, page G1.

Karlin, R. (2000). "Advice from a genius, age 7." *Albany Times Union*, November 17, page B1.

Kendrick, B. (1989). "Trial by Fire: Boy 'hero' story tests media." *FineLine: The Newsletter On Journalism Ethics*, August, 1, 4, page 5.

Koeig, P. (1998). "In the telecom trenches." *The Independent*, July 19, page 3.

Levine, S. (2002). "Cadaver Dogs Sniff Out the Clues; Highly Trained Canines Help Police Solve." *Washington Post*, June 16, page B3.

Lutz, W. (1990). *Double-Speak*. New York: HarperPerennial.

Massarella, L. and Delfiner, R. (2000). "IQ-UTE kid leads heady life—passing college classics at age 6." *New York Post*, February 15, page 4.

Masters, B.A. and Stern, C. (2004). "Former WorldCom CEO Indicted: Ebbers Charged With Fraud; Financial Chief Pleads Guilty." *Washington Post*, March 3, page A1.

Mehta, S.N. (2001). "Bernie Ebbers: Can Bernie Bounce Back? CEO Ebbers thinks he can resuscitate WorldCom's slumping stock with a renewed focus on fast-growing businesses like the Internet." *Fortune*, January 22, page 84.

Meyer, M. (1999). "Bernie's dream of 'WorldComination.'" *Newsweek*, October 18, page 48.

Olijnyk, Z. (1997). "King's ransom seen in private health care: Canada's biggest private facility expects its services to turn a profit next year." *Financial Post*, April 2.

Oliver, M. (2003). "Obituaries; A.E. De Mello; father pushed son to get a college degree at age 11." *Los Angeles Times*, June 5, page B12.

O'Reilly, B. (2000). "FORTUNE 500: The Power Merchant [ENRON, NO. 18] Once a dull-as-methane utility, Enron has grown rich making markets where markets were never made before." *Fortune*, April 17, page 148.

Poppen, J. (200 2). "Prodigy or pawn? The troubled saga of Justin Chapman." *Denver Rocky Mountain News*, March, denver.rockymountainnews.com.

Poppen, J. (2003). "Jail for mom who faked boy's genius." *Denver Rocky Mountain News*, December 3, rockymountainnews.com.

Powers, J. (1980). "The Queen gets skeptical looks." *Boston Globe*, April 22.

Powers, J. (1980). "Ruiz is out; BAA decision is unanimous." *Boston Globe*, April 30.

Reuters Business Report. (2000). "MCI WorldCom's Ebbers got $8.5 million in 1999." May 1.

Schroeder, A. (1996). *Scams, Scandals, and Skulduggery: A Selection of the World's Most Outrageous Frauds*. Toronto: McClelland and Stewart.

Shepard, J. (2000). "Blood-sniffing dog performs for murder jury." *Capital Times/Wisconsin State Journal*, June 16, page 3A.

Slaton, J. (2002). "That reporter done steered me wrong; How much should we blame journalists for the dot-com crash?" *San Francisco Chronicle*, September 19.

Smiley, B. (200). "American scene: Hounding the dead; A remarkable Michigan mutt sniffs out ancient human remains." *Archeology*, September/October, 53, 5, www.archaeology.org.

Smolowe, J., Kohan, J., and McWhirter, W. (1986). "World: East-West tale of a sundered city; After 25 years of the Wall, Berliners still long for unity." *Time*, August 18, page 32.

Stern, L. (1974). "Scheme to bilk the rich: $100 Million oil investment swindle probed." *Washington Post*, June 27, page A1.

United Press International. (2001). "Enron files bankruptcy and lawsuit." December 2.

Vulliamy, E. (2002). "Shattered life and mind of brightest boy on the planet." *The Observer*, March 3, www.guardian.co.uk.

Wechsler, P. (1997). "Who's Ebbers? A cowboy-boot-wearing maverick." *USA Today*, October 2, page 2B.

Wells, J. (2001). "Partners in Crime." *Toronto Life*, June, pages 70-84.

Wilkes, J. (1988). "Courageous Joey flying home; Burned Orillia boy has spent seven months in hospital bed." *Toronto Star*, October 21, page A23.

Chapter Nine: Fear, Stereotypes and Myths

Abbady, T. (2002). "Terror scare a possible 'hoax.'" *Associated Press*, September 13.

"All Things Considered." (1994). "Search for Missing Boys in South Carolina Continues." National Public Radio, broadcast transcript, November 2.

"All Things Considered." (1999). "Profile: Adelaide Abankwah granted political asylum two and a half years after fleeing Ghana over threats of genital mutilation, a common African practice." National Public Radio, broadcast transcript, August 19.

Anonymous. (1988). "Tearing apart Tawana's tale." *Time*, October 10, page 49.

Anonymous. (1989). "Gunman Kills Expectant Mother." *Los Angeles Times*, October 24, page 2.

Anonymous. (1989). "The Triumph of Evil." *Richmond Times-Dispatch*, December 6.

Anonymous. (2002). "Terrorist plot case heads to prosecutors." *Augusta Chronicle*, December 3, page B3.

Associated Press. (1989). "Suspect held in Boston slaying." November 12.

Associated Press. (1990). "Victim of Boston double shooting kills himself." January 5.

Associated Press. (1994). "MISSING: Brothers gone in S.C. carjack." *New York Newsday*, October 29, page A6.

Associated Press. (1999). "Would-be queen starts over: Newly freed Ghanaian aspires to finish school and get a job." *New York Newsday*, August 20, page A8.

Associated Press. (2000). "Asylum seeker called fraud: Ghanaian woman used false name; didn't face genital mutilation." Associated Press, December 20.

Associated Press. (2002). "Police shut down Florida highway due to 9-13 terrorist threat; 3 men detained." September 13.

Associated Press. (2002). "Coast Guard reports racist incidents in Port Angeles." April 29.

Associated Press. (2002). "Three men held for hours in Florida after report of 'alarming' comments." September 13.

Associated Press. (2003). "Coast Guardsman admits fabricating allegations of racial slur." *Seattle Times*, May 6.

Branigin, W. and Farah, D. (2000). "Asylum Seeker Is Impostor, INS Says; Woman's Plea Had Powerful Support." *Washington Post*, December 20, page A1.

Burritt, C. (1994). "South Carolina Carjacking: Authorities baffled by boys' disappearance; Town holds breath as police retrace steps, seek motive." *Atlanta Journal and Constitution*, October 29, page A3.

Burritt, C. (1994). "Parents' emotional plea to missing boys: 'Be brave, hold on to each other'; Search continues in South Carolina carjacking case." *Atlanta Journal and Constitution*, November 1, page A1.

Burritt, C. (1994). "Hopes soar, then crash in carjack; 'Exciting' lead fizzles; parents issue new plea for boys." *Atlanta Journal and Constitution*, November 2, page A1.

Canellos, P.S and Sege, I. (1989). "Couple shot after leaving hospital; baby delivered." *Boston Globe*, October 24, page 1.

Carlson, M. and Ajemian, R. (1990). "Presumed Innocent: Because Charles Stuart was white and affluent, he almost got away with murder. Now Boston must ponder why it so readily believed his lie." *Time*, January 22, page 10.

"CNN Breaking News." (2002). "Authorities Detained Terror Suspects on Alligator Alley." CNN, broadcast transcript, September 13.

CNN. "Man in terror scare says woman is lying." CNN.com, September 13, www.cnn.com.

Drudge, M. (2002). "Woman who reported 'threats' hospitalized." *Drudge Report*, September 16, www.drudgereportarchives.com.

Federal Bureau of Investigations. *Crime in the United States*, 2000, www.fbi.gov.

Glickman. L. (1998). "Without a home for the holidays." *Washington Times*, December 25, page A19.

Green, D. and Kidwell, D. (2002). "Federal sources say terrorism threat by 3 students was a hoax." *Miami Herald*, September 13.

Hays, T. (2003). "Ghanian found guilty in mutilation hoax." *Associated Press*, January 16.

Henderson, G. (1994). "Children's kidnapper still eludes authorities." *Spartanberg Herald Journal*, October 27.

House, B. and Werstein, L. (1988). "Panel: Brawley story a 'hoax'; Official: Advisors 'irresponsible.'" *USA Today*, October 7, 3A.

Hu, W. (1999). "Woman fleeing mutilation savors freedom." *New York Times*, August 20, page B4.

Jacobs, S. (1989). "Shooting victim Stuart leaves hospital; Reading man's condition is described as weak but improving." *Boston Globe*, December 6.

Jacobs, S. (1999). "Stuart reportedly reacted physically to suspect's picture." *Boston Globe*, November 23.

Kandel, B. (1988). "Ordeal turns N.Y. teen into recluse." *USA Today*, February 11, page 2A.

Kunen, J.A. (1988). "Incident at Wappingers Falls: The Case of Tawana Brawley puts New York justice on trial." *People*, March 7, page 42.

Leyden, L. (1999). "Adelaide Abankwah fled Ghana to avoid a tribal ritual. After 29 months in jail and along legal fight, she is finally… ; Getting Ready to Savor Freedom." *Washington Post*, July 21, page A3.

Loney, J. (2002). "Florida Police Find No Explosives in Highway Case." Reuters, September 13.

"Morning Edition." (1995). "An interracial couple complained to Rhode Island police that they were victims." NPR, December 19, broadcast transcript.

Morell, R. (1994). "A Town turns angry at dead boys' mother." *Seattle Times*, November 4.

Murphy, S. (1989). "Man probed as suspect in Stuart shooting." *Boston Globe*, October 30, page 21.

"NBC Nightly News." (1994). "South Carolina: Carjacking-Kidnapping." NBC, broadcast, October 31.

Parente, M. (1994). "Dead boys' uncle: We apologize to all blacks." *New York Newsday*, November 11, page A17.

Rowe, T. (1988). "The strange case of Tawana Brawley: Mystery deepens over alleged abduction and rape of black N.Y. cheerleader." *Toronto Star*, March 27, page D5.

Tamarkin, B. (1993). *Rumor Has It: A Curio of Lies, Hoaxes, and Hearsay*. New York: Prentice Hall General Reference.

Thompson, G. (1999). "No Asylum for a Woman Threatened With Genital Cutting." *New York Times*, April 25, page A35.

United Press International. (1989). "Slain woman's husband IDs suspect in Boston." December 29.

Unknown. (1988). "New Details reported in abduction of Black teen." *St. Louis Post-Dispatch*, March 11.

Waldman, A. (1999). "Woman Fearful of Mutilation Wins Long Battle for Asylum." *New York Times*, August 18, page B3.

Whitely, P. (1993) "Fax About Deadly Gang Initiation Called A Hoax." *Seattle Times*, September 24.

Chapter Ten: War Propaganda

Anonymous. (1914). "Belgian charges against foe laid before president tell of cities and villages destroyed by Germans; Men shot, women and children victims of outrages." *Washington Post*, September 17, page 3.

Anonymous. (1914). "Girls Mutilated, Children Beheaded, Wounded Foe Drowned By Germans." *Washington Post*, September 25, page 5.

Anonymous. (1915). "Torture of Canadian Officer." *Times of London*, 10 May, page 7.

Anonymous. (1915). "The Crucifixion of a Canadian: Insensate Act of Hate." *Times of London*, May 15, page 7.

Anonymous. (1993). "Envoy says some eating their dead." *Press of Atlantic City*, February 17, page A2.

Anonymous. (2003). "Marine shot in head four times and lives." *Times of London*, March 27, page 6.

Anonymous. (2003). "Bullet-proof helmet saves marine." BBC.co.uk, March 27.

Anonymous. (2003). "Bullet proof: Marine cheats death as helmet feels force." *Birmingham Post*, March 27, page 6.

Anonymous. (2003). "Corrections." *San Francisco Chronicle*, April 18, page A2.

Anonymous. (2003). "Mr. Lucky's Lotto." *The Sun*, March 28, page 14.

Associated Press. (1993). "Fierce shelling hits Sarajevo Canadian peacekeepers set to embark on aid operation." *Toronto Star*, February 17, page A3.

Associated Press. (2003). "Soldier's lucky break a hoax; helmet not worn when shot." April 17.

Biddle, F. (2003). "Helmet saves Brit from shots." Knight-Ridder News Service, March 30.

Bilski, A. (1990). "Witnesses to Terror: Refugees accuse Iraq of Savagery." *Maclean's*, October 22, page 22.

Christian, S.E. (1990). "Witnesses Tell of Iraqi Atrocities in Kuwait Congress: Members are shaken by what they hear. Kuwait's ambassador warns that 'time is running out.'" *Los Angeles Times*, October 11, page 6.

"CNN Inside Politics." (2003). "Explosions Rock Baghdad in Past Hour; Bush, Blair Hold War Summit." CNN, broadcast transcript, March 27, www.cnn.com.

"CNN Newsnight." (2003). "Frontline News, Arab Views." CNN, broadcast transcript, March 28.

Elsner, A. (1996). "Bosnian Serbs accuse Muslims of cannibalism." Reuters, May 31.

Ellul, J. (1965). *Propaganda: The Formation of Men's Attitudes*. New York: Vintage.

Evangelista, B. (2003). "Kevlar saving lives, minimizing wounds in Iraq / Technology first developed in 1965." *San Francisco Chronicle*, April 7, page E1.

Gallagher, B. (2002). "Baby-killing hoax led to first war in Iraq; now comes the rematch." *Niagara Falls Reporter*, September 24, www.niagarafallsreporter.com.

Gutman, R. (1992). "Death Camp Horrors Survivors detail Serbian atrocities." *New York Newsday*, October 18, page 3.

Holt, R.R. and Silverstein, B. (1989). "On the Psychology of Enemy Images: Introduction and Overview." *Journal of Social Issues*, 45, 2, pages 1-11.

Howell, T. (1997). "The Writers' War Board: U.S. Domestic Propaganda in World War II." *The Historian*, Summer, 59, 4, pages 795-813.

Hurst, P. (2003). "Helmet saved me from four Iraqi bullets." *Daily Record*, March 27, page 4.

Jowett, G.S. (1987). "Propaganda and communication: the re-emergence of a research tradition." *Journal of Communication*, Winter, page 97-114.

Kay, J. (2003). "Mr Lucky was not so plucky." *The Sun*, April 15, www.thesun.co.uk.

Keen, S. (1988). *Faces of the Enemy: Reflections of the Hostile Imagination*. San Francisco: Harper & Row Publishers.

Lakeman, G. (2003). "Shot four times in the head...and still smiling." *The Mirror*, March 27, www.mirror.co.uk.

Maass, P. (1993). "A Cry for Help From a Frozen Hell; Besieged Bosnian Town Uses Radio Link to Express Its Agony." *Washington Post*, January 13, page A1.

MacArthur, J.R. (1992). "Remember Nayirah, Witness for Kuwait?" *New York Times*, January 6, page A17.

MacArthur, J.R. (1992). *Second Front: Censorship and Propaganda in the Gulf War*. New York: Hill and Wang.

Pearl, D. and Block, R. (1999). "War in Kosovo Was Cruel, Bitter, Savage; Genocide It Wasn't—Tales of Mass Atrocity Arose and Were Passed Along, Often With Little Proof—No Corpses in the Mine Shaft." *Wall Street Journal*, December 3.

Reuters. (1990). "U.S. women, children flown from Kuwait; cruelty bared." *San Diego Tribune*, September 7, page A1.

Sande, G.N., Goethals, G.R., Ferrari, L., and Worth, L.T. (1989). "Value-Guided Attributions: Maintaining the Moral Self-Image and the Diabolical Enemy-Image." *Journal of Social Issues*, 45, 2, pages 91-118.

Shepard, S. (1990). "Iraqi invaders act like monsters, Kuwaiti refugees tell Congress." *Atlanta Journal and Constitution*, October 11, page A10.

Silverstein, B. (1989). "Enemy Images: The Psychology of U.S. Attitudes and Cognitions Regarding the Soviet Union." *American Psychologist*, June, 44, 6, 903-913.

Silverstein, B. and Flamenbaum, C. (1989). "Biases in the Perception and Cognition of the Actions of Enemies," *Journal of Social Issues*, 45, 2, 51-72.

"60 Minutes." (1992). "Nayirah," CBS television, September 6, broadcast.

"Special Report with Brit Hume." (2003). "Wartime Grapevine: Kevlar Proves It's Obvious Use; Iranian News Reports Civilians to be Used as Shields, Aid Ordered Cut by Ambassador." Fox News, broadcast transcript, March 27.

Sproule, J.M. (1998). "Propaganda, History, and Orthodoxy," *CSMC Review and Criticism*, December, 457-459.

Sun, M. (2003). "Luckiest man in Iraq—Shot four times in head and he lived—WAR IN IRAQ: MIRACLE SURVIVOR." *Daily Telegraph*, March 28, page 3.

Williams, N.B. (1992). "Kuwait Story of Babies Removed From Incubators Refuses to Die." *Los Angeles Times*, March 6, page 5.

Chapter Eleven: The Mistake

ABC. (1999). "Portrait of an angel." "20/20," April 26, broadcast transcript.

ABC. (1999). "Yes to God." "20/20," September 10, broadcast transcript.

Anderson, J. (2003). "Katharine Sergava, the Star Of 'Oklahoma!' Ballet, Dies." *New York Times*, December 4, page B9.

Aitken, V. (2003). "It's a boy!" *The Mirror*, October 30, page 1, 8.

Anonymous. (1996). "Guard has bee free with interviews." *USA Today*, July 31, page 2A.

Anonymous (2003). "Kathleen M. Connor-Allwarden: Teacher, helped seniors and children in need." *Milford Cabinet*, April 14.

Anonymous (2003). "A Curse of Their Own." *New York Post*, October 17, page 36.

Anonymous. (2003). "Kathryn Sergava." *The Telegraph*, November 11, www.telegraph.co.uk.

Anonymous. (2003). "Corrections." *New York Times*, November 19, www.nytimes.com.

Anonymous. (2003). "A Correction." *New York Times*, December 4, www.nytimes.com.

Anonymous. (2003). "N.Y. Times dancer obit dead wrong." *New York Daily News*, December 5, www.nydailynews.com.

Anonymous. (2003). "Biography for Kathryn Sergava." Internet Movie Database, undated, us.imdb.com.

Anonymous. (2004). "Lightning Gave Community More Than a Championship." *Tampa Tribune*, June 8, page 18.

Anonymous. (2004). "Kerry picks Gephardt: Mo. rep to get Dem veep nod." *New York Post*, July 6, pages 1, 4.

AP Worldstream. (2003). "Report: Mills gives birth to boy." October 30.

Associated Press. (1969). "Obituary Hoax Fatal." *Daily Oklahoman*, October 17.

Associated Press. (1997). "Super Scooper! an Im-Post-or Paper calls guy named Fiske, and guy named Fisk answers." May 18.

Associated Press. (1999). "Littleton teen: God remark was hers." September 29.

Associated Press. (2003). "Ex-POW Jessica Lynch says military manipulated her story." *National Post*, November 7, www.canada.com.

Associated Press. (2003). "Obituary for woman still living is printed in N.H." August 22.

Associated Press. (2003). "Man fakes death to avoid court appearance." August 28.

Associated Press. (2004). "NY paper picks wrong running mate." July 6.

Bauder, D. (2004). "Two networks Bungle Stewart verdict." *Associated Press*, March 6.

Becker, A. (2003). "Washington County: Dead man walking was live man faking." *St. Paul Pioneer Press*, August 28, www.twincities.com.

Blomquist, D. (1997). "Starr predecessor thinks probe's a bust." *New York Post*, May 16, page 4.

Bloomberg News. (2003). "It's another New York Post exclusive! Yankees lose!" *New York Daily News*, October 17, www.nydailynews.com.

Blum, R. (2003). "Yanks Nip Boston 6-5 in 11 to Win AL Flag." *Associated Press*, October 17.

Cohen, R. (2003). "On not admitting our mistakes." *Washington Post*, May 23, page A25.

Collins, J., Cohen, A., Sachs, A., and Shannon, E. "Society: The strange saga of Richard Jewell." *Time*, November 11, page 12.

Demetriou, D. (2003). "It's a boy! No, it's a girl! Newspapers get the baby blues." *The Independent*, October 31, page 2.

Donahue, D. (1999). "Mother nurtures legacy of a Columbine martyr; Book reveals girl's personal demons." *USA Today*, September 13, page 7D.

Dunn, M. (2004). "Bush to Announce Missions to Mars, Moon." *Associated Press*, January 9.

Eviatar, D. (2003). "The press and Private Lynch." *The Nation*, July 7. 277, 1 page 18.

Fechter, M. (2004). "Wrong Editorial Puzzles, Angers Lightning Readers." *Tampa Tribune*, June 9, www.news.tbo.com.

Fenton, B. (1999). "Doubts over faith of a schoolgirl martyr Confusion may have made wrong teenage victim the Angel of Columbine High, writes Ben Fenton." *Daily Telegraph*, September 30, page 4.

Fields-Meyer and Bane, V. (1999). "Sequel: For the record; 'Do you believe in God?' asked a Columbine gunman. Who really answered, 'Yes'?" *People*, October 18, page 129.

Gaskell, S. (2004). "Mike boos snooze in $1B tx-blitz blunder." *New York Post*, January 30, www.nypost.com.

Gelter, M. (2003). "A long, and incomplete, correction." *Washington Post*, June 29, page B6.

Gelter, M. (2003). "Capturing the faces of war." *Washington Post*, November 23, page B6.

Greigo, T. (1999). "Cassie Bernall 'the most beautiful blue-eyed...angel in heaven.'" *Denver Rocky Mountain News*, April 25, page 11A.

Harrison, E. and Clary, M. (1996). "Atlanta 1996; Guard who saw bomb now called a suspect; Investigation: Security officer who warned authorities shortly before Olympic blast is questioned." *Los Angeles Times*, July 31, page 1.

Kampfner, J. (2003). "The truth about Jessica." *The Guardian*, May 15, www.guardian.co.uk.

Kirkpatrick, D.D. (2003). "Jessica Lynch criticizes U.S. accounts of her ordeal." *New York Times*, November 7, www.nytimes.com.

Kitty, A. (2003). "Appeals to Authority in Journalism." *Critical Review*, 15, 3-4, pages 347-357.

Koric, S. (1996). "U.S. clears Richard Jewell of Olympic bombing." Reuters, October 26.

Lopresti, M. (1996). "Guard's alertness in park makes him an unexpected hero." *USA Today*, July 29, page 4A.

Lopresti, M. (1996). "Suspect or hero: My one-on-one encounter." *USA Today*, July 31, page 2A.

Lynne, D. (2003). "Spin behind Jessica Lynch story? Discrepancies in reports of POW's capture, rescue raise questions." Worldnetdaily.com, May 6.

Luzadder, A. and Kerwin McCrimmon, K. (1999). "Accounts differ on question to bernall; Columbine shooting victim may not have been asked whether she believed in God." *Denver Rocky Mountain News*, September 24, page 5A.

Martin, D. (2003). "Marvin Smith, 93, whose photographs defined Harlem life." *New York Times*, November 12.

Morehouse, M. and Walker, K.E. "Centennial Park bombing change of fortune: 'I just hope I never have to go through anything like this again." *Atlanta Journal and Constitution*, July 31, page A10.

Orin, D. (1997). "Lying lawyer admits he duped reporter chasing 'Fiske' story." *New York Post*, May 18, page 2.

Reuters Entertainment. (2003). Ex-Beatle McCartney has a boy—report." October 30.

Revah, S. (1997). "Will the real Robert Fisk(e) please stand up." *American Journalism Review*, July/August, ajr.org.

Rosato, K. (2003). "Former Broadway star still alive, despite what NY Times obit says." ABCnews.com, December 4.

Rosin, H. (1999). "Columbine miracle: A matter of belief; The last words of Littleton victim Cassie Bernall test a survivor's faith—and charity." *Washington Post*, October 14, page C1.

Saltonstall, D. (2004). "City under siege! Parking tix on pace to break $1B for year." *New York Daily News*, January 29, www.nydailynews.com.

Saltonstall, D. (2004). "We goofed on $1B tix tally." *New York Daily News*, January 30, www.nydailynews.com.

Scruggs, K. and Martz, R. (1996). "FBI suspects 'hero' guard may have planted bomb." *Atlanta Journal and Constitution*, July 30, X1.

Schmidt, S. and Loeb, V. (2003). "'She was fighting to the death': Details emerging of W. Va soldier's capture and rescue." *Washington Post*, April 3, page A1.

Sharp, D. (1999). "17-year-old's last words inspire other Christians." *USA Today*, June 1, page 3A.

Sherwin, A. (2003). "Oh boy, rivals crack up Mirror's baby blues." *Times of London*, October 31, page 5.

"60 Minutes." (1996). "It's a Lie," CBS, September 22, broadcast.

Strupp, J. (2003). "Col Allen Explains 'NY Post' Sox Win Editorial: Not Quite 'Dewey Defeats Truman.'" *Editor and Publisher*, October 17, www.editorandpublisher.com.

Strupp, J. (2004). "Ooops... 'NY Post' says Gephardt gets VP nod." *Editor and Publisher*, July 6, editorandpublisher.com.

Venezia, T., Kelly, K.J., and Garvey, M. (2003). "Dead wrong." *New York Post*, December 5, www.nypost.com.

Walker, K.E. (1996). "Guard's quick thinking saved lives." *Atlanta Journal and Constitution*, July 30, page S29.

Walker, K.E. (1996). "Bomb suspect had sought limelight, press interviews." *Atlanta Journal and Constitution*, July 30, page X3.

Wallace, B. (2003). "Quick takes: A new kind of battle of the sexes." *Los Angeles Times*, October 31, page 2.

Chapter Twelve: Reporter as Victim

Anonymous. (1988). "Minnesota." *USA Today*, February 26, page 5A.

Anonymous. (1992). "6 HIV students at Texas school top U.S. rate." *Los Angeles Times*, February 14, page 4.

Anonymous. (1992). "Texas AIDS counselor may have falsified files; Agency finds no proof students has disease." *San Francisco Chronicle*, August 1.

Anonymous. (1996). "Anyone for some heresy? Cobain church coming." *Chart Attack*, May 27, www.chartattack.com.

Anonymous. (1996). "Diana romp with Hewitt 'on tape.'" *The Independent*, October 8, page 4.

Anonymous. (1997). "Privacy: Cyber-terrorism." *Maclean's*, April 21, page 21.

Anonymous. (1998). "First Timers Hit The Big Time And Make Internet History: Virgin Teens To Go All The Way With Notorious Internet Entertainment Group As Web Hosts." *Business Wire*, July 16.

Anonymous. (1998). "Teenager's sex on the net is a hoax firms says." *Los Angeles Times*, July 18, page D1.

Anonymous. (1998). "'Teen virgins' step forward." Wirednews.com, July 22.

Anonymous. (1999). "The friends of Kristen Clougherty gathered on Friday, June 4th..." *South Boston Online*, June, www.southbostononline.com.

Anonymous. (1999). "Hurricane survivor's incredible journey." BBC.co.uk, June 29.

Anonymous. (1999). "Honduran boy travels 3,200 miles in search of dad; Hurricane survivor, 13, winds up in N.Y. with little money, but help from mayor." *Minneapolis Star Tribune*, June 29, page 8A.

Anonymous. (1999). "Relatives debunk Honduran boy's tale of long journey to find father." *Minneapolis Star Tribune*, June 30, page 9A.

Anonymous. (1999). "Honduran boy fools New Yorkers." BBC.co.uk, July 1.

Anonymous. (1999). "Anti-brothel crusader's blood-stained car found." *Charleston Daily Mail*, November 10.

Anonymous. (2002). "10-year old watched in horror as teens hanged his dog." *Ottawa Citizen*, February 4, page A3, also see www.drudgereportarchives.com.

Anonymous. (2002). "Fake 9/11 cop conned an entire Nevada town: NYPD." *New York Post*, July 24, page 24.

Anonymous. (2002). "Hitler diaries agent was 'communist spy': Heidemann received a four year jail term for hs role." BBC.co.uk, July 29.

Anonymous. (2002). "Clueless Fox taps humorist as Poundstone pundit." *Media Life Magazine*, March 7, www.medialifemagazine.com.

Anonymous. (2003). "Microsoft technology headed for toilet." *San Francisco Chronicle*, May 6, sfgate.com.

Anonymous. (2003). "Web-accessible 'iLoo' flush with MSN technology." *Hollywood Reporter*, May 12, www.hollywoodreporter.com.

Anonymous. (2003). "Microsoft: Internet potty just a hoax." *Seattle Post-Intelligencer*, May 13, seattlepi.nwsource.com.

Ashbrook Nickell, J. and Bryan, J. (1998). "Teens enter virgin territory." *Wired News*, July 15, www.wired.com.

Associated Press. (1988). "Boy, 16, charged in ax murders of 4 in his family in Minnesota." *New York Times*, February 20, page A50.

Associated Press. (1992). "School Officials question AIDS report." *Austin American-Statesman*, February 15, page B4.

Associated Press. (1992). "State asked to investigate reports of HIV at Northeast Texas schools." *Austin American-Statesman*, February 18, page B3.

Associated Press. (1997). "High-tech pest has plagued family since December—police, telephone company have yet to catch intruder." *Seattle Times*, April 11.

Associated Press. (1997). "Police and parents fooled by teenage cyber stalker." *Kent Daily Star*, April 22.

Associated Press. (1999). "Boy's tale of odessy from mudslides wins hearts in New York." *Washington Times*, June 30, page A6.

Associated Press. (1999). "Story of boy's trek to find father in Big Apple a hoax." *Seattle Times*, June 30.

Associated Press. (1999). "Woman charged with bilking donors." September 22.

Associated Press. (1999). "Anti-brothel crusader seen in Calif." November 11.

Associated Press. (1999). "Search goes go for missing prostitution foe and for answers." *Las Vegas Sun*, November 12.

Associated Press. (2000). "Woman who hatched cancer hoax earns probation, called callous." November 2.

Associated Press. (2002). "Man who crash-landed plane in Cuba sentenced." February 1.

Associated Press. (2002). "Police say bridegroom wasn't N.Y. firefighter." July 24, www.amarillonet.com.

Associated Press. (2002). "New York man involved in hoax may have married twice in Nevada." August 26.

Associated Press. (2003). "Microsoft: 'iLoo' Internet project a hoax." May 13.

Associated Press. (2003). "Microsoft has knickers in twist over iLoo." May 14.

Bacon, J., Johnson, K., and Capella, C. (2001). "2 Missing after small plane ditches off the Florida Keys." *USA Today*, August 10, page A3.

Berry, S. and Brownfield, P. (2001). "Comedian Paula Poundstone arrested; Crime: The stand-up comic is accused of lewd acts against a child and child endangerment." *Los Angeles Times*, June 28, page B1.

Boyd, G. (1996). "The Prince and the popper." *Eye*, April 18, www.eye.net.

Boyd, G. (1997). "Springtime for Sommy." *Eye*, April 24, www.eye.net.

Browning, D.R. (1993). "Warily, one city shop restocks sex videos." *St. Louis Post-Dispatch*, March 14, page 1D.

Brunker, M. (2003). "'Hunts' of nude women draw fire: Las Vegas firm charges men up to $10,000 to stalk 'prey' with paintball guns." MSNBC.com, July 16.

Castaneda, C.J. (1992). "Students stung by HIV stigma; Town feels neighbors' hostilities." *USA Today*, February 17, page 3A.

Castaneda, C.J. (1992). "No proof of teens' AIDS cases in Texas." *USA Today*, February 27, page 3A.

Castro, J. and Lessing, G. (1985). "Press: Judging the hoax that failed; Nagging questions remain in the Hitler diaries trial." *Time*, February 25, page 60.

Chang, G. (1997). "High-tech tools used to uncover 'low-tech lie.'" Discovery Channel Canada, April 24, www.exn.ca.

CNN.com (1997). "High-tech stalker turns out to be an insider." April 22.

CNN.com (1999). "Honduran boy's family says he is 'depressed and confused runaway': Edwin's relatives said he hasn't accepted the fact that his father died months ago of AIDS." CNN.com, June 30.

Crary, D. (1997). "Ghostly Ontario stalker harasses family by using high-tech electronic—unseen, he changes TV channel and turns lights on and off." *Associated Press*, *Seattle Times*, April 15.

De La Cruz, D. (1999). "Honduran boy makes 37-day trek to New York in search of father." *Associated Press*, June 29.

De Mara, B. (1996). "Dying mom, 27 robbed of hope; Purse snatcher takes her cash, medicine and son's bus ticket." *Toronto Star*, April 5, page A1.

Driedger, S.D. (1996). "A tangled tale, and a trust betrayed. (false theft report elicits public contributions to cancer impostor)." *Maclean's*, August 22, 109, page 17.

Drozdiak, W. (1983). "Hitler's diaries reported found." *Washington Post*, April 23, page A1.

Egan, M. (1998). "Cynics see hoax in U.S. Internet virgin sex plan." Reuters, July 15.

Egan, M. (1998). "Internet virgins fighting another man's cause?" Reuters, July 16.

Egan, M. (1998). "Internet virgins must find a new home." Reuters, July 17.

Everett, E. (2002). "Money in grave: Weird report claims rancher installed ATM on tombstone." *Bozeman Daily Chronicle*, August 17, bozemandailychronicle.com.

Exner, R. (2002). "Boy cried woof! Now says teens weren't involved in dog's death." *Edmonton Sun*, February 5, www.canoe.ca.

Foxnews.com. (2003). "Vegas 'game' has men hunting nude women." July 16.

Freed, D.A. (1996). "Donations, offers pour in for purse-snatching victim Dying mother overwhelmed by Easter gifts, cash from strangers." *Toronto Star*, April 6, page A3.

Gardiner, S. (2002). "Tahoe paper run 9/11 hoax story." *New York Daily News*, July 23.

Gardiner, S. (2002). "Man's tall tale of terror debunked: His story screamed 'hero,' but cops say it's a big lie." *New York Newsday*, July 24, www.newsday.com

Granastein, L. (1997). "Son, you are so grounded; A 'cyberstalking' turns out to be an inside job." *Time International*, May 5, page 35.

Griffith, M. (1999). "Search continues for missing anti-brothel crusader." *Associated Press*, November 9.

Hardy, A. (1996). "Parishioners find nirvana at the Church of Cobain." *Associated Press*, June 1.

Herring, C. (1991). "Testing, counseling important tools in fight against AIDS." *Mount Pleasant Daily Tribune*, December 15, A1.

Howell, R. (1999). "A mourner, an actor; 13-year-old boy longed for dad, but also stardom." *New York Newsday*, July 1, page A4.

Josey, S. and van Rijn, N. (1997). "Start wins 9 newspaper awards; record number of prestigious national prizes." *Toronto Star*, April 20, page 3.

Koleka, B. (1996). "Grunge worship." Reuters, May 26.

KVBC.com. (2003). "Another twist in the Hunt for Bambi story," undated, www.kvbc.com.

Lake, R. (2003). "Tracking naked women: Real 'hunts rack up attention, ire." *Las Vegas Review/Journal*, July 17, page 1B.

Lazar, K. (2000). "Emotions raw as Clougherty faces trial for cancer scam." *Boston Herald*, August 27, page 8.

Lindsay, G. (1998). "A tangled Web for virgins site; New details cast doubt on the "'Our first time' story." Salon.com, July 16.

Ljunggren, D. (1996). "British tabloid apologizes over Diana tape." Reuters, October 9.

Magnuson, E. (1983). "Hitler's forged diaries." *Time*, May 16, start page 36.

Marcus, J. (1996). "I was a media dupe: Even the most wary, seasoned reporter—like, say me—can fall for a hoax." Salon.com, July 25.

Mikkelson, B. and Mikkelson, D.P. (2003). "Hunting for Bambi." Snopes.com, July 28.

Moore, S. (1996). "Here's looking at you, Di." *The Independent*, October 9, page 21.

Nason, P. (2002). "Was Fox News had?" *United Press International*, March 8, www.upi.com.

Oliver, M. (2002). "Rescued from 9-11 rubble, policeman finally has wedding." *Tahoe Daily Tribune*, July 19.

Oliver, M., and Wood, S. (2002). "Man's story about being Sept. 11 hero doesn't pan out." *Tahoe Daily Tribune*, July 24.

Parker, K. (2003). "Hunting meaning in a base society." *Orlando Sentinel*, July 19.

Paynter, S. (2003). "Bambi hunt paints an ugly picture of women." *Seattle Post-Intelligencer*, July 18, seattlepi.nwsource.com.

Pietrucha, B. (1998). "Online live sex site can't keep up the hoax." *Newsbytes News Network*, July 22.

Proctor, D. (2003). "Proctor: The outhouse goes high-tech." *Denver Rocky Mountain News*, May 12, www.rockymountainnews.com.

Puente, M. (1992). "HIV report stuns Texas community." *USA Today*, February 14, page 3A.

Reaney, P. (1996). "Newspaper admits Diana spy video was a fake." Reuters, October 8.

Reuters. (1997). "Canadian family to move to avoid 'Cyber-punk.'" April 17.

Reuters. (1998). "Online pair say motives were pure, even if they are not." *Philadelphia Inquirer*, July 25.

Reuters. (2003). "World's first Internet loo planned." May 6.

Richmond, R. (2002). "Poundstone granted 'supervised' child abuse." Hollywoodpulse.com, February 25.

Richmond, R. (2002). "Fox News Deems *Hollywood Pulse* Legit News Site." Hollywoodpulse.com, March 4.

Rubard, J. (1996). "Cobain Communion hoax." *The Rocket*, June 12-26.

Sachs, S. and Blair, J. (1999). "Seeking Father, Boy Makes a 3,200-Mile Odyssey." *New York Times*, June 28, page A1.

Scott, J. (2003). "Protesters overshadowed by media, police." *The Post and Courier*, April 13, www.charleston.net.

Scott, J. (2003). "Embarrassing lesson: Duped reporter learns the hard way." *The Post and Courier*, April 20, www.charleston.net.

Sevlin, J. (1988). "Band's Puzzling link to murder case." *San Francisco Chronicle*, June 19, page 51.

Slinger, J. (1996). "Con job or not, 'tragic' case has lessons for us all." *Toronto Star*, April 13, page A1.

Snow, A. and Vogel, E. (2001). "Saga of stolen aircraft: Cubans move crashed plane." *Associated Press*, August 2.

Sonner, S. (1999). "Brothel basher leaves bloody trail; hoax may leave him with big bill." *Associated Press, Seattle Times*, November 20.

Sonner, S. (1999). "Vanishing Crusader just an expensive act—Nevada police to bill for anti-prostitution zealot's faked death." *Associated Press*, November 21.

Sorrell, L. (2003). "Bizarre Game Targets Women: Hunting for Bambi." KLAS-TV, July 10, www.klas-tv.com.

Squires, M. and Lake, R. (2003). "Officials: 'Bambi' an elaborate hoax: But man behind videos continues to tell media outlets that hunts are real." *Las Vegas Review-Journal*, July 25, www.reviewjournal.com.

Tamarkin, B. (1993). *Rumor has it: A Curio of Lies, Hoaxes, and Hearsay*. New York: Prentice Hall General Reference.

Treen, J., Demaret, K., Harmes, J., Stewart, B., and Carbo, R. (1992). "Epidemic or Hoax? A health care worker says rural teenagers in one part of Texas are facing a dramatic outbreak of AIDS—36 cases so far—but is she telling the truth?" *People*, March 2, pages 32-35.

United Press International (1988). "Band under self-imposed 'house arrest.'" May 14.

Vincent, D. (1996). "A dying mother says thanks you: 'I wish that I could everybody inside my heart so they would know how thankful I am,'" *Toronto Star*, April 10, A1.

Vincent, D., Mascoll, P., and Brazao, D. (1996). "Dying mom's sorry tale could be a hoax: Purse-snatching victim doesn't have cancer and she isn't dying." *Toronto Star*, April 11, page A1.

Vincent, D. and Brazao, D. (1996). "Mischief charge laid: Mom who moved nation arrested over report of purse-snatching." Toronto Star, April 12, page A1.

Vincent, D. (1996). "Heartbreak mom 'never meant to hurt anyone'." *Toronto Star*, November 7, page A3.

Vogel, E. (1999). "Anti-prostitution activist in LV, admits staging disappearance." *Las Vegas Review-Journal*, November 18.

Weber, D. (2000). "Cancer faker seeking deal—Prosecution wants donors paid back in alleged scam." *Boston Herald*, October 5, page 3.

Weber, D. (2000). "Cancer victim: Clougherty "preyed off" her illness." *Boston Herald*, November 1, page 24.

Wireless Flash. (2002). "ATM doles out inheritance." August 15.

Wolf, B. (1998). "Two virgins, one lawsuit: Internet sex hoax now a court battle." ABCnews.com, July.

Wolf, B. (2002). "But seriously folks...; Fox apparently takes humor site seriously." ABCNews.com, March 7.

Zeman, N. and Howard, L. (1992). "Periscope: texas is talking." *Newsweek*, February 24, 119, 8, page 8.

Chapter Thirteen: Reporter as Hero

Anonymous. (2000). "2000 Pulitzer Prize Winners—Beat Reporting." The Pulitzer Board, www.pulitzer.org.

Conner, N. (1999). "Media played complex role in the scandal: Reaction from public mixed." *St. Paul Pioneer Press*, November 21, page 8A.

Dohrmann, G. (1999). "'Experiment': Haskins sought counselor's move to athletic staff." *St. Paul Pioneer Press*, March 10, www.pulitzer.org.

Dohrmann, G. (1999). "Counselor: Haskins asked me to write papers in '86." *St. Paul Pioneer Press*, March 12, www.pulitzer.org.

Dohrmann, G., Morrison, B., and Shaffer, D. (1999). "Report: Eligibility fears fed problems: Papers allege program intervened for players." *St. Paul Pioneer Press*, April 14, www.pulitzer.org.

Dohrmann, G. (1999). "U basketball program accused of academic fraud." *St. Paul Pioneer Press*, March 10, www.pulitzer.org

Dohrmann, G. (1999). "Haskins praised employee in '95 letter: Gangelhoff sought recommendation for U master's program." *St. Paul Pioneer Press*, March 21, www.pulitzer.org.

Hammer, R. (2002). "Grand jury should investigate Escambia commission." *Pensacola News Journal*, February 7, www.pensacolanewsjournal.com.

Hauserman, J. (2003). "The wild rise and fall of Childers." *Petersburg Times*, May 16, www.sptimes.com.

Morrill, J. (1981). "Some of the Glitter Wasn't Gold: Embellishments Creep Into Rock Hill Teacher's Credentials." *Charlotte Observer*, June 12, page 1.

Morrill, J. (1989). "Too good to be true: Blowing the whistle on a lying source." *FineLine: The Newsletter On Journalism Ethics*, August, 1, 5, page 3, www.journalism.indiana.edu.

Shaffer, D. and Dohrmann, G. (1999). "Grad rate worst on Big Ten: A Pioneer Press analysis of the Gophers men's basketball team shows its graduation rate is 26 percent-half the conference average." *St. Paul Pioneer Press*, April 8, www.pulitzer.org.

"60 Minutes." (1992). "Nayirah," CBS television, September 6, broadcast.

Streater, A.K. (2002). "$6.2 million land purchases raise concerns: Broker makes $600,000 in one day buying, selling land to Escambia." *Pensacola News Journal*, February 3, www.pensacolanewsjournal.com.

Streater, A.K. (2002). "Junior's financial reports raise questions." *Pensacola News Journal*, February 3, www.pensacolanewsjournal.com.

Streater, A.K. (2002). "Indicted: 4 Escambia commissioners face felonies, misdemeanors." *Pensacola News Journal*, May 1, www.pensacolanewsjournal.com.

Chapter Fourteen: Reporter as Villain

Adler, A.L. (1993). "NBC admits using fire starters on truck used in test collision—network says spark, not toy rockets, started blaze." *Associated Press, Seattle Times*, February 9.

Anonymous. (1993). "Breach of Trust." *New York Newsday*, March 6, page 18.

Anonymous. (1993). "Letters: To our readers." *Time*, October 11, page 6.

Anonymous. (1998). "To Our Readers." *New Republic*, June 1, pages 8-9.

Anonymous (2001). "Monkey Business." Opinionjournal.com, June 8, www.opinionjournal.com.

Anonymous. (2002). "Reporter resigns after quotes, sources disputed: He Worked At 'Tribune-Democrat' For 9 Months." *Editor and Publisher*, October 10, www.editorandpublisher.com.

Anonymous. (2003). "Corrections to Articles by Jayson Blair." *New York Times*, June 11, page A1.

Anonymous. (2004). "To our readers." *Chicago Tribune*, March 3, www.chicagotribune.com.

Anonymous. (2004). "Obituaries: Kim Stacy." *Appalachian News-Express*, undated, www.news-expressky.com.

Anonymous. (2004). "Kimberly Stacy, reporter who fabricated stories, dies Kimberly Stacy, 38, wrote of fictitious battle with cancer." *The Courier-Journal*, March 12, www.courier-journal.com.

Anonymous. (2004). "Note to readers." *National Post*, July 2, page A2.

Ashley, B. (1999). "Newspapers would rather report news than be it: Being on other side of a news story is an interesting experience." *Owensboro Messenger-Inquirer*, May 23, page 2E.

Associated Press. (1981). "Washington faces suit over fictitious addict article." *New York Times*, August 8, page A7.

Associated Press. (1985). "Chicago paper fires reporter for apparent hoax story." November 29.

Associated Press. (1991). "Bergen fined for staging TV dogfight; Ex-reporter avoids prison, says she's 'glad it's over.'" *Colorado Springs Gazette*, October 5, page 5.

Associated Press. (1994). "High court upholds conviction of reporter who taped dogfight." *Colorado Springs Gazette*, November 17, page 4.

Associated Press. (1999). "Reporter who fabricated cancer story says she lied about AIDS." May 14.

Associated Press. (1999). "Writer fired for uncertain sources." August 21.

Associated Press. (2000). "San Jose newspaper investigates intern's articles." December 7.

Associated Press. (2002). "*AP* corrects crime story." September 12.

Associated Press. (2002). "*AP* fires reporter after source query." September 16.

Associated Press. (2002). "*AP* dismisses reporter after editors unable to verify experts quoted in his stories." September 23.

Associated Press. (2002). "*AP* corrects 40 Newton stories." October 22.

Associated Press. (2004). "Newspaper Columnist Who Fabricated Cancer Stories Dies." WKYT-TV, March 11, www.wkyt.com.

Associated Press. (2004). "Tacoma Reporter Quits After Editors Question Sources." *Editor and Publisher*, March 9.

Barbash, F. (2004). "USA Today finds fabrications in star reporter's stories: Foreign correspondent Jack Kelley denies charges." *Washington Post*, March 19, www.washingtonpost.com.

Barry, D., Barstow, D., Glater, J.D., Liptak, A., and Steinberg, J. (2003). "Correcting the record; Times reporter who resigned leaves long trail of deception." *New York Times*, May 11, page A1.

Bates, S. (1989). *If No News, Send Rumors: Anecdotes of American Journalism*. New York: St. Martin's Press.

Bercovici, J. (2001). "Ethics stink over Slate monkey business: Did reporter cook facts? Barbs fly back and forth." *Media Life Magazine*, June 15.

Bissinger, B. (1998). "Shattered Glass." *Vanity Fair*, September, pages 176-190.

Blair, J. (2002). "Officials link most killings to teenager." *New York Times*, November 10, query.nytimes.com.

Blair, J. (2003). "A Nation at war; Military families; Relatives of missing soldiers dread hearing worse news." *New York Times*, March 27.

Blair, J. (2003). "VETERANS; In Military Wards, Questions and Fears From the Wounded." *New York Times*, April 19, page A1.

Blair, J. (2003). "The Missing; Family waits, now alone, for a missing soldier." *New York Times*, April 25, page A1.

Carbonara, P. (1998). "Confabulation crisis; It's the battle of the Boston Blowhards as a scandal at the Globe raises questions about standards for columnists." Salon.com, June 26.

Carpenter, D. (2004). "Fired Chicago news writer: 'No regrets.'" *Associated Press*, March 4, story.news.yahoo.com.

Ciolli, R. and Fireman, K. (1993). "Time says its photos were bogus." *New York Newsday*, September 11, page 10.

Clark, R.P. (2000). "The Unoriginal Sin." Poynter Institute, July 28, www.poynter.org.

CNN.com (1998). "Boston Globe columnist resigns, accused of fabrications." June 19.

Collins, S. (2002). "NBC says there is 'no truth' to the New Times story." *Hollywood Reporter*, August 18.

Cooke, J. (1980)." Jimmy's World: 8-year-old Heroin Addict Lives for a Fix." *Washington Post*, September 28, page A1.

Daniel, J. (1996). "Get out." *St. Louis Post-Dispatch*, October 24, page 22.

Davidoff, K. (1993). "Follow up: Phony photos." *Columbia Journalism Review*, November/December, archives.cjr.org.

DiBacco, T. (1992). "Lift a glass to Fillmore, whose cup runneth under." *Washington Times*, January 7, page E1.

Drudis, E.R. (2000). "Girl apologizes for beating, accusing prom date of rape." Medill News Service, November 15.

Dumenco, S. (2002). "The Glossies: Would the Real Kurt Andersen..." *Folio*, October 4, foliomag.com.

Duran, M. (1991). "Former co-worker tell of Bergen plan; Ex-reporter decided it was time to recant story on pit-bull fight, witness testifies." *Denver Rocky Mountain News*, August 2, page 6.

Elias, J. (2004). "'Shattered Glass' turns the 'intrepid reporter' drama inside out." Knight-Ridder News Service, March 10.

Finkel, M. (2001). "Is Youssouf Malé a slave?" *New York Times Magazine*, November 18, www.nytimes.com.

Fishel, E.C. (1992). "Mencken's ghost must be amused." *Washington Times*, letter to the editor, January 20, page E2.

Foreman, J. (2001). "Monkeyfishing: Cruel and unusual? Or good sporting fun?" Slate.com, June 8.

Futrelle, D. (1996). "Esquire's sexy starlet is the hoax with the most." Salon.com, November 11.

Gaines, J.R. (1993). "From the managing editor." *Time*, August 16, page 4.

Germer, F. (1991). "Bergen blames ambition, fear of failure; Ex-reporter gratified by pit-bull verdict, but she can't forgive her breach of ethics." *Denver Rocky Mountain News*, August 11, page 10.

Glass, S. (1996). "Taxis and the meaning of work." *The New Republic*, August 5, pages 20-24.

Glass, S. (1996). "Hazardous to your mental health." *The New Republic*, December 30, pages 16-20.

Glass, S. (1997). "Don't you D.A.R.E." *The New Republic*, March 3, pages 18-28.

Glass, S. (1997). "Spring Breakdown." *The New Republic*, March 31, pages 18-20.

Glass, S. (1998). "The Vernon Question." *George*, April, pages 88-96,138.

Glass, S. (1998). "Monica Sells." *The New Republic*, April 13, pages 10-11.

Glass, S. (1998). "Hack Heaven." *The New Republic*, May 18, pages 11-12.

Glass, S. (2003). "Canada's pot revolution." *Rolling Stone*, September 4, 930, start page 79.

Green, B. (1981). "Janet's world." *Washington Post*, April 19.

Herman, E. (2004). "Trib to review stories by writer after learning of fake source." *Chicago Sun-Times*, March 4, www.suntimes.com.

Hernandez, M. (2003). "Texas soldier Calley mom awaits news of MIA son." *San Antonio Express-News*, April 18, page 1A.

Hernandez, M. (2003). "He stole a lot more than my words." *Los Angeles Times*, May 25, page M1.

Johnson, P. (1994). "Toning up and tuning up for a tender tv moment." *USA Today*, February 15, page 3.

Johnson, P. (1994). "All's well at ABC with Cokie Roberts, producer." *USA Today*, February 16, page 3.

Jurkowitz, M. (1998). "The Globe, columnists, and the search for the truth." *Boston Globe*, June 21.

Keating, G. "Disgraced journalist Blair signs L.A. book deal." Reuters, September 10.

Kelly, K.J. (2002). "The Devil in the Details." *New York Post*, August 23, nypost.com/business/kelly.htm.

Kennedy Jr., J.F. (1998). "Dear Reader." *George*, July, page 14.

Kinsley, M. (2001). "Editor's note: Was *Slate* had?" Slate.com, June 13.

Kinsley, M. (2001). "Monkeyfishing: *Slate* apologizes." Slate.com, June 25.

Kirkpatrick, D.D. (2003). "Fictional Nonfiction Fiction." *New York Times*, May 11, page 42.

Kurtz, H. (1994). "Fallout from faked photos; *Time* sued for libel by whistle-blower." *Washington Post*, August 12, page F1.

Kurtz, H. (1998). "New Republic writer fired for falsehoods." *Seattle Times*, May 11.

Kurtz, H. (1998). "Jordan receives apology from *George* publisher." *Seattle Times*, June 9.

Kurtz, H. (2002). "New York Times feature was fiction: Michael Finkel fired over slave story." *Washington Post*, February 22, page C1.

Kurtz, H. (2003). "*New York Times* story gives Texas paper sense of deja Vu; San Antonio editor cites 'damning similarity.'" *Washington Post*, April 30, page C1.

Mayer, P.J. and Levine, D.M. (2002). "An editor's note." *Tribune Democrat*, October 10.

Maynard, M. (1993). "GM suits attacks NBC report." *USA Today*, February 9, page A1.

McCampbell, M. (1996). "The Year that was 1996: The Truth hole, talk about a credibility gap. The media have turned fibbing into an art form." *Entertainment Weekly*, December 27, page 64.

Mencken, H.L. (1917). "A neglected anniversary." *New York Evening Mail*, December 28.

Mnookin, S., Smalley, S., Sinderbrand, R., Brant, M., Bailey, H., Wingert, P., Alter, J., Fineman, H. and Braiker, B. (2003). "*Times* Bomb: An ambitious reporter with a troubled relationship to the truth meets an aggressive editor eager to mint new stars. Inside journalism's perfect storm." *Newsweek*, May 26, www.msnbc.com.

Newton, C. (2002). "Violent crime continues to decline." *Associated Press*, September 9.

Oman, A. (pseudonym for Ortega, T.) (2002). "Survive This!: The two girls kidnapped and raped in the Antelope Valley are set to go Hollywood." *New Times of Los Angeles*, August 15, www.newtimesla.com.

Ortega, T. (2002). "Peacock Tease: New Times contributor is fired for faking story about nonexistent NBC 'reality' show." *New Times of Los Angeles*, August 11.

Ostrow, J. (1990). "Grand jury probe: TV journalists indicted for illegal dogfight." *FineLine: The Newsletter On Journalism Ethics*, October, 2, 7, page 3.

Pappu, S. (2002). "Who's the Devil in Details?" *New York Observer*, August 21, www.observer.com.

Pappu, S. (2003). "Jayson Blair Talks: 'So Jayson Blair Could Live, The Journalist Had to Die'." *New York Observer*, May 21, www.observer.com.

Petrina, R. (2003). "NYT editor said top brass was irresponsible in Blair case." *Society of Professional Journalists*, undated, www.spj.org.

Popham, P. (1996). "When glamour is beyond parody." *The Independent*, November 28, page 19.

Prendergast, A. (1991). "Wendy Bergen's Exclusive: The ace reporter promised her bosses at KCNC Denver a riveting story on illegal dogfights. Strange thing, it arrived in a plain brown envelope." *American Journalism Review*, October, ajr.org.

Reed, D. (2000). "Mercury News: intern's unverifiable sources 'serious breach' of ethics." Knight-Ridder/Tribune News Service, December 6.

Reuters. (1999). "Arizona paper details case against columnist." August 24.

Reuters. (2002). "Tennis: WTA fuming over magazine hoax." September 4.

Richburg, K.B. (1980). "Mayor says city ending its search for 'Jimmy.'" *Washington Post*, October 16, page C1.

Roeper, R. (2004). "No way to escape your life's defining moment." *Chicago Sun-Times*, March 18, www.suntimes.com.

Rupert, J. (1993). "From Moscow, photojournalism or photo fraud? Time investigating published pictures of 'child prostitutes.'" *Washington Post*, August 7, page D1.

Sager, M. (1996). "Janet's World." GQ, 66, 6, June, pages 200-211.

Sawyer, K. (1994). "Is it real or is it...? Digital imaging fiction leaves no footprints." *Washington Post*, February 21, page A3.

Schmetzer, U. (2004). "Short fuse is lit in Australia: Aborigines' anger turns into rioting after teen's death." *Chicago Tribune*, February 24, www.chicagotribune.com.

Schram, M. (1993). "NBC burned public trust along with a truck." *New York Newsday*, February 23, page 76.

Serrill, M.S., Crumley, B., Simmons, A.M., and Schoenthal, R. (1993). "Sex for Sale: Defiling the children; In the basest effect of the burgeoning sex trade, the search for newer thrills has chained increasing numbers of girls and boys to prostitution." *Time*, June 21, start page 52.

Sherill, M. (1996). "Dream Girl: Forget Gwyneth, forget Mira. Here's Hollywood's next The Allegra Coleman nobody knows." *Esquire*, November, Vol. 126, Issue 5, page 70.

Sloane, W. (1993). "'Sex for Sale': Did *Time* buy some phony photos?" *Columbia Journalism Review*, September/October, archives.cjr.org.

Smith, P. (1998). "A little girl's rite of passage." *Boston Globe*, April 13, page B1.

Smith, P. (1998). "In the long run, awe is for sale." *Boston Globe*, April 20, page B1.

Smith, P. (1998). "It all began with betrayal." *Boston Globe*, April 24, page B1.

Smith, P. (1998). "The cruel truth about cancer." *Boston Globe*, May 11, page B1.

Staats, E. (1999). "Reporter fired for cancer tale." *Associated Press*, May 10, www.aegis.com.

Stacy, K. (1999). "Reporter has no regrets as she faces death at 33." *Owensboro Messenger-Inquirer*, April 4, page 1A.

Stacy, K. (1999). "Normal life is vital; giving up job would be admitting defeat." *Owensboro Messenger-Inquirer*, April 11, page 1A.

Stacy, K. (1999). "Dying boy reaches out, offers hope, courage to others." *Owensboro Messenger-Inquirer*, April 18, page 1A.

Strupp, J. (1999). "Canned columnist claims to be clean." *Editor and Publisher*, August 28, 132, 35, page 9.

Strupp, J. (1999). "Who told you that?" *Editor and Publisher*, September 4, 132, 36, page 16.

Strupp, J. (2003). "Showtime plans Jayson Blair movie; 'Dark comedy' based in part on 'Newsweek' articles." *Editor and Publisher*, October 15, www.editorandpublisher.com.

Taranto, J. (2001). "In praise of online journalism; We helped bust Slate's hoax." *Wall Street Journal*, June 27.

United Press International (1999). "Newspaper apologizes for stories." May 11.

Urschel, J. (1994). "When roving correspondents stay at home." *USA Today*, February 17, page 10.

Vied, S. (1999). "Reporter fired after fabricating columns: Stacy did not have cancer." *Owensboro Messenger-Inquirer*, May 11, page 1A.

Weaver, T. (2004). "Book Buzz: truth or Blair Disgraced ex-reporter for Times spews out bad prose, self-delusions." *Atlanta Journal and Constitution*, March 5, page E1.

Wertheim, L.J. (2002). "Who's that girl? The WTA tour is desperately seeking a new star to embody its ideal of strength, attitude and sex appeal. Meet Simonya Popova." *Sports Illustrated*, September 2, www.cnnsi.com.

Chapter Fifteen: Academic and Scientific Hoaxes in the News

Adler, J. and Annin, P. (1992). "A hard lesson or hoax?" *Newsweek*, March 2, 119, 9, page 77.

Altman, L.K. (2002). "Blondes fading out? That's just a pigment of the imagination." *Seattle Times*, October 2, .

Anderson, J. (1978). "Human cloning claim challenged." *Washington Post*, June 16, page B19.

Anonymous. (1980). "A protein linked to photosynthesis." *Science News*, January 19,117, page 38.

Anonymous. (1992). "It's a boy." *USA Today*, May 28, page 9A.

Anonymous. (1992). "Complications...in a family way." *Washington Times*, June 15.

Anonymous. (1992). "Half-man, half-woman report is wholly untrue." *USA Today*, June 10, page 4A.

Anonymous. (1992). "'Pregnant man' is a fake!" *Miami Herald*, June 10, page 2A.

Anonymous. (1992). "'Pregnant' male nurse admits he staged hoax." *Seattle Times*, June 10.

Anonymous. (1997). "Divorce hurts kids for years: Researcher." *Toronto Star*, June 3, page A2.

Anonymous. (1999). "Search is underway for rare ox head." *Sarasota Herald-Tribune*, November 1.

Anonymous. (2000). "Effect Of Divorce On Children Not As Clear As 'study' Suggests." *Wisconsin State Journal*, November 13, page 6A.

Anonymous. (2001). "Cow horn crookery exposed: DNA analysis found the horns matched local cattle." BBC.co.uk, February 15.

Anonymous. (2001). "Horny Dilemma." *Science*, January 5.

Anonymous. (2002). "Extinction of Blondes vastly overreported: Media fail to check root of 'study.'" *Washington Post*, October 2, page C1.

Anonymous. (2002). "Natural Blondes to become extinct: Blondes to evolve into brunettes, redheads." nbc5.com, undated.

Anonymous. (2002). "Blondes are a dying breed: Fewer people have proper genetics." clickondetroit.com, September 27.

Anonymous. (2002). "Group says Blondes going extinct." nbc10.com, September 27.

Anonymous. (2003). "Cloning hoax?" *Odessy*, September, 12, 6, page 4.

Anonymous. (2003). "Lawmaker angry at delay in report of misconduct; Falsified data not included in AIDS study, officials say." *Washington Times*, December 9.

Anonymous. (2004). "Clone baby 'born in Australia." *The Australian*, February 11, www.news.com.au.

Associated Press. (2004). "Possible Meteorite Reported in Wash." June 3.

Babula, J. (2001). "Woman pursues human cloning." *Las Vegas Review/Journal*, September 2, page 1B.

Branswell, H. (2002). "WHO says reports it has predicted the demise of blonde hair is a semi-hoax." *Canadian Press*, October 1.

Broad, W. and Wade, N. (1982). *Betrayers of the Truth: Fraud and Deceit in the Halls of Science*. New York: Touchstone.

Burt, C.L. (1958). "The Inheritance of Mental Ability." *American Psychologist*, 13, pages 1-15.

Butler, B.E., and Petrulis, J. (1999). "Some further observations concerning Sir Cyril Burt." *British Journal of Psychology*, February, 90, 1, start page 155.

Chang, K. and Rutenberg, J. (2002). "Reporter becomes actor in human clone drama." *New York Times*, December 30, page A10.

CNN (2001). "Group: Clone research 'going very nicely.'" CNN.com, August 6, broadcast transcript.

CNN. (2001). "Human embryo created through cloning." CNN.com, November 26.

CNN. (2003). "Clonaid: Baby 'clone' returns home." CNN.com, January 1.

CNN Saturday. (2003). "Interviews with Brigitte Boisselier, Alta Charo." CNN, January 4, broadcast transcript.

Cooke, R. (1981). "Cancer findings may be wrong, scientists say." *Boston Globe*, September 10.

Culliton, B.J. (1978). "Scientists Dispute Book's Claim That Human Clone Has Been Born." *Science*, March 24, 199, pages 1314-1316.

Dixon, B. (1988). "John Maddox Offers Surprising Insights Into His." *The Scientist*, June 13, www.the-scientist.com.

Edelson, E. (1981). Cornell student quits over dispute." *Boston Globe*, September 11.

Fantz, A. (2003). "Cloning probe by Florida Court fails to confirm baby even exists." *Miami Herald*, January 23.

Friend, T. (2001). "Human cloning project may have begun." *USA Today*, March 29, page D8.

Friendly, A. (1969). "Britain's Toffs fight importing of high schools: A Two-track system." *Washington Post*, October 26, page B2.

Grossfeld, S. (1991). "'Safer' and in jail: women who kill their batterers; Trail of a father's abuse would switch if she could; Her story...their story." *Boston Globe*, September 2.

Haney, D.Q. (1978). "The Clonists: Is it nice to fool Mother Nature?" *Washington Post*, December 10, page F2.

Harris, C. (1976). "3 say Briton falsified data on IQ." *Washington Post*, October 29, page A1.

Hoffmann, B. (2002). "Study is a Blonde Bombshell," *New York Post*, September, 30, www.nypost.com.

Johnson, G. (2002). "At Lawrence Berkeley, physicists say a colleague took them for a ride." *New York Times*, October 15, page F1.

Johnson, P. "Reporter caught in the wreckage of Clonaid story." *USA Today*, January 8, page D3.

Lamb, K. (1999). "Measuring Minds: Henry Herbert Goddard and the Origins of American Intelligence Testing." *Mankind Quarterly*, 40, 1, page 121.

Lindsay, M. (1957). "Heredity Revived in Talent Search." *Washington Post*, May 30, page A16.

McCain, R.S. (2003). "Researchers fake AIDS study data." *Washington Times*, December 5, www.washtimes.com.

McCarthy, M. (1999). "Vietnamese jungles yield 'lost world' of the rarest animals." *The Independent*, July 17, page 9.

McFeathers, D. (2002). "Blonded by the light." *Scripps Howard News Service*, October 2.

Melnbardis, R. (2001). "Canadian cult says it was first to clone embryos." Reuters, November 26.

Miller, A. (2002). "'Clone' cult: Blessed event due soon." *New York Post*, December 20, page 23.

Reuters. (2001). "New species claim is bull: Scientists say a recently discovered, endangered mammal is a fake." February 14.

Peterson, K.S. (2000). "Unhappily ever after Children of divorce grow into bleak legacy." *USA Today*, September 5 page 1D.

Quinn, J. (1978). "$7 Million libel suit file over clone book." *Washington Post*, July 11, page A3.

Randal, J. (1978). "The First cloned baby? Despite denials, It is possible: Though scientists challenge the claim made in forthcoming book, All Elements Of Single-Parent Replication Exist In Laboratories." *Washington Post*, March 12, page C3.

Reliable Sources. (2003). "Should media have covered Raelians' cloning claims?" CNN, broadcast transcript, January 11.

Roig-Franzia, M. and Weiss, R. (2002). "Sect says 1st cloned human has been born." *Seattle Post*, December 28.

Scripps Howard News Service. (1999). "Two new heavy elements discovered." June 8.

Seife, C. (2002). "Heavy-ion physics: Heavy-element fizzle laid to falsified data." *Science*, July 19.

Service, R.F. (2002). "Breakthrough of the year: breakdown of the year: Physics fraud." *Science*, December 20.

Shermer, M. (1997). *Why People Believe Weird Things*. New York: W.H. Freeman and Company.

Sommers, C.H. (1994). *Who Stole Feminism: How Women Have Betrayed Women*. New York: Touchstone.

Spector, M., Pepinsky, R.B., Vogt, V.M., and Racker, E. (1981). "A Mouse homolog to the avian sarcoma virus src protein is a member of a protein kinase cascade." *Cell*, July, 25, pages 9-21.

Dtrupp, J. (2004). "*AP* Meteor crash report was a hoax." *Editor and Publisher*, June 3, www.editorandpublisher.com.

"Talk of the Nation." (2003). "Interview: Michael Guillen discusses his work researching the alleged cloned baby born in December." National Public Radio, January 10, broadcast transcript.

United Press International. (2002). "Company claims to have cloned human." December 27.

United Press International. (2003). "Researchers admit faking AIDS study data." December 5.

Wallerstein, J. (2001) *The Unexpected Legacy of Divorce: A 25 Year Landmark Study*. New York: Hyperion.

Watson, A. (1999). "Physics: Beaming into the dark corners of the nuclear kitchen." *Science*, October 1.

Weiss, R. (2003). "Cloning a copy of previous hoax?" *Seattle Post*, January 1.

Witze, A. (1999). "They're so heavy: New elements tantalize scientists with their stability." *Dallas Morning News*, September 13, 7D.

Wu, Y. Stanton, B.F., Galbraith, J., Kaljee, L., Cottrel, L., Li, X., Harris, C.V., D'Alessandri, D., and Burns, J.M. (2003). "Sustaining and broadening intervention impact: A longitudinal randomized trail of 3 adolescent risk reduction approached." *Pediatrics*, January, 111, 1, pages 32-38.

Zitner, A. (2003). "Journalist quits as clone evaluator; raises doubts." *Seattle Times*, January 7.

Chapter Sixteen: Sources and Investigation

Anonymous. (1982). "Would-be hero admits to hoax." *St. Catharines Standard*, March 3, page 13.

Anonymous. (2002). "Editor of *Times Argus* dismissed." *Times-Argus*, November 19, timesargus.com.

Anonymous. (2002). "*Times Argus* editor fired for questionable story." *New England Press Association*, November, www.nepa.org.

Anonymous. (2003). "Vermont paper fires editor over sourcing." *The Quill*, February 1, page 25.

Anonymous. (2003). "Journalist perpetrates online terror hoax." *Computerworld*, February 6, www.computerworld.com.

Anonymous. (2003). "Anarchists for a Better State." website, undated, anarchistsforabetterstate.4t.com/custom.html.

Anonymous. (2004). "You Make Me Feel Like 'Gancing'." *Wireless Flash*, March 3.

Barkovich, J. (1982). "Notaro insists he played in tourney." *Welland Tribune*, March 2, page 12.

Berdik, C. (2002). "Duped! When journalists fall for fake news." *The Quill*, May 90, 4, pages 22-26.

Cox, M. (1999). "Magazine criticized for parody." *Associated Press*, February 10.

Fletcher, S. (2002). "Heart and Hearth: One woman's post-Sept. 11 journey to peace." *Times-Argus*, September 11, page A1.

Fletcher, S. (2002). "It's here: Vermont used to be virgin territory for heroin dealers. Not anymore." *Times-Argus*, September 15, page 1.

Hernan, S. (2004). "Metrosexual Morons Gancing the Night Away." *Men's News Daily*, March 5, mensnewsdaily.com.

Johnson, R., Froelich, P., and Wilson, C. (2004). "Male-Dance Fever: Just Kidding, Guys!" *New York Post*, March 26, www.nypost.com.

Juniper, A. (1982). "'Gretzky Syndrome' sparked hoax: 'He needed to be a hero,' soccer player's lawyer says." *Globe and Mail*, March 3, page S1.

Kobell, R. (1999). "Buying time; Year-2000 madness has firms cashing in." *Washington Times*. December 11, page C9.

Krane, J. (2003). "'Computerworld' Duped by Hoax website." *Editor and Publisher*, February 7, www.editorandpublisher.com.

Lewis, F. (1999). "Secrets and Lies." *Philadelphia City Paper*, February 4-19, citypaper.net/articles/020499/onmedia3.shtml.

Malcolm, A.H. (1982). "Soccer hoax boomerangs on Welland Youth." *New York Times Wire Service*, Buffalo Courier Express, March 21, page C6.

Okeson, S. (2004). "Truth hidden in lies: Years after telling newspaper readers in Kentucky she was dying of cancer, journalist is overcome by diabetes in Peoria." *Peoria Journal Star*, May 16, www.pjstar.com.

O'Shube, G. (2003). "Our Own Smarty-pants: Yes, last week's "exclusive" was a ruse, but it still fooled a few cops and reporters." *New Times Broward-Palm Beach*, November 27 www.newtimesbpb.com.

O'Shube, G. (2003). "Anarchy in a Briefcase: Radicals plan to flood Republicans with mice, locusts, and chicanery." *New Times Broward-Palm Beach*, November 20, www.newtimesbpb.com.

Redshaw, W. (1982). "Nataro nets winner on a penalty shot." *Welland Tribune*, March 1.

Redshaw, W. (1982). "Notaro shoots winning goal." *Welland Tribune*, March 1.

Redshaw, W. (2004). Personal Interview, March 5.

Ricker, D.A. (2003). "Despite low poll numbers, HUD Secretary Mel Martinez to run for U.S. Senate seat from Florida." *Miami Herald*, December 9, www.miami.com.

Schulz, B. (2004). "Everybody Gance Now!" *Stuff Magazine*, April, www.stuffmagazine.com.

Stacy, K. (1999). "Normal life is vital; giving up job would be admitting defeat." *Owensboro Messenger-Inquirer*, April 11, page 1A.

Swierczynski, D. (1999). "Boys in the String Band: The secret life of the loneliest Mummer." *Philadelphia Magazine*, January, pages 85-94.

Verton, D. (2003). "Terrorist group claims responsibility for Slammer worm." *Computerworld*, February 5, www.computerworld.com.

Winston, R. (1982). "Humiliated hoaxer yanks award bid." *Hamilton Spectator*, March 5.

Chapter Seventeen: Logic Versus Emotion

American Psychological Association. (1994). *Diagnostical and Statistical Manual of Mental Disorders*, Fourth Edition. Washington, DC: APA.

Anonymous. (2003). "Following up on the hoaxes." *Washington Times*, November 8, washingtontimes.com.

Anonymous. (2003). "Search For Baby Ends With Dramatic Reunion: Baby Returned Safely Home." nbc4.com, November 6.

Boothman, N. (2002). "How to connect in business in 90 seconds or less." New York: Workman Publishing.

Bond, C.F., Omar, A., Pitre, U.L., Lashley, B.R., Skaggs, L.M., and Kirk, C.T. (1992). "Fishy-looking liars: Deception judgement from expectancy violation." *Journal of Personality and Social Psychology*, 63, pages 969-977.

Collins, A. (1987). "You're On!" *Canadian Business*, March, pages 38-44, 116, 118.

Fahrenthold, D. A. (2003). "SE Woman is charged over stolen baby report." *Washington Post*, November 2, page B1.

Feeley, T.H. and deTurck, M.A. (1995). "Global cue usage in behavioral lie detection." *Communication Quarterly*, 43, 4, pages 420-430.

Fiske, J. (1989). *Television Culture*. London: Routledge.

Lieberman, T. (2004). "Answer the &$%#* Question!: Ever Wonder Why They Won't? They've Been Media-Trained. And the Public Is the Loser." *Columbia Journalism Review*, January, cjr.org.

McGrath, M. (2000). "False allegations of rape and the criminal profiler." *Journal of Behavioral Profiling*, December, 1, 3.

Randi, J. (1982). *Flim-Flam!: Psychics, ESP, Unicorns and other Delusions*. Amherst: Prometheus Books.

Wagner, A. (2003). "SE woman charged with kidnap hoax." *Washington Times*, November 7, washingtontimes.com.

Chapter Eighteen: Deconstructing News Stories

Anonymous (2003). "Sportswriter fired for reporting off TV." *The Quill*, November, 91, 8, page 43.

Douglas, J.E., Burgess, A.W., Burgess, A.G., and Ressler, R.K. (1992). *Crime Classification Manual: A Standard System for Investigating and Classifying Violent Crime*. New York: Lexington Books.

Chapter Nineteen: Misdirection

Anonymous. (2004). "New doubts about Bush's WMD source." *New York Newsday*, March 29, www.newsday.com.

Associated Press. (1995) "Oh Boy! That's One Heck of a Hoaks." December 28.

Associated Press. (2004). "Kansas Woman Posed As 13-Year-Old Boy: 33-Year-Old Allegedly Tried To Enroll In Middle School." February 3.

Blomfield, A. and Alderson, A. (2004). "'This won't go away. What happened is much nastier than is being reported'." *London Daily Telegraph*, February 15, www.telegraph.co.uk.

Burke, K. and Sienaszko, C. (2004). "Affair's a lie, she says: Columbia grad denies romantic link to Kerry." *New York Daily News*, February 17, www.nydailynews.com.

Coman, J. and Laurence, C. (2004). "This time it's personal." *London Daily Telegraph*, February 15, www.telegraph.co.uk.

Drudge, M. (2004). "Campaign drama rocks Democrats: Kerry fights off media probe of recent alleged infidelity; rivals predict ruin." *The Drudge Report*, February 12, www.drudgereport.com.

Kurtz, H. (2004). "Woman Denies Affair With Kerry: She Calls Rumor 'Completely False'." *Washington Post*, February 17, page A6.

McGrath, M. (2004). Personal Interview, January 7.

Miller, J. (2003). "Illicit Arms Kept Till Eve of War, An Iraqi Scientist Is Said to Assert." *New York Times*, April 21, page A1.

Mitchell, G. (2004). "Keller Defends Judith Miller in Statement." *Editor and Publisher*, March 28, www.mediainfo.com.

Moore, J. (2004). "Kerry's Alleged Intern Identified, Taped Interview With Major Television Network," *Talon News*, February 16, www.gopusa.com.

Okrent, D. (2004)."Weapons of Mass Destruction? Or Mass Distraction?" *New York Times*, May 30, www.nytimes.com.

Parkinson, C. (1995). "Parents abandon boy at S.L. bus stop." *Deseret News*, December 15, page A1.

Polier, A. (2004). "The Education of Alexandra Polier: Falsely accused of having an affair with John Kerry, the "intern" sifts through the mud and the people who threw it." *New York Metro*, June 7, www.newyorkmetro.com.

Robinson, S. (2004). "Campaigners in crisis mode amid fear of 'bimbo eruption'." *London Daily Telegraph*, February 13, www.telegraph.co.uk.

Shafer, J. (2003). "Reassessing Miller: U.S. intelligence on Iraq's WMD deserves a second look. So does the reporting of the *New York Times*' Judith Miller." Slate.com, May 29.

Walczyk, J.J. (2004). Personal Interview, January 23.

Chapter Twenty: Eyewitness Testimony and Testimonials

ABCNews.com. (2004). "Without a trace: College student vanishes in Wisconsin." March 30.

Adams, B. (2004). "Clues are scarce in search for Audrey." Match 31, *Wisconsin State Journal*, www.madison.com.

Adams, B., Rivedal, K., and Schuetz, L. (2004). "One search ends... Hugs, laughter: Family friends celebrate the good news; Manhunt: Police comb marsh for armed kidnapper." *Wisconsin State Journal*, April 1, page A1.

Anonymous. (2003). "Vallejo Police Investigate Possible Kidnapping." vallejonews.com, November 5.

Anonymous. (2003). "Vallejo police probe alleged kidnapping." *San Francisco Chronicle*, November 6, www.sfgate.com.

Anonymous. (2004). "UW student missing." *Wisconsin State Journal*, March 28, www.madison.com.

Anonymous. (2004). "Worker founder Seiler laying alone in the marshy area." WBAY.com, undated.

Associated Press. (2003). "Assistant Principal Stabbed In N.Y. High School Bathroom." Local6.com, November 4.

Associated Press. (2003). "Cops: Principal Found Bleeding In School Bathroom Stabbed Himself; Man Charged With Falsely Reporting Incident, Making False Statement." Local6.com, November 18.

Associated Press. (2003). "Possible Kidnapping In Vallejo." abc7news.com, November 5.

Associated Press. (2004). "After mysterious attack, Wis. college student now missing." March 30.

Associated Press. (2004). "Wisconsin college student reportedly at a psychiatric facility." April 3.

Bacon, J. (2000). "Tampa student admits kidnap story was hoax." *USA Today*, March 31, 3A.

Boniello, K. (2003). "Twist in assault case shocks Hyde Park." *Poughkeepsie Journal*, November 18, www.poughkeepsiejournal.com.

Bonopartis, N., Boniello, K., and Davis, J. (2003). "FDR vice principal apparently stabbed by student: Man is stable; teen apparently attacked him." *Poughkeepsie Journal*, November 4, www.poughkeepsiejournal.com.

Bradfield, A. (2004). Personal Interview, February 16.

Callender, D. and Elbow, S. (2004). "Police believe missing student faked her abduction, have store videos of her buying rope and duct tape; 'We do not believe there is a suspect at large, period,' says chief." *The Capital Times*, April 2, www.madison.com.

CNN.com. (2004). "Police: Evidence doesn't support abduction claim; Search for suspect dropped." April 2.

Cuprisin, T. (2004). "Student's recovery has essential elements for live coverage." *Milwaukee Journal Sentinel*, April 1, www.jsonline.com.

Elbow, S. (2004). "Shaken by attack, Audrey took extra care, friend says." *The Capital Times*, March 31, page 1A.

Elbow, S. and Weier, A. (2004). "Mystery lingers; Cops still seek abductor, say Seiler was not raped." *The Capital Times*, April 1, page 1A.

Elbow, S. (2004). "Audrey's new story; Seiler tells police she 'wanted to be alone.' then was grabbed." The Capital Times, April 2, www.madison.com.

Fonda, D. (2004). "Abduction Overruled: A Wisconsin college student apparently faked her own kidnapping. Was the hoax a cry for help?" *Time*, April 12, www.time.com.

Furst, R., Adams, J., and Collins, T. (2004). "Minnesota family, friends search for student who disappeared in Wisconsin." *Star Tribune*, March 30, www.startribune.com.

Gardner, B. and Donovan, L. (2004). "College student leaves mystery." *St. Paul Pioneer Press*, March 30, www.twincities.com.

Haberstroh, J., Royce, K., Shaw, G., Hoswell, R. MCoy, K., Cooke, B., Cummins, H.J., Fagin, D., and Bowles, B. (1995). "Oklahoma City Bombing: Killer Blast in Midwast [sic] Many children among the dead in explosion at federal building." *New York Newsday*, April 20, page 3.

Jones, M. (2004). "Police searching for UW student; Sophomore has been missing since early Saturday." *Milwaukee Journal Sentinel*, March 29, www.jsonline.com.

Loftus E.F. and Palmer J.C. (1974). "Reconstruction of automobile destruction: An example of the interaction between language and memory." *Journal of Verbal Learning and Verbal Behavior*, 13, 585-589.

Loftus, E.F. (1974). "Reconstructing memory: The incredible eyewitness." *Psychology Today*, December, pages 116-119.

Loftus, E.F. and Loftus, G.R. (1980). "On the permanence of stored information in the human brain." *American Psychologist*, 35, 405-420.

Milgram, S. (1968). "Some conditions of obedience and disobedience to authority." *Human Relations*, 18, 57-76.

Mitchell, J. (2003). "Vallejo kidnapping was just a hoax." *Daily Republic*, November 7, www.dailyrepublic.com.

Nowlen, C. (2004). "Search on for student: She vanished Saturday." *The Capital Times*, March 29, www.madison.com.

O'Neill. (2003). "Burpee calls for perspective on stabbing." *Zwire.com*, November 13.

Richmond, T. (2004). "Police defend probe of faked abduction." *Associated Press*, April 3.

Ross. J.R. (2004). "Wisconsin student changes story in abduction: Woman says she was not taken from her apartment." *Associated Press*, April 2.

Salmen, J. (2004). "Search for missing student continues." *Badger Herald*, March 30, www.badgerherald.com.

Sifakis, C. (1993). *Hoaxes and Scams: A Compendium of Deceptions, Ruses, and Swindles*. London: Michael O'Mara Books.

Simms, P., Adams, B., and Treleven, E. (2004). "Police: No reason to think Seiler story made up." *Wisconsin State Journal*, April 1, www.madison.com.

Smith, J.J. (2003). "School principal stabbed." *Daily Freeman*, November 4, www.dailyfreeman.com.

Spinney, L. (2003). "'We can implant entirely false memories'." *The Guardian*, December 4, www.guardian.co.uk.

Tascio, L. (2003). "Police search follows report of kidnapping." *Contra Costa Times*, November 6, www.bayarea.com.

Treleven, E. (2004). "Missing UW student was attacked last month." *Wisconsin State Journal*, March 29, www.madison.com.

Treleven, E. (2004). "'It's totally unlike Audrey': Missing UW student was attacked downtown street last month." *Wisconsin State Journal*, March 30, page B1.

Wells, G. L., and Bradfield, A. L. (1998). "'Good, you identified the suspect': Feedback to eyewitnesses distorts their reports of the witnessing experience." *Journal of Applied Psychology*, 83, 360 -376.

Zaldivar, R.A. and Goldstein, S. (1995). "There are 'hundreds of potential suspects.'" *Macon Journal*, April 20, page 6.

Chapter Twenty-One: Forensic and Other Evidence

ABC World News Tonight. (1992). "MIA Hoax." Broadcast, February 27.

Anderson, D. (2004). "Funeral held for oldest man in county." *The Gazette*, March 2, www.gazette.net.

Anonymous. (1991). "Hoax Or Hope?—Disturbing Mia Photo Demands Investigation." *Seattle Times-Intelligencer*, July 18.

Anonymous, (1991). "Relatives say photo shows American POWS." *Watertown Daily Times*, July 17, page 2.

Anonymous. (1992). "MIAS Uncandid Camera." *Time*, March 9, page 31.

Anonymous, (2003). "*Stu*: Inside the premier issue." Torontolife.com, September.

Anonymous, (2003). "Stu editorial mandate." Torontolife.com, September.

Anonymous. (2003). "New anti-lad magazine to launch." *Masthead*, September 11, www.mastheadonline.com.

Anonymous (2003). "Stu magazine a hoax." *Masthead*, September 26, www.mastheadonline.com.

Anonymous. (2003). "Lundy, Albro Lynn Jr." Defense Prisoner of War/Missing Personnel Office, December 29, www.dtic.mil.

Anonymous. (2004). "William Coates, 114, possibly oldest man in U.S." *Cleveland Plain Dealer*, February 28, www.cleveland.com.

Anonymous. (2004). "Wanted: An 'Awareness Day' in Wake of Hate Crimes." ABCNews.com, March 11.

Arnold, D. (2002). DNA testing backfires for convicted rapist." *Boston Globe*, March 24, B1.

Arnold, D. (2002). "Convict's cause is tested: Supporters shaken by DNA findings." *Boston Globe*, March 28 2002.

Associated Press. (1971). "Cave Houses Termed Major Scientific Find." *Daily Oklahoman*, July 9.

Associated Press. (1971). "Lost Tribe Found on Island." *Daily Oklahoman*, July 9.

Associated Press. (1971). "New-Found Tasadays Shyly Emerge From Stone-Age Life to Modern World." *Daily Oklahoman*, September 11.

Associated Press. (1984). "Man gets life for beating and rape." *Associated Press*, February 19.

Associated Press. (1997). "M. Elizalde Jr., Found 'Tribe' Called Hoax." *New York Newsday*, May 6, page A51.

Associated Press. (2002). "Positive DNA Test Leaves Rapist's Supporters Feeling Betrayed." *FoxNews.com*, May 16.

Associated Press. (2002). "DNA testing links convicted rapist to scene." *Boston Herald*, March 23, 2002, www.bostonherald.com.

Associated Press. (2002). "DNA results cause soul-searching among convicted rapist's supporters." *Boston Herald*, May 12, www.bostonherald.com.

Associated Press. (2004). "William Coates, believed to be oldest man in U.S., dead at 114." *San Diego Union-Tribune*, February 25, www.signonsandiego.com.

Associated Press. (2004). "Professor suspected of staging hate crime." *San Mateo Daily Journal*, March 22, smdailyjournal.org.

Associated Press. (2004). "America's 'oldest' man actually 92, not 114." *Arizona Republic*, March 2, www.azcentral.com.

Associated Press. (2004). "Witnesses allege prof faked hate crime against herself." *USA Today*, March 18, www.usatoday.com.

Associated Press. (2004). "Tape purportedly shows San Francisco man beheaded." August 7, www.kesq.com.

Associated Press. (2004). " Video of U.S. man allegedly beheaded in Iraq a fake." August 7, thestar.com.

Associated Press. (2004). "Son of Late Officer Questions Bush Memos." September 9, abcnews.com.

Bostelaar, R. (2003). "A car-aaazy year: News and notes from 2002." *Windsor Star*, January 14, page B1.

Bruun, M. (2001). "La Guer alleges evidence hidden; Fingerprints not a match." *Worcester Telegram and Gazette*, December 12, page A1.

Castaneda., C.J. (1991). "Picture inspires hope; Disquieting image refires MIA debate." *USA Today*, July 18, page 1A.

Castaneda., C.J. (1991). "Authenticity of photo in question." *USA Today*, July 19, page 3A.

CBS Television. (2004). "New Questions On Bush Guard Duty." September 8, cbsnews.com.

CBS Television. (2004). "CBS: Bush Memo Story A 'Mistake.'" September 20, cbsnews.com.

Chin, P., Benet, L., Bacon, D., Eftimiades, M., and Sellinger, M. (1991). "A Last frail hope: A mysterious photo stirs longings—and anguish—for the families of three fliers missing in Southeast Asia." *People*, August 5, page 34.

Dobbs, M. (2004). "Questions Surround Man Who Provided Document CBS's: 'Unimpeachable Source' Is Ex-Guard Officer With History of Problems and of Attacking Bush." *Washington Post*, September 21, page A3.

Eckler,R. (2003). "Who wants a perfect guy, anyway?: Stu magazine is out to celebrate the 'adequate man'." *National Post*, September 24, www.nationalpost.ca.

Emery, T. (2002). "DNA Test Confirms Rape Conviction." *Associated Press*, May 16.

Guthrie, J., and Wallace, B. (2004). "Web hoax fools news services: S.F. man fakes beheading, proves need for verification." *San Francisco Chronicle*, August 8, page A1.

Harris, H.R. (1999). "No stopping centenarians." *Washington Post*, June 2, page M3.

Kurtz, H. (2004). "Document Experts Say CBS Ignored Memo 'Red Flags'." *Washington Post*, September 15, page A10.

Marquez, J. (2004). "Claremont colleges reel from hate crime." *Associated Press*, March 11, www.signonsandiego.com.

Marshall, E. (1989). "Anthropologists debate Tasaday hoax evidence." *Science*, December, 246, 4934, pages 1113-1115.

Milloy, C. (2002). "Key to Longevity Is Moderation—Or a 'Bloodwash'." *Washington Post*, July 3, page B1.

Nalder, E. (1991). "Missing Flier No Stranger To Bailouts—Family Clings Desperately To The Hope He's Still Alive." *Seattle Times*, July 21.

Nance, J. (1972). "Competition, Bad Felling Toward Others Almost Foreign to Tasaday." *Daily Oklahoman*, June 29.

Nance, J. (1971). "Worst thing in world for Tasadays in Thunder." *Associated Press*, June 16.

Schwartzman, P. (2004). "Census records cast doubt on age of Pr. George' man." *Washington Post*, March 2, page B1.

Shafer, J. (2002). "*Slate* Gets Duped: This week's Diary by an "automotive CEO" proves to be a hoax." Slate.com, March 5.

U.P.I. (2004). "114-year-old man dies in Maryland." *Washington Times*, February 25, washingtontimes.com.

Walczyk, J.J. (2004). Personal Interview, January 23.

Wallsten, P. (2004). "GOP Activist Made Allegations on CBS Memos." *Los Angeles Times*, September 18, latimes.com.

Wedge, D. (2002). "Convicted rapist says DNA will show innocence." *Boston Herald*, January 17, page 14.

Williamson, D. (2002). "Media fell for tactics of LaGuer ; Many were beguiled by convicted rapist." *Worcester Telegram & Gazette*, April 2, page B1.

Wilson, R. (2004). "Professor Is Accused of Staging Hate Crime by Vandalizing Her Own Car." *The Chronicle of Higher Education*, March 19, chronicle.com.

Xinhua News Agency (1997). "Laos Hands Over American Remains." October 28.

Zerbisias, A. (2003). "New 'men's mag' has limited readership." *Toronto Star*, September 26, www.thestar.com.

Chapter Twenty-Two: Getting All Sides

Allen, M. (2003). "Inside Bush's Top-Secret Trip: News to Reporters of Flight to Baghdad Was No Joke After All," *Washington Post*, November 28, page A47.

Allen, M. and Wright, R. (2003). "Bush Surprises Troops in Iraq: President Returns to Texas After Stealth Trip To Baghdad," *Washington Post*, November 28, www.washingtonpost.com.

Anderson, R. (2004). "C-J acknowledges false story." *Topeka Capital-Journal*, June 24, www.cjonline.com.

Anderson, R. and Purinton, C. (2004). "Decomposing body found in home: Woman also found inside ex-YW counselor's home." *Topeka Capital-Journal*, June 29, www.cjonline.com.

Anonymous. (1953). "City Families Open Arms to 'Lost Youth.'" *Daily Oklahoman*, August 21, page 1.

Anonymous. (1953). "Sheriff's Orphan Is Hoax." *Daily Oklahoman*, August 22, page 1.

Anonymous. (1970). "Oleo Heir Fails to See Nixon." *Washington Post*, January 20, page A6.

Anonymous. (1991). "Lenin for Sale." *Forbes FYI Supplement*, 148, 12, start page 58.

Anonymous. (1991). "True capitalism: Lenin for sale?" *USA Today*, November 6, page 6A.

Anonymous. (2003). "Sharp-eyed British pilot almost blows Bush cover." *Toronto Star*, November 28, www.thestar.com.

Anonymous. (2004). "Painful story: Juanita Smith talks reluctantly about her experiences as a Japanese prisoner of war." *Topeka Capital-Journal*, May 4, page A4.

Antilla, S. (1989). "Increase in hoaxes pester news services." *USA Today*, May 26, page 4B.

Associated Press (1970). "Heir Offer of Riches Draws Mob of Takers," *Washington Post*, January 17, A1.

Associated Press (1970). "Brody Claims He Has Ended Vietman War," *Daily Oklahoman*, January, 20.

Associated Press (1970). Oleo Heir Held in Mental Center." *Washington Post*, April 22, page A3.

Associated Press (1973). "Heir Who Sought to Give Fortune Away Kills Himself," *Washington Post*, January 27, page A3.

Associated Press. (1989). "NWA-Pan Am bid rumored New York halts trading after report of deal for both airlines." May 24.

Associated Press. (2003). "Is that Air Force One?'—Trip kept top-secret." November 28.

Associated Press. (2004). "Woman says she cpuldn't bury daughter." *Wichita Eagle*, July 1.

Banchero, P. (1996). "Sex ed remains a delicate topic for discussion." *Wichita Eagle*, February 14, page 13A.

Barbash, F. (2004). "USA Today Finds Fabrications in Star Reporter's Stories Foreign Correspondent Jack Kelley Denies Charges." *Washington Post*, March 19, www.washingtonpost.com.

Business Wire. (1999). "Trans-Global Holdings, Inc. Has Entered Into an Agreement to Acquire Sun Raye River Estates." May 25.

Cancela, J.C. (2000). "A tale of Cuba's reality." *USA Today*, March 14, letter to the editor, page 18A.

"CBS Evening News" (1970). "Joke on Reporters," CBS television, January 22, broadcast.

Chen, E. and Reynolds, M. (2003). "Can you keep a secret? Hop on." *Los Angeles Times*, November 29, www.latimes.com.

Crudele, J. (1989). "Sharpies sometimes dupe the financial press: All that's faxed isn't the fax." *Buffalo News*, June 5.

Curl, J. (2003). "Mum's the word on Bush's secret mission," *Washington Times*, November 28, washingtontimes.com.

Donlon., B. (1991). "ABC red-faced over Lenin report." *USA Today*, November 7, page 1D.

Fahlgren Rothschild, S. (2004). "Pregnancy prevention: World War Two experience spurred her to help others." *Topeka Capital-Journal*, May 2, page E1.

Fireman, K. (2003). "President Drops in on Troops: Bush secretly flies to Iraq for Thanksgiving Day visit." *New York Newsday*, November 28, www.newsday.com.

Fireman, K. (2003). "Changing a story on the fly." *New York Newsday*, December 3, www.newsday.com.

Hanna, J. (2004). "Topeka, Kan., editor resigns over story." *Associated Press*, June 24.

Hooper, H. (2000). "Spreading the word." *Topeka Capital-Journal*, September 24, page E1.

Hunt, T. (2003). "Bush Trip to Baghdad Kept Top-Secret." *The Guardian*, November 28, www.guardian.co.uk.

Hutcheson, R. (2003). "Pilot got a glimpse of Bush's secret flight." *Bergen County Record*, November 29, page A01.

Hutcheson, R. (2003). "Details of Bush's surprise trip still coming to light." Knight-Ridder News Service, November 28, www.sunherald.com.

Kelley, J. (2000). "Quest for freedom carries a price." *USA Today*, March 10, page 1A.

Kurtz, H. (2004). "USA Today Calls Work By Star Reporter Fake." *Washington Post*, March 20, page A1.

Milgram, S. (1968). "Some conditions of obedience and disobedience to authority." *Human Relations*, 18, 57-76.

Moran, N. (1970). "Heir on Drugs When Giveaway Idea Came: What a joke I've pulled on the world." *Daily Oklahoman*, January 19, page 1.

Morris, V. (2003). "Inside Dubya's Secret Mission," *New York Post*, November, 28, www.nypost.com.

Morrison, B. (2004). "Ex-USA TODAY reporter faked major stories." *USA Today*, March 19, www.usatoday.com.

Morrison, B. (2004). "Woman who died in Cuba story alive in USA." *USA Today*, March 19, www.usatoday.com.

Nair, L. (2004). "Body found at home of ex-professor: The police made the discovery after what a Kansas newspaper later called a false war story." *Roanoke Times*, July 2, www.roanoke.com.

Oppel, R.A. (1999). "S.E.C. Civil Suit Says Faxes About 12 Stocks Were False." *New York Times*, July 17, page C3.

Petterson, J.L. (2004). "Body found in Topeka home tentatively identified." *Kansas City Star*, July 1, www.kansascity.com.

Reid, T. (2003). "Flight of fancy." *Times of London*, November 29, page 24.

Reuters. (2003). "White House Version of Mid-Air Exchange Disputed." December 1, news.yahoo.com.

Reuters. (2003). "Who was the pilot who spotted secret Bush flight?" December 2, edition.cnn.com.

Reuters. (2003). "White House Changes Story on Bush Plane Incident." December 3, www.reuters.com.

Rosen, J. (2004). "Who knows Jack?" *American Journalism Review*, March 11, ajr.org.

Sardella, J. (2000). "Americans take all freedoms for granted." *USA Today*, March 14, letter to the editor, page 18A.

Steinberg, J. (2004). "Journalists Say Paper Failed to Stop Deceit of Reporter." *New York Times*, March 29, www.nytimes.com.

Trueheart C. (1991). "Is Lenin for sale? Of corpse not! Christopher Buckley's hoax fools *ABC News*, *USA Today*." *Washington Post*, November 7, page C1.

United Press. (1953). "'Motherless' Lad Revealed As AWOL." *Washington Post*, August 23, page M6.

United Press International. (2004). "*USA Today* finds reporter faked stories," *Washington Times*, March 19, washingtontimes.com.

Chapter Twenty-Three: Being a Savvy News Consumer

Alters, D. (1989). "Shhhhh... Some firms are busy spying on the nation's social activists, environmentalists, animal-rights workers and skeptics of biotechnology are targets of a lucrative trade." *Boston Globe*, July 9.

Bates, S. (1989). *If No News, Send Rumors: Anecdotes of American Journalism*. New York: St. Martin's Press.

Cauvin, H.E. (2003). "Top PR Firm Advises Zoo, Its Director After Deaths." *Washington Post*, September 25, page B01.

Collins, A. (1987). "You're On!" *Canadian Business*, March, pages 38-44, 116, 118.

Doyle, P. (2004). "*Star Tribune* draws Parker Hughes patients' criticism." *Minneapolis-St. Paul Star Tribune*, March 28, www.startribune.com.

Grimaldi, J.V. (2003). "Latest Check at Zoo Finds Rodents, Roaches Persist." *Washington Post*, September 30, page B1.

Hill and Knowlton Canada (2003). "H&K's 10 Rules of Crisis." www.hillandknowlton.ca.

Kurtz, H. (2003). "On Paper vs. In Paper; Ow! Hit by the Stories That No One Saw Coming." *Washington Post*, October 13, page C1.

Mann, B. (1994). "Straight talk: the value of effective disaster communications." *Emergency Preparedness Digest*, April-June, pages 2-4.

Reber, A.S. (1985). *The Penguin Dictionary of Psychology*. New York: Penguin Books.

About the Author:

Alexandra Kitty is a freelance journalist who has written for *Elle Canada*, *Maisonneuve*, *Presstime*, *Current*, *Quill*, *Critical Review*, *Skeptic* and *Editor & Publisher*, and the co-author of the book *Outfoxed* (forthcoming from The Disinformation Company). She has an Honors B.A. in Psychology from McMaster University and a Masters Degree in Journalism from the University of Western Ontario. She was a Professor of Language Studies at Mohawk College, and now teaches writing at the Sheridan Institute. She won the 2004 Arch Award from McMaster University and lives in Hamilton, Ontario.